British Planning

British Planning

50 Years of Urban and Regional Policy

Edited by

BARRY CULLINGWORTH

THE ATHLONE PRESS
London and New Brunswick, NJ

First published in 1999 by
THE ATHLONE PRESS
1 Park Drive, London NW11 7SG
and New Brunswick, New Jersey

British Library Cataloguing in Publication Data
*A catalogue record for this book is available
from the British Library*

ISBN 0 485 00404 6 HB
0 485 00604 9 PB

Library of Congress Cataloging-in-Publication Data
British planning: 50 years of urban and regional policy / edited by
Barry Cullingworth.
    p.   cm.
    Includes bibliographical references and index.
    ISBN 0–485–00404–6 (hardcover).—ISBN 0–485–00604–9 (paper)
    1. City planning—Great Britain.   2. Regional planning—Great
Britain.   I. Cullingworth, J. B.
HT169.G7B758   1999
320'.6'0941—dc21   99–22497
                                                                  CIP

Distributed in the United States, Canada and South America by
Transaction Publishers
390 Campus Drive
Somerset, New Jersey 08873

Typeset by RefineCatch Ltd, Bungay, Suffolk
Printed and bound in Great Britain by
Bookcraft (Bath) Ltd

Contents

List of Illustrations

Contributors

Paul Balchin is Reader in Urban Economics in the Faculty of the Environment at the University of Greenwich. He is author of several books on housing and urban economics, including *Housing Improvement and Social Inequality* (Saxon House 1979), *Regional and Urban Economics* (with Gregory Bull) (Harper and Row 1987), *Housing Policy and Housing Needs* (Macmillan 1981), *Housing Policy: An Introduction* (Routledge 1995, 3rd edition), *Urban Land Economics and Public Policy* (with Gregory Bull and Jeffrey Kieve (Macmillan 1995, 5th edition) and (as editor) *Housing Policy in Europe* (Routledge 1996).

Philip Booth is Senior Lecturer in Town and Regional Planning at the University of Sheffield. He is author and co-author of several books, including *Low Cost Home Ownership* (edited with A. D. H. Crook; Gower 1986) and *Controlling Development: Certainty and Discretion in Europe, the USA, and Hong Kong* (UCL Press 1996). He is currently working on a history of British development control, to be published in the Spon series on planning and planning history.

David Callies is the Benjamin A. Kudo Professor of Law at the William S. Richardson School of Law, University of Hawaii at Manoa, where he teaches town planning, property and local government law. He is author of several books including *Preserving Paradise: Why Regulation Won't Work* (University of Hawaii Press 1994), *Cases and Materials on Land Use* (2nd edition) with Freilich and Roberts (West Publishing 1994), *Land Use Law in the United States* (Kyoto 1994; in Japanese) and *Property Law and the Public Interest* with Hylton, Mandelker and Franzese (Michie / Lexis 1998). He is also the editor of *Takings: Land Development Conditions and Regulatory Takings After Lucas and Dolan* (American Bar Association Press 1996). He received his LL.M. (Town Planning Law) from Nottingham University in 1969.

Barry Cullingworth is Emeritus Professor of Urban Affairs and Public Policy, University of Delaware, and Senior Research Fellow in the Department of Land Economy, University of Cambridge. He is author of several books including *Housing Needs and Planning Policy* (Routledge and Kegan Paul 1960), *Problems of an Urban Society* (Allen & Unwin 1973), three volumes of the Official History of *Environmental Planning 1939–1969* (HMSO 1975–80), *Urban and Regional Planning in Canada* (Transaction 1987), *The Political Culture of Planning: American Land Use Planning in Comparative Perspective* (Routledge 1993), *Planning in the USA: Policies, Issues and Processes*

(Routledge 1997) and (with Vincent Nadin) *Town and Country Planning in the UK* (Routledge, 12th edition, 1997).

H. W. E. (Lyn) Davies is Emeritus Professor of Planning at the University of Reading. He has worked in local government and consultancy in the UK, Asia, Africa and Canada, and has been adviser to OECD, UNECE and the European Commission. Among his publications are (with Llewelyn Davies) *Urban Change in the United Kingdom since 1976* in *Sustainable Settlements and Shelter* (the United Kingdom National Report for the UN Habitat II Conference, Istanbul 1996 (HMSO)) and *Planning Control in Western Europe* (HMSO 1989)

Malcolm Grant is Professor and Head of Department of Land Economy at Cambridge. He is the editor of the six-volume looseleaf *Encyclopedia of Planning Law and Practice* and joint editor of the eight-volume looseleaf *Encyclopedia of Environmental Law*, both published by Sweet and Maxwell. He is also the author of several books, including *Urban Planning Law* (1982, with two subsequent updating supplements), *Rate Capping and the Law* (2nd edn 1986, Association of Metropolitan Authorities), *Permitted Development* (2nd edn 1996) and (with Hawkins, R) *Concise Lexicon of Environmental Terms* (Wiley, 1995). He is the Chairman of the Local Government Commission for England.

Peter Hall is Professor of Planning at The Bartlett School of Architecture and Planning, University College, London. He is a member of the Deputy Prime Minister's Urban Task Force, established in May 1998, and is currently Chairman of the Town and Country Planning Association. He has taught at the London School of Economics; at the University of Reading (1968–88), where he was Dean of the Faculty of Urban and Regional Studies; and at the University of California at Berkeley (1980–92), where he is Professor Emeritus of City and Regional Planning. He has written many books on urban and regional planning and related topics, including *London 2000* (1963, 1969), *The World Cities* (1966, 1977, 1983), *Urban and Regional Planning* (1975, 1982), *Great Planning Disasters* (1980), *Cities of Tomorrow* (1988), *London 2001* (1989), and *Technopoles of the World* (with M. Castells, 1994). His latest book *Cities in Civilization* will be published by Weidenfeld & Nicolson in 1998.

Ian Hodge is Gilbey Lecturer in the Department of Land Economy, University of Cambridge. He has previously taught at the Universities of Queensland and Newcastle upon Tyne. He is the author or co-author of *Countryside in Trust: Land Management by Conservation, Amenity and Recreation Organisations (Wiley 1996) (with Janet Dwyer), Environmental Economics: Individual Incentives and Public Choices* (Macmillan 1995) and *Rural Employment: Trends Options and Choices* (Methuen 1981) (with Martin Whitby). He has also published more widely in the areas of environmental management, property institutions and rural development.

Peter Larkham is Reader in the School of Planning, University of Central England, Birmingham and was previously a British Academy Doctoral Fellow at the University of Birmingham. He has published widely on urban form, conservation and planning. He is the author of *Conservation and the City* (Routledge 1996) and joint editor of *Urban Landscapes: International Perspectives* (Routledge 1992), *Building a New Heritage* (Routledge 1994) and *Changing Suburbs* (Spon 1998). He edits *Planning History* for the International Planning History Society and is Associate Editor of *Urban Morphology*, published by the International Seminar on Urban Form.

Vincent Nadin is Reader and Director of the Centre for Environment and Planning at the University of the West of England, Bristol. He is author (with Barry Cullingworth) of *Town and Country Planning in the UK* (Routledge, 12th edition, 1997) and recently led the preparation of the *EU Compendium of Spatial Planning Systems and Policies* for the Regional Policy Directorate of the European Commission. He is editor of *Planning Practice and Research*.

John Punter is Professor of Urban Design in the Department of City and Regional Planning at Cardiff University, Wales. He has held academic posts in urban studies, land management, and planning at the Universities of York (Canada), Reading and Strathclyde, respectively. He is the author/co-author of several books including *Planning Control in Western Europe* (HMSO 1989), *Design Control in Bristol* (Redcliffe 1990), *The Design Dimensions of Planning* (Spon 1997) and *Design Guidelines in American Cities* (Liverpool University Press, forthcoming).

Michael Purdue is Professor of Law at City University. He is author of several books on planning law, including *Sizewell B: An Anatomy of the Inquiry* with T. O'Riordan and R. Kemp) (Macmillan 1988), *Planning Law and Procedure* (with E. Young and J. Rowan-Robinson) (Butterworths 1989), *Planning Appeals: A Critique* (Open University Press 1991), *Planning Decisions Digest* (with V. Fraser) (Sweet & Maxwell 1992, 2nd edition), and *Negotiated Development Rationales and Practice for Development Obligations and Planning Gain* (with P. Healey and F. Ennis) (Spon 1995). He is Assistant Editor of the *Journal of Planning and Environment Law*, Case-Analysis Editor of the *Journal of Environmental Law*, and Consultant Editor of Butterworth's Planning Law Service

Brian Robson is Professor of Geography at Manchester University and Director of its Centre for Urban Policy Studies (CUPS). He has published widely in the field of urban studies: his books include *Urban Analysis* (Cambridge 1968), *Urban Growth* (Methuen 1975), *Those Inner Cities* (Oxford 1988). With his colleagues in CUPS he has been heavily involved in research on urban policy issues, producing: a major evaluation of the policies of the 1980s (*Assessing the Impact of Urban Policy*, HMSO 1994), an assessment of UDCs (*The Impact of UDCs in Leeds, Bristol and Central Manchester*, HMSO 1998), and the development of DETR 1991 and 1998 *Indexes of Deprivation*. He has played an active role in voluntary sector bodies in Manchester and the North West.

Yvonne Rydin is Reader in Environmental Planning at the London School of Economics where she is also Director of the MSc in Environmental Assessment and Evaluation. Her publications include *Housing Land Policy* (Gower 1986), *Remaking Planning* (with T. Brindley and G. Stoker) (Routledge 1989 and 1996), *The British Planning System* (Macmillan 1993) and its successor *Urban and Environmental Planning in the UK* (Macmillan 1998), and *The Language of Environment* (with G. Myerson, UCL Press 1996).

Paul Truelove lectures on the principles, methods and history of transport planning at Aston University. He has written a number of papers on the political aspects of public transport and road pricing proposals, and is the author of *Decision-making in Transport Planning* (Longman 1992).

Urlan Wannop is Emeritus Professor of Urban and Regional Planning, University of

Strathclyde. Previously he worked in new town planning (Cumbernauld, Skelmersdale, Northampton, Redditch and Irvine) and in regional planning. He is author of *The Regional Imperative* (Jessica Kingsley 1995), a comparative appraisal of regional planning in the UK, Europe and the USA.

Stephen V. Ward is Professor of Planning History at Oxford Brookes University. He is President of the International Planning History Society and a member of the Editorial Board of *Planning Perspectives*. His published works include *The Geography of Interwar Britain: The State and Uneven Development*, (Routledge 1988), *Planning and Urban Change*, (Paul Chapman 1994) and *Selling Places: The Marketing and Promotion of Towns and Cities 1850–2000*, (Spon 1998). He has also edited *The Garden City: Past, Present and Future*, Spon (1992) and co-edited (with John R. Gold) *Place Promotion: The Use of Publicity and Marketing to Sell Towns and Regions*, (Wiley 1994). In addition, he has written many articles, book chapters and papers on planning history. He is currently working on a major international study of the diffusion and global application of urban planning during the twentieth century, to be published by Wiley under the title *Planning the Twentieth Century City*.

Christopher Wood is Director of the EIA Centre and Professor of Environmental Planning in the Department of Planning and Landscape at the University of Manchester. Following an education in chemistry and town and country planning, he became a researcher in the University of Manchester Pollution Research Unit. He was then appointed an associate of Land Use Consultants, London before becoming a university teacher. He is convenor of the Royal Town Planning Institute's Environmental Techniques Panel, and was a founder council member of the UK Institute of Environmental Assessment and chairman of the Royal Town Planning Institute's working party on environmental assessment. He has published extensively on environmental planning, including *Town Planning and Pollution Control* (Manchester University Press 1976), *Planning and Pollution* (with Chris Miller) (Oxford University Press 1983, *Planning Pollution Prevention* (Butterworth Heinemann 1989) and *Environmental Impact Assessment: a Comparative Review* (Longman 1995).

Preface

The idea for this book came from a special issue of *Town and Country Planning* on 'Fifty years of the 1947 Act' (*Town and Country Planning*, vol 66, no. 5, May 1997, pp 129–57). This was well received and it seemed a good idea to attempt something similar on a larger scale. It was initially thought that it would be possible to present a fairly comprehensive range of papers, but this would have resulted in a bulky volume in which sheer quantity might prove overwhelming – certainly for the editor! So comprehensive coverage, like comprehensive planning, had to be rejected in favour of something more manageable. In deciding which issues to be covered – and, more difficult, which to exclude, a personal selection had to be made. Hopefully, it is not idiosyncratic, though critics will rightly point to the lack of chapters on planning for town centres, the revolution in retailing (production, distribution and marketing), recreation and leisure, and the role of 'planning implementation' – to name but a few that might have been included. The chapters do, however, illustrate the nature of British planning, its achievements and failures, and some of the issues it now faces. There is no attempt to devise a blueprint for change: that would require both a political endeavour for which modest academics are ill-suited, and a new 'vision' which shows little sign of emerging. Nevertheless, the authors have made their views clear, and I have added a postscript in which I focus on a number of issues which arise in several chapters.

Barry Cullingworth

chapter 1

Introduction and Overview

BARRY CULLINGWORTH

INTRODUCTION

The centrepiece of postwar planning policy was the control of land use. The 1944 white paper, which bore this title, waxed lyrically on the importance of 'provision for the right use of land, in accordance with a considered policy'. In majestic terms, the Minister of Town and Country Planning was given the duty of 'securing consistency and continuity in the framing of a national policy with respect to the use and development of land'. These were halcyon days, full of hope and determination to 'build a better Britain'. To quote from *The Control of Land Use:*

> Provision for the right use of land, in accordance with a considered policy, is an essential requirement of the government's programme of postwar reconstruction. New houses, whether of permanent or emergency construction; the new layout of areas devastated by enemy action or blighted by reason of age or bad living conditions; the new schools which will be required under the Education Bill now before Parliament; the balanced distribution of industry which the government's recently published proposals for maintaining employment envisage; the requirements of sound nutrition and of a healthy and well-balanced agriculture; the preservation of national parks and forests, and the assurance to the people of enjoyment of the sea and countryside in times of leisure; a new and safer highway system better adapted to modern industrial and other needs; the proper provision of airfields – all these related parts of a single reconstruction programme involve the use of land, and it is essential that their various claims on land should be so harmonised as to ensure for the people of this country the greatest possible measure of individual well-being and national prosperity.

Even more broadly, as Robson (in chapter 12) eloquently testifies, there was 'a fervent desire to make a better society, one which was fairer, more compassionate, and more equal'. There was, in a word, a vision. Translating that vision into operational realities was another matter.

Inevitably, the realities of the postwar years rapidly shattered the early dreams. Other issues dominated the political agenda; plans took much time and effort to bring to an operational level, and the resources available were grossly inadequate to implement them. Both public and private investment was held back. Thus 'positive planning' was limited, though the regulatory regime worked, partly because there was so little activity to regulate!

The 1950s, however, witnessed an accelerating rate of change, with a long period of economic growth and social transformation which set new challenges for all the agencies of state planning. The general nature of these changes presented unexpected problems. The planning system had been conceived on assumptions about the future which now moved further and further in unexpected directions. Those assumptions had included modest economic growth, little population increase (except for an anticipated short postwar 'baby boom'), little migration either internal or from abroad, a balance in economic activity among the regions, and a generally manageable administrative task in maintaining controls. Some of the changes that now emerged were the result of the release of pent-up demand which followed the return of the Conservative government in 1952 – a government which was wedded to a 'bonfire of controls'. One of the first acts of this government was a symbolic one: a change in the name of the planning ministry – from 'local government and planning' to 'housing and local government'. This reflected the political primacy of housing and the lack of support for 'planning' (now viewed, with justification, as restrictive). The regional offices of the planning ministry were abolished, thus dismantling the weak (but potentially useful) machinery for coordination.

As prosperity slowly took the place of austerity, structural changes occurred in the economy (though without the devastating social upheavals of the interwar years), new technologies spread, population growth continued at totally unexpected rates, housing demand and need grew, immigration filled low skilled job vacancies (and also provided new occupiers – and buyers – of inner city houses from which white households migrated to the suburbs). Private housebuilding boomed; and curiously so did council house building since this was the only way in which the Conservative government could meet its high housing targets. The birth rate (which – as expected – dropped steadily from 1948 to the mid-1950s) suddenly started a large and continuing rise. These and many other changes transformed the framework within which the planning system operated. With one major exception the system itself changed little. The exception was the abolition of development charges; but development rights remained (and still remain) in the public domain. Indeed, planning acquired an increasingly secure place in the governmental structure and, more important, in the political system. The new towns slowly got under way; city-centre redevelopment proceeded under new forms of public–private partnerships and comprehensive development plans. Development pressures grew as households increased even more rapidly than population, and as car ownership spread (the number of cars doubled in the 1950s and doubled again in the following decade).

Such changes as these had a big impact on British society, but there was little to mirror this in the planning world. There, debate focused on improving the 'efficiency' of the planning process – a recurring theme throughout the postwar period, and on finding an acceptable way of recouping land values. Attempts by Labour governments to do this failed twice. Both the Land Commission and the Community Land Scheme were unable to prove themselves (or even become established) before electoral fortunes reversed their political support. Yet there was no change in the foundation stone of publicly controlled development rights. Nor was there any attempt to change drastically the organization and operation of the planning system as was done later with health, housing, education and transport. The development plan system was updated in 1968–69 following the Planning Advisory Group (PAG) report, but the parallel reorganization of local government into unitary authorities, though accepted by the Labour government, was rejected by its successor. Since then, the local government map has become increasingly confused; making the need for a regional tier of planning urgent.

Some minor changes in the planning system were brought about through changes in planning controls, and in the introduction of enterprising initiatives such as urban development corporations and enterprise zones, but the system remained largely untouched. One foray into the development plan area proved both the political danger of change and the strong support that existed for the system. A proposal to abolish structure plans had to be abandoned after the painful political experience of attempting to deal with major land allocations for residential development through the central appeal process. (The Secretary of State – then Ridley – had his effigy burnt in the village square after his announcement that he 'was minded' to approve the private enterprise new town proposal for Foxley Wood in Hampshire.) It became apparent that it was politically much more comfortable to allow local authorities to deal with such sensitive issues through the development plan system. The burden of proving to the electorate that unwelcome developments were required thus fell to local government.

As environmental awareness grew into a political asset, environmental controls were extended, thereby strengthening the planning system still further. Increasingly, planning became to be seen as a valuable means of protecting high-quality living environments, and opposition to changes in rural areas merged with a range of other issues to form an unstable countryside alliance. Thus, though the planning system is largely unchanged, it has become a powerful mechanism for the resistance of change at the local level.   However, change is now in the air, and there is earnest debate about the way in which the planning system can be adapted to deal with current and emerging problems. It is against this background that this book has been written.

OVERVIEW

With the exception of the last chapters, the order is alphabetical by author. Paul Balchin's chapter on housing is the first, and this is an appropriate accident: housing has always been of higher political profile than planning, and the inter-relationships between the two areas of government are problematic. Balchin repeats a Department of the Environment (DoE) official's comment that 'the DoE planning directorate had more influence on government housing policy than the housing people did'. This, he claims, involved only a slight degree of hyperbole 'for planning guidelines shaped the entire pattern of national housing provision' (Hall 1997: 120). It would be interesting to explore this proposition further (and historically), but for present purposes the point is that the *location* of housing development has been a major preoccupation of the planning system (now given a new twist with mathematical juggling on household projections). Balchin explores a number of the relationships between the two policy areas. His depressing conclusion is that public policy in the 1980s and 1990s 'lamentably failed' to improve housing conditions. In his guide through the labyrinth of housing policies, he shows the complexities with which housing policy has to deal, and the additional complexities which it creates. It is incredible that with so much 'housing policy' and all our wealth, the current housing problem is so great. At least some of the blame for this must be laid at the door of our planning system; and the same system could help to rectify the situation, as Balchin points out 'in the development of a new generation of new towns'. But the majority of the electorate are well housed and will need much persuasion to support major programmes of new building (especially affordable housing), improvement and redevelopment. The spirit of 1947 is not in evidence.

The explicitly discretionary nature of British planning is analysed by Philip Booth. This is difficult to describe, let alone justify: what is a plan for if it can be over-ridden by 'departures', 'exceptions', 'policy guidance' from the central government, and a host of other 'material considerations' which are not defined by the legislation and are subject only to very broad judicial limitations? Most countries operate some form of zoning system in which the plan is a legal document and provides a greater degree of certainty, and many have a constitution which provides protection against arbitrary planning actions. In Booth's words, 'seen from without, the British system is distinctly odd'. However, all is not what it seems, and Booth's journey around the relevant issues shows that zoning systems typically incorporate an essential degree of flexibility, and therefore the very uncertainty that is a feature of the British system. Indeed, all systems have to trade off flexibility and certainty. This does not mean that improvements cannot be made. Booth suggests that there is real issue that 'planning policy nationwide could be led by government directive rather than determined locally in development plans' (a matter on which there could be very conflicting views). There is also some doubt about the purpose that development plans should serve – a subject which Davies examines further in chapter 4.

Development plans had a lengthy and chequered birth, with an initial conception of an 'outline plan' giving way to something similar to the prewar 'planning scheme' and eventually becoming the 1947 development plan. Davies traces the history of the debate on this within Whitehall. It is revealing to see the way in which the development plan emerged, and also how it changed over time. With the focus of hindsight, postwar planning appears like a continuing drama (some might say a tragedy of errors) played out against the background of changes in the political scene, in the structure of local government, in the role of the central government and in perceptions of what planning is about. Interestingly, the concept of an 'outline plan' kept resurfacing, partly because development plans had a habit of becoming too detailed and cumbersome, and partly because they confused (or at least masked) policy. It is now re-emerging. There was also a less obvious force for change: the reaction of Whitehall to the burden of coping with the sheer weight of plan submissions.

There are many fascinating byways, and it is to be hoped that others will follow the lead of Davies (and others [1]) in searching though the records now available in the Public Record Office. It is noteworthy how the changes in the compensation–betterment provisions of the 1947 Act influenced (and continue to influence) thinking on the nature of plans. In the run up to the 1947 Act, the nationalization of development rights, and the removal of the liability for compensation, implied that the function of a plan was not 'to determine the rights of owners, but to determine the pattern of future development' without regard to property values. One implication of this was that an adversarial public inquiry system was unnecessary: all that was required was 'a process of consultation with selected interest groups'. The idea was dropped, but it emerged in a different guise when the sheer avalanche of inquiries led to the introduction of the examination in public. Currently, development plans are again under review, this time in the context of an emerging regional tier of planning. In this review, note should be taken of the comment that Davies makes in reflecting on experience that perhaps the major mistake in the past has been to encompass two very different functions in the development plan: the strategic one (not requiring a statutory document) and the regulatory one which, 'given our mixed economy and the private ownership of land, does need to have legal status'. The power of the strategy of some of the postwar advisory plans is eloquent testimony to the usefulness of non-statutory guides to land-use planning, particularly at the regional level.

The centrality of the compensation–betterment issue is the subject of Malcolm Grant's chapter. He traces the sad story of the three attempts to devise a workable comprehensive solution; the 1947 development charge scheme, the 1967 Land Commission and the 1975–6 Community Land Scheme. Curiously, it was their very comprehensiveness that was a major part of their undoing: political forces supplied the death blow. Perhaps the schemes could have been amended and made to work had changes in government come somewhat later, but time ran out, and a succeeding government abolished them with the clarion call that they had 'no place in a free society'. The position was not quite as clear-cut as this, but the simple story lives on, and the experience is deeply embedded in the political psyche of successive Conservative governments.[2] Indeed, both parties now have (in Grant's words) 'no political will to revisit past failures'. This is a tragedy for the planning system for two reasons. First, the issue will not go away: it permeates the planning system, and, secondly it distorts planning policy and creates inequities on a large scale. Differing operations of planning gain cause inequities between different developments. Much more widely, it gives huge prizes to the winners in the sweepstakes of planning applications; but the losers get nothing. So is there a politically practicable answer? Grant argues that there is: both planning gain in its general sense, and the specific case of requirements for affordable housing provide the basis for an answer. The present 'gains' constitute 'a ramshackle device, which has been pressed already beyond its legitimate limits', but given rationalization it could serve as a workable alternative to a betterment tax. It would thereby serve to facilitate the implementation of planning policies and achieve greater equity in the land market.

The re-emergence of the regional planning of land use on the political agenda makes Peter Hall's chapter particularly timely. For most of the postwar period, there has been little of this type of regional planning: instead there has been a preoccupation with regional disparities – mainly in terms of employment. The policies which have been crafted to deal with this have sometimes had relationships with land-use planning (and vice versa), and also with urban policies, but typically they have been conceived and operated essentially in terms of creating (or saving) jobs. Significantly, the responsibilities for designing and operating these policies have rested unambiguously with central government. Local initiatives, where they have existed, have been supplementary, and largely restricted to advertising and – as a land use planning matter – allocating sites for industrial development. The short-lived regional economic planning councils (and their civil service boards) muddied the waters somewhat since, despite their titular emphasis on *economic* and their role in the Wilson government's ill-fated *National Plan*, they strayed into land use issues such as green belts, overspill and housing land. However, they were of little importance: they operated as talking shops for articulate local authority members, spiced with bemused local worthies. They were abolished, with little opposition or regret by Mrs Thatcher, long after they had any discernible function.[3]

Despite (or because of?) the central government's unchallenged role as the controller of regional policy, its objectives were unclear (except in terms of politics and real concern for the inequities created by regional disparities). Its implementation was erratic, partly because of the inherent uncertainties, partly because it was mercilessly buffeted by economic forces over which it had no control, and partly because there was always a doubt (shared by more than would admit to it) that its efforts were futile. The highly significant change in policy from regional assistance to national economic growth (started by Labour in the late 1970s) was in fact, to use Hall's phrase, a 'retreat from regional policy'. It acknowledged the transformation of the 'regional' problem. A new dimension was emerging with serious imbalances between well-off suburbs and rapidly declining and deprived inner cities. Already housing improvement policies had been supplemented by the educational priority area and urban aid programmes: these were now expanded into a wide-ranging set of measures heralded by a white paper *Policy for the Inner Cities*. Again it is significant that as with regional programmes the 'policy, consisted of a plethora of programmes of a confusing and incoherent nature' (discussed further by Robson in chapter 12).

A shift of focus and funds to inner cities was continued by the Thatcher government, spurred on by the opposition of their supporters to major programmes of housebuilding in the suburban and outer suburban areas, and with a greater concern for economic enterprise. Hall points to another facet of the changing regional economic geography, with the old-style 'regional problem' extending southwards to the midlands and even large areas of London. With 'the highest concentration of unemployment in the advanced industrial world, heavily concentrated in a few boroughs, and including a substantial proportion of long term unemployed', London is an outstanding case of the new-style regional problem. It remains to be seen how the 1997 Labour government's emerging urban and regional planning proposals will deal with this. So far as regional planning is concerned, the separate strands (particularly in the southeast) which Hall discusses give grounds for optimism.

If there has been a plethora of programmes for urban areas and for regional economies, there has been an avalanche for the countryside. New schemes have proliferated, sometimes at a bewildering rate. One is tempted to consider whether this is a result of a lack of clarity in policy formation, or, indeed, whether it is a case of governments being unable to face up squarely to the crucial issues. In chapter 7, Ian Hodge outlines what these issues are, mercifully resisting the temptation to give us a programme inventory. Essentially, there has been such a transformation of the countryside scene, both figuratively and literally, that traditional thinking on this policy area has become quite outdated. It is, however, easier to diagnose than to devise effective and (a different matter) acceptable policies. The hand of history is heavy particularly when the situation, theoretically at least, demands a turn around of large and upsetting dimensions. The history of the prewar and wartime years created a concern for agricultural protection and development which strengthened attitudes to the conservation of the countryside and the rural economy that sustained it.

The Scott report (1942) provided an analysis and policy prescription which commanded almost universal acceptance – that is apart from Dennison's minority report which anticipated declining agricultural employment (and therefore the undermining of a rural economy which had produced the admired landscape) and questioned the role of agriculture in environmental protection. Dennison was ignored, but he was right. The harmony between agricultural production, rural society, visual delight and urban containment was (like much else in the mid-1940s) a product of backward thinking rather than forward anticipation. The countryside was seen essentially as agricultural land: a crucially important national asset for food production, landscape enjoyment and (to a lesser extent) recreation, to which the planning system was not relevant – except to ensure that it was 'protected' from inessential development. Hence, it was exempt (along with forestry) from planning controls. At this time it was inconceivable that the agricultural industry could itself be a threat to the other virtues characteristic of the rural scene. The revolution(s) that have taken place in the 50 years that followed (and which Dennison foreshadowed) have been widely documented – they include changes in technology, ownership, management; agricultural surpluses of an embarrassingly huge size; the decline of the traditional rural economy; the suburbanization of the rural housing market, increased concern for landscape and environmental values; massive increases in countryside travel and recreation. And, of course, the impact of European policies. Vast areas of land have been taken into more intensive agricultural production (and over a 100, 000 miles of hedgerows have been lost). In the face of such changes, and the interest groups involved, it is not surprising that the policy responses, though numerous, have been less than impressive. Hodge illuminates this complicated scene, and points to the issues of ownership, property rights and management agreements, which abound. He notes that changes in policy can have far-reaching implications for compensation (where there is already a Gilbertian situation of farmers being compensated for grants foregone). He suggests that change may come about by a continuation of the erosion of the rights of agricultural landholders which has taken place on a scale that looks modest to the outsider, but fearful to landowners.

It is noteworthy how this issue of property rights arises in so many different planning areas: the repeal of the compensation–betterment provisions brought about a profound change in the character and operation of the planning system. Curiously, one area in which the strident controversy could have been expected is that of heritage preservation. Of course, there have been opponents of the clear interference with property rights from the 1870s when Lord Percy objected to ancient monument protection on the grounds that this was a 'control of private property not for public purposes, but for purposes of sentiment, and it was difficult to see where that would stop'. Lord Percy would certainly have been horrified at the case of Old Hall, Thurrock, where the redoubtable MP Theresa Gorman was fined for making illegal substantial alterations to the Grade II listed building. He would have been even more incredulous at the detailed nature of the controls and the insistence that alterations be carried out with original materials – no artificial plastic, even if it is a visually close 'match'. Heritage conservation has always been separate from the main arenas of planning debate. Its origins and history are different, it is the responsibility of a separate government department, and its distinctiveness has now been hallowed on the consolidation of planning legislation by the passing of a separate Planning (Listed Buildings and Conservation Areas) Act. It also has had a tradition of secrecy that is extreme even by traditional British standards (instructions to investigators responsible for listing were strictly secret). Larkham shows how some of these features of conservation are changing, particularly in their relationship with the mainstream planning system. Conservation has a wide degree of public support as well, of course, as a considerable tourist appeal. It may be devoting too much of its resources to designations and too little to management and the reuse of properties which have outlived their usefulness. This may because of its underlying ambiguity: Larkham concludes his survey with the oft-repeated, but valid, criticism that there is no underlying or consistent philosophy of conservation, nor is there any indication that one is likely to emerge.

Of all the unforecastable influences on postwar planning, perhaps that of Europe is the most unexpected. In chapter 9, Vincent Nadin traces the paths along which this has developed. The Common Agricultural Policy (CAP) is well known, if only by distorted repute. Directives on wild birds and on natural habitats are now part of the firmament of environmental policy. Local authorities, at least in areas which are or may be eligible for financial assistance, will know of 'structural funds'. Planners and geographers may be among the few who are familiar with the activities on 'spatial planning', which Nadin explains in some detail. This, of course, seems to be closest to the core of 'town and country planning' (a distinctively British term) but in fact it has a different meaning. Rather than being essentially concerned with land-use planning itself, 'spatial planning' is the coordination of all policy fields that have spatial objectives or impacts. 'Spatial planning seeks to coordinate the spatial impacts of all sectoral policy such as land use, transport, environment, regional, agriculture, and others. It is an integrating activity, ideally providing an umbrella of spatial strategy within which other sectors operate'. Despite its salience in planning circles, the spatial planning work of the European Community (EC) (particularly through the Committee on Spatial Development) operates in an informal manner. This seems curious: it is certainly very different from the environmental directives which are translated into national legislation. It follows from two factors. First, the Treaty provides no appropriate 'competence' in this area. Second, there is nothing unusual about informal working in Brussels: indeed, as Nadin points out, it is common practice. How far the ideas which emanate from the ministers and civil servants (UK and EC) on spatial programmes will have an impact in Britain remains to be seen. So far, 'the lack of institutional capacity and appropriate instruments at the regional and nation levels in the UK' has not provided fertile ground. However, the dramatic institutional change that is now beginning to take place in this country may transform the situation. Having started major constitutional reform, there is no saying where it will lead.

Few planning issues have proved as controversial as design. The controversy is not restricted to particular design styles: it extends to much wider questions. Is design a 'planning' matter at all? Are planners qualified to pronounce on design issues? Is it really possible to 'control' design or is it a matter of individual taste? What is the scope of 'design'? (The terms used in official advice over the years are revealing: elevational control, external appearance, aesthetic control, design, urban design, and perhaps in the future sustainable design.) John Punter analyses the issues and recounts the postwar history which, until recently, has been a dismal one. Good design is not easy to define. As Holford argued in an official handbook in 1953: 'design cannot be taught by correspondence; words are inadequate, and being inadequate may then become misleading, or even dangerous. For the competent designer a handbook on design is unnecessary, and for the incompetent it is almost useless as a medium of instruction'. This general agnosticism grew into outright hostility in the 1980s when controls were typically regarded as brakes on enterprise. Curiously, the attitudes in Scotland were quite different, and they have remained so with 'a flow of positive design advice' from the Scottish Office. South of the border, attitudes began to change, and a more positive note was sounded in the 1990s, particularly after the advent of John Gummer as Secretary of State. His personal opinions (with a 'passionate view about architecture, town and urban life') made a tangible impact, not only in promoting the cause of 'urban design' but also in broadening the terms of the debate on design. At the end of his chapter, Punter discusses the direction in which these should go – essentially to embrace 'a more sustainable approach to development and to questions of future urban forms and overall design quality'.

The role of the courts in the planning system is a limited one. This follows from the absence of a written constitution guaranteeing individual rights – particularly the right to property (see Callies' chapter 18), as well as the historical and cultural forces operating on the British scene. Whether the courts *should* play a more prominent role is a debatable question (which may no longer be a theoretical one following the Human Rights Act). Purdue, in chapter 11 on the changing role of the courts in planning, takes the view that at times 'the present line taken by the courts gives too much leeway to the decision maker'. It also gives inadequate guidance in areas where it is clearly needed, as with planning gain. However, following Grant's discussion in chapter 5, the alternative to judicial activism would be a clear statutory framework. The difficulty with judge-led policy formulation is that, in Purdue's words, the 'consistent trait of the role of the courts in planning cases has been the way they have disagreed among themselves'. Indeed, court decisions sometimes almost appear as a game, with the joker being the unpredictable. To the non-lawyer, Purdue's demonstration of the uncertainty and lack of clarity in the case law makes it difficult to see why issues such as third-party rights, or material considerations, should be left in limbo between the legislature and the courts. Presumably, governments have neither the time nor the inclination to devote scarce parliamentary time to legislation which could prove contentious: it would certainly make it necessary for some awkward policy decisions to be taken. Far better to let the courts decide and shoulder the blame if matters develop in an unpopular way! There will be time enough for legislation if public pressures mount sufficiently. An alternative might be some form of specialist court to which Purdue refers at the end of his chapter. There are many forms which this take and, rather than adjudicating on specific issues of legal contention, it could have a quite extensive role in rationalizing policy matters.

Brian Robson's chapter 12 on urban social policy is written in a distinctive style. It is both a personal testament about 'the irresponsible society' (to borrow the title of a tract by Richard Titmuss) and an attempt to summarize the complex of social/urban problems which are proving so resistant to policy initiatives. He draws on studies in which he has been deeply involved, at the behest of government, of analysing 'urban policy'. The conclusions of this research have not been entirely to the liking of those who commissioned it. This is an obstacle which confronts all who study in this area: it is one which bristles with difficulties for governments and the electorate – difficulties of comprehension, of public understanding and support, of overcoming prejudice about the poor (a way of dealing with what might otherwise be unacceptable), as well as the more general ones of finance and the organization of programmes which inevitably straddle established boundaries of departmental responsibility, funding and thinking. Robson recalls the vision of the wartime and postwar years, which is now largely forgotten and probably impossible to recreate. So we must battle on with the attempt to devise programmes that can be effectively targeted (to use contemporary parlance). The Wilson government was the first to declare (in 1968) an 'urban policy' which led to a 'welter of policy instruments'. Conservative governments placed faith in market forces and 'trickle-down' theories, but neither flagship policies such as urban development corporations nor a further proliferation of programmes had much coherence or impact. Attempts were made (more successful than earlier) to establish effective partnerships 'across the domains of the public sector, private sector and voluntary/community sector'. Building on these modest successes came the Single Regeneration Budget which added the important element of more integrated working across government departments. This recognition of the interconnectedness of the problems in deprived areas led later to 'joined-up thinking' and to the Social Exclusion Unit which refocused the agenda to emphasize social deprivation. The persistence of the problems to which these policy developments are addressed are mortifying: indices of social deprivation that refuse to show significant change. The solutions are elusive, and there are no easy routes ahead.

Robson's chapter points to the importance of public support for government policies; but which comes first? Is it the function of government to rally support for its policies, or the function of public participation to inform government what its policies should be? Of course, this is an impossible question: it is a conundrum rather than a question. It does, however, point up the crucial political question: how are policies to be decided in a democratic society where majorities effectively wield power over minorities? Yvonne Rydin raises these issues at the conclusion of chapter 13, after reviewing some postwar experiences of 'public participation in planning'.

The outcomes are not encouraging, and it looks as if frustration, incomprehension and the sheer impossibility of communication can easily turn public participation into a sham. Certainly, that is the verdict of those who view participation as a means of wresting power from governmental bodies. Rydin explores the various issues involved here, and pinpoints the underlying question of 'who should exercise power within planning?' She urges caution: it is very easy for all concerned in the planning process to subscribe to the notion of greater public participation, but at the same time have conflicting ideas on what this involves. Further, there are issues on which a higher authority must over-ride the wishes of local participants for the sake of wider public interests – Rydin lists some telling examples. She concludes that 'the real issue is over the legitimacy of the planning system and its robustness in the face of criticism . . . support for the planning system and its outcomes is as likely to arise from the extent to which the public feel that grievances have been adequately dealt with, as the quantum of public involvement in planning forums'.

The difficulties of public participation are well illustrated by the seemingly intractable problems with transport. The public want better transport facilities from which they will benefit, but they do not want new roads or railway lines close to their homes: the public in general is different from the public in particular. With road charges the division of publics is along different lines: between the public that would have to pay them and the public who do not. However, the problems of public participation in transport planning have been dealt with over much of the postwar period by ignoring or preventing it. (The farce of road inquiries continued until John Tyme made a thorough nuisance of himself, and recruited an active body of protesters – an approach copied with variations by Swampy and his colleagues in relation to the Newbury bypass a generation later; both eventually contributed to major changes in transport policy.)

Paul Truelove, in chapter 14, outlines issues such of these which illuminate the chequered history of transport planning. He notes that there was no conception of the extent to which traffic would grow and still less, of course, of the implications for land-use planning. (American experience was simply not considered relevant.) There were warnings as with J. M. Thomson's 1971 article on 'halfway to a motorised society' though, like all traffic forecasters, he underestimated the figures: we were far less than 'halfway'. Gradually, the scale of the growth and its impact became apparent. Buchanan posed the problem, and he also presented a clear choice. We could either undertake major roadworks and urban reconstruction to accommodate the growth in traffic, or we could deliberately limit the use of vehicles in towns. Being an experienced civil servant, he saw the possibility of steadily increasing traffic and only minor alterations to the urban fabric thus resulting 'in the worst of both worlds – poor traffic access and a grievously eroded environment'. Truelove's chapter spells out some of the ways in which this has been accomplished. The most extraordinary aspect of the history of transport policies is the persistent refusal to acknowledge the fundamental relationship between transport and land-use planning. Surely this must be among the first elementary lessons to be learned in a planning school? The school of politics is, of course, very different and, though it will be very difficult to bring about a renaissance in coordinated land use and transport planning, at least crucial elements are now accepted as a basis for an 'integrated transport'. The 1998 white paper *A New Deal for Transport* represents a first step.

Most of the chapters in this volume point up failures in postwar planning. It is therefore a relief to turn to one field of policy which has achieved considerable success (and international acclaim). The new towns' story is a long and oft-told one dating back to the later years of the industrial revolution, and the remarkable persistence of a small group of visionaries who not only campaigned for new towns, but actually ventured into building them at Letchworth and Welwyn Garden City. In chapter 15, Urlan Wannop (who has been a planner in six new towns) picks up the story with the birth of the Labour government's commitment to a policy of government sponsored and financed new towns. This was a difficult time for such an enterprise: both financial and material problems were acute. The wonder is that the policy was actually implemented; and without Lewis Silkin, the Minister of Town and Country Planning, it may well have been abandoned. The planning and start-up period was a long one, and there was strong local opposition to most of the sites chosen; but slowly the new towns took shape. As they got under way, there was a constant battle with the Treasury (concerned about costs) and the Board of Trade (concerned that the new towns were attracting industry that was needed for the regions suffering high unemployment). However, they gathered momentum, commitments were made and had to honoured, and the senior staff of the development corporations were constant in pressing the claims of their new towns. (Wannop comments on 'the impetus to self-perpetuation' : 'the career interests of their staff and corporations propelled them as much as most governments'.) Their fortunes improved when the Treasury realized that they represented an excellent long-term investment (which, of course, is what the theories about new towns claimed). The real mark of their political success, however, came with the decision of the Conservative government to start a 'second generation' of new towns, which was further expanded under the subsequent Labour government.

Wannop examines their 'success' in other directions. He points out that it is misleading to refer to the policy as a 'programme', except in the sense that they were the implementation of a policy. The 32 new towns differ widely in many ways. The 'programme' was added to irregularly, 'some intended additions never arrived, and many parts became distorted'. Judging their overall success is as difficult as deciding on the relevant criteria. Wannop submits that they provide a 'vision' for dealing with current and emerging problems of urban development. However, if further new towns are to be developed, it will be necessary to revisit the arguments about the form of the 'developing agency'. Of particular relevance today is some form of partnership.

It may come as a surprise to some that the concept of partnership in urban development has along history of implementation. Stephen Ward's chapter 16 traces its origins in the exceptional circumstances of the war and early postwar period when it was clear that local authorities would have to play a role in assembling land and redeveloping blitzed (and blighted) areas. Powers were provided to designate *comprehensive development areas* (CDAs) to facilitate this. The powers were broad and could be used in a variety of circumstances. Though the powers rested with local authorities, it was the private sector which had the skills required for commercial development: a partnership between the two was an obvious way forward. With the abolition of licensing, the freer availability of building materials, and the abolition of development charges in the mid 1950s, a more speculative market grew, particularly for offices. Partnerships with local authorities developed, either through the use of CDA powers or by way of planning agreements.

The commercial property development sector mushroomed – to the extent that it became 'the world's largest and most highly organised'. This put it a strong position to wield influence and to enhance profits; at the same time, local authorities could extract planning gain. Partnerships also developed in the large scale development of greenfield sites. Cramlington and, to a lesser extent, Killingworth in Tyneside were quasi new towns developed in partnership using CDA powers. (A similar proposal for the Bletchley area was rejected by the ministry and instead it was developed as the new town of Milton Keynes.) Other developments included South Woodham Ferrers, Essex (using CDA powers) and Lower Earley, Berkshire (on land largely owned by the builder, and using a planning agreement). Other agreements proved impossible to conclude because of the opposition of a number of county councils to the creation of 'new settlements'. Partnerships also operated in the field of urban regeneration, particularly after the importation of American ideas in the form of the *urban development grant* in 1982 (later *city grant*). These proved to be insensitive to the needs of inner urban areas, and their crudeness led to the formation of English Partnerships and the *single regeneration budget* discussed in Robson's chapter. Nevertheless, the partnership idea thrives on the standard formula of developer profits plus public interest equalling benefits for all. It has equally good currency with the Blair government, and it now seems that it 'permeates all aspects of public policy' and its future 'seems assured'. Yet it has to be recognized that private developers are not charitable organizations, and that their very purpose is to make private profits. Ward's final comment is that harnessing the profit motive 'to cross-subsidize publicly necessary projects, particularly those that will never be profitable, remains a goal that is still too rarely achieved'.

Environmental policy is currently very much to the fore, though this has certainly not always been the case, as Chris Wood explains in chapter 17. Many political analysts have commented on the way in which issues move up and down the political attention ladder, rising and falling in the concern of politicians and in their willingness to 'take action', or to promise 'to do something about it', or to deny that there is a problem, or to protest that there is no answer to it. Environmental policies illustrate this very human trend. Dramatic unexpected events can have equally dramatic policy changes: the disastrous London smog of 1952, which resulted in 4,000 deaths, led directly to extensive clean-air controls (and a longer term change in the use of domestic coal). The recent concern about 'mad cow disease' resulted in draconian controls on beef and major impacts on farmers' incomes. Sometimes, issues can merge and create an unstable coalition (as with the proposed ban on hunting, protection of the countryside, 'freedom to roam' and so on): here the individual issues may recede, but there is no doubt that 'the countryside' has risen in political salience. International and EC pressures can have an impact, as well as royal commissions and professional bodies. All these influences are seen with particular clarity in the environmental field, as Wood shows. There is also in this area the extraordinary 1988 conversion of Mrs Thatcher to an environmental ethic (in striking contrast to her previous preference for the removal of brakes on enterprise). Rarely can such a positive speech have had such an impact on environmental policy.

There have been two periods (in recent history) when environmental awareness (and policy) burgeoned. The first was the reaction to the environmental horrors of the industrial revolution (which Wood describes as an environmental origin of the UK planning system). The second came towards the end of the 1980s when a 'reviving interest' followed American and international concerns about the effects of inadequately controlled growth on the environment. In Britain, the establishment of the DoE and the Royal Commission on the Environment signalled the emergence of a new era of active environmental policies which are still developing. At present it certainly seems that environmental policies themselves are sustainable.

The last chapter, by David Callies, provides an American perspective on UK planning. There are some clear similarities between the two countries, as with development agreements and planning gain. There are also striking differences: the wide-ranging controls over development in Britain, and the extent of development freedoms as of right in the USA. This is the most important difference of all: it reflects the nationalization of development rights in Britain, and the constitutional rights to property in the USA, together with the historical and cultural framework which underpin these. Some of the features of the British planning system appear baffling to American eyes – the huge public inquiries on such major developments as the new terminal at Heathrow; the absence of constitutional protection of property rights; the limited role played by the courts. On the first of these points, there would be strong support in Britain for a change in the cumbersome and unsatisfactory nature of 'the big public inquiry' (as it was once called[4]). On the constitutional protection of property rights, current constitutional changes could make a significant change, and bring the British system closer to the American; and similarly with the limited role of the courts.

Callies emphasizes some points of possible convergence, as with the increasing prominence of plans as a framework for development control. Some of his comments may seem unconvincing to British readers – which makes them particularly interesting and challenging. For instance, will the emphasis on plan-led development lead to 'a more legalistic treatment of local plans in applications for planning permission'? Particularly telling is his comment that 'positive planning' is the Achilles heel of the British system: 'while it is relatively easy to halt development which is deemed inappropriate, it is extremely difficult to require "appropriate" development to take place'. However, it is not the editor's place to cross-examine a contributor. David Callies was invited to provide a 'perspective' on British planning because it was thought that he would produce a thought-provoking chapter, and this he certainly has.

To round off the volume, I add a short *postscript* which highlights some of the major planning problems which are discussed in the book. I argue the case for a more positive approach to planning, particularly at the regional level. The arguments will be familiar but, until recently, they have been academic. The first 18 months of the Blair government, however, led to the hope that some major changes in the planning system may come about. Certainly, there has been a host of ideas which are apparently being seriously studied. It remains to be seen, of course, what emerges as practical politics, but there do seem to be grounds for some cautious optimism.

chapter 2

Housing

PAUL BALCHIN

INTRODUCTION

It is sometimes argued that 'there is a great academic divide between studies of housing and studies of planning' (Ball 1983 : 193). Undoubtedly, housing literature focuses on legislation relating to households and tenures, and often ignores spatial considerations, whereas planning studies concentrate on the effect of planning policy on land markets and the spatial distribution of housing and other land uses. It might also be suggested, however, that housing and town and country planning 'are inextricably linked, both in the history that the two disciplines share and in some areas of overlapping contemporary policy and legislation' (O'Leary 1997: 122). This chapter, therefore, is an attempt to consider the relationship between housing policy and planning policy in Britain since the late 1940s.

Evidence suggests that there have been four major stages in the development of housing policy in Britain since the second world war although, from time to time, different stages overlapped (Boelhouwer 1991). The first stage of policy development was dominated by the urgency of reducing the large housing shortages in the late 1940s and early 1950s. The second stage, incorporating large building programmes, included a major concern for improving the quality of the housing stock. Initially marked by a concentration on slum clearance and redevelopment, it was subsequently focused on improvement and repairs. The third stage, commencing in 1971, was largely characterized by further shifts of emphasis, from supply-side expenditure to demand-side subsidies. These benefited the reasonably well-housed at the expense of the inadequately accommodated, in the belief that such a shift would reduce state intervention in the production process and, instead, promote the development of the free market. The fourth stage, commencing in the mid-1980s, saw the reappearance of quantitative and qualitative housing shortages, and an increase in state involvement. It is interesting to note that there was little close relationship between the different stages of housing policy and governmental change (Figure 2.1).

LOCAL AUTHORITY HOUSEBUILDING 1945–54

During the second world war housebuilding came virtually to a halt, and as many as 200,000 dwellings were completely destroyed and 3.5 million were seriously damaged. In 1945, it was estimated that there was a need for an additional 1,250,000

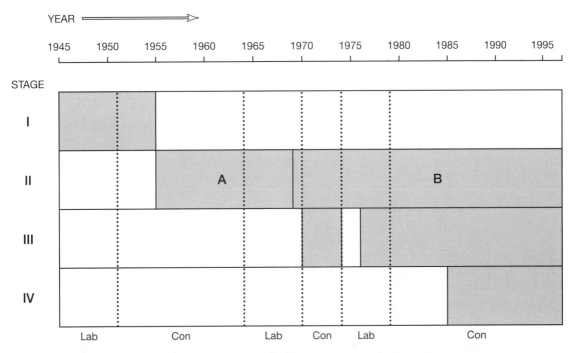

YEAR ⟹

STAGE

I High degree of government involvement, particularly in order to alleviate housing shortages.

II Greater emphasis on housing quality:
  A Improvement in the quality of the stock by slum clearance programmes and substitute new construction.
  B Emphasis on maintenance and improvement instead of slum clearance.

III Greater emphasis on problems of housing distribution and targeting specific groups, and the withdrawal of the state in favour of the private sector.

IV Reappearance of quantitative and qualitative housing shortages; state involvement increases.

Lab: Labour
Con: Conservative

Figure 2.1 The development of housing policy under successive Labour and Conservative governments 1945–97

dwellings – a figure that was later destined to increase with rapid population growth in the postwar period.

It was clear that the private rented sector would play little part in satisfying housing needs in the aftermath of the war, notwithstanding the fact that, in 1945, it had been the largest tenure (accounting for 55 per cent of Britain's housing stock). Privately rented dwellings were subject to controls restricting rents to their 1939 level (against the background of a doubling of the general price level by 1951). Although this helped to ensure affordability, it severely constrained supply since there was little or no incentive to new investment. As the main provider of new and affordable housing, the public sector thus dominated the period from 1945 until the late 1950s.

Under a newly elected Labour administration, local authority housebuilding was stimulated by subsidies and low interest rate government loans. Local authorities were also given priority for scarce building materials which, for the private sector, were subject to a licensing system. From the outset, it was emphasized that council housing was intended for general need to meet the acute housing shortage. The Housing Act 1949 thus removed the 'ridiculous inhibition' restricting local authorities to the provision of houses for the working class.

Between 1945 and 1951, a total of almost a million houses were built in Britain. Four-fifths of these were local authority dwellings. Overall this was a great achievement in view of postwar material shortages, the need to reconstruct industry, curb inflation and correct the balance of payments deficits. Of equal importance, the quality of new housing was improved. The minimum size of a three-bedroom house had been fixed at 750 ft² (75 m²) in the 1930s. In 1944, the Dudley Report recommended 950 ft² (95 m²). This was accepted, and local authorities were encouraged to adopt even higher standards where this was possible.

The Conservative government which was elected in 1951 was committed to an annual housebuilding programme of 300,000 houses. Aided by an increase in subsidies, the number of local authority completions increased from 163,000 in 1951 to 229,000 in 1953. The total number of council and private sector dwellings increased from 185,000 in 1951 to 314,000 in 1954. However, the achievement of the housebuilding target was not without its downside. Space standards were sacrificed in the public sector; fewer new local authority dwellings were earmarked for low income inner city households; more slums were being created by poor maintenance than were being removed by clearance; and imports of timber and other building materials were putting a strain on the balance of payments.

During the postwar years, housing policy was strongly underpinned by planning legislation. The 1947 planning act required all local planning authorities to prepare development plans for the whole of their areas, and these were to be submitted for ministerial approval. Notwithstanding the positive effects of development plans on the spatial development of housing (and other uses), the provisions of the 1947 Act relating to development rights and development values had arguably the greatest impact on housing development in the late 1940s and early 1950s. Under the Act, both development rights and development values were nationalized. All development required planning permission, while private development was subject to a 100 per cent development charge (equal to market value less existing use value).

Whereas the 100 per cent charge almost certainly deterred the development of owner-occupied housing (and other private uses) by drying up the supply of land, the development of housing in the public sector was facilitated by public powers of compulsory purchase of land at existing use value. To a significant extent, the effect of the 1947 Act on housing development in the immediate postwar years was thus marked by the very different levels of housebuilding in the two housing sectors. While there were only 402,000 completions in the private sector in Britain from 1947 to 1954, there were 1.4 million completions in the local authority sector. Also, whereas home buyers faced high prices for new private housing, council tenants did not have had to bear the development value of land in their rent payments (Merrett 1979: 241).

After the second world war, however, there was a need not only to build a large number of low cost houses in the public rented sector but also to provide housing to relieve the problems of London and other major cities and to further the redevelopment of the declining industrial regions. As discussed in chapter 15, fourteen new towns were designated between 1946 and 1950. Eight of these were to relieve the housing problems of London (Stevenage, Harlow, Hemel Hempstead, Crawley, Welwyn, Hatfield, Basildon and Bracknell); one to provide overspill housing for Glasgow (East Kilbride); four to assist regional development in Scotland (Glenrothes), Durham (Aycliffe and Peterlee) and south Wales (Cwmbran), and one to deal with employment growth (Corby).

Figure 2.2 Low-density semi-rural housing in Bracknell new town 1950

The expansion of country towns was a further means of accommodating population overspill from London and other major cities. Town expansion appealed particularly to the Treasury 'always mindful of the lower costs involved compared with new towns' (Cherry 1996: 154). Under the Town Development Act 1952, 'exporting authorities' (cities) were therefore encouraged to enter into agreement with 'receiving authorities' (country towns) to provide housing 'for the relief of congestion and overpopulation' in the congested areas. Houses were built by the receiving authorities with the assistance of Exchequer grants and contributions from the exporting authority. Tenants were nominated either from local authority housing lists or through an industrial selection scheme. A similar scheme was adopted in Scotland as a means of facilitating overspill programmes for Clydeside.

However, due to the need to compete for limited resources, both the new town and expanded town initiatives were slow to bear fruit. In the meantime, some of the major cities developed housing estates beyond their boundaries to provide an immediate solution to their more urgent needs. For example, a ring of 13 'out-county' estates were developed around London between 1945 and 1956 accommodating 150,000 people mainly from the housing list. This was a stopgap measure deemed necessary before new and expanded town schemes got off the ground.

SLUM CLEARANCE 1955–68

By the mid-1950s, the postwar housing shortage had been sufficiently reduced to permit a resumption of the slum clearance programme which had been halted by the war. In 1954, the law relating to clearance orders and the compulsory purchase of unfit houses was streamlined, and a new standard of fitness was introduced. Subsequently the subsidy for general needs housing was reduced, and a new subsidy introduced for public sector housing built to replace slums. At the same time, the subsidy structure was changed to encourage high-rise building. Local authority completions fell from 229,000 in 1953 to 114,000 in 1959 while over the same period private sector building rose from 63,000 to 151,000. This was a reflection of the policy to promote a 'property-owning democracy' promised in a Conservative election pledge. However, to prevent a continuing slide in the number of local authority completions and to reflate the economy, the government – perhaps rather reluctantly – reintroduced subsidies for general needs housing in 1961.

Under the 1964–70 Labour government, the number of housing completions in the public sector initially increased (from 141,000 in 1964 to 182,000 in 1968) in line with the commitment to build half a million houses a year across all sectors. It was intended, moreover, that local authority housebuilding would be stabilized at pro-grammed levels even if interest rates rose. To this end, the basic form of subsidy which had been in existence since 1924 was modified. Henceforth, the Exchequer would meet the difference between loan charges incurred by the local authority on borrowing for the financial year and charges which would have been incurred had interest rates been 4 per cent. The central government also attempted to stabilize spending by means of an 'approved cost element' measured by the 'cost yardstick', while quality was to be enhanced through the adoption of Parker Morris standards.

Rates of housebuilding in both the public and private sectors during the 1950s and 1960s were substantially influenced by planning policy in a number of different ways. First, inspired by the London green belt (launched initially in 1938), the Minister of Housing and Local Government, Duncan Sandys, extended the concept of the green belt to areas around provincial cities to check their outward growth, to

Figure 2.3 High-rise local authority housing of the late 1960s: 21-storey flats developed with the use of industrial systems, London Borough of Wandsworth

assist in safeguarding the countryside, to prevent the merger of neighbouring towns, and to preserve towns of historic interest. Development was severely restrained in designated green belt areas, and thus (so it has been argued) the shortage of urban development land was exacerbated, and land prices increased.

Second, since the 100 per cent development charge of the 1947 Act had led to a significant drying up in the supply of development land, it had become obvious by 1950 that a major change in the scheme was essential. But whereas the 1950–51 Labour government might have lowered the development charge to (say) 50 per cent, the incoming Conservative administration abolished it completely (see chapter 5). This provided a stimulus to private development for owner occupation. Private development became increasingly speculative throughout the property boom of the late 1950s and early 1960s (Marriott 1967).

Third, under a Labour government in 1967, a new approach to land policy was introduced by the Land Commission Act. This aimed to ensure that part of the

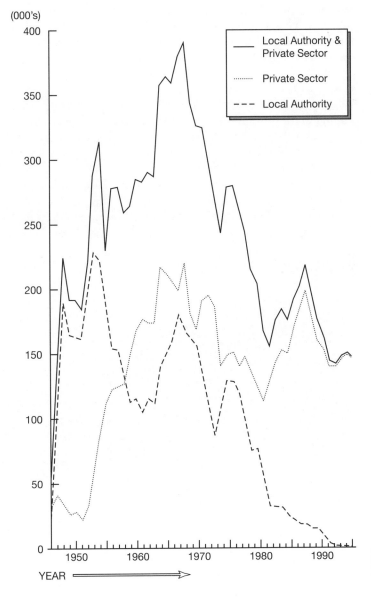

Figure 2.4 Housing completions, Great Britain, 1945–95

increased value of land arising from development was returned to the community; that the burden of the cost of land for essential purposes (such as housing) was reduced; and that suitable land was available at the right time for the implementation of national, regional and local plans. The Act failed to achieve its objectives and, worse still, land was withheld from the market, either because owners were unwilling or unable to pay the levy, or because they postponed sales in the belief that the government would lower the rate of the levy or that an incoming Conservative government would abolish the levy altogether. The effect was an inflationary hike in land prices which contributed to a substantial decrease in the number housing completions. From 1968 to 1971, the number of local authority completions fell from 170,000 to 134,000, while private sector completions fell from 212,000 to 192,000. Clearly from a pragmatic point of view, there was a need to amend the Act, but after the defeat of the Labour government in June 1970, it was repealed. The detailed story of the successive attempts to forge a land policy is given in chapter 5.

Fourth, since overspill policies were arguably crucial to the success of slum clearance programmes and to the perceived need to contain urban growth, both Conservative and Labour governments adhered to the 'filtration' strategy which involved the out-migration of households and employment and the subsequent clearance and redevelopment of vacated sites. Thus, with Glasgow's overcrowding and poor housing arousing increasing concern, Cumbernauld new town was designated in 1955. New towns for the northwest and the west midlands followed in the 1960s. Further new towns were established as part of regional growth strategies. The number of designated new towns doubled in the 1960s. To ensure that new towns would also help to satisfy the demand for home ownership, development corporations were urged to increase the proportion of houses built for owner occupation (see chapter 15).

Fifth, with regard to powers of land purchase, new town development corporations undoubtedly received 'preferential treatment'. Development corporations did not have to pay full market prices for the land which they acquired. In Hall's words (1974: 118) ' . . . to prevent the absurdity of a new town paying values which it had

Figure 2.5 Owner-occupied housing in Milton Keynes: comparatively high-density development with integral garages, built in the 1970s

itself created, a development corporation did not pay any value which resulted from its own actions around the land in question'. Thus, by being able to purchase land at a discount, and by buying mainly greenfield rather than brownfield land, new town development corporations often had a cost advantage over local authorities in the acquisition of sites for housing development. The 28 development corporations in England, Scotland and Wales built 178,000 dwellings from designation to December 1970, in addition to the 24,000 local authority and 23,000 private sector dwellings completed within the new towns over the same period.

Finally, expanded town development continued to supplement the new towns programme, though to a limited extent. Although, by 1970, there were 67 town expansion schemes in England and Wales, only 68,000 dwellings had been built since declaration, while in Scotland there were only 10,000 completions in the 42 schemes for Clydeside. Except in the case of a very small number of expanded towns, such as Swindon and Basingstoke, progress was adversely affected by the 'inability of small towns to become effective development agencies, the inadequacy of Exchequer grants, the tenuous nature of the agreements involving four parties (district, county, exporting city and government), and the frigidity of local support' (Thomas 1997).

HOUSING MAINTENANCE AND IMPROVEMENT 1969–97

The 1967 house condition survey revealed that there were still 1.8 million unfit dwellings in England and Wales (not 0.8 million as previously thought), many more lacked one or more basic amenities or required substantial repairs, and the majority of poor dwellings were in the private sector. At the same time, there was increasing evidence that rehabilitation was often far more cost effective than clearance and redevelopment (Needleman 1965; Hillman 1969; Stone 1970). In 1969, improvement took centre stage in the attempt to hasten the pace of renewal. Improvement grants (first introduced in 1949, but not promoted as a mainstay of policy) were increased in 1974 and again in 1980. Grants were also made more generous and subject to easier conditions.

Figure 2.6 Local authority housing developed under the Town Development Act: low-density development in Basingstoke, showing similarities with new town housing

By the mid-1980s, the Treasury was becoming increasingly concerned that a significant number of grants were going to private owners who could afford to finance improvement from their own resources and loans from financial institutions. Much greater selectivity in the award of grants was thus considered necessary. As a result, grants were targeted towards the worst housing and to households in greatest need. The new regime of means-tested renovation grants was introduced in 1989 in England and Wales. In Scotland, however, the improvement grant system of the 1970s was broadly retained. This led to the improvement of 352,000 dwellings north of the border between 1980 and 1990. More broadly, Scottish Homes became a leading actor in housing renewal across all sectors, having been given wide ranging powers under the Housing (Scotland) Act 1988.

Unlike the reduced rate of improvement in the private sector, renovations in the local authority sector throughout Britain remained at a comparative high level, and public expenditure on local authority renovation increased. However, it is of considerable concern whether the present level of council house renovation and the present regime of grants in the private sector will be sufficient to make serious inroads into the problem of poor housing. Leather and Morrison (1997) reported that there were still 1.6 million homes unfit for habitation in Britain (1 in 14 of the total housing stock), and a large number requiring urgent repairs. A sum of £20 billion needs to be spent on repairing council houses alone. Demolition of unfit housing, moreover, plummeted so dramatically over the period 1975–95 that, at the prevalent rate in England and Wales, new housing built at the end of the twentieth century would have to stand for 5,600 years before being replaced!

Though initially concerned with individual houses, the emphasis in improvement policy shifted increasingly to areas. In 1969, local authorities were empowered to declare *general improvement areas* (GIAs) of between 300 and 800 fundamentally sound houses capable of providing good living conditions for many years ahead. Together with enhanced grants, progress with these areas has undoubtedly made a significant contribution to the reduction in the number of unfit properties, although in some areas, such as parts of inner London, improvement was associated with gentrification and the displacement of low-income households (Balchin 1979). Because of this, social considerations were given increased importance in wider ranging comprehensive area-based strategies for *housing action areas* (HAAs). Local authorities, when declaring HAAs, were obliged to focus on areas of housing stress and, although the aim was to improve the condition of housing, importance was attached to areas containing a disproportionate number of pensioners, large families, single parent families and low-income households. However, although there were 1,217 GIAs and 384 HAAs by 1978, it was doubtful whether they were having little more than a patchy effect on housing in the inner urban areas.

Social considerations were given additional prominence in 1989 when *renewal areas* replaced the earlier area designations. To be eligible for declaration, more than 75 per cent of the dwellings of an area had to be privately owned, 75 per cent had to be considered unfit, and 30 per cent of households had to be in receipt of specified state benefits. Through the medium of renewal areas, a broader strategic approach was adopted whereby local authorities were encouraged to resume clearance (in addition to facilitating grant aided renovation), and promote partnerships to combine the initiatives of local authorities, housing associations, property owners and residents. DoE Circular 6/90, *Area Renewal, Unfitness, Slum Clearance and Enforcement Action*, placed clearance firmly back on the agenda, pointing out that some authorities had persisted with improvement even when it seemed that it was less cost effective than clearance. It was also emphasized that renewal areas with the participation of the private sector – should 'turn around' areas which had not yet reached their nadir, rather than immediately focusing on the worst areas. However, progress has not been dramatic despite the guidance of Circular 6/90. By 1995, 80 renewal areas had been declared with an average of 1,526 houses.

In Scotland, different legislation produced different outcomes. Since the Housing (Scotland) Act 1974, HAAs have been the foci of housing renewal and were not superseded by renewal areas as in England and Wales. By 1992, 41 of Scotland's housing authorities had declared a total of 1,654 HAAs containing 64,000 dwellings. Most HAAs were declared for improvement rather than for clearance and redevelopment, and, in contrast to England and Wales, housing associations undertook the majority of improvement (Bailey and Robertson 1994).

FROM SUPPLY-SIDE FUNDING TO DEMAND-SIDE SUBSIDIES 1971–97

Following its 1971 white paper, *Fair Deal for Housing*, the Conservative government set out to reduce the subsidization of council housing and to encourage better-off council tenants to become owner occupiers. This was to be achieved (it was hoped) by raising council house rents in stages, to private sector 'fair rent' levels. Low-income tenants became eligible for means-tested rent rebates, and a general subsidy was directed at those authorities where costs were not covered by rising rents.

By 1973, local authorities in England and Wales were making an overall profit of £20 million on their lettings, while the number of public sector housing completions in Britain had dropped to 88,000 (compared with 163,000 in 1969). A change in government in the following year led to a major, but short lived, change. The fair rent concept was abandoned, and local authorities were again able to determine and charge 'reasonable' rents based on historic costs (together with the rebate system). New subsidies were introduced with the aim of encouraging housebuilding, protecting local authorities from inflation and stabilizing rents.

In the late 1970s, and as part of the government's attempt to respond to pressure from the International Monetary Fund, investment in council housing became a victim of public expenditure cuts. Local authority completions consequently plummeted from 130,000 in 1975 to 76,000 in 1979. At the same time, it was clear that there were major problems relating to housing finance. While the average subsidy to council tenants was constant over a wide range of incomes, mortgage interest relief was rising as incomes increased. However, although the green paper, *Housing Policy: A Consultative Document* (DoE 1977a) suggested that housing assistance should be distributed more fairly and evenly, it dismissed all means of doing this and upheld existing arrangements governing tax relief on mortgage interest so as not to tamper with the 'natural desire' of home ownership. It also ignored the evidence that there was a growing concentration of poorer households in the public sector, with 55 per cent of tenants being eligible for rent rebates.

Stemming from the 1977 green paper, major changes in resource effectiveness and subsidization were introduced towards the end of the 1974–79 Labour administration. Local authorities were obliged to submit annual bids to the DoE for spending permission based on their *local housing strategies* and associated *housing investment programmes*, which took account of shortages and needs not catered for in the private sector. The DoE then allocated spending permissions on the basis of total demand and the amount which the Treasury thought reasonable. In effect, the green paper confirmed that even a Labour government regarded council housing as a 'residual' rather than a general needs tenure since the role of local authority housebuilding would, at best, be confined to filling the gaps left by the market.

Under a new Conservative government, the Local Government and Planning Act 1980 retained this procedure, but replaced allocations of borrowing permission with allocations of permitted capital expenditure. Expenditure could be supplemented by a proportion (initially 50 per cent) of the receipts from the sale of council dwellings emanating from new 'right to buy' provisions. These gave tenants a statutory right to buy their house, at generous discounts of 33 to 50 per cent, depending upon their length of tenure. As a result of these, and more generous discounts introduced throughout the 1980s, a total of around 1,500,000 council dwellings were sold between 1980 and 1994 – equivalent to a quarter of the 1980 local authority stock. Sales greatly exceeded the number of new local authority dwellings built, thus depleting the size of the sector, between 1981 and 1994, from 30 to 20 per cent of the national housing stock.

With strong central government controls over new local authority building, Conservative administrations in the 1990s were able to reduce housing investment in the local authority sector by 76 per cent in England (from £5.4 billion in 1979/80 to £1.2 billion in 1994/95, in real terms). There was a comparable reduction in housing investment in Scotland, although in Wales investment was broadly maintained by a dramatic shift of emphasis from new construction to renovation. The effect of the overall reduction in capital spending was that the number of housing completions fell from 75,600 in 1979 to a trifling 1,400 in 1995. Simultaneously, as part of a policy to marketize the sector, average weekly rents in England were increased significantly between 1980 and 1996: from around £11 to £38 in England, from £8 to £28 in Scotland and from £11 to £36 in Wales.

Conservative antipathy to council housing was in contrast to its support for private sector renting. In an attempt to boost the provision of alternative rented accommodation and to unleash market forces, most rent controls have been repealed, and a new form of tenure has been introduced (now termed *assured shorthold*, with rents at negotiated levels). Overall, Conservative policy succeeded in stemming the decline of the private rented sector. After falling from 11 per cent of the total stock in 1981 to 9.1 per cent in 1988, it expanded to around 10 per cent in 1997. However, over a comparable period (1980–94), there was at least a threefold increase in average 'fair' rents in the unfurnished sector in England, Wales and Scotland (to respectively £43, £35 and £29 per week) and (from 1989 to 1994) approximately a 50 per cent increase in unfurnished market rents in England and Wales (to, respectively, £65 and £54 per week)

STYLES OF PLANNING POLICY

Since the late 1960s, the planning arena has been transformed to accommodate an expanded free market economy. This has been marked by the demise of new town development corporations, by the failure to establish further overspill schemes, and by the introduction of market-led initiatives such as urban development corporations. Under the 1968 planning act, a system of 'process planning' was introduced whereby the county councils and county boroughs were required to respond to economic and social indicators in the preparation of development plans – in contrast to the previous system of 'blue print planning' which was essentially concerned with the determination of land use from a largely physical perspective. Whereas before 1968 it was expected (naively) that the market would be conditioned by development plans, after 1968 development plans were expected, to a varying extent, to conform to the market.

By 1980, however, central government had reverted to a predominantly land-use approach to planning. Under this comparatively relaxed regime, there was a tendency for local authorities to 'police' new housing demand, for example, 'allowing new development on infill sites or on the edge of larger towns and villages, but preventing development in the open countryside and in designated areas such as green belts' (O'Leary 1997: 132). Housebuilders consequently negotiated with local authorities for the release of land to permit the development of expansion schemes on the edge of towns and villages, or searched for vacant or under-used sites within urban areas. Older houses in large grounds were also targeted because they could be redeveloped to provide low-rise flats (O'Leary 1997: 133).

The demand for housebuilding land in widely fragmented locations would not have been so great had the new towns programme not been wound down. In 1976, the target populations of Milton Keynes, Northampton, Peterborough, Telford, Warrington and Central Lancashire were severely reduced. In 1980, the boundaries of the new towns were tightened both to restrict further development by the development corporations and to privatize the land outside of the new boundaries.

Urban regeneration likewise became market-led in the 1980s. Urban development corporations were established in the London docklands, Merseyside, Tyneside, Teesside, Sandwell, Trafford Park, Cardiff Bay, Bristol and Sheffield, ostensibly to tackle the problems that local authorities could not deal with alone, and where allegedly the private sector had been deterred from investing. Although the urban district councils (UDCs) had both planning and compulsory purchase powers (usurping local authority responsibilities), they lacked the powers vested in the new town development corporations and had to pay market value for land acquisitions. Although a total of 24,800 dwellings were constructed within UDC areas from designation until December 1992 (along with commercial, industrial and infrastructure development), housebuilding for owner occupation often squeezed out public sector development despite lengthy waiting and transfer lists.

Figure 2.7 Infill development of starter homes for the owner-occupied market 1997

Figure 2.8 Owner-occupied luxury flats built in the London Docklands during the 1990s

THE RE-EMERGENCE OF HOUSING SHORTAGES AND AN INCREASE IN STATE
INVOLVEMENT SINCE 1985

Although, in quantitative terms, housing need in Britain was largely met in the 1990s (there was a crude surplus of 822,000 dwellings in excess of households in 1991), and despite the improvement of the general quality of housing, there were serious causes for concern. Of the 23.6 million dwellings in 1991, over a million were unfit, lacking basic amenities, undergoing extensive conversion or improvement, or used as second homes, while there were about half a million concealed households. The total shortage was substantial, amounting to perhaps some 2 million dwellings in the early 1990s. This was an appalling outcome of public policy over the years, for which neither party of government can take pride. To eliminate the deficit, the Joseph Rowntree Foundation *Inquiry into British Housing* (1991) called for 228,000 – 290,000 houses to be built each year into the new millennium, and stressed that, within this total, 100,000 should be built for rent. In respect of England alone, Holmans (1995) suggested that in order to meet housing needs over the period 1991–2011, an annual output of about 240,000 new homes would be required, with approximately 40 per cent being in the social sector.

In the 1980s, Conservative governments attempted to renovate up to 1.3 million substandard or badly managed council dwellings – a policy that, had it been successful, would have made a major impact on housing conditions. An u*rban housing renewal* programme was launched in 1985 (renamed *estate action* in 1986) to provide assistance to local authorities in renovating their properties, and to supplement existing finance by drawing in new private sector funds and urban regeneration grants (Brunivels and Rodrigues 1989: 66). In addition, local authorities were enabled to sell off whole estates to developers to hasten the pace of renovation. Housing Action Trusts could be established to repair or rehabilitate housing estates prior to their transfer to housing associations or private landlords (subject to tenant ballot). Large scale voluntary transfers of council estates could be made to housing associations – again subject to tenant consent. Housing associations were now in a better position than local authorities to undertake both an improvement and an increase in the stock of social housing. Unlike local authorities, capital expenditure was not directly controlled by central government but indirectly through the Housing Corporation by means of a more flexible system of loans and housing association grants. Housing associations could also look increasingly to private financial institutions to fund both renovation and new housebuilding: thus, by 1997, 44 per cent of total investment in the housing association sector was provided by the private sector. Since public funding could therefore be spread more widely, the number of housing association completions rose from 13,000 in 1988 to 38, 000 in 1995.

Housing policy in the latter years of the twentieth century was accompanied by changes in planning practice which, to a greater or lesser extent, recognized the increasing problems of housing supply. Circulars and policy guidance notes have increasingly been used 'to provide direction to local authorities and the development industry on how central government expects the planning legislation to work in practice' (O'Leary 1997: 139). DoE Circular 7/91, *Planning and Affordable Housing*, for example, encouraged local authorities to take the need for affordable housing into account when formulating their development plans and making planning decisions, and to negotiate with developers to ensure that some affordable housing is included in their schemes. RPG9, *Regional Planning Guidance for the South East* (DoE 1994d), sets dwelling targets for authorities in the southeast of England. These figures are used by local authorities as a basis for indicating the broad locations for future residential development within their areas. PPG3, *Housing* (DoE 1992c) recommends the involvement of housing associations in the provision of housing for rent or shared ownership in an attempt to ensure that the benefits of affordability can be enjoyed by both initial and subsequent occupiers. Further guidance on the relationship between planning and affordable housing is provided by the revised circular on this issue (DoE 1996a). In rural areas, the problem of affordability is exacerbated by local people being unable to compete in housing markets with commuters, the retired, and those seeking second homes – and by a restricted stock of local authority housing resulting from the right-to-buy policy and the almost complete cessation of council housebuilding in recent years. In attempting to meet unsatisfied housing needs, rural authorities have sought to use legal agreements to restrict the occupancy of new affordable homes to local people (O'Leary 1997: 139).

It is sometimes argued, however, that the planning system (far from ensuring that there is an adequate supply of land for affordable housing) actually creates a shortage of development land and inflates prices, a view expressed by the House Builders Federation and supported by research by Evans (1988). However, research by Bramley *et al.* (1995) suggests that if land allocations for housing in development plans were significantly increased across the country, the effect on prices would be only slight since prices are affected primarily by market changes rather than by planning controls. There is, nevertheless, a continuing problem of land supply, particularly in the southeast. Despite a worsening housing shortage in the region and the continuing need to contain the outward growth of Greater London, the Conservative government in the 1980s and early 1990s was unwilling to resurrect the new towns programme, preferring to rely upon the free market to meet housing needs. It might have been thought that, within this context, private sector new settlements of between 3,000 and 5,000 houses would have provided a useful substitute for further new town development. However, private proposals for new settlements at Tillingham Hall and Northwick (in Essex), Foxley Wood (in Hampshire) and Westmere (in Cambridgeshire) were all rejected by the government.

During its last year in office, the Conservative government published a white paper *Household Growth: Where Shall We Live?* (1996b). On the basis of a projected 4.4 million additional households in England over the period 1996–2016, an estimated annual rate of 220,000 completions is needed for decades (equivalent to the level of housebuilding in the 1960s and 1970s). While the incoming Labour government initially accepted the previous government's preference for a 50/50 split between greenfield and brownfield development, in 1998 Labour accepted a 40/60 split in favour of brownfield development; but the debate continues. In the meantime, a task force chaired by Lord Rogers was appointed to investigate the extent to which urban locations could meet the forecast demand.

The new Labour government quickly formulated its policy on renovation. From the receipts of past council house sales (or from new borrowing if receipts had been used to pay off debt), £3.6 billion was scheduled in 1998 to make a start in tackling the backlog of repairs to council housing (the total cost of neglect being estimated at £20 billion) and a further £3 billion was allocated from the single regeneration budget for Britain's 50 most deprived areas. The extent to which these measures will satisfy future housing needs remains to be seen, but it is highly probable that a large-scale programme of housebuilding, particularly on greenfield locations, will also be necessary.

CONCLUSIONS

Since the second world war, there have been long periods of consensus in the aims and objectives of housing and planning policy. However, whereas policy was broadly central to the nostrums of social democracy and the maintenance of the welfare state until the late 1960s, subsequently there has been a 'neo-liberal' convergence of ideology, particularly since the emergence of Thatcherism in 1979. An emphasis on intervention was gradually superseded by the dominance of the market. During the postwar years, the gradual easing of housing shortages through major housebuilding programmes subsequently gave way to slum clearance – both programmes being underpinned to a significant extent by the development of new towns. In the last two decades of the twentieth century, the emphasis was on the extension of owner occupation, the privatization of municipal housing, rehabilitation rather than slum clearance, and a shift away from supply subsidies to household allowances.

Overall, public policy in the 1980s and 1990s lamentably failed to eliminate a substantial housing shortage and to reduce the number of dwellings in need of repair and improvement. Huge reductions in public expenditure on housebuilding and the malfunctioning of the market have left significant housing needs unsatisfied and, together with household growth, will continue so to do well into the twenty-first century unless there are radical changes in policy. The time has come for a 'return to the bulldozer'. Renewal areas should be increased in number and size, with a focus primarily on clearance and low-rise redevelopment rather than renovation. The introduction of a windfall tax on greenfield development could be a means of siphoning-off a proportion of betterment, and also of providing hypothecated revenue for investment in affordable housing in brownfield areas. Similarly, to accommodate the growth in the number of households, a resurrected new towns policy might ensure that the 'right housing gets built at the right price and in the right location'. Since the new towns (containing a population of over 2 million in the 1990s) 'represented the most active approach to public sector housing provision in the post-1945 period [and] were a major vehicle for meeting housing needs as well as other objectives' (Malpass and Murie 1990: 144), their like should be employed again to help tackle the problems of housing need away from the major cities. There should also be an important role for the Scottish Parliament, the Welsh Assembly and, perhaps in the long term, the new English regional authorities in the coordination of plans, in the redistribution of betterment, in the maintenance and extension of green belts, and in the development of a new generation of new towns.

FURTHER READING

Housing Policy
There is a range of good textbooks on housing policy such as Malpass and Murie (1994) *Housing Policy and Practice* (4th edition), Balchin (1995) *Housing Policy: An Introduction* (3rd edition), Holmans (1987) *Housing Policy in Britain: A History*. The best and most thorough analysis of the private rented sector is Harloe (1985) *Private Rented Housing in the United States and Europe*, while, among the many books on owner occupation, Forrest *et al.* (1990) *Home Ownership: Differentiation and Fragmentation*, and Saunders (1990) *A Nation of Home Owners* are important texts. Consisting of a wide range of chapters on contemporary issues, Malpass and Means (1992) *Implementing Housing Policy* is useful for an understanding of Conservative housing policy in the late 1980s and early 1990s.

Housing Renewal
Housing renewal, in its many different aspects, is examined in Balchin (1979) *Housing Improvement and Social Inequality*, Couch (1990) *Urban Renewal Theory and Practice*, Carley (1990) *Housing and Neighbourhood Renewal: Britain's New Urban Challenge*, Kirkby (1979) *Slum Housing and Residential Renewal: The Case of Urban Britain*, Merrett (1979) *State Housing in Britain*, and Roberts (1976) *General Improvement Areas*.

Housing Finance
Balchin (1995) *Housing Policy: An Introduction* includes a good introduction to this complex field. Malpass (ed.) (1986) *The Housing Crisis*, is particularly useful in providing a critical review of housing issues during the early years of Thatcherism. Both Gibb and Munro (1991) *Housing Finance in the UK* and Hills (1991) *Unravelling Housing Finance* provide useful information on funding and subsidies in the 1990s.

Urban Regeneration
Among the large number of useful books on urban regeneration are: Atkinson and Moon (1994) *Urban Policy in Britain: The City, the State and the Market*, Blackman (1995) *Urban Policy in Practice*, Imrie and Thomas (1993) *British Urban Policy and the Urban Development Corporations*, Lawless (1989) *Britain's Inner Cities*, Robson (1988) *Those Inner Cities: Reconciling the Social and Economic Aims of Urban Policy*, and

Thornley (1993) *Urban Planning under Thatcherism*. The renovation of privatized council estates, and the development of private housing in inner city locations are examined by the Public Sector Management Research Unit (1988) *An Evaluation of Urban Development Grant Programme*.

Land for Housing

The availability of land has been subject to much analysis and debate. Recent policies are examined in Bramley (1989) *Land Supply, Planning and Private Housebuilding*, Bramley *et al.* (1995) *Planning, the Market and Private Housebuilding*, Bramley and Watkins (1996) *Steering the Housing Market: New Building and the Changing Planning System*, Evans (1988) *No Room! No Room! The Costs of the British Town and Country Planning System*, Rydin (1986) *Housing Land Policy*, and Williams and Wood (1994) *Urban Land and Property Markets in the UK*. In considering new settlements as a means of containing growth in the southeast, Breheny *et al.* (1993) *Alternative Development Patterns: New Settlements* provides an analytical account of development proposals in the region in the early 1990s. The effect of green belts on housing supply is explored in Regional Studies Association (1990) *Beyond Green Belts*, Elson *et al.* (1993) *The Effectiveness of Green Belts* and Elson *et al.* (1996) *Green Belts and Affordable Housing: Can We Have Both ?*

chapter 3

Discretion in Planning versus Zoning

PHILIP BOOTH

INTRODUCTION

As a very broad generalizsation, systems of planning throughout the developed world can be divided into two types. First, there are those that can be described as regulatory, in which current and future land uses are identified in zoning plans, to which attach more or less detailed rules for new development. Regulatory, zoning systems of this kind derive from the pioneering work, first in Germany and then in the USA, at the end of the last century. In principle, they are characterized by a scientific rationalism in the way that land uses are allocated. They are intended to provide an unambiguous basis for future development that leaves as little to the vagaries of chance as possible. They do not, again as a matter of principle, allow scope for discretionary decision making. Zoning systems and zoning control of one form or another – and in detail there are wide differences between them – account for the majority of the world's planning systems.

The second type of system can be described as discretionary, and is represented by Britain and a very small number of systems that claim a British inheritance. Seen from without, the British system is distinctly odd. For where it might be supposed that planning is primarily about removing future uncertainty over the form and location of urban development, the British system appears to introduce deliberately a blurring of the relationship between policy and implementation. The legislative source of that blurring is well known. Section 70 of the 1990 Town and Country Planning Act, in direct succession to Section 14 of the 1947 Act, requires that local planning authorities in dealing with planning applications 'have regard to the development plan insofar as it is material to the application, and to any other material considerations'. The significance of this clause, as Davies (1980) and Booth (1996) have emphasized, is twofold. First, it substantially weakens the link between the plan and development control decisions, a link which is primordial in zoning systems. The development plan is potentially only one of a number of 'material considerations' that will inform the eventual decision on what is built where; it may not even figure in the decision at all. The plan can, therefore, never be more than an indication of the future pattern and development, and there is no guarantee of what will or what will not be acceptable. Second, Section 70 explicitly grants decision makers wide discretion. The local planning authority is at liberty to determine what considerations are material to the decision it takes. The penalty that this system carries, commentators such as McBride (1979) have argued, is uncertainty and delay which a more clearly defined relationship between development plan and development control would eliminate.

Whether the British discretionary system offers particular advantages in securing the objectives of land-use planning or represents instead an unhealthy arbitrariness in the policy process is to some extent the theme of this chapter. The rationale of zoning systems is to eliminate any tendency to arbitrariness. Certainty is the major benefit ascribed to zoning and the certainty that zoning provides accrues to all users of the system. For developers and landowners, it identifies with precision the nature of future land use and the limits of acceptable future development. For decision makers, it in theory alleviates the tension inherent in decision making: the parameters of decisions are articulated and defined. For third parties, it provides protection from unwanted intrusion. Residential values are maintained; unacceptable uses – and by extension, sometimes people – are excluded; views and wilderness are guaranteed protection.

For anyone reared in a discretionary system of planning, this presentation of the virtues of zoning is accompanied by a nagging doubt which is amply confirmed by the commentaries that have been written on regulatory systems. The doubt is whether zoning can in fact deliver the certainty which is an inherent part of its rationale. Sure enough, sooner or later, all zoning systems come up against a mismatch between the predicted future and the realities of the moment, and all zoning systems develop mechanisms for circumventing the rules which were supposed to set the limits of future action. Sometimes the mechanisms appear as an outright challenge to constitutionality or the rule of the law (Booth 1989, 1996). Sometimes they may be applauded for the imaginative way in which they surmount difficulties: such is the case with Wakeford's commentary on innovation in American zoning (Wakeford 1990). Whatever the case, the desire to modulate the zoning regulations carries with it a fundamental threat to the legitimacy of the system. How much better, we may conclude with British smugness, is a system which acknowledges the inherent uncertainty of planning for the future and makes explicit the need for flexibility by building in overt reference to discretionary action. Is such a conclusion warranted?

Figure 3.1 Sir Stamford Raffles zoned his trading port of Singapore by ethnic group: Little India, Singapore

PLANNING AND ZONING

So far we have considered discretionary systems of planning as being in opposition to zoning. Yet in one sense zoning has informed all systems of town planning regardless of their character. As early as the 1820s Raffles and his surveyor were laying out the trading port of Singapore in a way that specifically allocated areas for different ethnic groups (Bristow 1992), something which was to set a baleful precedent for the twentieth century. Zoning in the twentieth century owes most to the experiments in Germany, however. As Sutcliffe (1981) has shown, Germany began the process of planning for town extensions from the middle years of the nineteenth century. To begin with, these extension zones were developed under exactly the same kind of building regulations as applied to the existing built-up areas, and administrators aimed to create a uniformity in building control across the whole city. But beginning with Frankfurt in 1891, German planning began to develop the concept of differential regulations applied to defined zones within an overall plan. This allowed distinctions to be made between areas suitable for industry and those for housing in which industry could be excluded (Logan 1976). The advantages of such a system quickly spread. It commended itself to those who argued for a rational and scientific approach to urban development. But in the USA it took root because it came to be seen as a powerful mechanism for stabilizing the market in land and for protecting property rights and values (Boyer 1983).

Whether promoted because it responded to an ideal of rational decision making or because it helped reinforce the market in land, zoning systems also related admirably to a certain culture of decision making. In France, as in the USA, the constitution affirmed the rights to property. Zoning became an important means for reconciling the right to property with the desire and need for control over urban development. The zoning ordinance or plan with its regulations may have been a constraint on the absolute constitutional right to property, but it was also a means of guaranteeing, within limits, the rights that you had, whether as a landowner or as a neighbour. The zoning ordinance guaranteed your rights within the limits as defined. In principle, neither landowner nor administration was in doubt about the nature of the decision to be taken. In the event of dispute, the courts were available for adjudication.

THE NATURE OF DISCRETIONARY DECISION MAKING

By dividing systems of planning into the regulatory and discretionary, there is the implication that in regulatory zoning systems there is no discretion. This implication is false. As commentators have shown, zoning systems time and again yield instances of discretionary decision making (see Booth 1989, 1996, Wakeford 1990, Cullingworth 1993). We need to consider for a moment the nature of discretionary power to understand why this should be and what its consequences are.

Although the question of discretion is a complex one, there are two points which are relevant to this discussion. First, any system like zoning which relies on a series of rules, to be adjudicated if the need arises in courts of law, operates well in an environment of identifiable fixed limits, or as Jowell (1973) suggests, where the issue is one of 'more or less' on a simple axis. By contrast, fixed rules cope badly with the multi-polar problems which often characterize town planning. So codified regulations may have to be modified to reflect that fact. Second, absolute certainty in the application of rules is in practice unobtainable. As soon as an order is made to be carried out by someone other than the person who makes the order, the capacity for

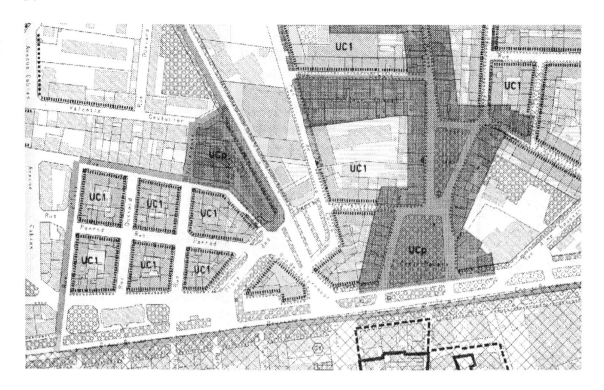

Figure 3.2 Part of a French *plan d'occupation des sols* (local land-use plan). Each parcel of land is allocated to a particular zone, identified by a letter to which a series of regulations apply.

slippage occurs. Equally, the application of a generalized rule to a specific place at a specific time requires an act of interpretation – be it never so slight – on the part of the decision. makers. From interpretation it is a relatively small step to the beginnings of adaptive mechanisms: the introduction of rules which offer decision makers choices, or in the American case, the move away from the fixed-zone-plus-fixed-rule to one in which the zoning is more or less open ended (Cullingworth 1993). The important point to note is that, although discretionary action is present in zoning systems because it has to be, zoning is legitimated by the absence of discretion, not its presence.

The distinction made by Bull (1980) between officer and agency discretion is helpful. Officer discretion is that which the individual decision maker exercises when he or she judges how a rule is to be applied in a particular case. Agency discretion is the discretion which is accorded formally by statute or directive to a given organization in carrying out an official function. Though officer and agency discretion can be found in both zoning and discretionary systems of planning, British planning law offers wide agency discretion as a fundamental principle of the system. By contrast, much discretion in zoning systems is covert, officer discretion and where there is agency discretion, it has come about as a response to problems, not as a fundamental requirement of the system.

THE ORIGINS OF BRITISH DISCRETIONARY PLANNING

Why Britain should have developed a system whose basic operation should have been so different from that of its continental partners requires an explanation that goes beyond the confines of the planning system itself. The explanation is to be found both in the British legal system and in the development of local government in the nineteenth century. Unlike those of Europe, Britain's legal system is not based on the civil tradition deriving ultimately from Roman law. From the Middle Ages, English courts had not only dealt with criminal cases but had begun to handle disputes between citizens. As the extent to which judges were called on to adjudicate in such disputes increased, the judges themselves developed a body of principles on which cases could be determined. Such principles did not bind judges in dealing with cases, but did act as a point of reference for a particular case which would be determined in the light of precedent and according to the circumstance of the case itself.

Common law came to be seen as increasingly inadequate to deal with the complexities of the developing mercantile and industrial society, and statute law enacted by parliament became the necessary means of establishing legal limits in advance of disputes. Common-law traditions did not die out, however. Judge-made law and reference to common-law principles and to legal precedent remained distinguishing features of the British legal system. In time, the tradition of legal decision making was then transferred to administrative decisions, particularly by local government in the nineteenth century. Action by reference not only to statute but also to a body of principles and the case-by-case approach became hallmarks of all local administration and was well established by the time of the first planning legislation.

The development of local government in Britain in the nineteenth century is marked by the hesitations about the proper balance between central control and local initiative. Though Lagroye and Wright's (1979) categorization of local governments in Britain as being a 'residual domain' (as against the 'conceded domain' of French local government) is now regarded as too simplistic a description of the reality of central–local relations in Britain, it nevertheless underscores the very considerable reluctance of central government to become involved in local affairs in the nineteenth century. Though the inefficiency of local administration was often castigated, the weight of political thinking tended to favour leaving local authorities to their own devices.

Much of the argument hinged on sanitary reform which was of course to be an important precursor of the planning system. In the first half of the century, some of the larger towns had promoted their own local acts of parliament to deal with sanitation and building control. By mid-century, policy favoured the passing of general public health statutes which allowed local authorities to make their own by-laws, a far more efficient process which still let the burden of responsibility fall on local shoulders. But at this point it became clear that not all municipalities were equal to the task, and central government issued model by-laws to guide local authorities, tentatively at first in 1848, and then in a much more detailed form in 1877 following the 1875 Public Health Act (Lambert 1962). These by-laws covered constructional standards for new housing and set minimum dimensions for the spacing of new buildings and street widths. The regulations where thus normative and universal in the areas to which they applied. Though local authorities were not obliged to adopt the model by-laws, the majority did, and it looked very much as though central government would no longer be able to take a back-seat role in local administration.

By-law regulation was in its own terms highly successful. The regulations were applied for the most part with considerable rigour and achieved a hitherto unknown spaciousness for working-class housing. Yet by the time the whole of the country had acquired representative local government and the use of by-law regulation to control building and sanitation was widespread, if not universal, there was already discontent with the dimensional norms. By-law housing was condemned as unaesthetic and economically wasteful, while not ensuring sufficiently high standards in new

Figure 3.3 By-law housing produced under the 1877 model by-laws was condemned for the wastefulness. South View Road, Sheffield, built *c.* 1895

housing. Critics demanded greater elasticity in the by-laws so that high quality housing at affordable cost could be achieved. But the sub-text of the discontent that resulted in a deputation to the Prime Minister in 1906 seems to have been the desire of local councillors and administrators in a now mature local government system to have a greater degree of control over the standards they set (Booth 1998b).

THE BEGINNINGS OF DISCRETIONARY DEVELOPMENT CONTROL

Into this frame came the 1909 Housing, Town Planning, etc. Act which marks the start of planning legislation in Britain. The inspiration for legislation was to a large extent the experience of Germany (Sutcliffe 1981). Indeed, the planning schemes of the 1909 Act can be readily assimilated to German town extension plans. They could and did contain the rudimentary zoning of land uses as well as laying down a pattern of new roads. What the 1909 Act did not do was to establish a separate mechanism for implementing such planning schemes. The expectation was that the housing would be put up in accordance with the by-law regulations, for which formal permission was necessary. For the rest, building which did not conform to the requirements of the plan could be demolished.

The difficulty with this system was that the time taken between announcing the start of the planning scheme and its approval by central government proved to be inordinately long. The result was that planning schemes which were intended to promote orderly urban growth had quite the opposite effect. No developer was willing to start a project if there was a risk that it would be demolished. Some local authorities got round the problem by entering into agreements with builders but, as Crow (1996) has shown, the solution advocated by the Town Planning Institute was to introduce a system for local authorities to issue permits to builders which in effect certified that development would not infringe the requirements of the plan once it had been approved. The system was implemented in 1921 and rapidly proved popular. Although introduced as an expedient device, interim development control, as it came to be known, nevertheless marked a decisive break with the implied zoning control of the 1909 Act and a return to discretionary decision making my local authorities nurtured within the twin traditions of case law and municipal independence.

Interim development control received a major impetus with the 1932 Town and Country Planning Act which for the first time allowed local authorities to prepare schemes for the whole of their area. Once again local authorities were empowered to issue permits once they had declared their intention to proceed with the preparation of a scheme. Moreover, control could now be exercised not just over building form and location but also the use to which land was put. The enormous popularity of this measure is evidenced by the fact that if, after 10 years, only 5 per cent of England was covered by approved planning schemes, no less than 73 per cent was covered by declarations of intent to prepare a plan, so conferring interim control powers on the local authorities concerned (Uthwatt Report 1942). This extension of control power further served to underwrite discretionary decision making in British planning.

Yet though development control was well established and widespread, it was not universal. It only applied where a declaration to proceed with a planning scheme had been made, and ceased once the scheme had been approved. Planning still operated on the assumption that sanctions against development that did not confirm to the plan were a sufficient means of control.

Both the experience and the weaknesses of the legislation enacted between the wars informed the character of planning for the period after 1945. Wartime bombing led to an extension of interim control to the whole country in 1943 regardless of the existence of a declaration of intent to prepare a plan. Simultaneously, a rather more profound debate on the proper relationship between plans and the control of urban development was being conducted (see chapter 4). One of the perceived defects of the 1932 Act was that a departure from the allocation in an approved town planning scheme required a modification to the scheme itself. Just as local officials had argued for elasticity in the public health by-laws, so now central government officials began to argue in favour of flexibility in the system of plans. There was agreement in the 1940s on the need for a universal and mandatory system of development plans, and a growing consensus that these plans needed to be flexible to respond to the need for new development (Cullingworth 1975). What had been an expedient interim measure became central to this conception: planning applications would be required for all new development which local authorities would consider in the light of the 'material considerations' This ensured that not only were development rights nationalized but that plans became indicative rather than legally binding. A land-use allocation in a development plan would not confer a right and the development control decision amounted to a good deal more than a certification that the proposed development conformed to the plan.

So the experiment with universal normative regulations for building control was finally set aside in favour of a return to the common-law tradition of each case on its merits and the administrative tradition of freedom of action for local authorities. Quite apart from legal and administrative traditions, the desire for flexibility was fuelled by a desire to promote, as much as control, urban development. The need for new housing after 1918 had been the inspiration for interim control. The need for housing and redevelopment after 1945 led once again to a perceived need for flexibility and a policy presumption in favour of development. A discretionary system suited both those who advocated greater control over development and those who believed that a flexible planning system would be the surest way to promote new building.

THE 1947 PLANNING SYSTEM

We need now to explore in more detail the character of the 1947 planning system. The 1947 Town and Country Planning Act offered essentially two discretionary freedoms. Of these, the most significant was the duty of local authorities to consider all material considerations, and not just the development plan, in reaching a decision on individual applications to develop. The second, less far reaching in its consequences but still important, was the power given to impose conditions on planning permission as the local authority 'should think fit'.

The impact of these discretionary freedoms has been to ensure that a great deal of weight attaches to the decisions taken on planning applications. This in turn has led to an unhealthy preoccupation with the time taken to decide as much as with the content of the decision itself. This as we shall see, came to dominate the debate in the 1970s. A second impact was the need to hold local authorities accountable for their discretionary decision making. To this end the appeal, with possibility of a public inquiry, came to play a major, and largely beneficial, role in the planning process.

In the first 20 years of the universal planning system the issue of discretionary freedom and the relationship between a system of plans and a system of development control did not appear to be particularly problematic. There were, after all, rather more difficult issues to resolve of which the most important had to do with compensation and betterment. When discontent with the 1947 planning system did begin to emerge, the focus was on the system of plans. The development plans which were intended to be flexible and swift to prepare proved in practice to be neither. The Planning Advisory Group (PAG) was set up in 1963 to explore new ways of representing land use policy which would be genuinely strategic and flexible and yet also provide the level of detail that might be needed in given circumstances. Significantly, the PAG report (PAG 1965) concluded that, while the development plans system did indeed require reform, development control was working in a broadly satisfactory way and only needed some marginal improvement in management rather than a fundamental review. The tenor of this critique was to inform the whole of the subsequent debate on development control.

The failure of PAG to treat development control as anything more than an administrative routine which only needed tightening up to be effective was to be reinforced during the 1970s. First, the property boom of the early 1970s led to a rapid increase in the number of planning applications and the consequent deterioration of the development control system. Then Dobry (1975), commissioned to advise on how the system could be improved in the light of this deterioration, addressed the problem as though it was primarily one of efficiency. The approach was further reinforced at the end of the decade by the report of the Expenditure Committee of the House of Commons. The committee's conclusions were entirely geared to the concept of development control as an administrative exercise being handled inadequately by inefficient local authorities. The 10 years to 1979 saw a perception of development control as time wasting and arbitrary becoming deeply entrenched. All it needed was a change of government to introduce changes designed to meet that perception.

DISCRETIONARY PLANNING IN OPERATION

But how was the discretionary planning system working in the 1970s? Certainly the evidence brought by developers to the House of Commons Expenditure Committee

(1977) was not very encouraging. By far the most notorious case was that of Queen's Park, Billericay, which took 18 months to be determined. The delay was caused essentially by a conflict between Basildon District Council and Essex County Council on the way in which detailed policy in the Essex Design Guide for Residential Areas should be applied. The case confirmed all the worst suspicions about the inadequacies of the British planning system. The processing of what should have been a straightforward planning application took an inordinate time. There was an inadequate policy base for the decision. There was conflict between the two tiers of local authority. There was an unpardonable arbitrariness in the behaviour of the county council. Discretionary power had been used to interfere unnecessarily in what was properly the developer's domain. The Queen's Park case could be taken as the epitome of the failure of development control.

Or could it? The Queens Park case was a failure because it had not delivered the results that the development industry expected. Indeed, the failure may have more to do with a tension between the presumption in favour of development which, as we have seen has been present since 1919, and the requirement to consider all material considerations in the public interest. A developer's expectations of the system, nurtured by the policy of successive governments to promote development, had been fouled on potentially legitimate concerns voiced by the local authority. But the case does illustrate how much, in a discretionary system of planning, is vested in the development control decision, not in the plan.

Two further reflections flow from the Queen's Park case. One is that because the development control decision assumes such importance, a failure to grant planning permission and a failure to decide as quickly as possible carries the potential for financial loss for the developers. By the same token, however, a favourable decision may result in a considerable speculative gain: for developers are by no means simply innocent victims of the system. Indeed, the British discretionary planning system may be partly responsible for fuelling speculation in land.

The second reflection has to do with the concept of delay. At Queen's Park, the time taken to make a decision may have been incommensurate with the problem to be resolved but, notoriously, critics have never been able to define delay or to distinguish between unnecessary delay and the time for due process. Moreover, a study in the late 1980s suggested that delay was rather more under the control of the developer than might be supposed. If the whole of the unremunerative period of the development was taken, that is to say from that moment at which the developer invests in land purchase to the first sales of completed housing, the processing of the planning application took well under half of the total time. The rest of the time was taken up by the developer's own decision making, as for example when to lodge a planning application, and by construction (Glasson and Booth 1992).

The Queen's Park case represents one aspect of the operation of discretionary planning and was held to epitomize its failures. It nevertheless gives only a partial picture. A rather different snapshot of the system is given by another case of the late 1970s, that of High Storrs Roughs in Sheffield. The Roughs was council-owned land in the form of partly derelict allotments for which the council wished to obtain outline planning permission in order to sell at a profit. The only detailed planning policy document was the initial development plan which was by then considerably out of date. This showed the site as 'white' land, that is to say land on which no future change was expected. The site did, however, form part of an advisory green belt that had been defined before the war by the Council for the Protection of Rural England. Though there was no formal policy document setting out this green belt, maintenance of green belt around Sheffield had been incorporated as a policy in the

Figure 3.4 Discretion in action: a valuable part of the green wedge penetrating the built-up area or derelict allotments whose appearance would be improved as well-landscaped low-density housing? High Storrs Roughs, Sheffield

Source: University of Sheffield

South Yorkshire county structure plan, then in the course of preparation. The case was called in by the Secretary of State and a local public inquiry held (Booth 1998a).

The city council, acting in this case as the developer, argued that the material consideration was that the site would be more attractive as low-density housing in landscaped grounds than as derelict allotments. Further, there was a demand for larger new housing that the few sites available could not meet. Though the council's argument was considerably disingenuous given their opposition to development in other parts of this informal green belt, it rested on the belief that an exception could or should be made. The case inevitably aroused widespread opposition from articulate and largely well-to-do local residents. Their argument was simple: the site was, as the inspector put it in her report, 'a valuable part of a green wedge penetrating the built up area of the city' and, as such, had been given recognition in the informal green belt and the policy of the structure plan. The inquiry found in favour of maintaining the Roughs as open space.

The case indicates both the strengths and the weaknesses of the British discretionary system. First, the ambiguity of the policy base is striking. The only detailed land-use plan was significantly out of date. The structure plan, though new, could not by its very nature define precise limits for the green belt, even if it made a policy generalization that by implication applied to the Roughs. The most definite policy was a green belt boundary that had been prepared by a pressure group some 40 years earlier. Second, the public inquiry proved to be a forum in which the arguments both in favour and against the proposal received an airing. It not only enabled those affected by the proposal to present arguments but also allowed those arguments to be tested by cross-examination. Finally, the recommendation made by the inspector was in itself a discretionary decision. She, just like a local authority, made a decision on the merits of the case, by reference to a mixture of committed policy, professional values and her experience which was as much implicit as explicit.

DISCRETION IN THE 1980S

If the failure to deliver appropriate decisions in an appropriate time can be seen as a strictly partial criticism of the way in which the British planning system was working by the 1970s, it was one that nevertheless had taken firm hold by the beginning of the 1980s. It found particularly fertile ground with the incoming Conservative administration because it fitted well with the general view of local authorities as obstructive and time wasting, an impediment to the proper operation of the free market. The way in which this philosophy found expression in the reform of the planning system is intriguing. Although there were attempts at modifying the planning system directly, either by limiting control powers or removing them from local authorities altogether, by far the most important change was in government policy expressed in DoE circulars. These circulars had become notorious for their content and for their tone: Circular 22/80 on development control in general, Circular 15/84 on land for housing, and Circular 14/85 on planning for employment. The most striking feature of these circulars was the way in which they encouraged local authorities to use their discretion to permit development that would aid economic development or new housing and, if needs be, to disregard policy in development plans.

The failure to develop a coherent policy on town planning as opposed to an ideology of free-market enterprise led to two important cases in the mid-1980s. Encouraged by the government's emphasis on flexibility in planning, a consortium of developers put forward proposals for two major housing developments in south-eastern England, in areas that would have hitherto been taboo. In both cases the developers believed that government policy aided by proposals for self-contained settlements would be sufficiently material to outweigh any land-use constraints in local development plans. The first case, Tillingham Hall in Essex, was in the metropolitan green belt, between Upminster and Basildon, and the policy base was clear. The local authority could argue that the purpose of the green belt was to contain the outward spread of continuous urban development, and that the proposal at Tillingham Hall would reduce the capacity of the green belt to act as a buffer. At the inevitable public inquiry the local authority's case was upheld.

The second case, at Foxley Wood in Hampshire, was apparently less clear cut. The land for the proposed development was not designated green belt, but Hampshire County Council argued that it was land that was not allocated for future development and that adequate provision for housing had been made elsewhere on more suitable sites. Once again there was a public inquiry which recommended that development was refused permission.

There were several aspects of these two cases that deserve comment. The fact that local authorities and residents had vigorously opposed both developments, and the fact that this opposition was largely from the ranks of the government's own supporters, was a political embarrassment. But both cases also showed that, quite apart from legal constraints, there were appropriate policy limits to discretionary action. Discretion could not simply be invoked in order to take expedient decisions to promote development. Discretionary planning could only operate by reference to some kind of policy framework, even it that framework was not wholly unambiguous.

By the end of the 1980s, the government began to realize that development plans could be a way of resolving disputes and eliminating wayward decision making, although the process of conversion was slow. The final stage in the process came with the Planning and Compensation Act 1991 which introduced the celebrated clause to ensure that the development plan would be the first consideration in planning decisions. At the time, the change caused considerable excitement because it apparently represented a complete reversal of previous policy and gave the planning system a new boost. It was even claimed that the Planning and Compensation Act was moving the British planning system closer to the zoning systems of continental Europe.

Yet the change was essentially ambiguous. The reference to 'other material considerations' was not abandoned; the wording of the section merely required that: 'where in making a determination under the Planning Act, regard is to be had to the development plan, the determination shall be in accordance with the plan unless material considerations indicate otherwise'. Though the section is now held to have introduced a presumption in favour of development in accordance with the development plan, it does not alter fundamentally the discretionary nature of the British planning system.

CONCLUSION: DISCRETIONARY PLANNING VERSUS ZONING

What, then, have been the benefits and disbenefits of the discretionary system? Discretionary planning allows responses to development proposals to reflect the circumstances that exist at the point at which the development is proposed. It ensures that inevitable change can be rapidly absorbed into the system without necessarily prejudicing the policy base in its entirety. In these terms, the quest for flexibility does seem to have been achieved.

The discretionary system has developed a mechanism for resolving disputes, the public inquiry, which has proved to be a remarkably effective means of exploring the impact of a proposal for development. It allows objectors to make a case, albeit by custom rather than law, and it ensures a measure of accountability for local authority decision making. There have of course been celebrated failures of inquiries to resolve the tension between national policy and local conditions, to which the Heathrow Terminal 5 inquiry looks set to be the latest addition. However, these failures do not call into question the undoubted success of public local inquiries in dealing with small and medium sized cases. Finally, the discretionary planning system in Britain has allowed the control of development to take place in the absence of formally approved plans or when a plan has become out of date. Necessary new development need not be jeopardized by the absence of an approved plan, and its impact is not subject to any less rigorous an examination. These are formidable strengths. But they are also strengths which carry with them some significant disbenefits.

We have noted how nationalizing development rights has led to the planning permission assuming an overriding importance as the one guarantee that development may proceed. This carries a twofold disbenefit. It creates – some would argue a pathological – uncertainty for developers. It has also allowed the focus on development control to be on efficiency of process rather than quality of decision. It may even have fuelled speculative dealing in land.

The 'other material considerations' clause has partly divorced plans from development control. This has led to considerable uncertainty about what plans should achieve or what the appropriate form of expression should be. Although there is no longer a tendency on the part of local authorities to defer the preparation of local plans, since plan making is now once again mandatory, there is still no clear vision of the purpose that plans should serve.

The criteria that are used to evaluate the effect of proposals are, as we have noted, often not explicit. The planning profession has been called on to use its judgement in advising elected representatives how to exercise their discretionary powers. In this way, decision making reflects professional values and prejudices which are not fully articulated.

Since government policy has long been recognized by the courts as a material consideration, there is a real danger, as Davies *et al.* (1986) have observed, that planning policy nationwide could be led by government directive rather than determined locally in development plans. Though that danger has receded since the mid-1980s, it remains an endemic threat.

The question that arises from this list of weaknesses is whether a stronger connection between development control decision and the development plan, as proposed by zoning systems, would in fact resolve the problems. As critics of the British system have noted, the two issues that do appear to have been resolved in zoning systems are those of uncertainty and delay. The preparation of a zoning plan indicates a degree of commitment which is binding upon the decision maker and confers a right on the developer or land-owner. Yet we have noted at the beginning of the chapter that zoning systems appear constantly to be kicking at the limits that the systems themself impose. Studies of zoning systems, whether in the USA (Wakeford 1990; Cullingworth 1993) or in France (Booth 1989, 1996), suggest that decision makers regularly try to circumvent the constraint of prior commitment, and all systems of planning find themselves constrained to develop mechanisms to allow some flexibility in the face of unforeseen change. The difficulty for regulatory systems is that all too often the means of building in discretionary freedom offer a challenge to the legitimacy of the system as a whole.

In rehearsing the arguments for and against both kinds of planning system there is sometimes a pardonable tendency to conclude that if only the British system of planning came a little bit closer to the zoning systems of continental Europe and the USA or if only regulatory systems could behave rather more flexibly, both types of system could be improved. Yet such a conclusion would be nonsense. Regulatory and discretionary systems of planning do not exist as independent phenomena to be changed at will by planners. They are creatures of the constitution and cultures which give rise to them. The significant strengths of a discretionary and regulatory systems carry with them weaknesses, which have to be resolved within the context of the system itself. It is in resolving those weaknesses that the real test of any planning system lies.

FURTHER READING

Zoning Systems

For European zoning systems, the description of planning in Denmark, France, Germany and the Netherlands contained in Davies *et al.* (1989) *Planning Control in Western Europe* remains the fullest account so far in English. Two works written from a British perspective provide comprehensive descriptions of American zoning systems: Wakeford (1990) *American Development Control: Parallels and Paradoxes from and English Perspective* and Cullingworth (1993) *The Political Culture of Planning: American Land Use Planning in Comparitive Perspective*. Logan's article, 'The Americanization of German zoning' (1976), is an excellent brief account of the development of zoning in Germany and its impact on the USA. American critiques of zoning are to be found in Haar and Kayden (1989) *Zoning and the American Dream*, Babcock (1966) *The Zoning Game*, and Babcock and Siemon (1990) *The Zoning Game Revisited*. A critique of zoning from an English perspective is contained in Booth (1989) 'How effective is zoning in the control of development?'

Discretionary Power and Discretionary Systems of Planning
Administrative discretion has exercised both legal experts and political scientists. Helpful discussions include those by Davis (1971) *Discretionary Justice* from an American perspective, and from a British one, those by Jowell (1973) 'The legal control of administrative discretion', and Bull (1980) 'The anti-discretion movement in Britain'. For a rather more detailed discussion of administrative discretion and the legal system in Britain, see Harlow and Rawlings (1997) *Law and Administration*. For discretion in town planning, Davies (1980) 'The relevance of development control' and Booth (1996) *Controlling Development: Certainty and Discretion in Europe, the USA and Hong Kong* are the key references. For the way in which discretionary power is used in British planning, see Brindley *et al.* (1996) *Remaking Planning*. Crow (1996) 'Development control: the child that grew up in the cold' is a detailed account of the almost accidental origins of the development control system in Britain.

Comparative Studies
A comparison of the effects of zoning and discretionary systems of planning forms the core of Booth (1996) *Controlling Development: Certainty and Discretion in Europe, the USA and Hong Kong*. Although mainly concerned with environmental management and control, Vogel (1986) *National Styles of Regulation* contains an admirable debate on the differences between British and American approaches to administrative action and includes a chapter on land-use planning. Davies *et al.* (1989) provide a comparative synthesis in the final chapter of *Planning Control in Western Europe*.

chapter 4

The Planning System and the Development Plan

H. W. E. DAVIES

INTRODUCTION

The 1947 Town and Country Planning Act received the Royal Assent on 6 August 1947 and came into operation on 1 July 1948. It was the culmination of a process which had started ten years earlier, with the appointment of a Royal Commission on the distribution of the industrial population under the chairmanship of Sir Montagu Barlow, analysing the problems of urbanization in Britain and the difficulties and defects of existing planning legislation. Its main conclusion was that national action was necessary because of the nature and urgency of the problems (Barlow Report 1940).

The 1947 Act was a response to this analysis (Cullingworth 1975). It completely altered the form and structure of the planning system; and it established the basis for an effective land policy, with payment of compensation and collection of betterment relating to changes in the value of land. The fundamental principles of the planning system have survived broadly unchanged since 1947. The same is not true for land policy which has altered with every change of government from the 1950s to the 1980s (see chapter 5).

The Act contained five key instruments for planning and regulating the development and use of land: a definition of development; a duty on a local planning authority to prepare a development plan; a requirement for planning consent by the local planning authority for the carrying out of any development; a right of appeal to the minister against a refusal of planning consent; and a power of enforcement against any breach of planning control. Four of those instruments have not changed substantially in 50 years; they remain at the heart of the current planning Act. The only one of the five that has altered significantly is the development plan.

Many factors have influenced the changes in the development plan. Planning, and with it the development plan, has passed through successive stages of 'positive' planning by the public sector in the 1940s; regulatory planning in response to private-sector development in the 1950s; emerging ideas about 'systems' planning in the 1960s and 1970s; an enabling function in market-led planning in the 1980s; and, in the 1990s, 'plan-led' planning for sustainable communities. Local government reorganization in the 1970s and 1990s, and changing relationships between central and local government, also have had their effect.

This chapter examines the origins of the development plan during the creation of the planning system in the 1940s, the successive changes in the following half-century, and how it might change in the Millennium.

THE ORIGINS OF THE DEVELOPMENT PLAN

Planning schemes

The Barlow Commission found serious defects in the prewar planning system. The essence of the system under the Town and Country Planning Act 1932 lay in what were called *planning schemes*. These were detailed land-use zoning maps, prepared by district and county borough councils and supported by detailed regulations for the layout and control of development, based on model clauses issued by the Ministry of Health for the guidance of local authorities (Cherry 1974: 100).

The main legal effect of the planning scheme after its approval by the minister and parliament was that it established a specific, local and restricted right over the development and use of land. Changes of use in accordance with an approved scheme did not require further permission. Although this gave an apparent degree of rigidity, in practice the regulations could be imprecise. Indeed, schemes were criticized by many because they were too indefinite.[1]

One problem was the cumbersome procedure for the preparation and approval of each scheme. As a result, by 1939 very little of Britain was actually covered by approved schemes, although there was interim control of development over half of the country where schemes were being prepared. Even more fundamental was the liability of local planning authorities for payment of compensation if a landowner's right to change the use of his land was restricted in certain ways. Thirdly, even if added together the schemes could never have amounted to a national plan; they were nothing more than 'a patchwork of schemes of varying size, and varying merit' (Barlow Report 1940: 106).

The Barlow Report concluded that a central planning authority was needed to formulate a policy to deal with the problems of the congested urban areas and a balanced regional development, with authority over all existing and future planning schemes in the national interest. Its recommendations were given greater urgency in the face of the problems of postwar reconstruction, not least those of the war-damaged cities. The 'principle' of planning as a national policy and the need for some form of central planning authority was accepted by the coalition government in February 1941 (Ward 1994: 88).

The first two tasks were to establish the central planning authority and to put a stop to development that might prejudice reconstruction. Two crucial Acts were passed, creating the Ministry of Town and Country Planning, and extending interim development control to the entire country. This latter change, the creation of what was described as the 'universal restriction' on development without the consent of the responsible authority, was the crucial move. It directly affected the question of the planning machinery and in particular the role of plans. If there was to be a universal restriction on changes in the use and development of land, there was no need for a specific and local restriction such as was afforded by the prewar planning schemes. Yet the responsibility placed on the new minister for a national policy with regard to the development and use of land implied the need for some form of plan.

The search for a new form of plan

The search for a new plan began with the idea of an *outline plan* which would initiate the planning of a particular area by drawing up 'a general picture of the town' showing only its broad features or structure. The main priority of this would be to present the concept underlying its reconstruction, rather than 'the assembly of complicated details which obscure the main concept of the plan' under planning schemes.[2]

The outline plan would be the framework within which the new reconstruction areas of war damage would be placed, and which would guide the minister when approving orders for the compulsory acquisition of land for redevelopment. The 'broad brush' outline plan would be supplemented by detailed plans showing the intentions for the redevelopment of these areas, especially where comprehensive redevelopment would be required. What was emerging was an outline plan 'to be implemented by a fluid programme of development or redevelopment as a process of time-planning'.[3]

There were several contentious matters. The first was who should prepare the plans, and for which areas? The choice lay between the central authority and local government and, within local government, the existing system of counties and county boroughs or the smaller county districts as under the 1932 Act. An idea was floated for dividing the country into 'economic units capable of being planned as a whole', each with an area planning council with representatives of both central and local government. This was rejected as it would have involved central government in 'a vast expansion of staff' and also raised problems about responsibility.[4] Local authorities successfully argued that the responsibility for preparing the plans and controlling development should remain primarily at their level.

A second issue concerned the process by which local people and interests were to be consulted, and their rights of objection. It was argued that the issues arising on an outline plan for a large town did not lend themselves to examination at a formal enquiry with representations and objections from all individuals. Furthermore, 'given a universal restriction, the function of a planning scheme would no longer be to determine the rights of owners, but to determine the pattern of future development'.[3] Instead of the traditional, adversarial inquiry, with full rights of objection, there should be a process of consultation with selected interest groups with a power, but not an obligation, on the part of the minister to hold a public inquiry.

The third matter was who should actually approve the plan. The minister himself made it very clear that 'we should try to get away with *not* laying the plan' before parliament, as had been the requirement with the 1932 planning schemes. Instead it (and major departures) should be formally approved by the minister.[5]

By the time of the 1944 white paper on *The Control of Land Use*, the early ideas about the planning system seemed to have undergone a complete reversal. The dominant plan was the detailed plan for the reconstruction areas, now extended to include areas of bad layout and obsolete development as well as the original areas of extensive war damage, but also the additional land needed for industries and population to be rehoused from such areas. The significant point was that neither the white paper nor the subsequent 1944 Town and County Planning Act referred to more general plans of any kind. However, a ministry circular made clear that 'the powers of the Act should be exercised in relation to a broadly conceived plan showing in outline how the town as a whole should be reconstructed' (MTCP 1944).

What was happening was a gradual return to the planning scheme. For the Plans Division of the ministry the outline plan would be similar 'to a good 1939 scheme except that the land is allocated more firmly and allocations can be more precise' following removal of the liability for compensation. The outline plan would then be followed by *development plans* (*sic*) and *redevelopment plans*, the former geared to the needs of controlling private development whilst the latter would be 'fairly precise and detailed, and will involve more formal treatment than development plans' as they will authorize changing existing layouts and involve public expenditure'.[6]

From model clauses to planning standards

Meanwhile the future of the model clauses under the 1932 Act was also being discussed. Their significance was that they had been the nearest to a national policy before the war, as they set out what the ministry would be looking for in reviewing planning schemes before their approval by parliament. The question was whether a new or revised version of the model clauses would be required. A small, technical committee, set up in January 1944,[7] accepted that 'under a universal restriction, nothing may be done without the consent of the authority; and the whole form of the provisions regulating development will be essentially different. Clauses in the ordinary sense would disappear'.[8] Thus the object of a new code would be to set out standards which would assist local authorities in drafting conditions in a planning permission, pointing the way to their use under the new planning system.[9] By August 1946, the committee's list of standards covered a streets schedule; use zones; residential density; floor space index; daylighting; limitation of height of blocks of flats; and orientation of dwellings (i.e. sunlighting).

Work continued on developing the standards, now becoming known as a *development code*, as the time drew nearer for the new planning bill which eventually became the 1947 Act. It was thought that such a code would be of the 'the greatest practical convenience' for planning authorities in giving consents to development. However, it was gradually realized that there were better alternatives to a single, comprehensive code – such as the emerging *general development order*, the development plan regulations, and the ministry's handbooks, manuals and circulars.[10]

COUNTY MAPS AND TOWN MAPS: THE MARK I DEVELOPMENT PLAN

The 1947 development plan

One of the officials who had been deeply involved in the discussions about plans, Blaise Gillie, remarked later that the main principle behind the 1947 Act was that 'in strict logic', it did not involve preparing a plan at all, since all changes in the development and use of land in future would only require the permission of a public authority (Gillie and Hughes 1950: 4). Nevertheless, a plan was 'a natural but not inevitable consequence' of that principle and the development plan was to be the main instrument of land-use planning policy, prepared by local planning authorities under the supervision of central government. As it finally emerged, the development plan was to indicate 'the manner in which they [the local planning authority] propose that land in the area should be used (whether by carrying out thereon of development or otherwise)' (s.5(1), 1947 Act). The Act provided that the plan 'may define the sites of proposed roads, public and other buildings and works, . . . or allocate areas of land for use for agricultural, residential, industrial or other purposes'. The plan could also designate land for compulsory purchase, in particular areas for comprehensive development.

The signs here were of a return to a greater rigidity in the form and content of the plan. No longer was it to be a general 'long term view of the ultimate structure, with a provisional time programme for carrying it out' which had figured among the early ideas.[3] The development plan regulations (MTCP 1948b) which followed specified in detail both the form and the content of the new development plans.

The Act stipulated that the local planning authorities in England and Wales were to be the 145 county and county borough councils, with similar arrangements in Scotland, as the old district councils under the 1932 Act were too small, and in general a wider area was required. The development plan for a county borough would be a *town map* on an ordnance survey base to a scale of 6 inches to a mile, showing areas for primary land uses, densities, principal communications, etc., and the location of areas for comprehensive development. It would be supplemented by more detailed *comprehensive development area (CDA) maps* to a scale of 25 inches to a mile. The development plan for a county would be a *county map* on an ordnance survey base to a scale on 1 inch to a mile, showing the settlement pattern and communications, and various land-use allocations and restrictions such as sites for minerals or areas of great landscape value, supplemented by such town maps and CDA maps as needed. Later, after 1954, *supplementary town maps* were added for areas needing the same detailed planning as in areas for comprehensive development, but without their powers for compulsory purchase of land. Each map was accompanied by a *written statement* summarizing the proposals of the plan.

The county map was a new concept, giving a very generalized picture of the future structure of a county but overlain by detail on land use matters such as mineral workings, designations of national parks or green belts and the like, and the boundaries of inset town and CDA maps. On the other hand, the town map was a comprehensive land-use zoning map using a standardized notation, in many respects similar in appearance to a prewar scheme (see Figure 4.3).

There were real differences compared with those prewar schemes. Five were significant. The plan was to be based on a comprehensive *report of survey* and *written analysis* which would have to be submitted to the minister at the same time as the draft development plan. Secondly, the idea of 'time-programming' was retained so that each county map and town map had to be accompanied by a *programme map* showing the stages by which the proposals in the plan were to be carried out. Thirdly, the plan was to be reviewed every 5 years, with a fresh survey and analysis. Fourthly, there was no indication of the form and layout of development such as had been provided by the model clauses and their incorporation into the schemes. Of course, there was a whole battery of guidance and regulations on planning standards, but these were the tools of development control rather than the development plan. Lastly, the development plan 'would have no direct legal effect and no directly compensatable financial implications so far as the planning authority were concerned' (Grant 1982: 81).

The removal of the liability on local planning authorities for compensation for a restriction of development freed up the preparation of plans; and the requirement for planning consent removed any specific development right in the plan. Nevertheless, once approved by the minister, the plan as a statutory document had a considerable indirect effect. It created at the very least a strong presumption in favour of development in accordance with the plan. This presumption was reinforced by the requirement that any departures from an approved plan be submitted to the minister for his comment and, if necessary, approval. The strength of the implied effect lay in the statutory right of objection on the draft plan, and the obligation on the part of the minister to give objectors a hearing, if necessary in a public local inquiry. Thus, a combination of regulations and rights of objection led inevitably to the need for precision and certainty in the plan instead of that original idea of an outline plan.

With the Act and regulations in place, the functions of the old Ministry of Town and Country Planning were merged with the local government, housing and environmental health functions of the Ministry of Health in a new Ministry of Local Government and Planning, renamed, following the election of the Conservative government a few months later, as the Ministry of Housing and Local Government (MLGP 1951).

The 1947 development plans in practice

Development plans were in being for most of the country by the late 1950s but the signs of dissatisfaction with the planning system, and development plans in particular, were increasing. Planning was in 'the doldrums', planners were unpopular (Cherry 1974: 161). Expectations aroused by the new development plans were not being fulfilled. The postwar period was proving to be one of rapid social and economic change; the assumptions on which many of the development plans were based were proving to be false, and the plans were becoming quickly out of date. Yet the procedures for review and alteration of plans themselves were complex, and applications for planning permission involving departures from the development plan were increasing. Disputes began to centre on the use of so-called *white land*, that is land not allocated for any urban use on the fringes of towns, but under pressure for development.

Another problem was that, for many, the plans were at the same time too detailed and not detailed enough: the main policy features in the county maps were obscured by a mass of detail, while the town maps were over-complicated yet inadequate as guides to development. One critic argued that simpler county and town maps were needed, with 'some thousands of supplementary town maps' laying down precise patterns of uses and road systems, and where appropriate building envelopes showing the general street picture (Keeble 1961: 98).

The first signs of a response from the ministry came with a new approach to the renewal of town centres, enabling the local authority to make a broad and relatively quick assessment of the problems and possibilities of the town centre which could be developed into a sound basis for more detailed decision, in effect an outline plan (MHLG 1962). This *town centre map* would be diagrammatic, produced quickly and non-statutory, and therefore could include many aspects which were neither required nor appropriate for a development plan. Together, Keeble's criticism and the town centre map pointed the way to the next big change in the evolution of the development plan.

STRUCTURE PLANS AND LOCAL PLANS: THE MARK II DEVELOPMENT PLAN

The PAG report and structure planning

Development plans prepared under the 1947 Act were still the prime instrument for planning policy in the early 1960s, but their weaknesses were becoming ever more apparent. They did not sit comfortably with the emerging regional planning, and they were increasingly unable to cope with the technical demands of the new planning issues, especially the relationship between land use and transportation, and the more complex redevelopment of town centres by public and private sectors. The government was concerned also about the workload in ministerial approval of development plans and their statutory reviews and was seeking a means of 'disengagement' (Delafons 1998).

Accordingly, in May 1964, a Planning Advisory Group was set up to advise on the technical quality of development plans and the levels of responsibility as between ministerial approval and local authorities. The group analysed the merits and defects of the existing system, concluding that development plans increasingly were technically unable to cope with the new challenges and that the delays in their preparation and approval exacerbated their technical defects. They were reinforced in their views by the anticipated 'surge of physical development on a scale that this country has not previously seen, . . . overwhelmingly in and around the towns' (PAG 1965: 8).

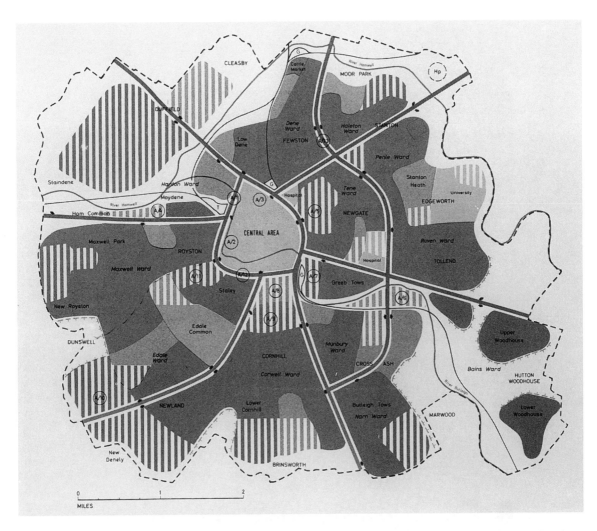

New kinds of plan would be needed to guide this development and promote efficiency and quality in the replanning of towns.

The key recommendation was to divorce strategic policies from their detailed implementation. *Urban structure plans*, prepared for county boroughs and towns of over 50,000 (and *county maps* with a similar function for the counties), would be the strategic policy plans, requiring approval by the minister. Their new feature was that they would be written statements of policy and its justification, illustrated by sketch maps and diagrams rather than a plan. The PAG envisaged a new form of plan setting out the strategic policies for the development of town (or county) as the main link between regional plans and local land use planning, in particular integrating land use and transport planning in a robust framework for more detailed planning. The plan would rely chiefly on written statements for the key strategic policies and proposals, excluding matters of lesser importance. It would be illustrated by a small map or diagram showing the broad outline of the town's future development and structure. Figure 4.1 shows the existing (solid) and proposed (hatched) areas of the main land uses, residential, industrial, commercial etc, and the primary road network and its points of access.

Local plans would be prepared for the implementation of structure plan policies and as a framework for development control. They too would be a written statement

Figure 4.1 An urban structure map, to illustrate the written policies in the new kind of development plan proposed by the Planning Advisory Group.

Source: PAG 1965: Figure 1
Crown copyright is reproduced with the permission of The Controller of Her Majesty's Stationery Office

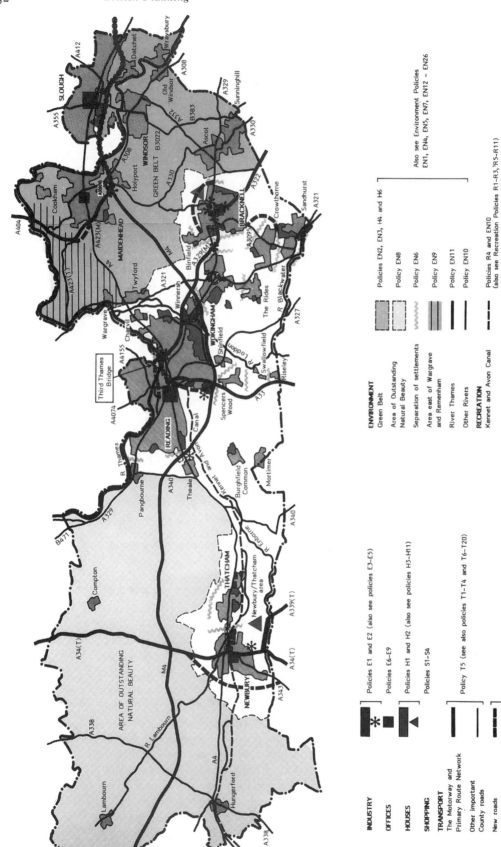

STRUCTURE PLAN FOR BERKSHIRE : KEY DIAGRAM

with a detailed *proposals map* on an ordnance survey base, rather than a land-use plan and omitting the idea of showing the programming or phasing of development. Local plans could vary in their style and content such as *action area plans* (replacing the CDA maps) and more general purpose *district plans*. All local plans would be approved by the local planning authority itself, in conformity with the structure plan provisions.

The recommendation which caught the imagination of many of the new generation of planners with a stronger base in social sciences than in the design disciplines was the emphasis on policy, with the changes in format and presentation and all that that implied for planning techniques. McLoughlin (1966: 258) summed it up in the recognition of a much clearer distinction between 'policies, objectives and standards' for the dynamics of urban growth and renewal . . . and the design of 'areas which will need to be planned as a whole and in detail'. For many others, it was the delegation of responsibility for self-approval of the new local plans which was seen as truly radical (Delafons 1998). Local authorities were more cautious in their response, concerned about the implications of the work load which the new system would generate and the new skills which it would require.

A 1967 white paper on *Town and Country Planning* broadly endorsed the PAG recommendations, and the new system was soon enacted in the Town and Country Planning Act 1968 with very little change. The development plan of a local planning authority would be the *structure plan*, with ministerial approval, and its *local plans*, including *action area plans*, the subject of self-adoption. Both kinds of plan would follow the traditional procedures for objections to the plan and a public inquiry if necessary. As a concession to local government fears, the new system was to be introduced gradually in different authorities; meanwhile, the old-style development plans would remain in force. As the new plans were approved, they would supplant the older plans.

One further change came in 1972 when the planning inquiry into objections to a structure plan was replaced by a new style *examination in public* in which only those invited by the minister could participate. This was based on the principle that its purpose would be to inform the minister more fully on the issues raised by the plan and its merits or defects before being approved, rather than protecting the property rights of landowners and others. Those rights would continue to be protected through the inquiry into objections to a local plan. Thus, the local plan inquiry would continue to suffer from the 'ambiguity of function' in the old, traditional inquiries, combining political and quasi-judicial elements, made worse by the local authority being in effect judge in its own cause (Grant 1982: 125).

The whole set of plans for an area, old and new, collectively would comprise the statutory development plan for the purposes of development control. The development plan in law continued to be a form of guidance rather than a master plan or mandatory blueprint. The change in 1968 was that the new structure plan would define clear objectives and strategic criteria for dealing with future decisions about the development and use of land, and the new local plan would concentrate on the proposals for change, including restrictions on change such as a green belt, rather than present a map of the future land uses in an area as the previous development plan had done.

The culmination of the new planning came with publication of a *Development Plans Manual* (MHLG 1970b). The manual gave detailed guidance on every aspect of the new structure, local and action area plans. It made clear that the context of the plan had widened since 1947. The new development plans were to be prepared and examined in the light of national and regional planning policies. They were to be

Figure 4.2 A structure plan key diagram and index to written policies showing new development concentrated between the metropolitan green belt and the area of outstanding natutral beauty

Source: Royal County of Berkshire Structure Plan, 1991–2006 *Reproduced from the Ordnance Survey map with the permission of The Controller of Her Majesty's Stationery Office, Crown Copyright MC 88785M0001, and Berkshire Unitary Authorities' Joint Strategic Planning Unit*

concerned not only with the use of land, but also with many other matters, in particular the full integration of land use and transport planning and creation of a good environment in town and country. They were also to be rolled forward at intervals when necessary. By 1995 for example the Berkshire Structure Plan was in its third revision (see Figure 4.2). The new, more flexible, plans and the distinction between strategy and detail would, it was hoped, simplify the planning system.

The retreat from PAG

It was not to be. PAG had not mentioned local government reorganization; counties and county boroughs were its unitary authorities for the purposes of town planning. The white paper acknowledged that the old development plans covered areas which were too small, dividing town from country. It referred to the work of the Royal Commission on Local Government in England which was expected to recommend unitary local authorities in place of the patchwork of county boroughs, counties and districts. That recommendation was broadly accepted in 1969 by the Labour government but, following the general election, it was rejected by the new Conservative government. The two-tier system of counties and districts was retained, the county boroughs being absorbed into the counties, though with a reduction in the number of district councils.

This created problems for the new planning system. The Local Government Act 1972 retained the upper tier of counties as planning authorities for the purposes of structure plans but made the new district councils the planning authorities for development control. County planning authorities were to prepare a development plan scheme, allocating responsibility for the preparation of local plans but retaining the duty of 'certifying' that any local plans conformed to the structure plan.

The new authorities came into being in 1974 in England and Wales, with broadly similar arrangements in Scotland a year later. So, at the same time as the new system of development plans was beginning, responsibility for planning was being split between two tiers, with new district councils taking over new responsibilities. The results were predictable. A further complication was the restriction in the 1968 Act that a local plan could be adopted only after its structure plan had been approved by the minister, a delay on average of two years from deposit to approval. Thus, the district planning authority which wished to have a clear, up-to-date local plan, say for an area under pressure for development, was prevented from doing so. This restriction was repealed in 1980, by which time most structure plans had anyway been approved.

The process of cutting back on the requirements for the new structure plans started in 1974. The DoE (1974b), noting that only half of the new plans had been submitted for approval, insisted that plans should 'concentrate on those issues which are of key structural importance' and that county authorities should be doing no more work than was essential. Nevertheless, it would be 1985 before the last structure plan was finally approved.

Next, the department downgraded local plans, emphasizing that they need not be for the whole of an area, but were to be prepared only where the extra detail seemed necessary or desirable (DOE 1977c). In the first round of their development plan schemes counties had identified a need for 3,500 local plans by 1980 (Mabey and Craig 1976: 71). By 1985 this had fallen to 1,525 with a disproportionate reduction in action area plans (Bruton and Nicholson 1987:135). The actual deposit of draft local plans and their approval were even more delayed than with the structure plans, and by 1985 only a third of the expected local plans had been deposited or adopted.

A significant factor was the change in the economic climate in the 1970s. The long-range population forecasts were proving illusory, economic growth was slowing, and the planning agenda was shifting from a focus on accommodating growth to responding to problems of urban decline. Action areas, with their assumption of rapid and comprehensive change in concentrated areas, were no longer what was required. Indeed, questions were posed as to whether any form of local plan was effective where there was no pressure for development or redevelopment. The two situations in which preparation of a development plan even of the new kind was useful and relevant were where there was still pressure for land-use change, namely, the central areas of many towns and cities, and the fringes of urban areas still experiencing growth (Healey *et al.* 1988: 193).

One consequence of the delays in producing the new structure and local plans was an explosive growth in non-statutory planning guidance being prepared and adopted, especially by district planning authorities. The trend was reinforced by the uneasy fit between the policy content of the statutory structure and local plans and the detailed planning considerations – the 'other material considerations' which those in development control could and did take into account when determining planning applications. Supplementary guidance of some kind was essential if development control was to be efficient and effective, consistent and equitable rather than relying on 'unwritten policies, local custom and practice, and professional skill, experience and judgement' (Davies *et al.* 1986: 13).

Abolition of the Greater London Council and the six metropolitan county councils in 1986 marked a further change. The new planning authorities in these areas were the London borough and metropolitan district councils who became responsible for new *unitary development plans*. These were prepared in two parts: part one had the same function as a structure plan, but for the smaller area; while part two was the detailed local plan. The function of the old county-wide structure plan was replaced by strategic planning guidance from the DoE.

The thrust of government policy through the 1980s was to 'release market forces' and to 'give people choice' (Thornley 1993). Planning was seen as part of the problem rather than the solution, especially in the declining inner urban areas. New instruments, such as urban development corporations and enterprise zones, were introduced, effectively supplanting the local authority development plan in their areas. From 1980, there was a progressive relaxation of development control. The significant moment for the development plan in this period of change came with a reminder that the development plan should be 'one, but only one, of the material considerations that must be taken into account in dealing with planning applications'. This was considered to be of particular importance given the fact that many development plans had been approved or adopted several years previously, with consequences for their relevance at the present time. They 'should not be regarded as overriding other material considerations'. This was clearly a warning shot (DOE 1985a: para 5).

This was quickly followed, in 1986, by a consultation paper on *The Future of Development Plans* (DOE 1986). The paper built up a powerful criticism of the state of development plans – as strong as that levelled against the 1947 plans by PAG. Most of the criticism was levelled at the structure plans, by now a complete set, each of which had an average length of 100,000 words; a written statement with 100 policies, many of them either irrelevant or trespassing on what should more properly be part of a local plan; and taking between 4 and 5 years to prepare and get approved. Local plans were characterized by length, complexity and cumbersome procedures, to which was added the slow progress in their preparation.

The paper concluded that the statutory county structure plan should be replaced by a non-statutory county statement, restricted to a limited number of topics relating

Figure 4.3 Extract from an old-style Town Map on the edge of a large town. It is a comprehensive land use map of existing and proposed new development, using a standard, national notation, with the phasing of land allocated for new development in the 5 and 20 year periods

Source: County Borough of Reading, Town Map: Programme Map, 1957 *Reproduced from the Ordnance Survey map with the permission of The Controller of Her Majesty's Stationery Office, Crown Copyright MC 88785M0001, and Reading Borough Council*

to its statutory responsibilities; and the statutory development plan should be a new, single-tier, district development plan prepared by district authorities for the whole of their area. Those conclusions were endorsed in a 1989 white paper on *The Future of Development Plans*.

Thus, after 20 years, the future of the development plan was once more under attack, even before the new, PAG-style plans had provided a complete coverage of the country – just as its predecessor, the old-style 1947 development plan had been under attack in 1964.

A MARK III DEVELOPMENT PLAN? THE PLAN-LED SYSTEM

No sooner was the white paper published in January 1989 than the reaction started. A new Secretary of State was appointed, and a major government statement was issued on environmental policy and sustainable development: the 1990 white paper *This Common Inheritance* made it clear that the development plan, including local plans and structure plans, would remain an essential instrument for town and country planning.

Planning policy guidance (PPG) *notes* containing statements of government's object-ives and policies covering a wide field had begun to be issued by the DoE in 1988.

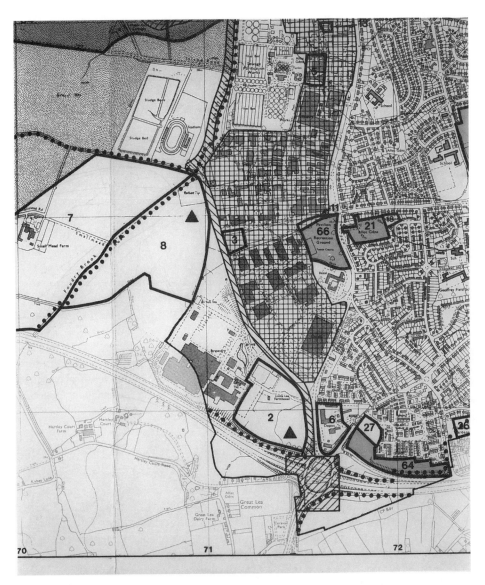

Figure 4.4 Extract from a Local Plan for the same area as in Figure 4.3. This new plan shows only the proposals for change, chiefly the new line of the A33 road, the new mixed industrial area, and developments around the motorway junction. Policies are defined in the written statement of the plan.

Source: Reading Borough Council, Reading Borough Plan, deposit draft Local Plan, 1992, Proposals Map *Reproduced from the Ordnance Survey map with the permission of The Controller of Her Majesty's Stationery Office, Crown Copyright MC 88785M0001, and reading Borough Council*

They followed the example of Scotland where *national planning guidelines* had been issued since 1974, responding initially to the pressures brought on by North Sea oil development and its on-shore impacts, but soon widened to a longer list of topics (Cullingworth and Nadin 1997: 75). PPG1 was a statement of general policy and principles, whilst other PPGs dealt with the preparation, form and content of development plans, and a range of subjects including housing, retail development, transport and green belts. These were supplemented by *regional planning guidance* (RPG) *notes*. The intention was to establish a consistent, systematic and up-to-date statement of national and regional planning guidance for the benefit of those preparing development plans. They quickly became a major, influential addition to the battery of policy statements and guidance, with the majority of PPGs being revised following publication of *This Common Inheritance* to take into account ideas about sustainable development.

The Town and Country Planning Act 1990 consolidated the various amendments to the previous 1971 Act, but it was itself amended the following year by the Planning and Compensation Act 1991. It was this Act which enshrined the most recent changes to the development plan system. The key changes were that the *structure plan* should be self-approved by the county council, provided that it had regard to national and regional planning guidance; the *local plan* would in future be a mandatory requirement for district councils, covering their entire area; and county councils would prepare a *minerals local plan* and a *waste local plan*. The most important change was a new section 54A in the 1990 Act, which provided that 'where, in making any determination under the planning Acts, regard is to be had to the development plan, the determination shall be made in accordance with the plan *unless* material considerations indicate otherwise' (my italics). This signalled the idea of a *plan-led system* in which the development plan would be the main component, with the expectation that there would be a substantially complete coverage of the new district-wide local plans by 1996 (DOE 1992a: para 3.7).

The legislative and policy changes were rounded off by advice on good practice in the preparation, form and content of development plans (DOE 1992b). As structure plans and unitary development plans were reviewed, as more local plans were adopted (albeit more slowly than had been hoped, with doubts whether 80 per cent coverage by the end of 1998 could be achieved) and as the suite of RPGs for England was completed by 1996, there seemed to be the prospect of what PAG had been seeking in 1964 actually materializing. That is, by the fiftieth anniversary of the passing of the 1947 Town and Country Planning Act there would be in place, or near to completion, an intelligible, comprehensive and effective hierarchy of plans, from national planning policy guidance, through regional planning guidance, to structure and local (or unitary development) plans.

THE FUTURE OF DEVELOPMENT PLANS

The concept of a development plan has survived for 50 years despite the vicissitudes to which it has been exposed as ideas about its function have shifted in response to a greater understanding of the forces underlying urban change and the limited power of the state to influence (let alone direct) those changes. However, it remains the weak link in the public's perception of planning as 'few people recognise the various types of development plan, or know who is responsible for their preparation' (McCarthy *et al.* 1995: iv). One reason for this lack of understanding is the technical complexity – even the obscurity – of the actual documents which make up the plan. Much has been done to improve that clarity, especially at the structure plan level, but the documents remain a barrier to understanding.

The plans are complex for various reasons. One is the concern about rights of objection. Discussions about the new plans in the 1940s had expressed the hope that the kind of planning typical of planning schemes would no longer be necessary. The removal of liability for compensation and the universal restriction together meant that the preparation of the plan and any representations and objections to its proposals could be treated purely on their merits for the proper planning of the town. That idea was lost, and the concern about property rights returned. Hence, plans and policies still have to be relatively detailed and specific, especially at the local level. The consequent risk is that the information and assumptions upon which a plan is prepared and finally approved 5 years or so later will leave at best 5 years of effective life before it ceases to be a realistic guide for future planning (Kitchen 1997: 79).

A second factor making for complexity in planning was for PAG the greater understanding of social and economic processes and interests in urban areas, and later the need for an enhanced awareness of development processes in the 1980s and of environmental concerns in the 1990s. There is now the challenge of sustainable development, and all that that implies for a development plan. Yet the planning system is essentially tied to the development and use of land in a specific, legal sense. Apart from widening the scope of concern beyond land-use into issues which are often beyond the capability of a land-use planning system, there are questions about the lengthening time horizons and widening spatial horizons for effective strategic planning; these extend well beyond the administrative boundaries and electoral timetables of current urban governance. There is even a question whether the very name *development* plan is too narrow, and should be replaced by *area* plan or some such term, reflecting the idea of 'planning for people and places' rather than just for development (Countryside Commission 1998e).

A further complication is that the Conservative government had initiated in 1992 yet another reorganization of local government. The aim was to simplify the structure of local government by doing away with the two-tier system, replacing it with a single tier of elected local authorities. The method in Scotland and Wales was arbitrary: the Scottish regional councils and the Welsh county councils were simply abolished, and new systems of unitary authorities established. But for England there was a long drawn-out process of local consultations which resulted in a complex patchwork of unitary authorities in some areas, usually cut off from their surrounding hinterland, and two-tier county and district councils in others. Joint planning arrangements for structure planning are being set up over much of England and Scotland between the districts of a dismembered county or region, or a new county borough and the remnants of its former county. It is too soon to say how they will work out. All of this means that the prospect of a new and perfect development plan system, which, from the vantage point of 1998, could be seen as something capable of being achieved, is once more in doubt.

The development plan has had two functions since 1947: a strategic one, in time and/or space; and a regulatory one which, given our mixed economy and the private ownership of land, does need to have legal status. Perhaps the mistake in the past has been to try to encompass both functions in the one development plan.

Structure plans seek to fulfil the strategic function. But they have been constrained by the requirements of statute, the limitations of county and borough boundaries, and uneasy relations both with higher authority and the lower tiers of local government – now still further constrained by the political dictates of joint arrangements. The strategic function is necessary but, with the strengthening of regions through regional development agencies and the review of RPG (DETR 1998f), the question can be posed whether the structure plan has outlived its day, and could be replaced by the new RPG, reinforced with statutory authority.

The regulatory function needs something like the local plan in its present form as a primarily land-based planning instrument, providing clear guidance for development control and the coordination of investment and infrastructure in the area. This, necessarily, has to be precise, with statutory procedures for protection of rights. But arguably the detailed, statutory local plan would be needed chiefly only for those areas where there are complex and competing claims for land. Elsewhere, land-use regulation through development control could be carried on with local regulations or by-laws and various kinds of supplementary planning guidance. A form of long range, non-statutory policy plan for that local area, in effect an outline plan, would give the clear sense of direction which the statutory plans are incapable of doing.

The development plan has been an imperfect but essential tool of planning for 50 years. It has evolved in response partly to changes in the demands made upon it by changing perceptions of planning, and partly to the perceived deficiencies of each preceding stage. Richard Pepler, Honorary Solicitor of the Town Planning Institute, said in 1949, one year after the coming into operation of the 1947 Act (Pepler 1949: 232):

> Here we are once more carrying out surveys and making plans. We seem to have done this before and no doubt we shall do it again and again before we are through. Perhaps some of us, on our more irritable days, discerning the millennium as far off as ever, feel even a touch of the chill hand of despair as we struggle on. This should not be. We are making great strides.

Well, here we are at the millennium, and we have made great strides, but still the search for a perfect form of development plan continues.

FURTHER READING

The Planning System
A detailed description of the creation of the planning system is found in Cullingworth (1975) *Environmental Planning 1939–1969 Volume 1, Reconstruction and Land Use Planning, 1939–1947*. A more general and well illustrated history is Ward (1994) *Planning and Urban Change*, while Cherry (1974) *The Evolution of British Town Planning* weaves into the story the perspective of the Royal Town Planning Institute. Cherry's last book (1996), *Town Planning in Britain since 1900*, presents a more general and critical account of the history of planning.

The standard account of the planning system is given in Cullingworth and Nadin (1997) *Town and Country Planning in the UK*. The 12th edition (1997) is the most recent, and the first to have a reasonably full account of planning in all four countries of the UK. Like earlier editions, it contains full listings of statutes, regulations, circulars and other government publications on planning as well as very comprehensive bibliographies. Earlier editions give an interesting perspective on how the system has changed since the first edition (1964), such as the ninth edition (1985), the last to have a chapter on new towns, or the 10th (1988), the last with regional planning, while the 11th (1994, the first with joint authors), was the first with a chapter explicitly on planning and the environment. A different, more theoretical approach reflecting debates about planning, the market and the state is Rydin (1998) *Urban and Environmental Planning in the UK*.

Planning and Development Plans
A very clear insight into the professional education and work of town planners in the 1950s with a strong emphasis on plan making is given in what for many years was the standard textbook on the 1947 system: Keeble (1st edition 1952; 4th edition 1969) *Principles and Practice of Town and Country Planning*. His later book (1961), *Town Planning at the Crossroads* gives a more critical review at a time of change.

Three books that give accounts of planning with a strong focus on the preparation and use of development plans in the 1970s and 1980s are Cross and Bristow (1983) *English Structure Planning*, Bruton and Nicholson (1987) *Local Planning in Practice* and Healey *et al.* (1988) *Land Use Planning and the Mediation of Urban Change*. Brindley, *et al.* (1996) *Remaking Planning: The Politics of Urban Change*, presents a comparative analysis of development planning in four different kinds of situation in the late 1980s, while Kitchen (1997) *People, Politics, Policies and Plans* gives an overview of development planning in one city (Manchester) from the 1940s to the present day.

chapter 5

Compensation and Betterment

MALCOLM GRANT

INTRODUCTION

Compensation and betterment have been the two heroic planning themes of the past 50 years. Like the opening sequence of a Rachmaninov piano concerto, they made a bold appearance in 1948, only to be banished abruptly shortly afterwards; then recreated with greater subtlety, in different disguises and with different instruments; then, somewhat more gently reintroduced as a main theme in the second movement (1965–1970); dropped, then resurrected and abandoned once again in the third movement (1975–1979). But those were the headline themes. The real development of the theme was always occurring elsewhere. There has been little change to the principal theme on compensation: there is in Britain no compensation for loss of development rights, only for the physical taking of land (i.e. for the acquisition of title). But many new tunes have been played with betterment, often quietly and dispersed, and some of the best have been those which have been improvised. In this chapter we review not only the virtuoso displays of 1948, 1965 and 1975, but also the sub-themes whose staying power and contribution to the work as a whole has actually been the greater.

THE STARTING POINT

It is necessary to recall that the 1947 Act did not start in a vacuum. A planning system had been in operation since 1909 but, despite its steady strengthening in successive Acts, it suffered from fundamental defects that made it largely unworkable. There was widespread agreement about this. The defects were well captured in the official wartime reports that were to become the pillars of the postwar system: in particular, both the Scott Report and the Barlow Report had identified the resolution of the betterment/compensation issue as the key to effective planning. The Barlow committee had been sufficiently concerned about it to recommend that the matter be examined further by a body of experts, and this recommendation was implemented in 1941 with the appointment of Mr Justice Uthwatt to chair a distinguished committee whose task was held out as a non-political exercise. The committee was asked to 'make an objective analysis of the subject of the payment of compensation and recovery of betterment in respect of public control of the use of land' and to advise, *inter alia*, on 'possible means of stabilising the value of land required for development or redevelopment'. These terms of reference were as explicit as they were narrow: they invited recommendations for an interventionist system. Indeed, the more interventionist they could be on the recovery of betterment, the less the need to worry about compensation or even land value stabilization, because the less the significance of market forces.

Hence, the Uthwatt committee's report was predictably radical, and nonetheless so for being meticulous in its analysis and dispassionate in its language. Though they narrowly rejected the general nationalization of land as an answer, they were happy to agree that it would present a logical solution to the problem presented to them to examine. On balance, however, they felt that general nationalization would be 'impracticable, at least in the short term'. The committee did support limited nationalization, though of rights other than title. They recommended:

(1) The rights of development in all land lying outside built-up areas should be vested immediately in the State, subject to payment of fair compensation. The land itself would then be acquired by the State as and when it was needed for development. Such arrangements would deal with the problems of 'shifting value' and 'floating value' which had arisen from the compensation provisions of the 1932 Act, because the values could be fixed and the compensation paid as at one fixed date, ignoring any subsequent increases due to increased development demand.[1]

(2) For already developed areas local authorities should have broader compulsory purchase powers, though the committee found difficulty in justifying a compensation base below market value.

(3) There should be annual site value rating as a continuing means of taxing increases in land values. This recommendation was one the committee believed could stand on its own, whether the other recommendations were accepted or not. In the event, it did stand on its own: it was rejected.

THE 1947 ACT

The Uthwatt proposals were not accepted in full by either the wartime coalition[2] or the postwar Labour government. But their influence upon the radical scheme of the 1947 Act was clear. There were two primary principles, which can be labelled the 'no compensation' rule and the 'land taxation' rule.

The 'no compensation' rule

The Act imposed first a general prohibition against any development without permission. It then ensured that permission would not be granted by the development plan, but only on a case-by-case basis, and with a broad discretionary power given to the local authorities. They would be expected generally to follow the plan, but they were entitled to depart from it in an appropriate case. Next, the Act adopted the general principle that no compensation should have to be paid if planning permission were refused, except in certain limited cases[3]. Instead, landowners were left with a claim against a global sum of £300 million in respect of any loss of development value caused by the Act. A scheme for distribution of the fund was to have been effected by mid-1953. It was a limited scheme, and its purpose was more to inject confidence into the market by meeting hardship cases than to provide an objectively measured level of compensation for loss of development rights. Admitted claims for loss were met at the rate of 16 shillings in the pound (80 pence) prior to the winding up of the fund in 1953, and the government had secured its objective: the nationalization of development rights in land (Parker 1965: 64).

The 'no compensation' rule was a product of its time. The postwar government acted with the knowledge that electors would not easily understand or forgive a spate of speculation and profiteering in land, and would not understand why land-owners (or 'landlords' as they were often pejoratively referred to in the parliamentary debates) should be compensated for diminution in values that had accrued whilst the war was continuing. Yet it remains the foundation stone of the British planning system today, and its effect is powerful. It has allowed the green belts to be protected from development without any payment of compensation, or any need to negotiate protective agreements on a case-by-case basis with landowners; and it has similarly reinforced the statutory protection of nature conservation areas and historic buildings. That is not to say that planners have been able to ignore the market or the adverse financial impact of refusals of permission. The hard line of the law has been mitigated by the courts' willingness to allow planners to take account of 'the human factor' [4] (i.e. to relax their usual requirements in exceptional cases to meet the needs of individuals) and even to allow them to manipulate the system so as to generate land-value enhancements which can be used to provide social benefits[5].

Nonetheless, the effect of the general rule is that, in place of substantive rights to develop, British landowners have only procedural rights: principally, the right to have a planning application determined in accordance with the development plan and other material considerations, and the right to appeal to the Secretary of State against a local authority's refusal of permission or conditions imposed by them. They also share collectivised rights, such as the right to participate as an objector to a development plan or to lobby local authorities and government ministers with proposals. All of this is in marked contrast to the situation in other countries where there has been no such historical watershed and where, as in the USA, there has been a constitutional guarantee of enjoyment of private property rights without uncompensated government interference. In Britain, the only live issue since 1948 has been that of entitlement to the value generated in land when government releases development rights back to the landowner, through the grant of planning permission.

The land taxation rule

This is because on land taxation, there has been no comparable stability of policy. The 1947 Act took an equally strong line, but the model that was adopted lacked any potential for political survival. The Act imposed a development charge (in practice set at 100 per cent) upon development value accruing to land by virtue of planning permission or otherwise. The intention was that the existence of the charge would result in market transactions taking place at current use value, since any sum paid in excess of that amount would be payable by way of charge to the Central Land Board. Hence, it was not a conventional tax or even a charge, because no impost set at 100 per cent of the value arising from an activity can be expected to generate any serious revenue in a voluntary market. What it could be expected to do, however, and did, was to dissuade landowners from bringing development land on to the market, particularly given the Conservative opposition pledge to repeal the charge in the event of their party becoming the next government. It was expected from the outset that the Central Land Board would have to play an interventionist role in a sluggish market, through use of compulsory purchase powers to bring land on to the market, and it was anticipated that they would be prompted in their acquisitions by requests from individual developers for particular sites. That did not eventuate. The Board's powers were effectively frozen while a legal challenge to them went as far as the House of Lords,[6] and almost outlived the charge itself.

The repeal of the betterment taxation rule

On their return to power at the end of 1951, the Conservatives abolished development charges and froze claims against the £300 million fund. A free market was restored in development land with a vengeance. There was no differential charge on increases in development value, nor in many cases was there any charge to ordinary taxation. An anomalous exception remained, however, which demonstrated the ad hoc character of the reforms. Compensation for acquisition by public authorities remained pegged at existing use values, so that there developed a dual market in which prices grew steadily further apart. The matter was not rectified until 1959, when market value was restored as the general basis for compensation assessment, though with an important exception to which we shall return below. But even when this anomaly had gone, a larger one remained: the planning system had become one in which the winner took all. Not only was there no differential tax on increases in land values, but until 1963 there was no capital gains tax on any increases in assets value.[7]

THE SECOND MOVEMENT: THE LAND COMMISSION

The enthusiasm of postwar Labour administrations for land taxation remained unabated, and emerged again in the mid-1960s. Land speculation in the new marketplace had become a matter of political concern. The Conservative Chancellor in 1962 had introduced a short-term speculative gains tax designed to catch 'the man who buys land in the hope of a quick speculative profit through a sale to a genuine developer',[8] and the incoming Labour government in 1964 moved quickly to introduce a new 30 per cent capital gains tax on all capital gains. But the government quickly showed its lack of familiarity with property economics by introducing a measure which, perversely but predictably, became one of the most extraordinary generators of profit that the property market had ever seen. This was George Brown's office ban of 1965, which, by declaring a moratorium on new office building in central London, immediately drove up demand and rents for offices already constructed or for which contracts were signed by midnight that night (which produced a flurry of Cinderella business deals whose effect over time was to increase greatly the volume of office space in London).

The Land Commission Act 1967 was conceived in part as an answer to the government's critics and in part as a continuation of the unfinished business of 1947. It readdressed the question of differential taxation for land, and introduced a levy set initially at a rate of 40 per cent of development value, with the intention that it should rise over the long term. In many ways it resembled the 1947 measure, in that its implementation and collection was given to an independent commission to act on behalf of the government, with powers itself of land assembly and promotion of development. There were two principal and related differences: first, the higher levels of tax were to be phased in over time, allowing the market the opportunity to adapt; second, the levy was intended to generate revenues. In practice, the market showed great reluctance allow it to do so, and the seeds of failure were there from the beginning. Again, the Conservative opposition were pledged to repeal; and in the period during which the measure was in effect (1967–1970) there was a significant problem in the supply of development land, and a sharp upturn in land values. Hence, the measure failed to achieve the key role that had been planned for it. Its abolition by the Heath government in 1970 was widely welcomed (Grant 1982).

THE THIRD MOVEMENT: THE COMMUNITY LAND SCHEME

The third attempt by a Labour administration to introduce a centralized system of development land taxation came with the enactment of the Community Land Act 1975 and the Development Land Tax Act 1976. The former was a radical scheme for land assembly through local authorities; the latter a more conventional system of centralized land taxation. The community land scheme reverted to a land national-ization philosophy, under which it was to be possible for local authorities to acquire development land, initially on a highly selective basis, but ultimately as the sole suppliers of development land to the market (Grant 1976, 1978b). They would, in the second phase (which was in the event never implemented) have had the duty to acquire all development land in their areas at existing use value, and then to have sold it on to the marketplace at full market value. Thus, the ultimate goal of the scheme was to cream off all development value for local authorities. This meant that the development land tax was in a sense a transitional measure. It was to have imposed a tax on development values in land, starting initially at 80 per cent (though with a reduced rate of 66.6 per cent in respect of the first £150,000), but increasing over time to 100 per cent.

The scheme was an administrative disaster (Grant 1979). Central government proved unable to provide local authorities with the necessary finance to implement it, or the loan sanctions necessary for them to acquire the land available; it also (except in Wales) approached the implementation of the scheme with an exception-ally heavy-handed centralized style which served its purpose of stifling all local authority initiative. There was no surprise when, in 1979, the new Prime Minister, Mrs Thatcher, announced its repeal. Development land tax survived longer, and its retention through the early 1980s symbolized a rare commonality of approach to land policy between the two main political parties. But in truth it was doomed from the start, as a highly complex, heavy-handed instrument of central taxation which, des-pite the ambition of empowering local authorities, actually ended up with little relationship to local land policy considerations.

THE SUB-THEMES: ALTERNATIVE APPROACHES TO BETTERMENT

Discussion of the phenomenon of betterment is not assisted by the lack of agree-ment as to what it involves. In a broad sense, betterment refers to any increase in the value of a parcel of land that can be attributed to factors other than the effort or investment of the owner or occupier of that parcel, sometimes referred to as the 'unearned increment'. No plot of land has inherent value in itself: all land value stems from its relationship with other land. In order to understand whether the State should be able to recoup betterment on the basis of a theory of unearned increment, it is therefore necessary to distinguish (1) between the impact of the effort or investment of the owner and the owner's predecessors, and (2) other 'external' effects.

As to the first, the starting point will commonly be the purchase price paid by the owner for the land, and capital taxation systems based on land value increase will normally focus only on the enhancement of value during the period the land remains in the hands of the current owner. The occasion of a sale or lease of the land is used as the trigger for liability to pay tax. That was the basis of the betterment levy and the development land tax.

As to the second, there tend in practice to be three broad categories of land value enhancement, attributable to:

(i)   local physical improvements carried out by a public agency, such as the construction of London's Victoria embankment or the rebuilding of Kingsway: here it may be possible to identify a specific impact;

(ii) the impact of regulation as it affects the demand for the particular parcel and the supply of other parcels; and

(iii) any other factors affecting demand for the land and supply of substitute land, such as improvements by adjacent landowners and improvements in social infrastructure (Grant 1991).

The case for betterment recoupment weakens as one moves down the list, yet it has proved impossible in practice to distinguish the impact of each category on the value of land. Buyers and sellers of land will recognize the value that is added to land under each of these categories, but will not engage in an abstract exercise of distinguishing and weighting their different characteristics. For this reason, the capital values tax approach to betterment recoupment that was used in the three principal occasions outlined above had to rely upon a simplified approach which set out to capture all value attributable to demand for the land for development. They distinguished between the value of the land for its existing use and its market value: the difference was its development value. Tax was then levied on enhancements in that development value occurring during the ownership of the taxpayer. Such an approach excludes betterment accruing under heading (i) above to the extent that it enhances the value of the land in its existing use; but it includes betterment arising under all headings to the extent that it affects development value.

The problems of this approach were not just those of political instability, but also of technical difficulty. An approach based on taxation of capital values is expensive to administer and slow in operation. Calculation depends upon a valuation in each case and also upon the calculation of set-off and allowances (e.g., for the landowner's own investment in improvements), and in exemptions for different categories of land (e.g., for private dwellinghouses). Final computation might not be achieved until some years following the completion of the sale or the development which triggered the liability.

Pre-empting the accrual of value: the new towns
The legislative scheme for new towns exempted the development corporations from having to pay enhanced land values when acquiring land in their designated areas. In calculating compensation, the valuer was entitled to assume that planning permission would be granted for the development for which the land was being acquired (e.g. housing, commercial, industrial), but to do so in a 'no-scheme world', ignoring the whole of the new-town development that was taking place, and hence the services that the scheme was bringing to the area. This had the effect of enabling the corporations to acquire land net of betterment, yet being able in due course to sell land on at market value. A similar formula was extended in due course to the town expansion schemes (under the Town Development Act 1952). It was later applied also to urban development corporations, but its application within existing urban areas was to prove more difficult than for greenfield sites. Projects to provide infrastructure some time after the designation of the area also confronted the problem that investment expectations had already risen (which indeed was one of the objectives of the exercise), yet the land that was needed for, say, a new road scheme, could be acquired only at the lower statutory value.

User Charges

An alternative approach is by way of user charges. These are at first sight dis-
tinguishable from betterment devices, because they involve charging landowners for
publicly financed improvements directly benefiting their land. However, there is
relatively rarely any need for the public sector to become involved in providing
private goods (though securing access to a public highway may be an example).
Publicly funded goods are most commonly non-excludable and may benefit several
landowners. Hence, any recovery from benefiting landowners calls for a collective
scheme.

However, there is a point of distinction, which is that a user charge is assessed not
in terms of benefit recoupment, but of cost recovery. The cost of providing the
benefit is charged to the landowner(s). The two models employed in parallel under
the Water Industry Act 1991 illustrate the distinctions. Under the first, a developer
may requisition from a water utility company the laying of a sewer or water main to
service a new development, but must undertake to meet the cost. This is normally
through a one-off capital contribution, but it may be through a revenue contribution
over a 12-year period. That is a long-standing arrangement. Under the second, introduced upon privatization in 1989, the developer is also required to pay an infrastructure charge to the water utility company, at a standard rate per dwelling, which
is fixed by the economic regulator (OFWAT) for each water company. The first is an
individual user charge, the second a collectivized contribution to off-site water
infrastructure.

Hence, although the principal distinction between a user charge and a betterment
charge is that the former relates to cost and the latter to value, the distinction is less
sharp in practice. Collectivized contributions are not always assessed with a methodological rigour that allows a *pro rata* allocation of responsibility, but may be more in
the nature of a tax at a fixed or variable rate, like the water infrastructure charge.

'Voluntary' contributions: the case of planning gain

In the absence of a national scheme of land taxation, local authorities turned increasingly to a different approach. The shared assumption postwar had been that developers' responsibilities were limited to servicing the facilities that they provided on
their own land, such as on-site streets and roads and street lighting, and that any
necessary off-site facilities would be provided out of general tax revenues.

That assumption came increasingly under strain in the late 1960s, when the introduction of the betterment levy coincided with the sharp increase in demand for land
for development that took place from 1967 onwards. Local authorities proved unable
to provide servicing at anything like the rate which developers sought. The only
course open to them was to negotiate with developers for contributions towards off-
site costs, and this was strongly encouraged by the government of the day. There
was a strong economic incentive for developers to agree to bring land forward
for development earlier, and there was a simple mechanism through which this
could have been achieved, which was by imposing planning conditions on a grant
of planning permission. That approach would have allowed local authorities to
establish clearly the level of contributions they required in order to allow development to go ahead, to have spread contributions liability between different landowners and developers whose development contributed to the overall requirements
for infrastructure for an area, and to have allowed developers the opportunity to
appeal to the Secretary of State against high levels of contribution requirements.

But it was not to be. The route was blocked as a result of a dogmatic approach
taken by the courts towards the use of planning conditions. Two leading cases

effectively destroyed the capacity of planning conditions to meet these requirements. In the first, *Pyx Granite v Minister of Housing and Local Government,* Lord
Denning announced the rules which were to govern the imposition of planning
conditions, drawing to some extent from previous advice issued by the ministry
itself. Although the legislation allowed authorities to impose 'such conditions as they
think fit', Lord Denning insisted that to be valid, a condition must relate fairly and
reasonably to the development being permitted, that it must be for a planning
purpose, and that it must not be manifestly unreasonable.

Those were reasonable requirements, but it was the third of these tests that was to
create difficulties in the subsequent case of *Hall & Co Ltd v Shoreham-by-Sea UDC,*
where a planning condition had been imposed requiring the landowners to make up
an estate road on their land, and to allow access along that road to neighbouring land,
in the interests of opening up the whole site for development. To the Court of
Appeal, Lord Denning's first two tests were amply satisfied, but not the third. This
was such an interference with landowners' rights, which could have been achieved
under other measures available to the local authority involving the payment of compensation, that it could not have been envisaged that parliament was intending to
authorize it through the use of planning conditions. It followed from that ruling that,
if planning conditions could not be used to require the provision of public goods by a
developer, then equally a planning condition could not be used to impose a financial
charge whose purpose it was to achieve the provision of those public goods.

That doctrine remains today, and its effect has been perverse. It has driven planning gain off the public record and out of the ambit of the Secretary of State's control
through the appeals system. Instead of imposing planning conditions, local authorities came to negotiate private agreements with developers. Private contract became
the medium of public control. This became possible because, coincidentally, in 1968
the former requirement that the minister give his consent to any agreement entered
into under planning legislation had been abandoned, largely because it had been so
rarely used. Hence the planning agreement power (now section 106 of the Town and
Country Planning Act 1990) came into use as a means not merely of providing a
formal mode of transaction for developers' contributions to off-site infrastructure,
but also for ensuring that a local authority could tie those liabilities to the land itself
and make them operable against subsequent landowners. In a speculative land
market, in which transactions might take place through intermediaries, this was a
necessary safeguard.

This gave rise to both good and bad practice. Some developers complained that
local authorities were abusing their powers by requiring contributions that bore no
relationship to the development for which they sought permission, and were naked-
ly pursuing a betterment taxation policy in the name of planning gain. Attempts
thereafter by the courts to grapple with this phenomenon produced at first some
dismal jurisprudence (Grant 1994), which was not set aside until the 1990s, when
attitudes began to change. Initially, it changed because the courts started to
approach planning gain from a commercial perspective, rather than from a doctrinal
perspective.[9] Next, the House of Lords simply announced the withdrawal altogether
of the courts from the task of assessing the lawfulness of planning gain in cases
where developers (or third parties) complained that too much was being sought or
paid.[10]

Indeed, the courts have contributed far more to the problem of planning gain
than to its solution. Yet, curiously, successive governments have resisted all
pressure to legislate on the matter. Although the amendments in 1991, which introduced planning obligations in place of planning agreements, were taken by the

courts as an indication of a change of parliamentary policy, their intended effect was actually more technical than substantive. The government's approach has been to prefer to guide planning gain through policy advice, now Circular 1/97, *Planning Obligations* (DoE 1997b), rather than to formalize it through a legal framework.

Does planning gain constitute a betterment recapture device? There is a view that it does not because its purpose is said to be to mitigate the impact of new development (Fordham 1993). But that approach is too simplistic. It ignores the negotiated character of the impost and it ignores the relationship between off-site investment and land value. In the absence of clear standards or guidelines against which such impact can be measured, such as the impact fees system which is used in several US jurisdictions, the developer/landowner's potential liability is open-ended, in theory up to the total development value in the land. Should the local planning authority seek no contribution, there is no impost against that development value. The reality is usually somewhere in between, but with significant variations. Where agricultural land is being brought into development, the uplift in value which results from public improvements and regulatory impact is normally hundreds of times the existing use value. Those who negotiate on behalf of local authorities generally comprehend this phenomenon, and may invite – or be offered – contributions towards facilities whose need is only to a small extent necessitated by the development. That practice, indeed, was upheld in 1995 by the House of Lords in *Tesco plc v Secretary of State for the Environment*. The capacity to make such contributions derives from the uplift in development value that the grant of planning permission is expected to confer, and it follows that such a transaction effects a recoupment of betterment, albeit hypothecated to the provision of a particular public good rather than paid into the Consolidated Fund.

Second, there is an indivisible relationship between development value in land and the provision of off-site services. Under the old regime, the state provided all public goods from general taxation and hence felt able to sustain a case for the taxation of betterment to recoup its expenses from the increase in land value resulting from its expenditure. Under the planning gain regime, the relationship is more direct, but it is essentially the same. The developer/landowner contributes the cash upfront to secure the provision of the facility which enhances the land value. True, it may only enhance the land value because the local planning authority have decided that planning permission will not be forthcoming for the development without that facility, so the cost of providing it is the price of the permission. Interestingly, the model bears a closer resemblance to the 1947 development charge than to the two subsequent land taxation attempts, because it has the effect of bringing down land price by internalizing into it some of the required external costs of the development, rather than by recovering tax revenues to meet those external costs.

Cross-subsidization: the case of affordable housing
There is one instance of betterment recoupment which requires special analysis, because it has followed a different path. In the early years of the planning system, providing affordable housing was almost exclusively a public responsibility, and it was a major commitment for all postwar governments through to the 1980s. The principal vehicle was the construction and management of low cost housing by local authorities and new town development corporations. That approach came under attack from the Thatcher Conservative administration in the 1980s. Council houses were sold at a discount to sitting tenants, and the provision of new housing became restricted to particularly vulnerable groups. Housing associations came to play a

more significant role, and some local authorities disposed of all their housing stock to such associations.

Some authorities were able during the 1980s to negotiate contributions from private developers towards the provision of social housing, either as part of a private-housing scheme or as a contribution towards the cost of providing housing elsewhere. Another, parallel, initiative was to allow local authorities to grant planning permission for low-cost housing for local people in rural areas on land not allocated for housing in the development plan: its effect was to allow land to come on to the market without the significant uplift in land values that would follow a development plan allocation. In effect, the low cost of the housing was made possible because of the low cost of the land, for which this type of housing was the highest and best use.

However, in 1990, the government ventured upon a more general scheme of shifting to the private sector the cost of providing affordable housing. This has been achieved, not through legislation, but through policy advice to local planning authorities. The process started under the Conservative government and has been continued, in nearly identical terms, by the Labour government elected in 1997. Although the current circular, DETR Circular 6/98, *Planning and Affordable Housing*, uses the language of voluntary provision and relies upon developers' contributions being secured through negotiation, neither the purpose nor the effect of its requirements is voluntary. The government believes it appropriate that private house-builders should, on housing schemes over a certain size (25 dwellings or one hectare of land; rather less inside London), provide affordable housing in addition to market housing. By 'affordable housing' is meant both low-cost market housing and also subsidized housing (irrespective of tenure, ownership or financial arrangements) that will be available to people who cannot afford to occupy market housing. The objectives are to secure that any new housing development of a substantial scale incorporates a reasonable mix and balance of housing types and sizes to cater for a range of housing needs. Once a local planning authority has established that a requirement for an element of affordable housing is appropriate, it is entitled to insist that it should be provided as part of the proposed development. The circular makes it clear that, if the developer is unwilling to make this contribution, then planning permission may be refused. Given that this is a statement of government policy, an appeal by the developer to the Secretary of State will not be successful in challenging its principles, only its application to the particular case.

It is again difficult to resist the conclusion that this is a form of betterment recoupment, and a more telling instance of it than for planning gain generally, because it proceeds from a different base. Instead of being a public good, the need for which is generated in whole or in part by the developer's proposals, affordable housing is a public good the need for which is generated by a shortfall in housing supply generally and in particular by the government's withdrawal from providing affordable housing as a tax-borne public good. The tenuous character of the link drawn in the circular between private and affordable housing is demonstrated by the government's willingness for the obligation to be commuted to a financial contribution by the developer, towards the provision of affordable housing elsewhere in the local authority's area. Separate provision may indeed be preferable in land policy terms, depending on the circumstances of the local area, and an ability to commute the liability is a sensible and pragmatic approach which allows the local authority to secure the provision of affordable housing where it wishes. But it then becomes more difficult to portray the process as a planning instrument rather than as an instrument of taxation.

Legislative base	Policy objective	Instrument	Character of instrument	Extent of direct local benefit	Extent of hypothecation
Town and Country Planning Act 1947	Stabilize land values; tax development values	Development charge, set at 100% of development value	Capital taxation based upon valuation of difference between market value and current use value	None	None
New Towns Act 1948	Land acquisition for new town development	Compulsory acquisition of land at pre-new town values	Pre-emption of land value increase	High in sense that underwrote viability of development of new towns	High
Town Development Act 1952	Land acquisition for expanded towns	Compulsory acquisition of land at pre-scheme values	Pre-emption of land value increase	High: land value released to scheme; sites sold on at market value	High: land value released to scheme; sites sold on at market value
Land Commission Act 1967	Promote land supply for development; tax development values	Betterment levy, set at 40% of development value rising to 100%	Capital taxation based on land value	None	None
Community Land Act 1975 and Development Land Tax Act 1976	Promote land supply; tax development values; partial nationalisation of land	Development Land Tax coupled with special powers under Community Land Act 1975	Capital taxation based on land value	Partial, through net of tax local authority acquisition arrangements	None
Water Industry Act 1991	Supply water services to new development	Requisitioning power	Specific user charge, though greater capacity may be required to meet future development	High	High

Water Industry Act 1991	Secure contribution to off-site servicing costs for new development	Infrastructure charge	A general user charge, but not reflecting direct costs; assessed as fixed-rate charge per dwelling, payable by developer	Not necessarily any: payment to regional water plc, though may contribute to broader improvements in local water infrastructure	Ring-fenced to water services
Town and Country Planning Act 1990, s.106	Planning gain, of which examples: (1) off-site services directly for benefit of site; (2) provision of community benefits from development	Planning agreement/ obligation	In practice across spectrum of: (1) user charge; (2) betterment tax	High	Generally high: may be a contractual requirement
Town and Country Planning Act 1990; Circular 6/98	Secure private sector provision of affordable housing	Planning obligation; Grampian condition	Negotiated contribution, but within nationally prescribed framework	High: payments made, and/or land vested in, local agency such as housing association	High

Figure 5.1 Comparative table of betterment instruments

Incidence

Who actually pays when a developer contributes planning gain or affordable housing? There are at least three likely candidates: the developer; the landowners through whose hands the land has passed on the way to the developer; and the purchaser of the developed product, such as a house buyer. Only the first two of these are the potential beneficiaries of betterment.

In earlier times, and even in some quarters today, there was a tendency to regard developers' contributions as generous benefactions to the public good. But that view was never seriously tenable. Developers contribute because that is the price payable for allowing the development to go ahead. Contributions do not come from the developer's philanthropic funds, but are a factor in the price of producing the final product. A developer may, of course, seek to pass the cost forward in house prices, but the characteristics of the housing market, with reasonably high competition, are against this. Instead, the obvious outcome is that the cost passes backwards to landowners, and British developers and landowners have, over the past 50 years, devised a means of doing this through the use of land options.

For example, most housing land in Britain is acquired by housebuilding developers, not as freehold land ripe for development, but through the exercise of an option that may have been entered into many years previously. The option allows the developer to exercise the rights of acquisition at any time, and for the cost of the land at the time of sale to be calculated in accordance with a specified formula. There are many variants, but their common effect is to ensure that any contributions the developer is required to make to off-site costs will be deductible from the purchase price. One approach is to apply a 'market value' formula, but require that the land be valued in the real world, with off-site liabilities to be met before it can be developed. Hence, those liabilities are pushed back into land price. Other, more complex formulae, allow for an element of profit sharing in land value between landowner and developer. All have the primary object of placing liability for off-site costs and affordable housing with the land value.

CONCLUSIONS

Planning and public investment have a powerful impact on land values. Planning regulation rations the supply of land for development and it redirects demand for it. In 1947, the government saw tackling the betterment/compensation problem as the key to the success of comprehensive development control. It approached the issue from a strongly ideological perspective, which also underlaid its approach in 1965 and 1975. The land issue loomed large in the Labour government's priorities.

Today, the issue lies largely ignored, and there is no political will to revisit past failures. Regimes of capital taxation are largely discredited as being too clumsy and slow and incapable of achieving local land policy objectives. Yet the imbalance in the system remains. Compensation is not payable for the refusal of planning permission, and land markets have adapted to the implications of that rule by discounting appropriately for the risk of permission not forthcoming and by the use of option agreements to minimize upfront commitment and to internalize off-site liabilities. There are still significant increases in land values as greenfield sites are brought into development. Betterment is today captured from those sites not by way of a differential national tax, but primarily by a set of informal arrangements that have developed pragmatically through the planning system. Their ostensible objective is to internalize into the land price the external impact of the development. This is a more direct means of requiring landowners to pay towards the local public goods which contribute to betterment on their land. The theory is patchy in its application and it is tenuous in the case of affordable housing. That case is, in essence, an attempt to establish a national betterment taxation system, hypothecated to the provision of a particular public good.

The planning gain approach to betterment has shown great practical advantages. It secures private contributions to the provision of public goods. Liability is triggered at the point of maximum economic opportunity for the developer, as the price for granting planning permission. But it is still a relatively ramshackle device, which has been pressed already beyond its legitimate limits and which requires review and modification if it is to continue to develop as a surrogate, or an admitted, betterment tax. It has two defects that presently inhibit its further pragmatic development: a lack of certainty and predictability as to the demands likely to be made by a local planning authority which, were they more readily forecastable, could more readily be translated into land price at a earlier stage; and the inherent conflict between the collective character of the outcome, in the form of public goods, and the individual character of the process, in the form of privately negotiated contribution.

Betterment recoupment will continue to be as important an issue for the next 50 years of planning in Britain as it has for the last, but the mechanisms for delivering it need careful review and overhaul.

FURTHER READING

The starting point for any review of the postwar betterment debate is Cullingworth (1980) *Environmental Planning 1939–1969 Vol 4: Land Values, Compensation and Betterment*, which contains a detailed history of the political and administrative battles that were waged. An international perspective is given by Hagman and Misczynski (1978) *Windfalls for Wipeouts*. A useful collection of essays on the subject, prepared in anticipation of what was in due course to become the betterment levy, is to be found in Hall (1965) *Land Values*.

chapter 6

The Regional Dimension

PETER HALL

INTRODUCTION

Regional policy occupies a strange place in the history of British planning: separate from it, but always closely related to it, so closely indeed that it has provided a set of key parameters or constraints on the operation of the local land-use planning system. Save for a brief and ultimately disastrous episode in 1964–6, there has never been an attempt to emulate the French system of regional planning within the framework of a national economic plan; and during the 1980s a systematic attempt was made to scale down regional policy, which was seen as an unnecessary impediment to local enterprise. However, regional policy survived, thanks in large part to the increasing role of European policies in UK affairs, and, despite the lack of anything resembling a blueprint, regional policy has powerfully helped to shape decisions at local levels, not least because in practice it tends to reflect and in turn reinforce local attitudes to growth: crudely, the assisted areas of the country want it; the rest of the country resists it.

OBJECTIVES OF POLICY

Not the least strange fact about the policy is that its objectives have seldom if ever been clear. Gordon Cameron (1974) argued that national efficiency has not been the central aim; rather, the policy has been driven by arguments for social equity. Ever since the great depression of the 1930s, the base of this equity problem has been disequilibrium in the regional labour markets: the peripheral regions – Scotland, Wales, the northern region of England – have operated short of full employment despite continuous net out-migration, while others have experienced persistent labour shortages despite continuous in-migration, both from other regions and from overseas. In the peripheral areas, unemployment rates typically run 50–100 per cent above the national rate, while the southeast has rates below the national rate. This is despite the remarkable fact that, over the entire period 1921–61, the occupied population declined in Northern Ireland and remained relatively stagnant in Wales, Scotland and the northwest, while increasing by no less than 41 per cent in the southeast.

It is true that some indices, such as GDP per capita and real consumption per head, show that differences between regions are not great, with the possible exception of Northern Ireland. Despite a strong and persistent net migration trend out of these regions, natural increase has meant that no region has actually suffered a declining population. Overall, Cameron concluded in 1974:

> The differences in welfare across the British regions are small; rural depopulation has already occurred to a very great extent; the domination of the primate city has declined at least if measured in terms of population and despite interregional migration processes which constantly shape the balance of population in favour of the southeast, the southwest, east Anglia, and the west and east midlands; and the overall regional changes in population distribution, both historically and forecast, are on a modest scale. However, a high rate of unemployment in some regions, low activity rates, and generally appalling environmental conditions create a continuing need for active measures to improve regional economic performance and the regional physical environment (Cameron 1974: 77).

THE ANTECEDENTS OF REGIONAL POLICY: 1928–45

The story starts even before the great depression, with a policy of taking the workers to the work. In 1928, the *industrial transference scheme* and *juvenile transfer scheme* provided small grants and loans for unemployed workers to move to other regions. As many as 40,000 were helped to move in the boom years 1929 and 1936, and even in the depth of the depression in 1932–3 the figure was 14,000 a year. About a half of them stayed at their destinations, at least until the end of the scheme: a total of 50,000 over 10 years. But they were only about 1 in 10 of the half-million who moved out of the less prosperous areas in those years (Armstrong and Taylor 1993: 363).

In 1934 came a major shift: the Special Areas (Development and Improvement) Act designated four special areas in south Wales, Scotland, the northeast and west Cumberland. Two special areas commissioners were appointed to administer a programme of loans and financial aid. This was the effective start of a policy of positive discrimination which was to last over 50 years: gradually, incentives and assistance were forged to promote industry in the special areas, and by 1938 these included loans to private industry, provision of industrial premises by non-profit trading estates, contributions to rent, and rates and income tax liabilities of new firms. They were remarkably effective: 17 per cent of new factories opened in 1938 were in the special areas. However, most were small and they made little impact on the overall position.

World War II effectively abolished the problem of the depressed areas; wages and monetary demand shot up, and direct controls on manpower, plus the absence of male adults on active service, brought full employment everywhere. Further, the former depressed areas were a long way from Germany, so 22 million sq. ft of factory space were built in what, after the war, became the development areas. Moreover, some basic industries enjoyed a wartime boom: above all shipbuilding, where naval work grew nearly ten–fold between 1938 and 1944 (Brown 1972: 285).

The war years also laid the foundations of postwar policy. In 1940, the Barlow Report recommended radical policies to redistribute population and industry in order to reduce unemployment and ease congestion in Greater London. The 1944 white paper *Employment Policy* committed the government to a 'high and stable level of employment' by influencing the location of new enterprises in areas of high unemployment, encouraging labour mobility between areas and occupations, retraining labour and maintaining a high level of total spending.

1946–50: THE ORIGINS OF POSTWAR POLICY

The 1945 Distribution of Industry Act, passed by the wartime coalition government in its last days, laid the foundations of postwar regional policy. The old special areas were enlarged and redesignated as development areas. Responsibility for regional policy was given to the Board of Trade, which was empowered to provide loans and grants to firms within designated *development areas* and to facilitate the financing, building and leasing of trading estates. A radical provision was the retention of the wartime system of building licences as a means of controlling expansion in prosperous regions. Two years later, the 1947 Town and Country Planning Act effectively made permanent the wartime system of building controls, by introducing *industrial development certificates* (IDCs). These were required for all new manufacturing establishments and extensions of over 5,000 sq. ft. This was the only real difference compared with the prewar years: effectively, it provided one arm of a 'carrot and stick' approach which would be used, with varying degrees of enthusiasm, for the next 35 years.

The basic mechanisms were now in place, though other legislation provided additional powers and money. More significant was the fact that the powers were energetically used. There was a real concern that depression would again descend on the development areas; there was a huge stock of redundant wartime munitions factories; everywhere, there was a shortage of industrial premises and manpower; and, because of the serious problems of postwar reconstruction, it was politically possible to retain the wartime system of building licences through the IDC scheme.

The results were spectacular. During 1945–47, more than half the new industrial building in the country was in the development areas, compared with 5 per cent prewar, though these contained less than a fifth of the population. By 1955, these factories employed 86,000 people, mainly due to location decisions in the immediate postwar years. Luttrell's research showed that these firms had moved in search of premises and labour, and that suitable factory space owned by the Board of Trade, either newly built or converted from wartime use, was the biggest single magnet (Luttrell 1962). But, once the surplus space was occupied (by 1947–49), the proportion fell to 17 per cent. There was also a policy shift: a new emphasis on exporting, related to the balance of payments crisis (Brown 1972: 286).

1951–61: THE PERIOD OF WEAK REGIONAL POLICY

1951 saw the arrival of a Conservative government and an immediate further weakening of regional policy. Between 1946 and 1949, some £9 million a year was spent on regional policy, and 64 per cent of all job moves throughout the country went to the peripheral areas. In the years 1952–9, expenditure under the Act averaged £5 million a year, but the number of job moves to the peripheral areas fell to a mere 29 per cent of the jobs in all moves. This was not due to lack of powers: the main reason was that IDC policy was much more laxly applied. In any case, wartime shortages were a thing of the past, and the incentives to move were far fewer. There was now less incentive to pursue strong regional policies since the great postwar boom was under way.

1960–62: THE SHIFT TO TARGETED POLICES

The year 1960 brought a major change: the Local Employment Act of that year replaced the familiar map of development areas by a patchwork of development districts, mechanically scheduled (and descheduled) on the basis of unemployment rates exceeding 4.5 per cent. But, within these newly defined areas, the powers of the Board of Trade were actually strengthened and extended through easier loans and building grants. Controls over the location of industry were retained.

Government expenditure on factory building, loans and grants now received a big boost, increasing seven times between 1952–59 and 1960–63. But the major achievement of this period was the steering of major new investments in the motor industry away from the midlands and the southeast to Merseyside and Scotland – a result, doubtless, both of financial incentives and Board of Trade reluctance to grant IDCs for growth in the traditional motor-manufacturing areas. There was an immediate impact: during 1960–3 some 25,000 new jobs a year were created in the peripheral areas and had survived by 1966. These constituted 58 per cent of all moves nationally, and two and a half times as many as in 1952–9 (Brown 1972: 288).

Unfortunately, the very flexibility of the 1960 Act proved its undoing. It soon was evident that the continual scheduling and descheduling of development districts produced uncertainty about the future. The Act's other feature – the virtually automatic link to the local unemployment rate – actually militated against intelligent regional policy, which increasingly suggested concentrating development in growth points that had good growth potential near to the problem areas, rather than directly inside them. In 1963, the National Economic Development Council report *Conditions Favourable for Faster Growth* advocated the 'growth pole' concept, and this was embraced by the 1963 white papers on central Scotland and the northeast. Critical of the development district approach, they instead defined growth areas (Irvine, East Kilbride–north Lanarkshire, Cumbernauld, Falkirk–Grangemouth, Livingston and central Fife; and east Durham–southeast Northumberland) and guaranteed that they would continue to enjoy assistance.

1963–70: THE GOLDEN AGE OF REGIONAL POLICY

Between 1963 and 1970, traditional regional policy reached its apogee. There were now massive benefits to investment in the development districts. In addition, in 1965 the Labour government set up a Highlands and Islands Development Board with extensive powers of loans, grants, equity participation and new factory building for a wide range of economic activities. The *National Plan* was launched with great fanfares in September 1965: the first and only attempt in this 50-year history to create a system of national–regional planning on the French model. Yet the plan was officially and ignominiously abandoned within a year, when the government was forced to introduce the most severe deflation since the war in order to handle an escalating balance of payments problem. In retrospect, it seems clear that throughout the first two years of the Wilson government, there was a tension inside the government between its formal commitment to 'growth through planning' and a real commitment to traditional deflationary strategies based on the preservation of the exchange rate between the pound sterling and the US dollar, fixed since 1949, and a liberal trading system, formalized in a struggle between the Treasury and the new Department of Economic Affairs (Morgan 1980: 15).

1966 saw significant changes in the system of financial aid: the much-criticized development districts were abolished, and 165 small areas were replaced by five large development areas covering 40 per cent of the area and 20 per cent of the population, so that regional strategies could be based on the fashionable growth zone principle. These were being prepared for each standard region by the Regional Economic Planning Councils and Boards, set up in 1965–6 by the newly formed (and short-lived) Department of Economic Affairs. Even more significant was a massive boost in expenditure on regional aid: from £22 million in 1962–3 to no less than £324 million in 1969–70 (1970–1 prices). The Labour government also lowered the threshold for IDC controls, and enforced them more strictly.

A major shift in policy came in relation to service industry, above all offices. In 1963 the Conservative government had established the Location of Offices Bureau to encourage the movement of office employment from London. It had a notable success, but not quite what was intended: 2000 office firms and about 160,000 jobs left London during 1963–79, but 75 per cent went to the outer southeast. Then, under Labour, the Control of Offices and Industrial Development Act 1965 introduced *office development permits* for developments above 5,000 sq. ft in the London area. This was later extended in scope and geographical spread – to all of the southeast, east Anglia and the west and east midlands regions. To a limited extent, the government also relocated the civil service: 55,000 jobs were moved out of London between 1963 and 1975.

In 1966 came a *selective employment tax*, payable by employers in the service industries. But manufacturing firms in development areas were entitled to a *selective employment premium* (37.5 p per male worker per week) and a *regional employment premium* (REP) (£1.50 per male worker per week, with lower rates for women and juveniles). These schemes were abolished by the incoming Heath government in 1970.

In 1967, the map of regional assistance was again redrawn: *special development areas* were established in Scotland, the northeast, west Cumberland and Wales, with additional incentives and rent-free premises from the Board of Trade for 5 years, 35 per cent building grants and some operating cost subsidies. Even that was not the end: in 1969 came the Hunt report on *The Intermediate Areas*, which recommended the introduction of a strong set of policies for these so-called grey areas. The government, by this time beleaguered by economic difficulties, did not fully accept the proposals; but, in the 1970 Local Employment Act, seven *intermediate areas* were added to the map, eligible for government-built factories, building grants and derelict land clearance grants. All this looked impressive: fully one-half of the area and population of the UK now enjoyed some form of regional aid, the most extensive system of regional assistance ever undertaken in the UK.

1970–8: THE SHIFT TO URBAN POLICY

At first, the incoming Heath government made only minor changes to the system: a return to cash grants for capital expenditure in manufacturing (the *regional development grant* scheme), an initial allowance of 40 per cent on new industrial buildings, and 100 per cent free first-year depreciation on all plant and machinery investment throughout the country, both in industry and services; phasing out of the regional employment premium; an end to IDC controls in development areas and special development areas; selective assistance for industry; increased training grants in the assisted areas; and an extension of grants and low-interest loans to cover service industries in these areas. However, these changes were all within the well understood parameters of traditional regional policy. Further, intermediate area status was extended to all of the northwest and Yorkshire–Humberside areas. A major change was that the aid was no longer limited to projects providing employment and became available to existing as well as new firms. This recognized that the number of footloose firms that could be attracted to development areas was limited; the new emphasis was on modernization through investment in order to survive.

More momentously, 1973 saw the UK's entry into the European Economic Community (EEC). From now on, the UK assisted areas would have access to loans, grants and other assistance from the EEC. This was to prove very important because two years later the European Regional Development Fund was established specifically to assist depressed areas through investment grants and interest rebates on Community loans for industrial, craft, service and infrastructure projects. Each member state was guaranteed a predetermined share (or quota) of the fund. In return for membership, however, the UK had now to adhere to strict EEC competition policy controls, including limits on investment subsidies in the so-called central regions of the EEC, which included the intermediate areas. Most important, subsidies to employment, such as the regional employment premium, were now suspect under EEC rules. It was finally abolished in 1977.

The main innovation of the incoming Wilson government of 1974, however, was the establishment of a National Enterprise Board (NEB) with an initial £1 billion available for wide-ranging intervention in the private sector through planning agreements with firms to assist depressed areas. It was followed in 1975–6 by the establishment of the Scottish and Welsh Development Agencies (SDA and WDA). The SDA, in particular, received major powers to invest in industry, create new companies, provide finance and advice for industry, build and manage industrial estates, lease or sell factories, reclaim derelict land and rehabilitate the environment. Significantly, the Scottish Office abandoned a proposed new town at Stonehouse in order to divert funding to the Glasgow Eastern Area Renewal scheme (GEAR) – a precursor of a policy shift that would soon become more widespread.

Generally, however, both the Heath and Wilson governments maintained continuity in regional policy. Throughout most of the 1970s, manufacturers in the assisted areas could get automatic regional development grants of 20–22 per cent for new industrial buildings, plant and machinery, and could write off for tax purposes 100 per cent of investment in new plant and machinery and 44 per cent of the construction cost of new industrial buildings. In 1976, grants and rent relief, plus preferential loans, were extended to firms in services and the office sector locating in assisted areas. So no one could call this a time of weak policy.

Gathering recession brought a turning-point in 1976, when an emergency July budget reduced and delayed payment of a number of grants. In yet another crisis mini-budget, in December 1976, further most drastic cuts were made. In April 1977, the government announced that there would be no further assisted areas, while north Yorkshire and Aberdeen were reduced to intermediate area status – the first downgrading since 1966. In 1977, the government announced that it would move to selective, against general, assistance measures.

These were drastic changes in response to radically new conditions. Indeed, it was already emerging that 1973 had marked the end of the 'Long Boom' and that the UK was experiencing an unprecedentedly large and accelerating loss of manufacturing employment. Growth in services did not compensate, and so unemployment rose from under 2 per cent in 1966 to an average of 6 per cent in 1978–9 and over 12 per cent by 1982 – a total of 3 million.

There was a deepening cyclical recession, but longer-term structural forces were at work, leading to big and possibly permanent losses of manufacturing jobs and affecting industries and areas previously thought immune. This was particularly so in industries like motors and electrical engineering and cities like London and Birmingham, where unemployment was rising faster than in the assisted areas. London's employment fell by a tenth, and by over 30 per cent in manufacturing, between mid-1974 and mid-1982. The west midlands lost a seventh of total employment and a third of manufacturing employment; by 1976 it was already recording unemployment above the national average.

This was the reason for the new industrial strategy to back economic growth and industrial winners wherever they could be found, even at the expense of employment. It was no longer possible to believe that national economic growth would produce a pool of investment that could be persuaded to move to less prosperous regions. Thus, the retreat from regional policy began under Labour in the late 1970s; between 1975 and 1976 and 1979 and 1980 expenditure declined by 60 per cent in real terms; the Conservatives merely continued this trend. Even by 1980, Keeble could conclude that 'regional policy had ceased by 1976 to exert a measurable impact on the spatial pattern of manufacturing employment change in Britain' (Keeble 1980: 957)

Hence, also, the diversion of effort from regional aid to urban aid. This, marked by the 1977 white paper *Policy for the Inner Cities* and the Inner Urban Areas Act of 1978, was perhaps the most important single decisive break in 50 years of British regional/urban policy. Responsibility for it had already, in 1976, been transferred from the Home Office to the DoE. Expenditure on the urban programme was dramatically increased, from £30 to £165 million a year; and a total of seven partnership authorities, 15 programme areas and 14 'other' districts were designated, plus five 'other' areas in Wales. Each had powers to provide 90 per cent loans for land acquisition and site preparation, to make loans or award grants to cooperative or common ownership enterprises, and to declare industrial improvement areas, within which grants could be awarded for improvement or conversion of old industrial or commercial property. In Scotland the arrangements were different, with the SDA financing GEAR. In England, out of 41 designated urban areas, only eight were in the south, all in London. From then on, regional policy was increasingly transmitted to the north via inner-city rather than traditional regional support, and through DoE rather than Department of Trade and Industry (DTI) spending. There remained a difficult divided responsibility between the DTI, which kept responsibility for the industrial aspects, and the DoE which had charge of infrastructure and planning machinery plus housing, transport and local government, and had a hold on the new programme expenditure; the two were seen as competing rather than complementary.

THE THATCHER YEARS: 1979–90

From 1979, almost immediately on entry to office, Margaret Thatcher embarked on a further sustained attack on traditional regional policy: regional aid was cut from £842 million in 1979 to £540 million in 1983 (1980 prices); regional development grants were reduced or restricted; the boundaries of the assisted areas were cut back from 44 to 27.5 per cent of the population; office development permits were abolished and industrial development certificate controls were eased, before being abandoned entirely in 1982; selective financial assistance was retained but was to be provided only where necessary for a project to proceed; and the regional economic planning councils were summarily abolished. All this happened at a time of rapidly rising unemployment: between 1979 and 1984, from 4.9 to 11.7 per cent nationally, and 7.9 to 16.3 per cent in the northern region. Apart from ideology, these changes responded to two major criticisms of traditional policy: that it had exacerbated rising unemployment in the southeast and west midlands and that it had aided capital-intensive industries that had generated few if any jobs.

In 1984, as the national economy began to emerge from recession, Thatcher began her second attack. There would be cuts of £300 million in annual expenditure on regional policy by 1987/88, from £700 to £400 million; the special development areas were abolished (mostly downgraded to development areas), and the boundaries of the development areas were narrowed from 22 to 15 per cent of the working population; a cost-per-job limit of £10,000 was imposed on regional development grants, save for firms with less than 200 employees, with the alternative of a subsidy of up to £3,000 for each new job created. There were some concessions, but the general drift was clear: from automatic grants to selective assistance. That was continued in 1988, when *regional development grants* were totally abolished, and the funds (initially unchanged) were switched to *regional selective assistance*. The idea was to target schemes that would be viable, would benefit the region or the country, but also would not happen without subsidy.

Overall, as Balchin (1990: 74) argues, 'In broad terms, it was very evident that Conservative governments, in both 1979 and 1983, did not believe in a strong regional policy'. They saw it merely as politically expedient and as a device to attract inward investment. Expenditure on regional policy, as a percentage of GDP, plummeted by three quarters between 1970 and 1984. Balchin notes that though Thatcher governments cut regional aid, they were having to pay out much more as welfare benefits: while regional assistance was less than 1 per cent of planned public spending, social security spending had increased by nearly a third to 30 per cent of total government spending. Much other spending actually widened the north–south gap, particularly defence expenditure which went disproportionately to the south.

THE NEW EMPHASIS

This ignores three important considerations, in all of which Thatcher was merely continuing the policy shifts of the previous Callaghan government.

Indigenous growth
First, Thatcher was recognizing that the bases of traditional policy had been destroyed, almost certainly for ever. Keynesian spatial redistribution policies were seen as irrelevant; the problem was no longer lack of demand but of improving regional competitiveness. Subsidies for capital investment were condemned as poor value for money in employment generated; too much emphasis had gone on manufacturing and on branch plants, externally controlled and with limited multiplier effects, while office dispersal had gone to the outer southeast; most fundamentally, there had been too little emphasis on self-reliant regional growth. Regional policy must now be diverted into regional restructuring. Though this fundamental shift coincided with a change in dominant political ideology, the more basic reason was the 1980–3 depression, which caused a sharp fall in investment, especially in manufacturing. Equally important, it was realized that with increased unemployment everywhere, redistribution of industry was simply shifting jobs around with no net growth: the policy therefore collapsed (Martin 1988: 28; Taylor 1992: 292).

Instead of attracting firms from outside, it was argued, the emphasis should be on indigenous development: especially on encouraging new firm formation, helping small firms to grow and encouraging firms to adopt the latest technology. By creating the right conditions (low inflation, lower taxes, less government intervention, fewer state-owned companies) the government looked to small firms to create a more dynamic and competitive economy. There were two problems in this. First, most small firms stay small and a high proportion go out of business within one year; the small firm sector is less important than in the 1930s and it provides a minority share, albeit a respectable one, of new jobs – 19 per cent, in 1986, from firms with under five employees. Second, the conditions for small firm generation (such as greater wealth, a better educated workforce, easier access to finance, and continuous net inward migration) are more favourable in the south than in the north. Unsurprisingly, there is a clear north–south divide in new firm formation; London and its semi-urban hinterland dominate the picture. Traditional industrial areas seem to do particularly badly in entrepreneurship. Related to this, the southeast is strikingly the most innovative region in the country: it had one-third of innovations between 1945 and 1980, with only one-quarter of manufacturing employment (Armstrong and Taylor 1993: 263).

The new dependence on Europe

Second, in a rather simple way, Thatcher was replacing regional aid from London by regional aid from Brussels. In 1993–4 expenditure on regional industrial policy in Great Britain had fallen to £287 million, a quarter of its level in the early 1980s, while between 1994 and 1996 the UK's share of the EU's targeted regional funds totalled £980 million per year, increasing to £1115 million if the funding of Community initiatives is added (Lloyd 1996: 61).

There were major changes in European regional policy in these years: in 1984, the abolition of the distinction between quota and non-quota sections of the European Regional Development Fund (ERDF), with member states receiving a share of the fund lying within an indicative range, and a gradual shift of fund expenditure from projects to programme contracts comprising a number of initiatives and projects to meet specified objectives. In 1989, there was a major reform of the ERDF in response to the Single Market process, with a doubling (in real terms) of EC allocations for regional policy proposals between 1989 and 1992, and a coherent definition of EC objectives for its Structural Funds. From then on, regional policy objectives affecting the UK would be three in number: *Objective 1* (development of regions which are structurally backward); *Objective 2* (the conversion of regions in industrial decline); and *Objective 5B* (rural areas). Within these, there was to be a further shift of emphasis from project assistance to programme assistance, with Community programmes most favoured. The 1992 Maastricht Treaty added a new Cohesion Fund (in addition to the ERDF), initially set at 1.5 billion ecu (£1.05 billion), in order to help member states with particularly serious regional problems (Armstrong and Taylor 1993: 372).

The shift to urban aid

Third, Thatcher continued the Callaghan government's policy of diverting money from regional to urban aid, perhaps because economic decline was by now so heavily concentrated in the inner cities rather than in mining or heavy industry. She made radical changes in the mechanisms.

First, *urban development corporations* (UDCs) were created in the London and Merseyside docklands, with powers to reclaim land and provide infrastructure, renovate old buildings and provide new factories. The leverage effect was variable: by 1987 London Docklands Development Corporation had spent £500 million to attract over £2 billion of private funds; in Merseyside the figures were £140 million and £20 million. In 1987 further UDCs were created in the north: Trafford Park, Sandwell, Teesside, Tyneside and Cardiff Bay. Generally, UDCs failed to reduce local unemployment, and the new jobs tended to be filled by newcomers.

Second, *enterprise zones* (EZs) were created with special concessions: These included a simplified planning procedure; an exemption from all rates on commercial and industrial buildings for 10 years from declaration; a 100 per cent first-year depreciation allowance on commercial and industrial buildings; and a major reduction in government requests for statistical information. By 1981, 13 EZs had been declared; a further 14 were added in 1984, but not all were in the inner cities, while all but two were in the north. They were attacked for being ineffective. Nonetheless, Thatcher pressed on with a related reform: in 1984, six *freeports* were designated at various airport and dockland sites in the UK. In these enclosed zones, customs duties were payable only when goods left the freeport for the UK or EC.

Action for Cities, in March 1988, announced mini-UDCs for Bristol, Leeds and central Manchester. Though there was a big increase in spending on the *urban programme*, from £165 million in 1979–80 to £302 million in 1987–8, this was compensated for by cuts in grants to local authorities in the form of rate-support grants and housing subsidies. Manchester got only £10 million in *urban programme* grants but lost £350 million in other grants. The main stress was on programmes that bypassed local authorities altogether (Balchin 1990: 92).

THE CONTINUING NORTH–SOUTH DIVIDE

This reflects a fundamental shift in the economic geography of the country, already noticed: away from a regional distinction between north and south, and towards an urban distinction between cities and suburbs, and cities and countryside. True, the north–south divide weakened in the 'Long Boom' of the 1960s, but even then it was noticeable (Law 1980: 224). Since then, but fully recognized only from the mid-1970s, there have been three fundamental changes.

First, growth has been far slower, with much longer periods of recession. During the 'Long Boom', national unemployment ranged between 1 and 4 per cent. Some 240,000 jobs were steered to the assisted areas; and this was assisted by out-migration from the north, totalling 504,000 1965–73. By the 1970s, regional policy was having much less impact: during 1971–6 121,000 jobs were created or saved, during 1979–81 the total was only 73,000. But the decline of manufacturing and mining in the 1980s hit the north.

The significance is that traditional regional policy has assumed national growth in which some areas are experiencing excess demand and some excess supply; but when all regions are suffering from slump, it is necessary to develop policies aimed at creating jobs across the entire economy. True, there are also social equity arguments but these are more politically difficult to justify, especially as employers had less incentive to relocate.

Second, all regions and sub-regions have been profoundly affected by structural changes, specifically the parallel processes of de-industrialization and tertiarization. There have been two long-term trends: de-industrialization and tertiarization or post-industrialization. Over the entire period 1966–83 over 3.1 million manufacturing jobs (40 per cent) were lost. All the northern regions, except the east midlands, had a greater loss of manufacturing jobs than the south; in aggregate the north lost 32 per cent, the south 23 per cent. At an urban level, the contrast is even more striking; most of the fastest-growing towns were in the southeast, the southwest and East Anglia. Notably, high-technology industry is highly concentrated in the southeast and is negligible in Yorkshire, Humberside and south Wales. Service industry has always been highly concentrated in the southeast, and although that concentration weakened in the 1960s and 1970s, it strengthened again after 1979. Two service groups (distribution, hotels and catering, and business and financial services) are particularly strong in the southeast.

Third, the north–south divide has become more complex in its geography: de-industrialization, tertiarization and technological innovation have worked in parallel to impact most seriously on the industrial conurbations, including London, the west midlands and northwest, which have suffered massive de-industrialization and failed to compensate fully through tertiarization. At the same time, dispersal has continued to the attractive semi-rural areas of the outer southeast, east Anglia, the southwest and parts of the east midlands, assisted by better communications. There are some prosperous parts of the north (the so-called 'northern lights') and non-prosperous parts of the south. Thus, the terms 'core' and 'periphery' no longer have a simple meaning. Wales, the northwest and Yorkshire–Humberside can be regarded as periphery–transitional, leaving northern England, Scotland and Northern Ireland as the true periphery, remote and over-dependent on declining industries. The resulting north–south dividing line now runs from the Severn to the Wash, with only three prosperous regions; the 'north' has spread south, and parts of London are really part of the north (Damesick 1987b: 23; Martin 1988: 29).

Within the 'north', it seems that industrial structure was less significant than the dependence on a few large firms, especially in the west midlands. Large-scale activities, like coalmining, shipbuilding, iron and steel and heavy chemicals, offered little scope to the would-be entrepreneur. Mergers and acquisitions have favoured rationalization, with an obvious threat to the peripheral areas; firms tend to be increasingly controlled from outside, and the headquarters of big companies, as well as R&D, are strongly concentrated in London and the southeast. Though the industrial structure of the assisted areas has become more diverse, increasing the opportunities for new firm formation, social factors such as working class solidarity and industrial background have proved inimical to entrepreneurship. Overseas inward investment is very strongly concentrated in the southeast (Law 1980: 149).

The result is that the north suffers from what can be called a branch plant syndrome. Job loss through closure was far higher than in southern England, not because the north was dominated by branch factories, but because they tended to be routine production-oriented units without significant headquarters R&D functions; branches in the south tended to have been takeovers with a more independent existence. The northern closures were often small factories producing goods for which there was a structural decline, like men's suits or typewriters. They were archetypically *peripheral*, not *core*:

> Old style regional policy was effective in influencing the location of new investment when firms wanted to expand but it failed to influence the 'centre of gravity' of firms' operations. The headquarters staff, the R&D, and the more sophisticated products stayed where they had always been. The new branch plants in the assisted areas were small offshoots, intended to accommodate routine overspill production of mature products. They were always the marginal plants – the ones that would be opened in good times and closed down in bad. . . . The core–periphery distinction is ultimately the reason why during the 1980s so many branch closures were concentrated in the northern parts of the UK (Fothergill and Guy 1990: 170).

Also significant were environmental attractiveness and government spending on defence, which favoured the outer southeast. Studies suggest that transport costs are fairly insignificant for firms, and that there is little advantage in a central location as against a peripheral one. However, the south benefits from access to the wealthiest markets and from skilled labour plus suitable premises (Law 1980: 203). 'In contrast the peripheral regions appear to have had few advantages except those given by regional policy' (Law 1980: 130).

London is a rather massive special case. It lost manufacturing jobs more quickly, and gained service jobs more slowly, than the UK as a whole. Between 1960 and 1985 its manufacturing workforce halved, while most kinds of service employment also contracted (finance and business services excepted). In absolute numbers, London has the highest concentration of unemployment in the advanced industrial world, heavily concentrated in a few boroughs, and including a substantial proportion of long-term unemployed (Balchin 1990: 110, 120).

EVALUATING REGIONAL POLICY

During the 1960s and 1970s, there were several major attempts by economists to quantify the outcomes of regional policy. A. J. Brown concluded that it had produced 'a massive diversion of moves to the peripheral areas, which went on more or less continually, reached its maximum extent about 1963, and is almost certainly to be associated with the series of administrative and legislative changes of the time'. The share of IDC approvals going to the development areas rose from 15.5 per cent in 1960–2 to 19.6 per cent in 1963–5. The proportion of employment coming from IDC approvals rose from 22.6 per cent in 1956–9 to 49.1 per cent in 1966–9. Brown estimated the effect of the shift at 30,000 or more jobs a year in manufacturing and other 'basic' industries, implying a growth in all employment of about 50,000 a year, possibly much more (Brown 1972: 294).

Brown's overall estimate was that the four high-unemployment regions improved their regional growth of employment in manufacturing, mining and agriculture, apart from structural components, in relation to the rest of the country by about 28,000 a year between 1953 and 1959 and 1961 and 1966; this corresponds roughly to his estimate of the effect of policy changes. (Brown 1972: 317).

In a 1986 study, Moore, Rhodes and Tyler calculated throughout the period 1960–81 regional policy created a total of 604,000 manufacturing jobs in the development areas, an average of almost 29,000 per annum. However, some 154,000 or about one-quarter were lost before 1981, leaving some 450,000 surviving jobs in 1981. Using a conventional medium-term regional multiplier of 1.4, a further 180,000 jobs might have been generated in service industries, giving a grand total of 630,000 surviving jobs in 1981: 'a real and substantial achievement' (Moore *et al.* 1986: 9). Almost half the net jobs had been contributed by regional policy in the 1970s; thus, 'regional policy continued to be effective in the 1970s'. Indeed, it continued to be effective even in the recession from 1976 to 1981, generating some 23,000 manufacturing jobs per annum. Unfortunately, about half of these were needed to offset the continuing losses of regional policy jobs created before 1976; to that, net job creation fell to 12,000 manufacturing jobs per annum. They conclude: 'Given the depth of recession this remains a significant achievement'.

Investment incentives, represented in the 1980s by *regional development grants*, have been by far the most important policy instrument, accounting for about two-thirds of the total net jobs created by 1981, compared with 16 per cent for the IDC policy. REP accounted for very few jobs because it was abolished in 1976 and many of the jobs it had created subsequently disappeared. Even at its peak, however, it was the least effective of the instruments. Regional Selective Assistance was introduced only in 1972, but by 1981 it had generated over 40,000 new manufacturing jobs (Moore *et al.* 1986: 10). Even allowing for wide margins of error, the most effective instrument was the IDC, because it did not involve significant Exchequer expenditure, though there were other real costs associated with it.

Earlier, in 1971, Rhodes and Kan had looked at the impact of the office decentralization policies that the government had been pursuing since 1963 through encouragement and since 1965 through controls. These policies had proved successful because they reinforced market forces: an office moving out of London can expect to enjoy up to a 20 per cent reduction in operating costs, equal to about £500 per year per employee at that time. The transitional costs averaged £470 per new job created in the decentralized location, so that the majority of offices paid off the expenses, in the form of lower moving costs, within one year. The controls had the short-term effect of reducing the amount of floorspace receiving planning permission; between 1967 and 1970, they did restrict the rate of building in central London, and this accelerated the rise in office rents there (Rhodes and Kan 1971: 98). However, most movement had been over relatively short distances, mainly within the southeast region. Of the recorded 70,000 office jobs decentralized from central London between 1963 and 1970, only 1 per cent had moved into the development areas. This was because, in general, operating costs were as low 40–60 miles from London as further afield, including the development areas, particularly because transitional costs are higher over the longer distances.

Thus, regional policy in its heyday was effective in moving inward investment into the development areas, and this investment generated substantial numbers of jobs. What it failed to do was to create self-sustaining growth in the assisted areas.

Writing at the end of the 'Long Boom', Cameron reached a mordant conclusion on regional policy, which reads even more strikingly a quarter century later:

> The history of regional policy in the United Kingdom is rather like that of a man with a grumbling appendix. Every now and then he feels acute pain and is forced to take a bunch of medicines. Although his condition improves, he is never quite sure which of the medicines, singly or in combination with others, actually did the trick. However, at least he can forget about his discomfort and can turn his attention to other more pressing affairs. Then, sadly, his pain returns. This time he changes the dosage and hastily adds a few new medicines to his treatment. The new combination seems to work and once again he feels confident that the problem has been solved. Sadly, disillusionment is just around the corner (Cameron 1974: 65).

Cameron concluded that

> while there is no doubt that policy did have substantial success during the sixties, especially in terms of extra employment created in the development areas, the task remains dauntingly large. . . . In particular, far greater effort will have to be given to encouraging that part of the private service sector which is not tied to local consumption requirements to locate or to expand in the development areas. He was of course right, but history was to take a different course, and all that happened was that the north–south boundary moved south to occupy the midlands and even large parts of London.

CONCLUSION: REGIONAL POLICY AND REGIONAL PLANNING

As argued at the start of this chapter, since 1945 the UK has had regional policy but only fitful attempts at regional planning. In the era of the Attlee Labour government, a determined effort was made with regional offices of the Ministry of Town and Country Planning, but these promptly disappeared after the Conservative return to power in 1951. In 1965, the Wilson Labour government made the most ambitious attempt of all: the regionalization of the National Plan, through the regional economic planning councils serviced by the regional economic planning boards. As seen, in essence this collapsed in 1967, but the councils continued in being until their abolition by Mrs Thatcher in 1979. During the late 1960s they were engaged in regional planning exercises, some of them ambitious, as with the Southeast Strategy of 1967, which ran into opposition from the local planning authorities and led to the jointly commissioned *Strategic Plan for the South East* of 1970. This, produced by an ad hoc team of Whitehall officials, seconded local government officials and academic talent, was perhaps the most ambitious planning exercise of the half-century, deliberately designed as a worthy successor to Abercrombie's *Greater London Plan* of 1944. Its proposals for major polycentric developments in the outer southeast – in south Hampshire, Reading–Wokingham–Aldershot–Basingstoke, Crawley–Gatwick, south Essex and Milton Keynes–Northampton – evoked fierce local opposition throughout the 1970s, even though central government reaffirmed its support for the plan in 1978. A major problem here was the failure to implement the recommendations of the Redcliffe–Maud Commission on Local Government in England, in 1969, for a system of local government based on city regions. Instead, the reorganization actually introduced by the Conservative government through legislation in 1972, implemented in 1974, introduced a system essentially based on existing counties plus enlarged districts which, as intended, acted as an obstacle to implementation of this or any other plan for large-scale development in the countryside.

In the event, it was perhaps remarkable that in the later stages of Mrs Thatcher's administration, from 1987 onward, there developed a remarkably effective system of regional advice from regional standing conferences of local planning authorities followed by regional guidance from government, fortified in 1994 by the establishment of government offices in each region which took over responsibility for producing the regional guidance. In effect, though under Conservative governments the word could never be used, this was a system of regional physical planning, effective in handling the politically delicate matter of housing allocations, though less so in developing the bold approaches characterized by the 1970 Strategic Plan and similar exercises in other regions.

The incoming Labour administration, in 1997, at first intended to replace this system by one of directly elected regional authorities, but – with the sole exception of Greater London – this step was postponed until a second term of office. Instead, the government announced its intention to proceed with the creation of appointed *regional development agencies*, essentially to promote inward investment: a step which in many ways recalled the 1965 establishment of the regional councils, though it also entailed the creation of a major implementation agency for physical development through the regionalization of English Partnerships, the 'roving development corporation' recommended by Michael Heseltine and eventually created by the Major government in 1994. The government also proposed to give the regional standing conferences 'ownership' of RPG through a shared responsibility with the government regional offices, though it remained clear that they intended to reserve final powers of decision – for reasons that became clear when, for a time in 1998, the Southeast Regional Conference refused to accept the government's figures for housing provision contained in the government's own projections. At the time of writing, with legislation for the regional development agencies about to be introduced, their precise relationship with the new system of guidance remains to be clarified.

FURTHER READING

There is no single recommended source for British regional policy, but there is a number of sources which provide a useful background. They include Armstrong and Taylor (1993) *Regional Economics and Policy*, Damesick and Wood (1987) *Regional Problems, Problem Regions and Public Policy in the United Kingdom*, Law (1980) *British Regional Development since World War I*, Townroe and Martin (1992) *Regional Development in the 1990s: the British Isles in Transition*, and Parsons (1988) *The Political Economy of British Regional Policy*. Balchin (1990) *Regional Policy in Britain: The North–South Divide* provides a distinct perspective with plenty of statistical support. Cameron (1974) 'Regional economic policy in the United Kingdom' is still a good picture of the position in the heyday of regional policy. Hallett *et al.* (1973) *Regional Policy for Ever? Essays on the History, Theory and Political Economy of Forty Years of 'Regionalism'* and McCrone (1969) *Regional Policy in Britain* give a useful summary of the evolution of policy down to that time.

On the evaluation of regional policy, Brown (1972) *The Framework of Regional Economics in the United Kingdom* and Moore *et al.* (1973) 'Evaluating the effects of British regional economic policy' was followed by Moore *et al.* (1986) *The Effects of Government Regional Economic Policy*. Diamond and Spence (1983) *Regional Policy Evaluation: A Methodological Review and the Scottish Example* is a useful summary account.

For the increasingly important European aspects, see Williams (1996) *European Union Spatial Policy and Planning*; also Albrechts *et al.* (1988) *Regional Policy at the Crossroads: European Perspectives*, Alden and Boland (1996) *Regional Development Strategies: A European Perspective*, Artobolevskii (1996) *Regional Policy in Europe*, Bachtler and Turok (1997) *The Coherence of EU Regional Policy: Contrasting Perspectives on the Structural Funds*; and Martin (1988) 'The new economics and politics of regional restructuring: the British experience'.

Wannop (1995) *The Regional Imperative: Regional Planning and Governance in Britain, Europe and the United States* is a uniquely valuable source relating regional policy to other regional initiatives.

chapter 7

Countryside Planning
From Urban Containment to Sustainable Development

IAN HODGE

INTRODUCTION

The world in 1947 was very different from that in 1997, and yet in many respects the basic framework which was established after the war for countryside planning has remained intact. Rather than change the basic approach, additional layers of policy have been built on this initial framework. The initial emphasis was on giving priority to agriculture and protecting rural areas from the threats associated with urban development. However, it became clear that more positive conservation management was required than could be delivered through the statutory planning system. Various forms of countryside management were first applied to areas of particular conflict and later applied to a wider range of areas. The more recent objective of sustainable development requires attention to all areas, recognizing and managing distinctive characteristics at the local level.

THE POSTWAR FRAMEWORK

Urban containment and agricultural support

The framework established for the general protection of rural areas in the postwar period centred around the twin policies of urban containment and agricultural support. It was strongly believed that urban development represented the major threat to the quality of a countryside whose character and quality depended upon its maintenance by a prosperous agricultural sector.

In the prevailing view taken in the 1940s, as represented for instance by the Scott Committee on *Land Utilisation in Rural Areas* (Scott Report 1942), no essential contradiction was seen between agricultural progress and efficiency and rural amenity and the rural economy. Written during the second world war in a Britain under blockade, food security was inevitably seen to be of paramount importance. The Scott Committee believed that support for agriculture would have the effect of reviving country life and bringing about an improvement in the physical and social standards of country areas. Beyond this, a prosperous agriculture was seen as the only way of preserving the traditional appearance of the countryside. These views were rejected in a minority report by Dennison. He anticipated declining employment in agriculture and questioned agriculture's role in protecting the environment. However, the majority view of the committee reflected the received wisdom of the time, and this underpinned the postwar legislative framework for agriculture and rural areas.

The approach towards agriculture and rural planning was founded on a clear belief in the capacity of government to identify desirable outcomes and to move the system towards them. The 1947 Town and Country Planning Act provided the means for urban containment, thus safeguarding the countryside for the production of food. The use of land for the purposes of agriculture and forestry was expressly excluded from the definition of 'development' which was to be controlled under the Act. Further, certain other building and agricultural operations that would otherwise have required planning permission were given permitted development rights under the General Development Order. There was then a general view that controls over agriculture were unnecessary. For example, a 1950 circular commented that 'farm and forestry buildings are erected only for essential purposes: experience has shown that the degree of flexibility on siting is almost always governed by the purpose for which they are needed, and choice of materials is limited by the cost as well as local tradition'. As a result of this happy circumstance, there was confidence 'that farmers will respond to encouragement from local planning authorities to co-operate voluntarily in ensuring that the best local traditions are maintained' (quoted in Grant 1996: 32).

The basis for postwar agricultural policy was established in the 1947 Agriculture Act. The central objective was to establish 'a stable and efficient industry capable of producing such part of the nation's food as in the national interest it is desirable to produce'. Despite changes to the mechanisms of agricultural support, particularly the switch from deficiency payments to the maintenance of market prices, the general philosophy of rural policy was maintained through UK entry into the European Community. Even in the 1970s, two white papers concentrating on agriculture, *Food From Our Own Resources* (1975) and *Farming and the Nation* (1979), continued to advocate an expansion of food production, although by 1979, with emerging concerns for agricultural surpluses and the high cost to the Exchequer, this view was coming under increasing criticism.

These elements placed agriculture at the centre of rural policy: to secure food supplies from efficient agricultural production, to maintain rural amenity through a well-tended agricultural landscape and to support the rural population and services through a prosperous agricultural sector.

Protected areas
Alongside these national considerations, it was recognized that particular areas deserved some special protection. Thus a further element of postwar rural policy was the designation, through the 1949 National Parks and Access to the Countryside Act, of areas of particular pressure, notably *national parks, areas of outstanding natural beauty* and *sites of special scientific interest* (SSSIs). Yet, even in these areas, protection of the environment was to be achieved primarily through the exclusion of urban development; agriculture itself was not regarded as a major environmental threat. The establishment at this point of different systems for the designation and protection of areas of special landscape and areas of special nature conservation value introduced the divide between landscape, recreation and amenity issues on the one hand and the 'scientific' protection of habitat on the other. While this still remains today in England (Sheail 1993), legislation in 1990 and 1991 has ended the divide in Wales and Scotland with the establishment of the Countryside Council for Wales, and Scottish Natural Heritage: these have taken over responsibility for the administration of both landscape and conservation issues.

A CHANGING CONTEXT FOR COUNTRYSIDE PLANNING

The most immediate influences on the effectiveness of countryside planning were associated with the changing characteristics of agricultural systems. Relative price levels and the security of output prices guaranteed through agricultural policy together with the availability of new technology, stimulated greater intensity of production, higher use of chemical inputs, investments in the agricultural 'improvement' of the land by land drainage, reseeding, removal of natural features and rationalization of field patterns. The substitution of machinery for labour (and animal power) increased the scope for economies of size, both in terms of enterprises within holdings and in terms of the holdings themselves. The pattern of land use has changed considerably as illustrated in Figure 7.1.

These changes were successful in boosting agricultural production, but only at what has come to be seen as an excessive cost. The budgetary cost of operating the *Common Agricultural Policy* (CAP) became a major bone of contention within the European Community, especially from the perspective of the UK which was a major net contributor up until the time that Mrs Thatcher negotiated the Fontainebleau agreement. (This provided for reimbursement to the UK in respect of the net cost of membership of the EC.) At the same time, the environmental impacts of the changes became apparent. Agricultural production has cut into the rural landscape, decimating those parts where production potential had previously not been realized. In the 40 years following the second world war, about 95 per cent of lowland meadow was lost, 80 per cent of chalk downland, 60 per cent of lowland bogs, 50 per cent of lowland marsh and 40 per cent of lowland heath (Nature Conservancy Council 1984). The length of hedgerows declined from 495,000 miles in 1947 to 386,000 in 1985 (Countryside Commission 1986). The evidence suggests that the decline has continued since then. In the third of a series of studies of changes taking place in the landscape over a 25-year period in seven parishes, the Countryside Commission (1998c) found that features continued to be lost, although at a slower rate than in previous periods. There is also continuing concern at the loss of wildlife, recent studies emphasizing that this is an indirect consequence of pesticides which have killed important food sources in intensively farmed areas (Campbell *et al.* 1997).

At the same time, there has been an increase in the popularity of recreation in the

	1947	1997
Wheat	840	1,905
Barley	760	944
Oats	794	72
Oilseed Rape	46	383
Potatoes	381	127
Turnips, swedes and mangolds for stockfeed	250	36*
Linseed and Flax	21	72
Bare fallow	197	21
Total tillage	3,940	4,265
Temporary grass	1,277	735
Total arable land	5,217	5,000
Permanent grass	3,564	2,913
Sole right rough grazing	1,077	700
Set-aside scheme land	–	260

Figure 7.1
Agricultural land use in England, 1947 and 1997 (1,000 hectares)

* Other mainly fodder or compounding crops, excludes peas, field beans and maize.

countryside. Incomes and leisure time for the majority have increased, and the population has become much more mobile. It is now possible to visit areas, once relatively inaccessible to urban residents, even for quite short periods of time. Improved clothing and equipment make even the most remote areas of Britain accessible to a much wider section of society. Countryside Commission surveys have demonstrated the popularity of visiting the countryside. A 1996 survey suggested nearly 1.5 billion day visits to the countryside in Britain in a year. However, the detailed trends are complicated by difficulties of definition. In fact, Curry (1997) comments that national participation in countryside recreation peaked in 1977 and has exhibited a decline since then.

There have also been fundamental changes in the socioeconomic composition of the rural population, widely associated with the process of counter-urbanization. First described in Britain from the results of the 1981 census (Robert and Randolph 1983), more recent analysis has suggested a continuing growth of population across most rural areas although some easing of its extent (Champion 1994). A number of processes are involved, such as the movement of employment to rural areas, retirement migration and increased commuting. Each of these is in turn affected by different factors. The phenomenon is thus complex and spatially variable. The scale at which changes are analysed has an important influence on the pattern that emerges. The common pattern is of population decline in the larger conurbations and growth of smaller settlements in rural areas. However, there is often a continuing decline of population within the smallest villages (Weekley 1988). There is thus both a net increase as well as a redistribution of population within rural areas. At the same time, as demonstrated by the Rural Development Commission surveys of rural services, many of the collectively provided services in rural areas have continued to decline, especially public transport, shops, post offices and schools in the smaller villages.

THE DEVELOPMENT OF COUNTRYSIDE MANAGEMENT

The postwar policy framework was successful in several ways, but by no means in all respects. Agricultural production levels were raised and national self-sufficiency was effectively achieved in major temperate products, but only at significant cost both in financial and in environmental terms (Shoard 1980; Bowers and Cheshire 1983). The planning system has been most effective in containing the spread of urban development, but again there is debate about the costs involved (Evans 1991; Corkindale 1998). Taken together, changes in the socioeconomic composition of rural areas have divorced the rural resident population from the economy of agriculture. Rather than being seen as the source of economic activity in a local area, agriculture's role is increasingly viewed in terms of its influence on the landscape.

These changing pressures led to new conflicts within the countryside, and recognition that the conservation of the countryside requires positive management: it cannot be achieved by urban exclusion alone. The first efforts at a more positive approach towards countryside management were directed at areas where the urban pressures on the countryside were the greatest. Concerns over the potential consequences of increased recreational pressures on areas of natural beauty were behind the establishment of country parks under the 1968 Countryside Act. These were intended to divert pressures away from more sensitive environments (Curry 1997). There was also the development of management within areas of land under particular urban pressures (Davidson and Wibberley 1977). This led to the development of a more proactive approach with the explicit development of countryside management. In the urban fringe, this began with the *urban fringe management experiment* in Hertfordshire (Hall 1976) and the *upland management experiment* (Countryside Commission 1976) in the Lake District. This model now has more widespread application in the national parks and has been developed into the 'Groundwork' approach in urban fringe areas (Jones 1989; Dwyer and Hodge 1996).

The voluntary principle and the management of agricultural change

A more fundamental challenge to the basic assumptions of the 1947 legislation arose with the recognition of the impacts of changing agricultural practices on the rural environment. It became clear that agriculture could not be relied upon as the guardian of rural amenity and that a more direct influence over agricultural production decisions was required. Much of the wildlife and attractive landscapes which are valued have developed in response to the operation of particular agricultural systems over long periods of time. They are often not supported by the newer agricultural systems that have been introduced in the postwar period. Thus, the protection of the value of the countryside often depends upon positive actions to maintain particular agricultural practices. This has been implemented very largely through the use of management agreements.

Management agreements on SSSIs

The management agreement model had been under consideration for some while. Leonard (1982) attributes the proposal that agreements should be used in the conservation of valued landscapes to a suggestion by Hookway (1967), and their use in national parks was recommended by the Sandford Report (1974). However, their widespread application came only with the 1981 Wildlife and Countryside Act.

The Act was introduced following a lengthy and contentious passage through parliament (Cox and Lowe 1983). This established the 'voluntary principle' into rural environmental policy, and set a model of countryside management for a range of subsequent environmental initiatives. A major part of the Act concerned the arrangements for the protection of *Sites of Special Scientific Interest* (SSSIs). Up to this point, protection had depended essentially on special consideration being given to these sites within the operation of the planning legislation. This proved to be insufficient in the face of the pressures associated with the modernization of agriculture. The chosen solution was to permit the Nature Conservancy Council to enter into management agreements with landholders who agreed not to undertake potentially damaging operations. The compensation payable was calculated following financial guidelines that assessed the value of the opportunities foregone in entering the agreement, including the value of any agricultural grants that would have been payable. This was backed up ultimately by powers of compulsory purchase, although this is a sanction that has very rarely been applied in practice.

These arrangements made the rights of landholders explicit. In almost all circumstances, the landholder had the right to alter the countryside while the state had to compensate farmers to forego that right. The inclusion of compensation for agricultural grants foregone indicated that farmers had a right to grants, irrespective of the environmental impacts that they might have had. There was thus the irony of one UK government agency being obliged to buy out the subsidies being offered by another funded through the EC. There was also the concern that incentives were created for landholders to threaten changes simply as a lever to extract compensation payments. A relatively small number of very large payments to particular individuals brought the system bad publicity.

The rise of agri-environmental policy

While this approach accommodated many of the problems faced within notified sites of particular conservation value, there was also a broader concern for the consequences of 'agricultural improvement' in the wider countryside. Matters came to a head in the early 1980s on the Halvergate Marshes, an area of wetlands in the Norfolk Broads. The relative profitability of cereal production, boosted by the CAP, made it attractive to drain wetlands and convert the land for wheat production. This became a source of public controversy, and there was a search for a mechanism to extend environmental protection to the wider countryside.

A planning response could have been possible. Land drainage represents development but, under the General Development Order, it could be undertaken without seeking planning permission. This raised the possibility that Article 4 directions, revoking this general planning permission, might be used to require that permission be sought for land drainage operations. This would have allowed control through the planning system, but would have been purely negative in effect and would have obliged the payment of compensation where permission was refused.

In fact, the approach taken extended the voluntary principle, further signalling the ascendancy of countryside management over planning. The major difficulty concerned the cost. In the Halvergate Marshes an experimental scheme was introduced offering flat rate payments to farmers who agreed to adopt a standard package of conservation measures. This proved to be successful: uptake was high, despite the fact that the level of payments was significantly lower than those available within SSSI management agreements, and the policy presented a more positive political image than the individually negotiated payments on SSSIs. The model was subsequently incorporated into the CAP in the form of the *environmentally sensitive areas* (ESAs) (e.g. Whitby 1994), first to be permitted and then to be part-funded by the European Commission. This approach has formed the basis for the *countryside premium* scheme on set-aside land, the *countryside stewardship* scheme, and for the reduction of nitrate leaching in *nitrate sensitive areas*. These or similar schemes have been implemented throughout the UK. The principle was further advanced across Europe in the agri-environment package of measures accompanying the 1992 CAP reforms (Whitby 1996). The ESAs and the countryside stewardship scheme represent the major schemes in England.

Environmentally sensitive areas

The scheme for ESAs was introduced in 1987 through the encouragement of appropriate agricultural practices in designated areas of high environmental value. Areas for designation must be of national environmental significance, where conservation depends on adopting, maintaining or extending particular farming practices. Detailed environmental objectives are agreed through a process of consultation with farming and conservation bodies. Within the designated areas, farmers and agricultural land managers are able to enter 10-year management agreements with the Ministry of Agriculture, Fisheries and Food (MAFF) (with an option of termination after 5 years). A farmer receives annual payments on each hectare of land entered into the scheme.

Each ESA has one or more tiers. These are illustrated in Figure 7.2, each tier prescribing a specific set of agricultural practices to be followed. Details of the practices will reflect the specific objectives of individual ESAs. Payment rates are based on income foregone, although they also take into account any incentive that may be required to encourage the agreement holder to change his management approach. Typical payments range from £20 – £50 per hectare (ha) for upland

Each ESA has one or more tiers of entry

These tiers include:

> the protection and management of existing features
> the reversion of arable land to grass
> the traditional management of hay meadows
> the maintenance of high water levels in wetland habitats
> the establishment of arable field margins
> the maintenance of stockproof walls and hedges
> the enhancement of heather moorland
> the promotion of public access

All ESA scheme participants are prohibited from converting grassland to arable and must comply with restrictions on the amount of fertilizer and chemicals that may be applied to their land

Figure 7.2 The environmentally sensitive areas scheme

grassland, £100 – £200 for lowland grassland and £240 – £310 for reversion from lowland arable. The highest currently payable is £415 per hectare for raising water levels to create wet grassland in the Somerset Levels and Moors.

The English ESAs were designated in four separate stages – in 1987, 1988, 1993, and 1994. There are currently 22 ESAs in England covering an area of over 1.1 million ha, of which an estimated 0.9 million ha are potentially eligible for entry into the ESAs scheme. This excludes urban areas, roads and other land that would not be suitable. By the end of March 1996, some 46 per cent of the eligible area had been entered into the scheme, representing 7,800 agreements covering 427,000 ha. The take-up rates vary considerably between individual ESAs, from 94 per cent in West Penwith in Cornwall to 10 per cent on the Essex Coast.

A review in 1996 of environmental monitoring in the first round of ESAs to be designated concluded that the scheme had been generally successful in maintaining the traditional character of the landscape and arresting environmental decline, but that it was too soon to see statistically significant evidence of wildlife enhancement. There were however some localized concerns about continuing environmental degradation (NAO 1997b). Total expenditure on ESAs in England almost doubled from £22 million in 1992–3 to £43 million in 1996–7 as the number of ESAs designated and the take-up rate by farmers increased. Administration costs exceeded grants paid to farmers in the earliest stages. However through time they have shown some decline, reflecting the more established procedures and easier administration of the scheme.

The countryside stewardship scheme

The *countryside stewardship* scheme was first introduced as a pilot by the Countryside Commission, but was taken over by the MAFF in 1996. Similarly to the ESAs, it offers payments to farmers and other land managers to enhance and conserve landscapes, their wildlife and history and to help people to enjoy them. The major difference lies in the fact that there are no designated areas so that it is in principle available throughout England outside of the ESAs. The scheme is directed at the conservation of specific landscapes and targets are set annually in consultation with local interest groups to reflect current priorities and the progress made in previous years. Countryside stewardship agreements usually run for 10 years and each is drawn up individually to address particular management objectives and local circumstances.

A significant difference from the ESAs is that the scheme is discretionary and therefore not all applications are accepted. Thus, from 1991–4, 72 per cent of applications to enter the scheme resulted in agreements. Of the 'unsuccessful' applicants, 31 per cent were the results of applicants deciding not to proceed with the application; the remaining 61 per cent were rejected (Countryside Commission 1998a).

By 1996, about 107,000 ha had been entered into the countryside stewardship scheme involving over 6,225 agreements. A majority of these agreements related to field margins and waterside areas. In fact the administrative costs appear to be somewhat lower that those of the ESAs, although this may be attributable to differences in conventions in defining and accounting for the costs involved. According to the Countryside Commission (1998a), administration costs as a percentage of all expenditure fell from 28 per cent to 14 percent in the period 1991–6.

Limits of environmental contracts

These agreements accept that farmers will continue in occupation of the land and that they hold the rights to use the land in particular ways. Agreements are voluntary. It is assumed that any specialist knowledge can be provided to farmers, either within or in association with the particular contracts on offer. It is also assumed that fair compensation levels can be provided through standardized contracts.

This approach to agri-environment policy involves certain limitations (Hodge 1998). There is a strong element of central direction in the determination of environmental choices, and the range of options possible is limited by the need to negotiate and write requirements into enforceable contracts. Even so, the contracts guarantee conservation management only over relatively short time periods in relation to the periods that may be necessary to achieve the ecological objectives. Once the term of the contract has expired, there can be no guarantee that the conservation assets will continue to be maintained. The approach relies on regular payments on an indefinite basis. This is likely to imply a more critical scrutiny of the legitimacy of these payments and the return gained in competition with the many other demands made for on public expenditure. Questions will be asked as to whether, at least in some instances, the conservation of the environment should not be a duty of landownership. This returns us to the issue of the role of regulation.

TOWARDS SUSTAINABLE DEVELOPMENT

More recently, sustainable development has become the key criterion for all forms of environmental management and as such a guiding principle for the management of rural areas too. Government advice on the role of the planning system in relation to the countryside (PPG 7) comments that 'sustainable development is the cornerstone of both the government's rural policies and its planning policies'. A fuller extract from this PPG is given in Figure 7.3. Whatever the precise definition of sustainable development, the concept has a number of implications for the approach to be taken to countryside planning. It

- takes account of the interrelationships between economic and social needs and ecological limits, within a long-term perspective;
- takes account of all significant resource values, not just those regarded as being of the highest quality;
- recognizes the particular circumstances for management at a local level;
- indicates a need to co-ordinate values associated with different institutional arrangements, such as landscapes or nature conservation.

Sustainable development includes integrating the government's objectives to:

Figure 7.3
Planning policy
guidance – the
countryside:
environmental
quality and
economic and
social develop-
ment (PPG 7,
1997)

- meet the economic and social needs of people who live and work in rural areas, by promoting the efficiency and competitiveness of rural businesses, and encouraging further economic diversity to provide varied employment opportunities (especially in areas heavily reliant upon agriculture);

- maintain or enhance the character of the countryside and conserve its natural resources, including safeguarding the distinctiveness of its landscapes, its beauty, the diversity of its wildlife, the quality of rural towns and villages, its historic and archaeological interest, and best agricultural land;

- improve the viability of existing villages and market towns, reduce the need for increased car commuting to urban centres, and reverse the general decline in rural services, by promoting living communities, which have a reasonable mix of age, income and occupation and which offer a suitable scale of employment, affordable and market housing, community facilities and other opportunities;

- recognize the interdependence of urban and rural policies

Management across all areas

This implies the comprehensive management across the wider countryside as a whole, beyond designated areas: all areas have the potential to generate country-side goods that are likely to be neglected in the market. This shift is recognized in PPG 7:

> Since the second world war conservation efforts have concentrated on desig-nating and protecting those areas of countryside which are most important for landscape and wildlife. The priority is now to find new ways of enriching the quality of the whole countryside while accommodating appropriate develop-ment, in order to complement the protection which designations offer

Over the postwar period, numerous and varied countryside designations have been introduced (Bishop *et al.* 1997). These first demarcated areas of special value where particular efforts were to be made to exclude development. With time it has come to be recognized that this was insufficient and, in almost all instances, more attention has been given to the active management of the valued resources. Indeed, more recently designations have been introduced primarily for the purpose of identi-fying local areas where particular management approaches are to be introduced, such as in nitrate-sensitive areas or in ESAs. But if sustainable development requires a more active approach towards resource management across all areas, the role of designation becomes somewhat different. It shifts the emphasis from designation as a means of selecting areas with special qualities towards a means of identifying the constraints and appropriate management across all areas.

The *Character of England* map, produced jointly by the Countryside Commission and English Nature (1996), suggests an element of this approach. The map repre-sents a coordinated effort to define areas with similar landscape and nature conserva-tion characteristics across the whole country, without making judgements about their relative worth. It begins to define the particular qualities of resources and thus provides a framework for the determination of appropriate countryside management decisions in all areas. While this is perhaps better termed characterization rather than designation, it points to the importance of signalling information to decision makers as to the public values of all resources and the wider implications of decision making.

The Countryside Commission argues that the ideas of the countryside character approach should be included in regional planning guidance and structure plans, and from there be incorporated in subsequent plans as the approach develops (Countryside Commission 1998b). However, it is not a substitute for local designations, and the map itself provides no powers of protection (Swanwick 1997). Judgements about the relative values of different areas are still required.

Community and partnership

It is commonly argued that there is a close link between the economic success of communities in rural areas and the quality of the environment. For example, the 1995 English white paper *Rural England* stated that 'rural communities need to be economically viable if they are to maintain and enhance a countryside so significantly man's work'. This begs many questions, and the linkage between economic and environmental performance in rural areas is a topic that deserves further attention. However, the concept of sustainable development recognizes both of these aspects and indicates a requirement for integrated planning.

The rural development strategy in Scotland has done most to incorporate a socioeconomic element into sustainable development. The overall aim of all policies for rural Scotland, set out in *Towards a Development Strategy for Rural Scotland* (Scottish Office 1997), is to foster and enable the sustainable development of rural communities. In this, sustainable development depends 'on taking an integrated approach to each of the three main policy objectives: economic, social and environmental'. This places particular emphasis on the influence of local people on its achievement.

Real sustainable development therefore cannot be a top down or prescriptive process carried out by government. On the contrary, it is a major challenge facing local people and local communities, which to be effective should be based on local analysis of local needs. A grass-roots, bottom-up approach to sustainable rural development is likely to be a relatively slow process – there are no instant solutions – but it is a more durable approach because it has its roots firmly planted in rural communities themselves. Further, 'the planning system has a key role to play in promoting sustainable development. It is one of the mechanisms available to communities to identify and promote future development opportunities whilst conserving the natural and built heritage'.

In Scotland in particular, the question of sustainable development has been linked with the ownership of land. This is an issue raised by the Land Reform Policy Group (1998), established by the government to identify and assess proposals for land reform in Scotland. This group has accepted sustainable rural development as the overriding objective and that land reform should remove land-related barriers to that objective. Some forms of landownership may represent barriers, for instance where 'what are in effect local monopolies may stifle local development', where land is owned by individuals or companies from outside the UK or by absentee owners. This links issues of property rights with issues of sustainable local development.

The relationship here between community characteristics and performance and the physical environment is more obvious in the more remote rural areas, where economic activity relies to a greater extent on the local natural resource base and where settlements and their economies are less open than is the case in parts of England. However, the merger in England of the Countryside Commission with the national advisory and countrywide responsibilities of the Rural Development Commission to form the Countryside Agency in 1999 may promote a similar integration of environmental and socioeconomic elements of sustainable development there also (Countryside Commission 1998d).

As has been noted, the exclusion of agriculture from the definition of development in statutory land-use planning and its essentially negative emphasis have tended to direct attention towards more positive forms of countryside management. While the 1947 settlement significantly attenuated the rights of landowners in general to undertake development, the right to farm was left intact. Indeed, it was extended to an apparent entitlement to enjoy agricultural subsidies associated with agricultural land use. The 1981 Wildlife and Countryside Act essentially confirmed the rights of landowners to make alterations to the natural features on their land. Perhaps the high-water mark in rural landownership came in the mid-1980s with compensation payments being made to farmers in respect of grants foregone in order to comply with the conditions of management agreements.

Yet the planning system is a major factor in determining the rights enjoyed by landowners. Planning defines property. Changing social values and attitudes leads to changing rules of land ownership, often implemented through alterations to the planning system. Of course, the rights of landowners are defined in many ways, such as through environmental regulations and definitions of rights of way. This regulatory framework sets the context within which countryside management takes place.

While there has been relatively little development of a statutory planning approach towards the conservation of the countryside, there have been proposals for it. Shoard (1980) advocated the extension of planning controls to cover the changes taking place in the countryside. Cox *et al.* (1988) rejected a comprehensive extension of controls, arguing that the negative controls available would be insufficiently sensitive to deal with the dynamics of organic change. However, they did regard the exemptions provided to agriculture through the General Development Order as an 'indefensible anomaly'. Instead of comprehensive planning controls they proposed an extension of a general order-making power to prevent the removal or alteration of a specified landscape feature or the undertaking of a notifiable operation that might damage the conservation interest of a site. Regulation could thus be introduced on a piecemeal and responsive basis and amended in the light of experience and circumstance.

Despite the emphasis on countryside management, since the mid-1980s there has still been a gradual but significant erosion of the rights of agricultural landholders in response to the changing circumstances. The General Development Order was amended in 1988 to introduce restrictions on the building of intensive livestock units (Marsden *et al.* 1993). In changes introduced in 1992, development is (in certain cases) subject to a requirement to give prior notification to the local planning authority, to enable them to determine whether their prior approval should be required with respect to siting, design and external appearance. This applies for instance to new farm buildings, to significant extensions and alterations (to all extensions and alterations in national parks) and to farm roads. Further controls introduced in 1997 require the removal of buildings erected under agricultural permitted development rights, where the building ceases to be used for agricultural purposes within 10 years of their substantial completion, and where planning permission has not been granted for reuse for non-agricultural purposes (DoE 1997a).

Nevertheless, the UK Round Table on Sustainable Development has recently (1998) commented that

> the lack of clarity of current planning controls over agricultural buildings and
> over the carrying out of excavations or engineering operations for the purposes
> of agriculture, and the general inconsistency of approach in comparison with
> the requirements which apply to other industries, is unjustifiable. It is import-
> ant that controls do not stifle legitimate diversification of the economy in rural
> areas. But all development should be subject to proper control.

They recommend that 'the government should introduce requirements for full
development control on all agricultural buildings and on the carrying out of excav-
ations or engineering operations for the purposes of agriculture'. The issue of the
exemptions of planning controls over agricultural development has also recently
been raised in Scotland by the Land Reform Policy Group (1998).

A government consultation paper (DETR 1998i) on the protection and management of SSSIs includes proposals that conservation agencies should be empowered
to refuse permission to landowners to undertake potentially damaging operations
and to remove the presumption in respect of compensation in the form of net profit
foregone. It also raises the possibility of conservation agencies being given powers to
enforce positive conservation management orders, similar to the powers already
available in relation to the built heritage.

Other evidence of the erosion of landholders' rights can be seen from changes
taking place both within and outside the planning system. There have been several
attempts to introduce legislation for the control of hedges and this was included in
the 1995 Environment Act. This provides for the introduction of regulations for the
protection of important hedgerows, although concerns remain among environmental
groups that the regulations are too narrow and that local authorities lack the manpower and resources to enforce them. Outside of the planning system, there have
been restrictions on rights, for example, through the introduction of a ban on straw
burning, limits on the use and applications of pesticides, and regulations seeking to
limit nitrate leaching in nitrate vulnerable zones. Discussions of the provision of
access to open countryside in England and Wales raise the possibility of introducing
a general right to roam (DETR 1998e).

It is possible that the operation of countryside management may itself influence
views as to the appropriate duties of landownership. The establishment of a higher
standard of environmental quality through the operation of environmental contracts
might come to be regarded as the status quo that landowners have a duty to maintain. This might, for example come to be regarded as a duty of sustainable land
management and not something for which farmers should receive payment. Again,
the implication is that the public would reject the continuation of payments for
environmental contracts of this sort. This approach has been made explicit in the
proposal by the UK Round Table on Sustainable Development (1998) for a 'duty of
care' for landowners and land managers that would provide a uniform and basic level
of legal obligation.

THE PROSPECTS FOR COUNTRYSIDE PLANNING

Two major difficulties now face the rural conservation planning process, as indeed
they do in many other areas of government: the absence of a clear consensus as to the
appropriate objectives for policy, and a recognition that government cannot simply
command the system to deliver. The adoption of a goal of sustainable development
adds further complication in requiring that account should be taken of all relevant
values, thus undermining the more conventional objective of economic efficiency.

In planning terms the postwar problem seemed much less complex. The widely accepted priority was to secure the domestic production of certain identifiable and marketed products, to keep agriculture at the centre of the rural economy and to keep land in and available for production. The problem now is to determine a mixture of intangible countryside goods that are not readily measurable, let alone priced in a market. They are locationally specific, and judgements of their value are coloured by associations of heritage and nostalgia.

In the past, landscapes have emerged either as an incidental by-product of particular combinations of prices, technical relationships and institutions, or else for the private enjoyment of a privileged minority. The challenge now is to develop new landscapes for public enjoyment. But in the planning system the emphasis tends to be on what is not wanted rather than on what *is*. The application of centralized guidelines tends towards standardization, often referring back to the past for ideas for the future in a search to re-establish a 'traditional countryside' based on 'traditional' agricultural systems. But we can never be sure that what is regarded as traditional is the most appropriate for the future.

Though significant progress has been made with new forms of countryside management, we are in many respects still exploring the possibilities and implications. The emphasis is increasingly on the provision of countryside 'goods'. This is a novel project in public policy: the creation of new landscapes for public enjoyment. A major challenge here is to promote variety and local distinctiveness. Public policy is more often concerned with and generally better suited to promoting homogeneity and the planning system at opposing change.

The *countryside stewardship* scheme and the *Character of England* map suggest two elements of a general approach towards countryside management for sustainable development. The countryside stewardship scheme is generally not limited to particular places, but rather identifies desired outputs, and landowners have the opportunity to demonstrate their capacity to provide them. This provides an incentive for resource managers to look for opportunities for generating greater public benefits from the resources at their disposal. The character map offers a comprehensive framework within which judgements about priorities may be made.

In the longer term, a satisfactory outcome will only emerge from a complex of policy mechanisms and other institutions that articulate public demands to support local environmental solutions (Hodge 1998). Local groups, through government and collective action can demand particular countryside goods from local landholders. Efficiency can be improved through competition for contracts to produce them. Alternative landowners, such as non-profit trusts or perhaps new country house-owners, will make their own contribution to a varied landscape. Coordination amongst landholders can widen the range of options available.

Future developments may well involve constraints over the options available to landholders, perhaps defining the duties of landownership in terms of sustainability or the duties associated with the receipt of payments from the state. This implies the need to maintain a continuing balance between the planning and countryside management approaches to set the limits inherent in the ownership of land and to provide suitable incentives for positive actions to promote the public interest.

FURTHER READING

A number of books review various aspects of the history of countryside planning. Cherry and Rogers (1996) *Rural Change and Planning: England and Wales in the Twentieth Century* recount the changes in the countryside through this century. Blunden and Curry (1989) *A People's Charter? Forty Years of the National Parks and Access to the Countryside Act 1949*, review the role of designated areas and public access. Social change in rural areas is analysed by Newby (1985) in *Green and Pleasant Land? Social Change in Rural England*. In Marsden *et al.* (1993) *Constructing the Countryside: An Approach to Rural Development*, the authors offer a conceptual framework for the analysis of the development and restructuring of the countryside. Changes in agricultural and environmental policy are described by Winter (1996) *Rural Politics: Policies for Agriculture, Forestry and the Environment*. Curry (1994) *Countryside Recreation, Access and Land Use Planning* provides a detailed account of recreation and access policies and plans. Adams (1996) *Future Nature: A Vision for Conservation*, reviews the provision of nature conservation in the UK and offers his own perspective of the options. Allanson and Whitby (1996) *The Rural Economy and the British Countryside*, have provided a series of essays on resources and policy in rural areas. A recent report by the UK Round Table on Sustainable Development (1998), *Aspects of Sustainable Agriculture and Rural Policy*, provides an up-to-date review and recommendations on the development of policy.

The formal government statement on rural planning is provided in DoE (1997a) *The Countryside: Environmental Quality and Economic and Social Development* (PPG 7), but this was written before the change in government. Subsequent to this, a number of discussion documents have been published, including DETR (1998e) *Access to the Open Countryside in England and Wales*, DETR (1998i) *Sites of Special Scientific Interest: Better Protection and Management* and Scottish Office (1997) *Towards a Development Strategy for Rural Scotland*.

chapter 8

Preservation, Conservation and Heritage

Developing Concepts and Applications

PETER J. LARKHAM

THE CONTEXT OF CONSERVATION

There is a well known quotation by Michael Manser, former President of the Royal Institute of British Architects, that 'conservation is a comparatively new idea' (quoted in Knevitt 1986). In fact the reverse is true: conservation *does* have a lengthy history. This is true both in terms of records of individual action and statutory concern. There is also some confusion between 'conservation' and 'preservation'. Although the terms are often used together in UK guidance, and interchangeably by many writers, 'preservation' tends to be the older concept and implies retention without significant change. 'Conservation', very much a twentieth-century usage, implies a need for change but awareness that change should be directed in order to retain key valued elements. Even more recently, 'heritage' has come to imply the process of evaluation, selection and interpretation – perhaps even exploitation – of things of the past.

This understanding of the temporal dimension and of the evolution of concepts underlies this exploration of the development of UK conservation and the impact of the 1947 Town and Country Planning Act. However, with reference to the theme of this volume, it is significant to note that the path of conservation has always been gradual. Although Ross (1996: 22) notes that the 1947 Act 'laid the foundations of the regime that we have today', the development was incremental. It is thus pertinent to begin with a brief review of conservation before 1947, and the provisions and context of the 1947 Act.

It is now widely known that it was a broadening of interests in history and archaeology, together with reactions against contemporary developments and crude 'restorations', that spurred the UK's first conservationist legislation. This was Sir John Lubbock's repeated Ancient Monuments Bills of the 1870s, a watered-down version of which became law in 1882. This afforded only minimal protection to a small number of 'monuments' and specifically excluded ecclesiastical buildings in use. Nevertheless, there was strong sentiment among legislators and landowners that this represented an unwarranted state interference with private property rights. Lord Percy complained that the bills proposed to take control of private property not for essential public purposes, but 'for purposes of sentiment, and it was difficult to see where that would stop' (Delafons 1997a: 24).

Ancient monuments legislation was regularly amended and extended in the early twentieth century. Importantly, the 1913 Ancient Monuments Consolidation and

Amendment Act introduced the concept of a *preservation order* (although each one required parliamentary confirmation) and additionally gave the Ancient Monuments Board and the Commissioners of Works the duty to prepare lists of 'monuments and things . . . the preservation of which is a matter of public interest by reason of the historic, architectural, traditional, artistic, or archaeological interest attaching thereto'. Despite this wide remit, the board restricted itself to the established traditional scope of monument control.

Conservation received a surprising (and overlooked) boost in the 1923 housing act. This provided that:

> Where it appears to the minister that on account of the special architectural, historic or artistic interest attaching to a locality it is expedient that with a view to preserving the existing character and to protect the existing features of the locality a town planning scheme should be made . . . [the minister may authorise such a scheme to be made] prescribing the space about buildings, or limiting the number of buildings to be erected, or prescribing the height or character of buildings.

Cocks (1998) demonstrates that this unusual clause, establishing novel planning principles (in an Act which did not contain the word 'planning' in its title) was developed at the instigation of influential lawyers and parliamentarians, graduates of Oxford University, who were concerned to protect the character of that city. However, little or no use seems to have been made of these novel provisions. The 1932 planning act rather diluted this wide definition of interest, referring to 'protecting existing buildings or other objects of architectural, historic or artistic interest'. It did, however, introduce the term 'amenity' and building preservation orders, thus extending the familiar form of monument control to inhabited buildings. It also contained a number of significant procedural and practical flaws (Delafons 1997a: 39–40). Of more direct conservation interest than this legislation were local Acts such as the 1937 Bath Corporation Act.

The need for reform of the planning system resulted in the 1943 and 1944 Town and Country Planning Acts; the debate on the latter, in particular, touched upon conservation and the possibility of requiring local authorities to prepare lists of historic buildings (Delafons 1997a: 56). This resulted in new clauses empowering the minister to compile such lists, requiring owners to give notice of alterations or demolition, and extending the scope of building preservation to cover alteration as well as demolition. Thus, by 1947, the majority of the critical conceptual components of conservation planning were in place, though some were unused and others required further development of procedural mechanisms.

THE 1947 ACT

The 1947 Act was therefore not particularly radical (in this area). Conservation was only a tiny part – two clauses – of a long and complex bill. There was no discussion of these clauses in the House of Commons, and the debate in the House of Lords 'was not on the whole up to the standard of the earlier ones' (Kennet 1972: 44). One key amendment in the Lords, however, changed the minister's power to compile lists of historic buildings into a statutory duty. In introducing this amendment, Lord Salisbury also used the term 'national heritage' for probably the first time in parliament (Delafons 1997a: 60). More notable, perhaps, is the Act's reiteration, and assumption of an agreed interpretation, of the phrase 'expedient in the interests of amenity'

(Stuttard 1959). Amenity is an ill-defined but prominent theme in UK planning (Smith 1974; Cullingworth and Nadin 1997: 129), and the 1947 Act certainly embedded it in the planning consciousness – from whence it resurfaces from the 1967 Civic Amenities Act to the many refusals of planning permission as being 'detrimental to the amenities of the neighbourhood'.

The 1947 Act fitted well into the centralist framework of control, part of the ruling political philosophy of the time, as reflected also in measures such as the 1946 New Towns Act (Cherry 1996). The application of centralized control to conservation lay first in the listing system. Later, when the novelty of such control had worn off, the planning application mechanism was extended first to listed buildings, then to the demolition of unlisted buildings in conservation areas and then to ancient monuments. In all areas, the application of this quasi-judicial system of state control (at national and local level) has brought problems.

The following sections illustrate the slow development of the system in response to rapidly changing circumstances; the changing nature of buildings, areas and monuments that were found to be worthy of conservation, particularly as conservation became a popular public movement; and the problems of flexible policy and loose definitions, especially when appeals, court cases and the notion of 'precedent' came to dominate the way in which conservation was carried out.

It should also be recalled that other activities in this period were raising the general consciousness of conservation. One was the issue of countryside conservation, both in terms of scenery and recreational access, and of scientific conservation – resulting in the National Parks and Access to the Countryside Act (1949) and the setting up of the Nature Conservancy – showing an unfortunate split in ministerial responsibilities (Cherry and Rogers 1996). Second was the increasing shift in emphasis of the National Trust towards the acquisition, protection and public display of country houses, particularly spurred by the activities of James Lees-Milne (Mandler 1996). However, the ethos of new-town construction and widespread central area clearance redevelopment from the late 1940s into the 1970s led to a rather different view of the planner's attitude towards conservation (Figure 8.1).

LISTED BUILDINGS

Having such long antecedents, listing proceeded leisurely, hampered mainly by lack of resources. Yet 'the fieldworkers had very little background and almost no training.

"This is Mr Trimp from the Town and Country Planning Department. He's here to demonstrate the proposals for the old town"

Figure 8.1 Caricature of the 'evil planner' approach to conservation

Source: Reproduced by permission of *Private Eye*

[They surveyed] what was a completely unknown quantity to an impossible time-scale ... with additional constraints like petrol rationing' (Robertson 1993: 22). Criteria for listing were drawn up by the minister's advisors, particularly the architectural historian John Summerson. But the criteria were slanted towards pre-Victorian urban polite architecture, rather than rural vernacular (Figure 8.2).

Another procedural problem (recurring until the creation of the DoE and then again following the creation of the Department of National Heritage) has been the split in responsibilities between departments. The overlap with monument protection in the Ministry of Works and historic buildings in the Ministry of Town and Country Planning puzzled the Gowers Committee, a Treasury committee set up in 1948 to report on the preservation 'of houses of outstanding historic or architectural interest':

> It is absurd that the preservation of historic buildings should depend on two largely independent codes, overlapping at some points but differing in the Departments responsible for them, the manner of their administration, the powers they confer, and the types of buildings to which they apply. It is even more absurd that the question of which code applies should depend, as it sometimes does, on which Department finds itself there first (Gowers Report 1950: para 67).

In part a reflection of the disparate origins of UK preservation, the confusion persisted as this part of the Gowers Report was ignored.

The slowness of the survey, with the last volume not appearing until 1970, allied

SURREY   LEATHERHEAD U.D.
LEATHERHEAD

No 33, CHURCH STREET

VIEW FROM SOUTH-WEST

CONSTRUCTION: Brickwork, with contrasting quoins, stone coping, tile-hung gable, and tile-hung wing at south end. The front of the house is a very good example of 18th century provincial design, and has a panelled door and sash windows.
GARDEN: The house is separated from the street by a brick wall and a small well-kept garden containing fine clipped yews beside the front door.

Figure 8.2 Early List entry: 33 Church Street, Leatherhead by John Harvey

Source: Reproduced by permission of the Ancient Monuments Society

with the speed of postwar reconstruction and a developing academic and lay appreciation of architecture (both vernacular and post-Georgian) led to a national resurvey being approved by the then minister, Richard Crossman, in 1966. The priority was for speed:

> to get as many buildings protected as quickly as possible, so this meant min-
> imum inspection time, buildings looked at only from the street, almost no
> interiors inspected and no more background research than could be done
> during the inevitable rainy days in the field (Robertson 1993: 25).

Other factors intervened, including the local government reorganization rendering previous lists almost impossible to use; and the government agreed to accelerate the resurvey after the Firestone Building in west London was hastily demolished over a Bank Holiday and before it could be listed. Most recently, as the accelerated country-wide resurvey has been completed, English Heritage has been pursuing thematic reviews of particularly vulnerable building types, such as postwar education buildings. The resurvey took 1,000 man-years and cost over £4 million; it added about 300,000 buildings to the list (Robertson 1993: 93).

These efforts have resulted in approximately half a million structures being listed. The definition of 'building' has become very elastic, with examples ranging from milestones, telephone boxes, temporary prefabricated houses, to the Anderton boat lift, and a lift testing tower. The criteria for listing have been refined, and listing investigators are better trained. Listing has been extended to more recent buildings: it is now possible to list key buildings over 10 years old if they are under threat. It is this extension of listing to postwar structures that has brought about the greatest challenge in terms of public reaction.

Indeed, one of the problems with the listing system over time has been the secrecy with which it has operated. For example, an Advisory Committee on Listing was set up as early as 1945 and it developed instructions to investigators. However these were strictly secret, as John Delafons found when he became secretary to the committee in 1959: 'I was told of the instructions' existence but it was gently explained to me that neither my predecessor nor I was entitled to see a copy since they were confidential to the Investigators' (Delafons 1997a: 67).

However, he found a copy in a plain brown envelope in the Public Record Office and published extracts in his 1997 book. Similarly, it has always been the minister who makes the decision on listing, albeit on advice from experts (the Advisory Committee, now English Heritage). No reasons are given for listing or refusal to list, and there is no appeal (save on errors of fact). Yet no minister has been trained in the architectural or aesthetic appreciation of buildings. This secrecy and personalization of power were questioned both in the controversy surrounding postwar listings – where Nicholas Ridley listed only 18 of the 70 suggested by English Heritage in 1987 (English Heritage had thought that 'in recognition of the sensitivity and novelty of the whole issue, the expectation was that a significant number of the recommendations – perhaps 20 – might be rejected': Page 1992: 2) – and in the specific case of the wartime nondescript outbuildings of Bletchley Park, wherein the German 'Enigma' codes were broken, and which the minister of the day (Peter Brooke) refused to list.

A more fundamental change was the extension of real power to protect the structures that had merely been placed on the minister's list. The 1968 Town and Country Planning Act introduced the system of listed building consent (LBC) whereby separate approval has to be sought for the demolition or alteration of a listed building. This separate system has distinct criteria, so that in seeking both planning permission and LBC for the same alterations it is quite possible to receive one and be refused the other. The accompanying Circular 61/68 (MHLG 1968) also introduced a 'presumption in favour of preservation', and this became an increasingly doctrinaire approach. The 1972 Town and Country Planning (Amendment) Act introduced similar control over the demolition of unlisted buildings in those conservation areas where the local planning authority made a specific direction, while the 1974 Town and Country Amenities Act (another private member's measure) extended this power to all unlisted buildings in all conservation areas.

Two sets of events have tested building conservation concepts. One is the series of high-profile disasters, including the fires at York Minster (1984), Hampton Court (1986), Uppark House (1989) and Windsor Castle (1992). Each has generated debate, ranging from the basic principles of why these buildings were conserved and for whom, and whether they should be restored at all, to the minutiae of how restoration should be implemented. Yet each case rests on the peculiarities of the situation: Uppark, for example, proved a spectacular restoration and has drawn many thousands of visitors. Yet the scale of the restoration was made possible by the wording of the insurance policy, which provided some £20 million for reconstruction to the pre-fire state: and no other form of conservation would have been allowed under the terms of the policy (Rowell and Robinson 1996).

Secondly, a number of court cases have tested the interpretation of statute and guidance and thereby have set legal precedents. Suddards and Hargreaves (1996) chronicle many such cases in detail, but two are worth brief mention. The case of Old Hall, Thurrock, Essex caused considerable publicity, almost entirely since its owner was the high-profile Conservative MP Theresa Gorman. Substantial alterations had been made without LBC to a Grade II listed farm complex. Thirty-three summons and 14 enforcement notices were served, and in 1996 the Gormans were convicted of 29 breaches of LBC regulations.

Another key case is *Shimizu (UK) Ltd v. Westminster City Council*, which reached the House of Lords in 1997. The case revolved around the proposed demolition of

Figure 8.3 The burning of Uppark

Source: © National Trust Photograhic Library and Ian West

chimney-breasts in a listed building. The Lords extensively discussed the definition of 'building', 'demolition' and 'alteration' and, in a novel interpretation, held that 'demolition' implies the 'destruction, or substantial destruction, of the unit comprising the 'listed building''. The previous common interpretation, that LBC was required for any demolition no matter how partial, is thus overturned. There are important procedural consequences both for listed building control and for the control of demolition within conservation areas (Brainsby and Carter 1997). The editor of the Institute of Historic Building Conservation's journal has suggested that 'a short swift amending Act would have been helpful to correct the aberrant interpretation of the Law Lords' (Kindred 1997: 3).

AREA-BASED CONSERVATION

The move from individual buildings and monuments to general acceptance of area-based conservation came slowly, despite the obvious precursor of the 1923 Act. A key case was that of the *Earl of Iveagh v Minister of Housing and Local Government* (Court of Appeal 1964), where the Earl challenged building preservation notices and the issue of 'group value' listing (Ross 1996: 30). The new system introduced in France by André Malraux, the Minister of Culture, in 1962 was also influential. Three powerful personalities shaped a new UK policy direction. One was Richard Crossman, Minister of Housing and Local Government (1964–6), who encouraged the Ministry's Townscape Group which, in 1965, was 'working on a new policy document which suggested that the preservation of ancient buildings should be concerned not merely with individual listed buildings but also with groups or streets or small areas of old towns' (Crossman 1975). He also commissioned the four major studies of Bath, Chester, Chichester and York (published in 1968). The second personality was Lord Kennet, parliamentary secretary in the ministry (1966–70) (Delafons, 1997a). The third was Duncan Sandys, a former minister, founder and President of the Civic Trust, who won first place in the ballot for private members' bills in 1966. With Crossman's backing, he introduced the Civic Amenities Bill, which became law in 1967 with all-party support. It introduced conservation areas: 'areas of special architectural or historic interest, the character or appearance of which it is desirable to preserve or enhance'. Local authorities were given a statutory duty to make such designations and to pay special attention to planning applications in such areas. The link with the terminology of the 1923 Act is clear.

Only a relatively small number of areas were originally envisaged, and (mirroring attitudes of the time) these were implicitly assumed to be specifically urban, pre-Victorian or, preferably, medieval or Georgian. Over 30 years, however, this has changed substantially: there are now approximately 10,000 designations across the UK as a whole. Data collected annually by English Heritage help to assess the take-up rates of conservation areas, generally over time and geographically across the country. In general, the number of designations has risen quite steadily since 1967 and, although there was a slightly higher rate until the mid 1970s and a slightly lower rate until the late 1980s, these differences were relatively slight (Larkham 1996a). The fear of a continual rise in new designations into the mid 1990s did not occur, with the figures for 1992–4 being significantly lower than those of 1989–91. The concerns in the professional press about over-designation in the late 1980s/early 1990s relate to a quite short period, but are nevertheless worth brief investigation.

One issue was that of the reactions to continued designation. The question of whether continued designations devalue the concept, effectively 'debasing the

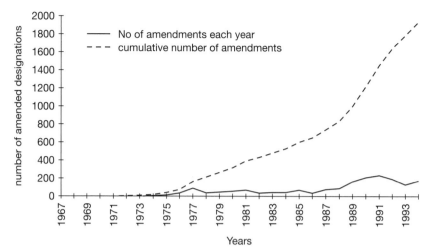

Figure 8.4 The
inexorable rise of
conservation area
designations to 1994

Source: English
Heritage data

coinage', has been examined by Morton (1991). He found that the process of designation is neither rigorous nor democratic. Moreover, in some cases, the reasons for designation are not well understood (it would appear that this criticism is applicable both to the public and to planners). Others have suggested that, since the criteria for designation are only loosely governed by statute, the system is open to abuse – and is being abused (Graves and Ross 1991). There are current concerns of continual erosion of character through numerous unsympathetic proposals for minor alterations (e.g. uPVC windows) and inadequate maintenance, with some local authorities being accused of 'incompetence and lack of concern' (Robinson 1982).

The vast majority of designations appear to be officer-led. They predominantly aim to control development and demolition, to protect the 'very special' and to encompass familiar and cherished townscapes. In some cases, designation is the result of a systematic initial townscape appraisal by officers. However, this is certainly not usual and most appear to be a response to actions which challenge what is 'very special' or familiar. In such cases, designations are stimulated by threats of demolition: a situation that may become less commonplace as measures to control demolition become more widespread.

A further explanation for patterns of designation, forming at least an administrative motive, is provided by changes in legislation and practice. Peaks in designation can be related closely to new legislation, to the publication of guidance reminding local authorities of their statutory duties and to administrative changes such as the 1974 local government reorganization. An increasing recent impetus is given by the growing importance of the development plan system. As local planning authorities prepare new plans, they use the process to review areas, amend or make new designations, and thus 'bursts' of activity occur.

Motivations for designation are questioned: 'snob zoning' to prevent change and development, political motivation, and designation to enhance development control powers all devalue the process and deviate from the original Act (Stansfield 1991). Reade's critique of the system, based on a study of Upper Bangor, sharply criticizes the system of designation and management (Reade 1991–2). He argues that designation is of real value only where significant policies are developed and resources allocated for their completion. Without this, designated areas will inevitably stagnate or even decay, rendering designation eventually fruitless and (by implication) de-designation inevitable.

What has been designated has also changed over time. Designations now include

Victorian and even mid-twentieth century urban landscapes, together with rural agricultural landscapes, parkland, cemeteries, canals and the Settle–Carlisle Railway. Not only have the types of area changed, but the scale has increased immensely. Early designations were small and tightly drawn; recently there is a trend towards 'giant' areas, exemplified by the Yorkshire Barns and Walls areas, covering tens of square kilometers. Bath, too, shows a peculiar growth pattern of its single conservation area over time, until it covered 1,914 hectares, or some 66 per cent of the city's area (Figure 8.5).

From the late 1980s, the conservation area concept has been tested and refined more through the courts than through the more usual policy development channels. In the case of *Steinberg and Sykes v. Secretary of State for the Environment and Another* ([1989] JPL 259), two residents in a conservation area were aggrieved at a grant of planning permission at appeal for a two-storey house in Camden. Steinberg and Sykes challenged the Secretary of State's decision in the High Court on the ground that the inspector had failed to take into account the statutory requirement of the local planning authority to pay 'special attention' to the application. In particular, the court agreed that there was a duty to ensure that development in a conservation area should positively preserve or enhance the area. Subsequent cases have moderated this view, for example by agreeing that development having a 'neutral' impact (i.e. not positively preserving or enhancing) is also permissible.

Millichap (1989a) examined a number of post-*Steinberg* appeal decisions,

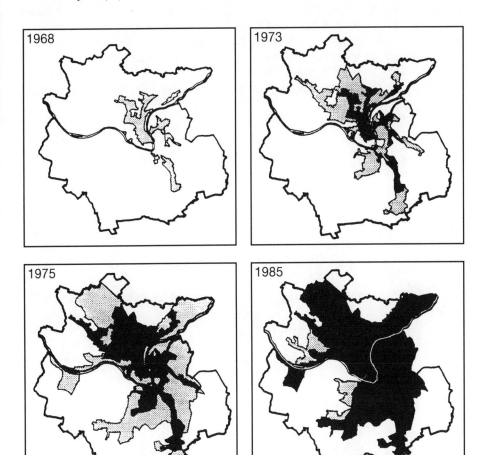

Figure 8.5 Bath: growth of a conservation area

Source: Redrawn from Bath City Council, 1993

noting the problems of identifying 'demonstrable harm' and the tendency to treat 'preservation' and 'enhancement' as alternatives, although many decision letters refer to preservation *and* enhancement rather than preservation *or* enhancement, as does the legislation. He also discusses the problems of distinguishing 'character', 'appearance', 'preserve' and 'enhance' – which he analyses lucidly (Millichap 1989b). He concludes that applicants and decision makers should beware of the ability to promote the interpretation of the section that favours their aims.

MONUMENTS AND ARCHAEOLOGY

As has been seen, the origins of UK conservation policy lie in the ancient monuments legislation of the 1880s. From the turn of the century, 'ancient monuments continued to attract the attention of legislators from time to time over the next eighty years. . . . The objectives did not materially change: it has been a matter of progressively tightening the girdle' (Delafons 1997a: 30).

The scheduling of ancient monuments has continued throughout the century and, as the entire process has largely been carried out by a separate government department (formerly the Ministry of Works), the impact of the 1947 Act has been negligible. There have been some (though few) confusions when scheduled monuments have also been listed. The main intellectual trend, as distinct from procedural developments largely concerning grant making powers, has been the gradual widening of the scope and date of features found acceptable for protection as 'ancient monuments'. This has been spurred by two factors: first, increasing archaeological awareness that remains are not discrete 'monuments' but part of landscape systems; in part spurred by the development of aerial photography and geophysical techniques (Figure 8.6). Second, there has been a growing awareness of the destruction of remains by development, road construction, and changing agricultural

Figure 8.6 Avebury: a scheduled ancient monument

Source: English Heritage Photographic Library

techniques (see the influential report of the Council for British Archaeology, edited by Heighway in 1972).

A key major development was the 1979 Ancient Monuments and Archaeological Areas Act. This replaced the former preservation order system with a centrally directed system of consent applications modelled on the listed building consent system. The second part seemed to promise a protection for important archaeological deposits similar to that afforded by conservation areas. However, this proved not to be the case. Only five such areas were ever designated, in 1984 (Canterbury, Chester, Exeter, Hereford and York). After various reviews of the procedure (Pagoda Associates 1992), there has been a firm decision not to proceed with additional designations. Indeed in 1994 there was a suggestion that this section of the Act should be repealed (Suddards and Hargreaves 1996: 337). Archaeological areas are very different from conservation areas: there is no presumption in favour of preservation, rather for the (necessarily destructive) investigation of remains. It is this approach that has changed since the Act.

The publication of PPG 16 on archaeology (DoE 1990a) has marked a significant change in policy and practice (Champion 1996). First, it shows a move away from the ancient monuments legislation, the key concepts of which are over a century old, towards the use of planning law. It asserts that archaeological remains are a material consideration in planning. It gives a presumption in favour of such remains, particularly those of national importance, being preserved *in situ*; and it puts the onus upon the developer to present appropriate evidence of the nature of archaeological remains, which may necessitate funding excavation. Second, allied with a change of philosophy at English Heritage, it has resulted in a move away from large-scale excavation to the protection of sites. Thus, the system 'has responded to changing threats and the growing perception of the nature and extent of the archaeological evidence, but is still rooted in its nineteenth century origins' (Champion 1996: 56).

This can be seen to advantage in the high profile case of the Rose Theatre, remains of which were discovered during development in 1989. The courts held that the Secretary of State was not bound to schedule the remains once identified. He did not do so (though he later changed his mind). Third parties (here including the Rose Theatre Trust Co.) had no legal standing to apply for judicial review. The costs of delaying the approved development were £1 million; the redesigned foundations of the new building added £10 million (Eccles 1990).

THE RISE OF 'HERITAGE'

'Heritage' has become a key word of the late twentieth century, often with negative connotations (Hewison 1987). Yet it is ill-defined, although many have attempted to show how heritage became prominent (Hunter 1996). In the UK, it seems likely that it links with the nineteenth-century emergence of concepts of nationalism and identity, particularly as reflected in landscapes (Lowenthal 1991). This raises the issue of 'heritage', and the idea that there is no 'correct', abstract, conceptualization of what should and should not be retained. 'Heritage' has become an increasingly significant term in the conservation/preservation debate from the early 1980s. Polemics such as Hewison (1987) argue against the rise of 'heritage', the selectivity and sanitization of the images of past places presented, and the dependency on a museum-based industry and culture.

'Heritage' is neither history nor place: it is a process of selection and presentation of aspects of both, for popular consumption (Figure 8.7). 'Heritage is history processed through mythology, ideology, nationalism, local pride, romantic ideas, or just

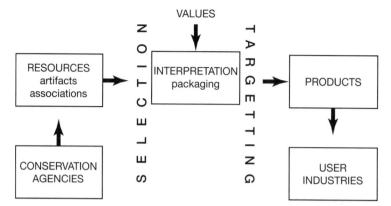

Figure 8.7 The
heritage process
Source: G.J. Ashworth

plain marketing, into a commodity' (Schouten 1995: 21). It is a form of commodification. Therefore, 'heritage' means something quite different from 'conserved relict
historical resources', and selection is central to the process. The management and
interpretation of the past as heritage raises problems: 'some of what now purports to
be heritage has been antiqued, not only in appearance but, rather more sinisterly,
in being presented as if it was significant historically as well as being ennobled by
time' (Fowler 1989: 60). The concepts of conservation and heritage are thus quite
separate, although in recent years there has been a tendency to confuse them.

Ashworth (1994) has suggested that there is a historic progression of ideas and
practices through 'preservation', in the early identification of monuments for retention, to 'conservation', and the involvement of the functioning of entire historic
districts, to 'heritage' with its commodification and consumption, rendering irrelevant earlier concerns over authenticity and historical 'correctness'. This can clearly
be seen in UK practice.

In the UK system, however, there is little awareness of this theoretical debate.
The term 'heritage' was first used in Parliament in the debate on the 1947 Act
(Delafons 1997a: 60). There it rested; subsequent legislation referred to other terms,
including 'civic amenities' (the 1967 Act). The heritage concept was reawakened
with European Architectural Heritage Year (1975), an idea first raised at a conference
in Brussels in 1969 by Sandys. Two of its objectives were to awaken the interest of
the European peoples in their common architectural heritage, and to protect and
enhance buildings and areas of architectural and historic interest.

The term was used in an official publication celebrating the year, compiled by
Lady Dartmouth (DoE 1975). It then resurfaced in what eventually became the
National Heritage Act (1983) although, as the Delafons quote (above) shows, there
was considerable official reluctance to use the term. But not only did it emerge in the
Act's title, it was also embraced in the everyday name of the body thus created:
English Heritage in preference to the formal title of the Historic Buildings and
Monuments Commission for England.

English Heritage (and the later Department of National Heritage) played a key
role during the 1980s and 1990s in extensive debates over the issue of heritage and
its place in planning. Some of these debates took place in the courts as, increasingly,
high-profile cases tested both the wording and interpretation of relevant Acts, but
also – implicitly and explicitly – the heritage concept (the many examples given by
Suddards and Hargreaves, 1996, show the range of this debate). The policy documents issued, principally DoE Circular 8/87 and its 1994 replacement PPG 15 (DoE
1994c), and English Heritage's policy notes (e.g. English Heritage 1995) all clearly
demonstrate the intellectual concept of 'heritage' becoming embedded in practice.

Figure 8.8 Heritage as selected and enhanced: the Barns and Walls conservation area of Swaledale, probably England's largest single conservation area

Source: Reproduced by permission of the Yorkshire Dales National Park

There are issues of selection, improvement (usually termed 'enhancement'), marketing and promotion, and interpretation. Over all, however, is an impression that the implicit values and attitudes remain those of a well educated élite (Thomas 1994).

One area where, arguably, 'heritage' values have outweighed those of preservation/conservation is that of façadism; where an historic wall or shell is retained, behind which a modern structure is constructed (Richards 1994). This has been an increasing trend in the past 15 years; in some cases, as in Birmingham, granted on appeal following refusal of consent by the local planning authority (Barrett and Larkham 1994). This is often successfully argued as the only way of retaining buildings, other options being too costly or impracticable (for related cases see Suddards and Hargreaves 1996: 160). Yet this widespread acceptance is a reversal of the policy shown when an application to demolish some nineteenth-century cottages was approved since any attempt at restoration would 'preserve a shell, but not the outward appearance, ambience or atmosphere of the original dwellings' (Suddards and Hargreaves 1996: 137).

CONSERVATION IN THE CONSERVATIVE YEARS

Is conservation a conceptual juggernaut – slow to get moving, slow to change direction but, having gained momentum, almost impossible to stop? Its origins and the apparently minor impact of the 1947 Act, so fundamental to other areas of planning even today, suggest so. In exploring this issue further it is instructive to review the events of the Thatcher years, which saw such fundamental changes in planning thought and application.

In many respects, conservation since 1979 simply continued along lines already laid down. However, there have been some important developments. The Mentmore Towers sale in 1977 provoked an inquiry by the House of Commons Expenditure Committee and a white paper by the outgoing Labour administration. The new Conservative government then 'moved surprisingly quickly. By the Spring of 1980 a

British Planning

new Act reached the statute book setting up an entirely new body, the National Heritage Memorial Fund, with independent trustees appointed by the Prime Minister' (Gaze 1988: 155). The National Heritage Act of 1983 established a new quango, English Heritage, with a wide range of heritage responsibilities; there are similar organizations for Scotland and Wales. The government felt that 'a more imaginative approach' needing 'commercial and entrepreneurial flair' was needed (DoE 1981), or, as Delafons (1997a: 137) critically comments, 'in the Brave New World, ancient monuments were expected to improve their performance'. English Heritage has emerged as a key, and sometimes controversial, player.

In the 1990 consolidation of planning legislation, the detachment of conservation from the mainstream of planning was epitomized and hallowed by the passing of a separate Planning (Listed Buildings and Conservation Areas) Act. Furthermore, as the planning system moved towards a plan-led system, with the 1991 Planning and Compensation Act (inserting Section 54A into the 1990 Town and Country Planning Act) emphasizing the importance of the development plan in planning decision making, the courts have held that this does not apply to decisions on listed building consent or to conservation area consent (Suddards and Hargreaves 1996: 110). The plan-led system has caused other confusions in conservation planning and policy making (Morton and Ayers 1993; Larkham 1994).

Organizational changes at the central government level further underlined the separateness of conservation, with the creation of an entirely new government department, the Department of National Heritage, taking responsibility for built environment conservation policy from the DoE (which retained planning-related decision making powers). Again, this separation of roles has been potentially confusing; and the new department was castigated as the 'Department of Nothing Happening' (Ravenscroft 1994; Amery 1995). (The renaming of this department by the new Labour administration – as the Department for Culture, Media and Sport – has done little, apart from marginalizing the position of 'national heritage'.) The importance of privatization and market forces, so evident in other aspects of Conservatism, are also evident in the changing role of English Heritage into the 1990s, and the urge to seek funding for conservation from business and community sources or from the new National Lottery.

So the overall direction of conservation under the Conservatives is difficult to elucidate. Certainly there have been notable increases in the numbers of listed buildings and conservation areas. Heritage venues remain as key tourist attractions and income generators. The National Trust, a major non-governmental heritage organization, celebrated its centenary amidst great public fanfare, and the media profile of conservation remains high. Yet much concern has been expressed, in the public media and professional press, over the direction that conservation is taking. Is Britain now dominated by the 'heritage industry'? Do we have too many conservation areas and listed buildings? Are we in danger of leaving important heritage issues, and even monuments, to the mercy of market forces?

CONCLUSIONS

This chapter has, somewhat unfairly, focused largely on conservation in England. Scotland has its own system, and Historic Scotland has a similar role to that of English Heritage; but the problems are similar: Horne (1993), for example, argues that vernacular buildings are under-represented in the listing procedure. Wales has virtually adopted the English system, save that the Secretary of State for Wales has not issued the equivalent of Planning Policy Guidance Notes; the relevant quango is

CADW (the Welsh word for preservation), which again has not issued detailed guidance in the manner of English Heritage. In Northern Ireland, conservation is largely in the hands of the DoE (Northern Ireland), including the designation of conservation areas; here, a very different view is taken compared to individual local planning authorities in the remainder of the UK, and the province has only some 50 areas (Hendry 1993).

Three decades of operating the UK conservation area system suggest that this is a strong and popular planning concept, and it is likely to continue. Designations will continue; new and different types of area will be designated, and minor amendments to the system can be expected. It is far from perfect, but has also suffered far less adverse criticism than have other area-based conservation systems. Fifty years of the listed building system result in similar conclusions: it is not perfect, but well understood and adequate in most cases.

Clearly, one important aspect in the development of these systems has been the reliance on key people in key positions at the right time. These have included Crossman, Sandys and Kennet, together with other MPs who have moved private members' bills ever since Lubbock in the 1870s. For conservation is rarely an issue felt by governments as being deserving of parliamentary time. This reliance upon the individual can, clearly, be a weakness – as shown by the lack of motivation in the DoE to progress the first listing, until the advent of Heseltine in 1980.

Various reviews of the conservation systems have been undertaken. That of the Preservation Policy Group under the chair of Lord Kennet merely tinkered with grant regimes, finding that 'what are needed are not more powers but the will, the skill, and the money to use the powers that already exist' (MHLG 1970a). More recently, in reviewing the character of conservation areas for the Royal Town Planning Institute, the author and colleagues were repeatedly warned by the Institute's steering group not to suggest radical legislative changes, for which there was no prospect of parliamentary time being made available. Most recently, there has been a heritage green paper (Department of National Heritage 1996) seeking public reaction to a range of questions. Although it suggests some worthwhile, largely minor, amendments, Delafons (1997a: 189) is rather critical of its general thrust: 'it steers well clear of any wider policy matters' such as are discussed in this chapter. Interestingly, Theresa Gorman MP, fresh from her brush with the LBC system, commented that

> it's really an eye-opener because it takes for granted that the role of the government is to interfere and protect listed buildings ... the tone of the document is extremely authoritarian, without hardly a note of the fact that what we are talking about is privately owned property from which the state has removed the rights of the owner (Hirst 1996: 3).

Perhaps Mrs Gorman, who pleaded ignorance and overwork in her own case, is equally ignorant of the entire thrust of 50 years of planning control? Although the 'lively debate' that the document wished to encourage did occur, no conclusions have been forthcoming.

Reviewing the operation of the system, particularly its popularity and its procedural and definitional shortcomings, one might suggest some alternative future directions. First might be 'designate and be damned', retaining the current system on the grounds of its successes in identifying and designating monuments, buildings and areas. But, as we have seen, the system has its shortcomings. Secondly might be the 'Section 54A' approach, with the explicit recognition and justification in development plans of all conservation-related policies, and with judicious review and refinement of the legal definitions and policy mechanisms. More radically might be the free-market initiative, the blanket removal of all conservation controls (the 'Circular 22/80 philosophy', after the Conservative circular arguing against aesthetic control). This is an extreme view and, however plausible in terms of the patterns of past urban development, will not find public or political favour at present. Conservation is still too high on the public agenda. But for how long?

Of major importance has been the development of strong links between conservation (including preservation) and the emerging discipline of urban design, reflected in the coverage of standard texts on the subject (Manley and Guise 1998) and the explicit recognition of the place of familiar and valued historic monuments and landscapes in achieving high-quality new urban design (Parfect and Power 1997). Conservation issues are very common in urban design-related control and advisory mechanisms such as design guides (Chapman and Larkham 1992) which themselves form a considerable extension of the spirit of the 1947 planning control system.

Further, increasingly, conservation has become linked to the concept of sustainability, which is implicit in aspects of PPG 15 including its focus on economic and transport-related issues. Delafons (1997b: 118), however, criticizes the lack of explicit recognition of this issue, partly because conservation and town planning 'have tended to drift apart in recent years'. In theory at least, the wise use and reuse of the existing spatial and cultural resources, and the investment of past generations, found in historic areas and buildings 'has more in common with the aims of sustainable development. . . Indeed, it can be argued that the historic city in many ways is a model for a sustainable city' (Manley and Guise 1998: 86). English Heritage (1997)

Key principles of sustainability

Developing stronger understanding of the historic environment and promoting wide awareness of its role in modern life

Taking a long-term view of our actions

Looking at the environment as a whole

Achieving greater public involvement in making decisions about society's needs and the environment

Deciding which elements of the environment are

    (i) to be conserved at all costs ('critical' assets)
    (ii) subject to limited change provided that the overall character of the resource is maintained ('constant' assets)
    (iii) suitable for exchange in return for other benefits ('tradable' assets)

Keeping our activities to levels which do not permanently damage the historic environment

Ensuring that decisions about the historic environment are made on the basis of the best possible information

Figure 8.9
Developing the
concept of
sustainable
conservation

Heritage values to consider

Source: English
Heritage – *Sustaining
the Historic
Environment: New
Perspectives on the
Future*, 1997

Cultural values
Educational and academic values
Economic values
Resource values
Recreational values
Aesthetic values

has begun work on this issue, recognizing the need in particular for a long-term management perspective Figure 8.9. I would argue that the future of UK conservation surely lies in these last two areas: development of a concept of sustainable conservation, and linking conservation with urban design and promoting its contribution to the creation of high quality places.

The 1947 Act, and the general acceptance of state control over development that it engendered, has been an enduring cornerstone of the UK conservation system: its influence gradually permeating the areas of monument, building and area conservation. That underlying control mechanism has not been problematic. On the other hand, a key difficulty with UK conservation has been that 'there is no real or consistent policy' on conservation and this reflects 'the absence of any philosophy of conservation' (Harvey 1954). This call has been regularly repeated (Worskett 1982; Larkham 1996b, ch. 11) but there seems no immediate likelihood of such an approach – even after over a century of monument conservation and half a century of the 1947-based system.

ACKNOWLEDGEMENTS

Parts of this paper are developed from the author's review papers in the *Journal of Urban Design* (1996a) and the *Transactions of the Ancient Monuments Society* (1997). Others have benefited from joint work with Dr Andrew Jones (Chesterton Consulting) and Dr Heather Barrett (Worcester University College).

FURTHER READING

In a chapter of this length one is forced to skate over many fascinating and relevant details. The reader is referred to John Delafons' recent detailed account of an insider's view of the official position: *(Politics and Preservation: A Policy History of the Built Heritage 1882–1996* (1997a). This volume provides the best available historical overview from the perspective of a senior civil servant; though it is intentionally focused on that view: the activities and ambitions of other agencies are not covered. Some of the thematic essays in Hunter (1996) *Preserving the Past: The Rise of Heritage in Modern Britain* are also valuable: this is a very readable collection of essays on specific aspects of UK conservation, from monuments to conservation societies. It contains an excellent comprehensive bibliographical essay by the editor. A broad, authoritative review of the past and its interpretation and use as 'heritage' is given by Lowenthal (1985) *The Past is a Foreign Country*. In *Our Vanishing Heritage*, Binney (1984), a key pro-conservation campaigner, provides a case study view of how UK conservation actually works – or does not. Probably the most comprehensive overview of the UK system (omitting the legal minutiae of the legal texts) is Pickard's *Conservation in the Built Environment* (1996). Comprehensive legal texts are Suddards and Hargreaves (1996) *Listed Buildings* (which, despite the title, covers the whole range of conservation issues) and Mynors (1995) *Listed Buildings and Conservation Areas*. An overview by the present author of conservation from the broader perspective of urban morphology, including some overseas comparisons, is Larkham (1996b) *Conservation and the City*. Robertson (1993) 'Listed buildings: the national resurvey of England' is a very useful detailed commentary on the politics and practices of the resurvey, with comments from a wide range of participants.

English Heritage produces a range of helpful shorter documents – discussion documents and policy guidelines – including *Conservation Area Practice* (1995), *The Monuments Protection Programme 1986–96* (1996), *Developing Guidelines for the Management of Listed Buildings* (1996), *Something Worth Keeping? Postwar Architecture in England* (1996), *Conservation Area Appraisal* (1997a) and *Sustaining the Historic Environment* (1997b).

chapter 9

British Planning in its European Context

VINCENT NADIN

INTRODUCTION

Until the 1990s, the idea of a European dimension to town and country planning would have been considered rather esoteric, but global economic and social forces spurred on by increased political and economic integration mean that it is no longer possible for any European country to plan in isolation. Even those who would deny this cannot escape the growing influence of the European Union (EU) in environmental protection, regional policy, sustainable development and the spatial coordination of Community sectoral policy.[1]

This chapter opens with a discussion of the early stages of European integration since the second world war. The focus then shifts to the major planning initiatives that have a European dimension, and the ways in which these have influenced – and also been influenced by – the UK. The impact that 'Europe' has had on planning in the UK can be divided into five periods (Davies *et al.* 1994). These follow the important steps in European integration as marked by the signing of European Treaties, which also correspond to significant increments in European planning related initiatives. The landmark events which separate the periods in this chronology are the accession of the UK to the European Community in 1973; the Single European Act in 1987; the Maastricht Treaty on European Union, and the signing of the Amsterdam Treaty in 1997.

THE CREATION OF THE COMMUNITY 1947–72

Contrary to popular myth, the UK has been a consistent and strong advocate of European integration in the interests of securing a lasting peace. After the war, Winston Churchill went so far as to call for the creation of a 'United States of Europe' (Tillotson 1996). Of course, he did not anticipate that the UK would be part of the integration process. Instead, Britain would lead the building of a continental economic federation whilst retaining its own liberty in favour of maintaining stronger links with the USA and the Commonwealth. Britain also emphasized working at the European level through other looser groupings such as the European Free Trade Association, the Organisation for Economic Cooperation and Development, and the Council of Europe. But, in the face of an increasing balance of trade deficit and a weakening pound, pragmatism won over chauvinism, and the first application was made to join the Community in 1958.

De Gaulle vetoed this first application, and it was not until 1973 that the UK eventually joined. By then, the circumstances were very different. Membership came at the cost of onerous economic conditions, and the negative effects were exacerbated by the oil crisis. The result was that Britain did not benefit economically from the early years of EC membership. Disputes over accession and the limited immediate benefit of joining hardened anti-Community sentiment in some quarters, and fuelled entrenched attitudes of autonomy which linger today (Radice 1992; Ward 1996).

The early years of the Community were dominated by economic questions, which had little direct impact on planning, but which have significant spatial development implications in the longer term. In particular, rapid integration in the agricultural sector through the Common Agricultural Policy (CAP) provided price guarantees to farmers to increase productivity and improve agricultural standards of living. This set in train a systematic and progressive loss of habitats, valued natural environments and landscape features as financial incentives led to higher demands for agricultural production (Cheshire 1985, Potter 1998). UK planners, with very limited powers over rural change, have had to watch from the sidelines, although intense lobbying from environmental interests eventually brought reforms to the CAP in the 1980s.

There was no official recognition that Community membership might extend beyond the economic sphere into other areas of public policy, although the foundations for broader action were already being put into place. The Paris Summit of 1972 prepared the path for UK entry, and was also the point at which the European Commission began a campaign to expand its competences into other fields such as the environment. Again there was only limited impact initially, but the effects were to be felt during the 1980s with major consequences for town and country planning.

At this time, it was the Council of Europe that provided the main arena for progress on the European dimension to planning. It established a Conference of European Ministers of Aménagement du Territoire (CEMAT) which has since provided a forum for discussion of planning issues by its members (now numbering 40). CEMAT began work on a European regional/spatial planning strategy to cover the whole of Europe. The rationale was simply that a common approach was needed to regional planning so that European integration did not aggravate existing geographical differences (Williams 1996). The UK played its part in those discussions, but the lead was taken elsewhere. In planning law and practice, Britain was taking a different course from that of most other European countries.

The Town and Country Planning Act of 1947 replaced the legally binding prewar planning 'schemes' with a system of development plans and development control characterized by a high degree of discretion. Most other countries continued to operate a legally binding zoning system. The significance of this parting of the ways has perhaps been overstated, since in practice, zoning systems are often implemented with considerable flexibility (see Booth, chapter 3). Nevertheless, it should be noted that, apart from academic studies, there was little if any consideration of how planning in the UK compared to that in other countries – a situation that has barely changed today.

THE ENTRY OF THE UK INTO THE EC 1973–85

Ireland and Denmark joined at the same time as the UK, extending both the territory and range of interests in the Community. Over the next 15 years, the influence of the EC steadily increased, especially in raising awareness about the transnational nature of environmental problems and regional economic disparities. The

Community began taking action in the environment field, and adopted the *First Action Programme on the Environment*, although acting on general provisions in the Treaty rather than on any specific legislative base. The accession of Greece in 1981, and Portugal and Spain in 1986, sharpened the contrasts in economic and environmental conditions among regions, with British regions beginning to make (not always favourable) comparisons with others in Europe.

The Council of Europe's work on spatial planning continued with the adoption of the *European/Regional Planning Charter* (1983) (known as the Torremolinos Charter), making a strong case for effective planning at the supranational (European) and transnational (between countries) levels. The Council also saw a European dimension in domestic planning issues, and in 1980 began the *European Campaign for Urban Renaissance* with a programme of ad hoc conferences, various reports and 'resolutions' on such matters as health in towns, the regeneration of industrial towns, and community development. A 1992 conference adopted the *European Urban Charter*, promoting principles of good urban management at local level. The principles relate to a wide range of issues, including transport and mobility, environment and nature in towns, the physical form of cities, and urban security and crime prevention. Both the idea of the supranational planning and a European role in urban management have been adopted by the EU in more recent years.

During the early years of its Community membership, the UK planning and local government systems were reformed, but there was no serious attempt to decide what type of authority might best realize the opportunities offered by Europe (Barber and Millns 1993: 13). The characteristics of local government structure in the UK – much larger local authorities than most comparable countries, and no regional tier – helps to explain many of the differences in approach to planning. Trends in planning practice tended to widen the gap between the UK and other countries. Public sector spending restraints and free-market ideology shifted the balance of the UK planning systems in favour of business and enterprise, and the private sector became more significant in facilitating development and infrastructure provision. Comparable north European countries continued much longer with a strongly public sector led development process, although they were to follow suit in later years.

The general influence of European integration, and actions of the Community began to be felt in the planning profession as elsewhere. On the surface, successive governments made much public show of defending the sovereignty of Britain against European federalism, whilst in reality recognizing the inevitability of European integration and signing up to waves of new European legislation. The recognition of economic realities and the need to facilitate European integration was evident in the most important 'European decision' of this period – the agreement to build the Channel Tunnel. This aside, there was little awareness at the time of how influential the Community was becoming in shaping domestic law and policy.

AFTER THE SINGLE EUROPEAN ACT 1986–91

The Single European Act of 1986 marked the start of a much more intensive period of European legislation and action, which was to have major impacts on development and planning in the UK through environmental, urban, transport and regional economic policy. Its main objective was to get the faltering programme of economic integration back on track and the completion of the single market (Ward 1996). Although the provisions for environment and transport policy may seem more relevant, it is the contribution that the Act made to the single market and laying the foundations for monetary union that may eventually be seen as its most important consequence for spatial planning. The spatial development implications of economic integration are fundamental, although as yet poorly understood.

The immediate effect of the Single European Act was widely felt. This is the period when many UK planners first became familiar with the workings of the European Commission. Local authorities started to recruit European officers and set up offices in Brussels. The objective was to secure a share of the structural funds – the principal regional policy instrument of the Community. The Act gave a major boost to the funding of European regional policy: the Community budget was increased substantially, with half the increase going to the strengthening of structural and regional policy to address disparities. Between 1989 and 1999, the funds will amount to 200 billion ecu – about £140 billion, or nearly £400 for each person in the Community, although this is concentrated in areas that can benefit most from Community funding. Two thirds of funding has gone to *Objective 1* areas (lagging behind in development). In the UK, only the Highlands and Islands, Merseyside and Northern Ireland qualify. The other objectives which are limited in their territorial application are *Objective 2* (declining industrial areas) and *Objective 5b* (vulnerable rural areas). The UK has benefited extensively from both, although designation presents some anomalies; for example, the Highlands and Islands has not been designated for assisted area status in the UK (Coombes 1994).

The structural funds are largely responsible for the 'European dimension' finding its way into the activities of many planning authorities (and a few consultancies have carved out a niche in the field too), but whether there was any fundamental impact on the planning systems and policy in the UK is questionable. Until recently, the single programming documents which set out the priorities for Community investment have rarely mentioned the spatial dimension of investment. The structural funding and development planning processes often appear quite separate, operating as they do on very different timescales. For the most part, the impact of structural funding has been to emphasize Europe as another source of money, rather than as an instrument for shaping spatial or planning policies and systems. In other countries, efforts were underway to ensure that the planning system played a more central role in coordinating investment decisions.

Other direct impacts on planning arose from the environmental provisions in the Single European Act and the steady flow of European legislation on environmental policy that followed. The Act extended the powers of the EC so that it could more effectively promote common actions designed to 'preserve and protect the quality of the environment and ... ensure the prudent and rational utilisation of natural resources'. The well known Directives on environmental assessment (1985 and 1997), wild birds (1979) and natural habitats (1992) are probably the best known European law amongst planners. It should be remembered here that the process of influence is not one-way: the UK has played an active role in the formulation of EU environmental law and policy, and the wild birds Directive, for example, drew heavily from British experience. This was a busy period for legislators, and other directives on metrication, public procurement, drinking water, waste and the recognition of professional qualifications have all had effects on planning practice in the UK.

From the late 1980s, the main arena for debate in western Europe on the European dimension to planning moved from the Council of Europe to the Community. The Commission's *Directorate General XVI: Regional Policy and Cohesion (DG XVI)* took up the cause, strongly encouraged by some member states. In 1989, the French government planning agency DATAR published an analysis of European spatial development trends, drawing attention to the increasing concentration of economic growth in the heartland of Europe – the now infamous 'blue banana' – a belt of cities stretching from London through the Benelux and Germany to northern Italy. The report spelled out the implications for spatial development in France, much of which is outside the core area of economic activity. French national spatial and transport policies have since been directed at bringing France closer to the centre of Europe. The Dutch government followed with its own analysis of development in northern Europe and called for spatial planning at the Community level to ensure the maximum benefit from the single market and EC investment. Whilst UK government departments were not enthusiastic about supranational spatial planning, the European Commission was, unsurprisingly, a keen advocate, and in 1991 published its own analysis of the changing patterns of spatial development in *Europe 2000* (CEC 1991).

Europe 2000 was intended to provide a reference point for planners working on their national and regional policies, providing planners with information and understanding of the wider processes shaping spatial development and change at the European scale (Martin 1992). It marks the point at which the process of incorporating a stronger spatial dimension to Community policy began in earnest. Eight transnational regions were identified which, it was argued, exhibited similar spatial development characteristics and problems, and these became the focus for further studies. Three transnational regions involved the UK – the Centre Capitals, the North Sea, and the Atlantic Seaboard (as shown in Figure 9.1). Increasing international cooperation between local authorities in the UK with partners overseas within these regions was accelerated through the *Europe 2000* studies.

The rationale for the EU interest in spatial development planning is simple and convincing. The fundamental goals of the Community are economic and political cohesion, the balanced development of economic activities and standards of living amongst its member states and, since 1997, sustainable development. It is axiomatic that these goals have a spatial dimension – not least the great disparities in wealth, jobs, investment and access to services across different regions. Some disparities, especially between the north and the south, are widening. Economic and political forces will ensure that they continue to do so. Mobile business continues to concentrate in the core cities, with decline in peripheral regions and those hardest hit by the economic recession of the early 1990s (CEC 1994). The single European market tends to reinforce such trends.

The Community response through regional policy funding had grown to account for more than a third of the total Community budget, with recognized impacts on economic growth and development patterns (CEC 1996a). Other Community policies such as transport and the environment also had very significant spatial impacts. Thus, by the 1980s, the Community was, in one sense, already heavily engaged in spatial planning. Certainly, Community actions have considerable impact on spatial development patterns and the quality of places. But there was, and perhaps still is, little coordination of the spatial impacts of Community policies as a whole, and Community and member state policies do not always act in concert (CEC 1994). Therefore, the argument is that coordinating Community and member state policies around a spatial strategy at the European level would have benefits in increasing their efficiency and effectiveness.

It is important to note that the Commission is primarily concerned with spatial planning rather than town and country planning (which strictly describes only the UK system). Spatial planning in its European sense, and as used by the Community, means the coordination of all policy fields that have spatial objectives or impacts. Town and country or land-use planning is an important policy field, but it is only one. Spatial planning seeks to coordinate the spatial impacts of all sectoral policy such as

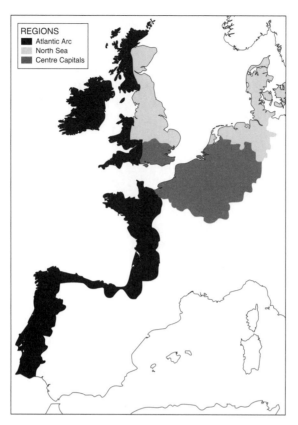

Figure 9.1 The
Transnational
Regional Study
Areas involving
the UK (from
Europe 2000)

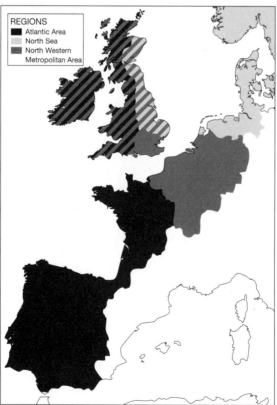

Figure 9.2 The
Transnational
Interreg IIc Regions
involving the UK

land use, transport, environment, regional, agriculture and others. It is an integrating activity, ideally providing an umbrella of spatial strategy within which other sectors operate. Spatial planning is also used as a generic term for all European planning systems, such as *aménagement du territoire* in France, *ruimtelijke ordening* in the Netherlands and *Raumordnung* in Germany. All forms of spatial planning are undertaken with the aim of creating a more rational organization of land uses and the linkages between them, but some have a much broader scope similar to the Community idea of spatial planning, whilst others are more narrow, such as planning in the UK. The term spatial planning has not been widely employed in the UK and, until very recently, there has been some resistance to the idea in government.

EU ministers responsible for spatial/regional planning in the member states have met since 1989, and on a regular six-monthly cycle as an informal Council since 1992 (Williams 1996). Such meetings are not part of the Council because it has taken the view that the Treaty does not give it competence to take action on spatial planning. As a result, the meeting cannot make any recommendations in respect of Commission proposals for legislation, but it has certainly provided an impetus to further cooperation on supranational planning. In response to a Dutch proposal in 1991, the informal meeting of ministers agreed to set up a Committee on Spatial Development (CSD) comprising senior bureaucrats from each member state and the Commission. The UK delegation has included civil servants from the DETR, the DTI and the Scottish Office. Working through an informal committee where the Community has no competence (intergovernmental working) is common practice, and in other fields has been recognized as one method by which the Community has explored and prepared for the extension of its competence (Edwards and Spence 1997: 17).

Intergovernmental working is slow. All parties need to agree any action, and the chair and leadership role change with each presidency. The close involvement of DG XVI does give some impetus and continuity, but its formal standing on the Committee is uncertain and the intergovernmental process has been criticized for delaying action on supranational planning, which might have been promoted more effectively had the Commission more competence in this field (Wulf-Mathies 1998). The UK has been a strong voice against any transfer of sovereignty to the Community, and disagreements between the UK and other member states about the form and content of any supranational spatial planning policy has been a major feature of the CSD.

During this period, UK local authorities particularly affected by European integration also established programmes of cooperation with neighbouring countries – in some cases with the incentive of European funding. International cooperation on planning was already established in some parts of Europe (although with varying levels of effectiveness) but this was a new venture for Britain.

Local authorities have also been keen to promote transnational networks with places sharing similar types of planning problems. The networks have helped local governments to learn from experiences elsewhere, to stimulate innovation, and perhaps most importantly, to lobby for resources for their particular problems (Parkinson 1992). The largest networks are the *Eurocities*, which provide a forum for exchange of experience and promote the interests of European cities to European institutions. Many others have emerged to cater for specific interests, such as the *Commission de Villes* which represents small and medium sized cities, *METREX* for spatial planning authorities in the major metropolitan regions; and *Quartier en Crise* (neighbourhoods in crisis) which addresses the problem of urban renewal and regeneration.

The education sector has led the development of international collaboration on planning, making extensive use of the *Socrates–Erasmus* initiatives launched in 1987 for funding staff and student exchanges, and curriculum development. The significance of European integration and understanding of other planning systems are now more prominent features of initial planning education, and specialist postgraduate education is becoming available. There is a steady supply of graduates with some experience in Europe who are able to assist planning authorities to make the most of transnational collaboration, but this is not reflected at higher levels. In comparison with other countries, few senior planning officers have a grounding in European matters or transnational planning, a situation which applies across the whole of the public sector in the UK. British applicants have been less successful in gaining jobs in the Commission, despite government initiatives to help prepare civil servants for the admission process. So far only one local authority planner has been seconded to the Commission. Nevertheless, planning authorities, consultancies and planning schools did establish effective European links during the late 1980s which are now well established. As by far the largest body of professional planners in western Europe, the Royal Town Planning Institute also took the lead in helping to set up the European Council of Town Planners (ECTP), which now formally represents the interests of the profession to Community institutions.

ESTABLISHING THE EUROPEAN UNION 1992–96

The Maastricht Treaty (on European Unity) of 1992 gave a further boost to transnational cooperation on planning by strengthening the commitment to cohesion within what has since been described as the European Union. It is perhaps best known in planning circles because it introduced into the English version of the treaty the actual words 'town and country planning' and 'land use'. This was seized upon by some advocates of increased European action on planning, but in fact it was introduced to ensure that whenever the Council enacts environmental legislation affecting town and country planning and land use (and the other matters mentioned) it has to be by unanimity and not by qualified majority (Bastrup-Birk and Doucet 1997). It was not introduced to give the Community any competence in town and country or land use planning. The Commission has stressed on several occasions that it does not have a competence to act directly either in town and country planning or spatial planning (although it might justify action under general provisions). Nevertheless, from the early 1990s, planning in the UK has been increasingly affected by Community initiatives supported by the structural funds; European legislation in other sectors, especially environment and transport; and in a more informal way through the many studies undertaken by the Commission (Davies *et al.* 1994; Institute for European Environmental Policy 1998).

The treaty gave added impetus to regional policy measures to tackle disparities and promote economic competitiveness. This paved the way for a much larger share of Community funding being allocated through the structural funds. Another significant development was the setting up of the Committee of the Regions (CoR), a consultative body which gives local and regional government a stronger voice in EU affairs. This Committee has taken great interest in regional and spatial planning: it has become a strong advocate of increased funding to support transnational planning actions, and increased coordination of spatial policy at the European level.

The signing of the Maastricht Treaty coincided with the 1992 Earth Summit and its strategy for the implementation of the sustainable development concept through Agenda 21. It strengthened the environmental protection powers of the EU and provided a basis for a Community response to Agenda 21 in the *Fifth Environmental*

Action Programme: Towards Sustainability. A very ambitious and positive set of measures were proposed, focusing on the anticipation of problems and the precautionary principle, and identifying the key tools for achieving more sustainable development. Town and country planning is identified as a principal means for promoting change. *Towards Sustainability* made commitments for action up to the end of the century, many of which affect local planning authorities (Morphet 1993) including the strategic environmental assessment of all spatial plans, policies and programmes. The review of planning policy guidance in England was undertaken with this and other emerging principles in mind, with the result, for example, that development plans should now be subject to environmental appraisal, although there is as yet no formal requirement in European legislation.

Towards Sustainability developed ideas first presented in the *Green Paper on the Urban Environment* (CEC 1990). This was an initiative of the Environment Directorate of the Commission together with a number of European cities who wished to move the balance in Community policy from rural to urban areas. The green paper led to the establishment of the *EU Expert Group on the Urban Environment*, on which the UK has played a prominent role. The main product of the expert group's work was the *European Sustainable Cities Report* (CEC 1996d) which makes recommendations on how the concept of sustainability can be applied in urban areas, and on the institutional capacity of local government to deliver sustainability. The expert group also organized the first European Sustainable Cities Conference and the creation of the *European Sustainable Cities and Towns Campaign* which many UK local authorities have joined. These activities contributed to a much stronger urban dimension in the *Towards Sustainability* programme, which has more recently been taken up by the Regional Policy Directorate.

The Commission continued its work programme on spatial development patterns in Europe and in 1994 published *Europe 2000+*, taking forward the Commission's thinking on spatial development with a focus on problems of urban sprawl more typical of southern Europe. But there were also messages for the UK, especially in the document's advocacy of 'decentralised concentration' and polycentric urban systems. The nature of thinking here may be as important as the content. Although Britain may claim some success in the physical containment of cities, concepts of spatial structure are less widely employed or understood in the UK, and even by the late 1990s there is limited understanding of spatial development patterns and trends at the national and regional levels in comparison with comparable countries in northern Europe. The British systems of forward planning concentrates more on the amount of development; much less attention has been paid to questions of 'urban structure', although the sustainability debate has recently brought this into focus. *Europe 2000+* also summarized the findings from the transnational regional studies (CEC 1995, 1996b, 1996c). Perhaps their most important effect was simply to raise awareness of the Community's interest in planning in the UK (and the scenario maps showing regional development trends in the UK were certainly a surprise to many planners) and also to demonstrate that spatial development trends in the UK are closely interlinked with those of its neighbours.

Also in 1994, the German government presented the first paper to the Committee on Spatial Development on a *European Spatial Development Perspective* (ESDP). The proposal took forward the earlier work of the Council of Europe (CoE) for a supranational spatial planning framework establishing principles for spatial development in the interests of social and economic cohesion. The German paper (known as the Leipzig principles) established agreements on the significance of spatial planning in pursuing the objectives of social and economic cohesion; the overriding need to ensure that future growth was sustainable and balanced; and the need to respect the principle of subsidiarity, with policies being non-binding on member states (Committee on Spatial Development 1994). The UK's position reflected the politics of the time, with reservations being made about the references to the contribution of spatial development to economic and social cohesion, and the implementation of Community policies.

The Treaty of Rome gave the Community competence to produce a common transport policy, but until 1992 there had only been limited action. The Maastricht Treaty made the creation of guidelines for European networks in energy, telecommunications, and transport a specific task for the Community. It also provided for Community funding to support their development. The transport strategy builds on existing or proposed national routes within the EU and linkages outside the EU territory. It identifies 14 priority transport projects of common interest. EU intervention has been mostly restricted to facilitation and coordination in the transport field, but there is a growing concern that national and regional development policies should make the most of the emerging trans-European networks and support cross-border cooperation. German reunification, the transition to market economies in central and eastern Europe, and the accession of the three relatively peripheral countries in 1995, Austria, Finland and Sweden, also drew attention to the need to improve linkages beyond the core of Europe and to external countries. This trend will not work in favour of the UK, although the likely consequences have not yet been widely discussed.

THE AMSTERDAM TREATY AND BEYOND 1997–

The Amsterdam Treaty prepares the Community's institutions for enlargement and extends its competences in employment, social policy and justice. The main planning issues are the provisions that make sustainable development one of the Union's objectives and require that environmental protection be integrated into the definition and implementation of other Community policies. In addition, the European Commission has undertaken to prepare an environmental impact assessment for any proposal which has significant environmental implications. The effect of these changes will be to provide more weight to sustainability and environmental considerations in Community policy and to help tackle contradictions in actions supported by the Commission which damage the environment. They will also give the Commission more power in challenging member states where they fail to implement Community environmental measures. More than 500 actions are now being taken to make up the backlog. Decision making on environmental measures is also simplified, but unanimity is still required for measures concerning town and country planning.

In 1997, the First Official Draft of the *ESDP* was published (CEC 1997a). Until this date, under a Conservative administration, the UK was a reluctant partner in this venture, but the publication of the draft coincided with the new Labour administration and its more positive stance on Europe. The UK government has since instituted a review of its relations with Europe in all policy areas seeking a more effective role for the UK. Before the start of the UK Presidency in the first half of 1998, planning minister Richard Caborn expressed enthusiasm for the ESDP, saying that it 'could make a significant contribution to achieving sustainable development throughout Europe'. He committed the UK government to preparing a revised and more complete version for presentation at the end of the UK Presidency. That the UK government should take such a positive attitude to this type of transnational cooperation on planning would have been unthinkable only a year before. In the event, the UK's proposals for revising and simplifying the text were not all to the liking of other member states, and the *Complete Draft of the European Spatial Development Perspective* (CEC 1998) was not very different from the original. It has proved particular difficult to reach agreement on policy, and the question of what spatial planning needs to be addressed at the European level is still very much open to debate.

Whilst the CSD has debated the form and content of the ESDP, the European Commission has used its funding powers to provide strong incentives for regional and local government to engage in transnational spatial planning from the bottom up. One initiative provides 415 million ecu (11 million for the UK) for innovative transnational actions on spatial planning. This is an extension to the programme for cross-border cooperation but in this case, and for the first time, European funding is specifically targeted at spatial planning initiatives (though much is earmarked for planning measures on flood and drought). The programme is intended to foster common territorial development policies and to improve the impact of Community policies on spatial development. The UK will be involved in three transnational groupings based on the mega-regions defined for the Europe 2000 studies, though now substantially altered, as shown in Figures 9.1 and 9.2. The content of the operational programmes that will guide the bidding process and allocation of funds follow closely the agenda of the ESDP in a top-down relationship. It remains to be seen what projects will come forward and be funded in the much more bottom-up process of formulating proposals.

The Amsterdam Treaty also makes recommendations in relation to the impact of enlargement, taken forward in the Community document *Agenda 2000*.[2] The cost of assistance to the accession countries is estimated at 75 billion ecu. However, since no significant increase to the Community budget would be allowed by member states, the outcome has to be a major readjustment of policy and spending. There are two major implications for planning in the UK – a reorganization of the structural funds and a reduction in the number of Community initiatives, with much more emphasis on spatial planning and coordination of policy. It is proposed that the objectives for structural funds be reduced, with greater concentration of resources and stricter enforcement of the criteria for eligibility. There will be major changes in the UK, although they will be mitigated to some extent by a transition phase which will assist areas no longer eligible for funding. The UK receives £9 billion in the current round of structural funding, and if Northern Ireland and the Highlands are to lose their objective 1 status, which seems likely, much of this could be lost (Healy 1998), although South Yorkshire, Cornwall and London may benefit from the changes.

Of special interest to planning in *Agenda 2000* is the proposal to reduce the 13 Community initiatives to only three, including one on 'cross-border and transnational inter-regional cooperation to promote harmonious and balanced spatial planning' and a second on 'rural development'. New initiatives will provide considerable opportunity for the UK planning authorities to establish partnerships on spatial planning with others overseas. The emphasis on Community involvement in the relatively prosperous countries is switching from funding support (although it will be maintained in the most deprived areas) to spatial planning and the coordination of Community and member state policies.

Whilst now more positive on the ESDP, and the notions of supranational and transnational planning, the UK approach to the European dimension is still distinctive in comparison with many of its partners. The discretionary, programmatic and private sector planning culture in the UK contrasts with the more directive and public sector dominated forms of planning elsewhere in Europe. The UK contribution is also hindered to some extent by its narrow focus on land-use planning. This is a feature of other systems, but there has been less willingness in the UK to address a broader spatial planning approach in addition to land use, except perhaps for a period of regional planning in Scotland. There is certainly no experience of spatial planning at a national level in the UK in the way it is undertaken in other countries. No national government policy is expressed in any spatial form (again with minor exceptions for Scotland). Even the spatial expression of regional planning guidance is mostly limited to descriptions of existing patterns.

At the transnational level, island geography has until recently sheltered the UK from the most obvious cross-border and transnational spatial development problems that have been recognized for many years in northern Europe. Thus, whilst the UK government recognizes the value of international planning collaboration, it tends to emphasize the value of agreeing general planning principles and the potential of exchanges of experience in dealing with common planning problems, rather than the adoption of universal planning policies and their expression in map form. In the Netherlands, Germany and France (which have led the European spatial planning debate) regional and national plans are much more explicit in setting out a preferred spatial strategy for development.

It should be emphasized that these differences in approach are not necessarily the product of anti-European sentiment (although particular ministers may have given this impression). The approach to planning in the UK is a product of historical, legal, socioeconomic, political and, above all, cultural factors which are particular to this country, as they are to any other country. The UK has a particularly strong tradition of an independent and professional civil service (including planners), of discretion in public administration and planning, of a single and central source of power in government, and of finding pragmatic solutions to planning problems. This is not the place to elaborate on the situation in other countries, suffice to say that it will take considerable time and effort for different viewpoints to converge.

THE FUTURE

Over the next few years, European funding will support many more transnational spatial planning projects. They will encourage and contribute to an analysis of the position of the UK regions in European spatial development, and raise awareness of the characteristics of the British approach to town and country planning in comparison with other countries. The lack of institutional capacity and appropriate instruments at the regional and national levels in the UK will become more evident. European collaboration will contribute to increased regional autonomy in deciding priorities and providing for a territorial dimension to the allocation of public expenditure rather than solely the aspatial, departmental budgets used by the Treasury (Roberts and Hart 1994).

In the longer term, the notion of transnational planning strategies will become well accepted. Structural funding will be reviewed, and the areas eligible will be reduced, with a greater concentration of resources. Authorities with a stake in the structural funds will start to look very hard at the relationship between development plans, funding bids and European planning policy. It will be essential to build a closer relationship between funding programmes (especially EU funds) and town and country planning. This means that government will have to embrace spatial planning as well as land-use planning, although it is to be hoped that this is not done by tacking more responsibilities on to the already overloaded development plans (see Davies, chapter 4).

The economic discipline now being exercised across Europe in order to meet the economic convergence criteria has important consequences, not least in the way that governments are looking increasingly to the private sector to provide development and infrastructure. As a leader in this field, there may be lessons and warnings that the UK can offer. Other countries will certainly seek to learn from UK experience in managing private sector investment and partnerships. But there is also an important lesson from monetary union for UK planners. It seems strange that some planners can so easily dismiss the idea of convergence of planning systems as unlikely or even impossible when there are so many examples of convergence and even harmonization in other sectors, not least fiscal policy and regulation. There will undoubtedly be a tendency towards further harmonization as countries work together: in many cases, this will be no more than a continuation of the convergence of systems already identified (Healey and Williams 1993).

Looking back over 50 years of European planning, it is ironic that the country with the largest body of people that call themselves planners has made only a half-hearted contribution to the European planning debate (with apologies to those who have contributed enthusiastically). Since the 1980s, a European dimension to planning policy has been more widely accepted. During that time the UK has played only a minor role in the development of transnational planning tools and policy. Instead, at various times, the European planning debate has been led by Germany, France and the Netherlands. It seems that the same forces that have generated such a strong profession in the UK have also tended to make it parochial in outlook, and focused attention on the fine grain rather than strategy. The parting of the ways in 1947 is much less significant now than it was then. The end of the 1990s promises a much more positive contribution from the UK. Planning across Europe is changing to cope with the pace and scale of development pressures that could hardly have been imagined in 1947, and as a result the European dimension is going to be a major feature over the next 50 years of town and country planing in the UK.

FURTHER READING

The history of spatial planning at the European level is told in Williams (1996) *European Union Spatial Policy and Planning.* This is the only textbook on the subject and provides an explanation of the historical development of the institutions, instruments and policies of spatial planning and spatial policy at the European level. There are many general accounts of the making of the EU, including Borchardt (1995) *European Integration, the Origins and Growth of the European Community,* and Dinan (1999) *Ever Closer Union?: An Introduction to the European Community.* For a more critical account see Chisholm (1995) *Britain on the Edge of Europe.* The texts on *EC Law* by Tillotson (1996) and Craig and de Búrca (1995) are useful in their own right, and these are also updated regularly and provide brief summaries of the history of the EU. The history of each policy area in which the Community has acted, including regional policy, environment and transport, is given in Moussis (1997) *Access to the European Union Law, Economics, Policies.*

There has been a great deal of progress on European spatial planning over the last few years, and the reader is recommended to consult the original sources, especially the Community study *Europe 2000+* (CEC 1994) and *The European Spatial Development Perspective* (CEC 1998). These documents provide a summary of the recent history of European spatial planning policy. For a general account see Shaw *et al.*

(1996) 'Toward a supranational spatial development perspective'. A more detailed history of the ESDP is Fit and Kragt (1994) 'The long road to European spatial planning'. For an update and view from the Commission, see Bastrup-Birk and Doucet (1997) 'European spatial planning from the heart', and Faludi and Zonneveld (1997) 'Shaping Europe: the ESDP'. An excellent summary of the likely impact of the Amsterdam Treaty is given by Shutt and Colwell (1998) *Towards 2006: European Regional Policy and UK Local Government*. On the question of harmonization of systems see Davies (1993) 'Towards a European planning system?'. Two recent texts provide comparative accounts of changing approaches to planning in European countries: Healey *et al.* (eds) (1997) *Making Strategic Spatial Plans*, and Newman and Thornley (1996) *Urban Planning in Europe* (which also includes an overview of different European 'families' of planning). For a fuller account of the variation in approaches to spatial planning in the Community see the *EU Compendium of Spatial Planning Systems and Policies* (Nadin *et al.* 1997).

chapter 10

Design

JOHN PUNTER

INTRODUCTION

This chapter examines the issue of design within the practice of town and country planning in the UK. It begins with a discussion of the changing and limited conception of design that has underpinned planning intervention and moves on to discuss why design has been such a controversial area of planning practice. The status and evolution of design control in the postwar planning system is then explored in discussions of the critical reactions to development in the 1950s, the rise of the conservation ethic in the 1960s, the debates about delay and design guidance in the 1970s, the deregulation and demise of control in the 1980s, and the role of design in the post-1991 plan-led system and a more quality conscious era. The chapter concludes with a general assessment of the achievements of control, the problems of measuring these, the controversies and criticisms which continue to dog the development of policy, and a discussion of the barriers to further improvements in practice.

THE PROBLEMATIC OF DESIGN

The concept and role of design as a facet of town and country planning in the UK has always been problematic. For a start, the concept of design has tended, until recently, to be equated with merely the external appearance or elevations of development, leaving design control as a matter of aesthetic, superficial and largely subjective judgements. While the principle of judging the external appearance of proposed developments in relationship to their surroundings and of protecting amenities was enshrined in development control from the outset, it took a long time for notions of surroundings to embrace more than just townscape and to incorporate the social and ecological character of both site and context. Similarly, it was not until the 1990s that the central government recognized that in design the spaces between buildings were as important as the buildings themselves, and that the public realm thus created had a critical social dimension as well as an aesthetic character. This broadening concept of urban design has begun to incorporate public perceptions through the emphasis on public consultation, and is beginning to develop a concept of environmental design through consideration of sustainability principles (walkable layouts, mixed use, etc.). The titles and subtitles of government circulars and advice notes demarcate the evolution from elevational control (1966) and aesthetic control (1980) to design (1992) and, latterly, urban design (1997), but remain some way from articulating concepts of urban environmental design which must underpin sustainable development (Punter and Carmona 1997).

Again, until recently, the view of design has tended to be a static one of an end product, a particular piece of built form, rather than a dynamic one of a process, a creative problem-solving process where the accommodation needs of a client are translated into a building that is functional, efficient and attractive (as well as profitable and economical) and which can be easily serviced while providing both public and private amenities. Design, like development itself, is a social process drawing, to various degrees, on a range of design skills and expertise, the resources of developers and investors, and the aspirations of client and future user/occupier/owner. Within this process, notions of design 'control' by the planning authority are clearly problematic, even though ultimately officers recommend and councillors decide on application approvals or refusals. Government advice now clearly stresses that the chief responsibility for design quality rests with the client and the designer, and notions of design 'control' (never supported by the central government) have now generally given way to those of a collective pursuit of design quality.

The arena of design has been problematic for other reasons, principally perhaps because it has been a contested area for competing professions, some prominent architects claiming a monopoly on building design skills, resenting any controls on the same, and being rightly sceptical of planners', councillors' and the public's design expertise (Manser 1983). Meanwhile, highway engineers have retained considerable controls over the public realm and the spaces between buildings through their traffic engineering principles. Planners have struggled to defend their design expertise, not least because they have not clearly articulated their design remit. It was only in 1997 that the design professions came together to end their unprofessional bickering and to develop a common urban design agenda (Urban Design Alliance 1997), and it will be interesting to see whether more positive collaborations ensue.

Finally, there has been a widely held view that design freedom is an integral component of development rights, that an 'Englishman's home is his castle' and that, except in areas designated for their historic, architectural and landscape quality, the developer/householder has a right to express his/her own design aspirations and tastes. Government has often defended this right in the interests of technological

Figure 10.1
'Vicwardian' housing in Cardiff, built in 1997 and typical of most suburban development in England and Wales. There is much professional antipathy towards the designs of the mass housebuilders, but not from the public

development (Sharp 1969: 181), market appeal (DoE Circular 22/80) and even design quality itself (Heseltine 1980), though in truth the most common argument for freedom in recent years has been on grounds of decision-making speed and efficiency (Punter 1986–7).

For all these reasons, it has taken almost exactly half a century for government to enshrine a broad definition of urban design at the heart of planning practice (in the 1997 edition of Planning Policy Guidance Note 1):

> Urban design should be taken to mean the relationship between buildings and the streets, squares, parks, waterways and other spaces which make up the public domain; the nature and quality of the public domain itself; the relationship of one part of a village, town or city with other parts; and the patterns of movement and activity which are thereby established: in short, the complex relationships between all the elements of built and unbuilt space.

Ironically, that definition has been offered at the very moment when a conception of environmental design should have been set out to embrace all the key dimensions of sustainability – energy efficiency, protection of biodiversity, pollution minimisation, minimal disturbance of natural processes – alongside the 'new' concerns about the quality of public space, comfort, safety and vitality (Punter and Carmona 1997; Bentley 1990).

DESIGN CONTROL IN POSTWAR PLANNING

The 1947 Act extended development control to all land and although there were crucial exemptions (notably for agriculture, for the operational land of statutory undertakers and for government departments) the vigilant local authority could control external appearance within the limits of ministerial tolerance. But design control had been relegated to a minor role in planning by concerns with regional economic development, land policy and rural prosperity, and pride of place was given to development plans and particularly to land acquisition, clearance and development powers and the recoupment of betterment. Matters of design were not mentioned in the legislation, and there were only peripheral references to the protection of amenity, but the provisions for the General Development Order noted that the local planning authority might wish to approve the design or external appearance (note the interchangeability of the terms) of development proposals.

The control of the design of private development was not really an issue for the incoming Labour government because their reforms presumed a major role for the public sector in development. Central government provided a series of manuals to provide guidance on the drawing up and execution of public schemes. The 1944 Dudley Report revamped the standards for public housing design, and the Ministry of Health's 1949 *Housing Manual* gave advice on site planning layouts, access, views, spaces and house styles, while the 1947 *Advisory Handbook on the Redevelopment of Central Areas* (MTCP 1947b) introduced modernist concepts of land-use segregation, open planning (daylight/sunlight and plot ratio) and traffic circulation efficiency (road hierarchies and parking provision), leaving only isolated 'historic buildings' as landmarks (Punter 1986: 371). Each of these documents had enormous impact in shaping publicly initiated development, but with the advent of a Conservative government in 1951, bent on restoring primacy to private development, their influence on the latter was more subtle.

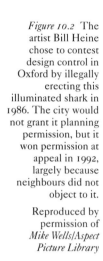

Figure 10.2 The artist Bill Heine chose to contest design control in Oxford by illegally erecting this illuminated shark in 1986. The city would not grant it planning permission, but it won permission at appeal in 1992, largely because neighbours did not object to it.

Reproduced by permission of *Mike Wells/Aspect Picture Library*

The original 1948 General Development Order was very tightly drawn and kept a wide range of street furniture, garden walls and the like under control. It proved largely unworkable and, in 1950, both the General Development Order and the Use Classes Order were revised to allow householders to carry out minor alterations, extensions and improvements to their houses without having to seek permission. In 1953, the MHLG published advice in *Design in Town and Village*, but in the foreword the minister argued that 30 years of control had had a generally 'dull and depressing' effect and that since design questions were 'matters of taste and . . . individual opinion' an official manual on design was inappropriate (Punter 1987: 30). It was not until the late 1990s that these agnostic and pessimistic views began to change. The manual also noted that 'more compact building leads to better and more attractive grouping as well as saving land and reducing costs', and this was one of the signals of a move to increase residential densities progressively, particularly in public-sector housing developments under the Conservatives.

OUTRAGE, COUNTER-ATTACK AND THE TOWNSCAPE PHILOSOPHY IN THE 1950S

Criticisms of the results of postwar design control were not slow in emerging. The most informed and constructive of these came from the *Architectural Review* which was highly critical of urban sprawl and advocated more compact development. The special issues of the *Review – Outrage* (Nairn 1955) and *Counter-Attack Against Suburbia* (Nairn 1957) – were careful to note the fragmentation of planning control as well as the failures of advertisement control. Their particular target was the tyranny of highway and planning standards and by law regulation which they saw as wasteful, preventing appropriate design responses to particular localities and blurring the differences between city, town and country. The *Review* had begun to develop a

DEVELOPMENT CONTROL OFFICER TO MAN-IN-THE STREET: "Just think what would happen if he was let loose uncontrolled and we were not here to protect you ! "

Figure 10.3 In response to proposals for reform of aesthetic control, Louis Hellman posed the key question about the quality of its outcomes in the mid-1970s in his usual acerbic way.

Reproduced by permission of Louis Hellman

picturesque approach to urban design and gradually this took shape as the *Townscape* gospel (Cullen 1961) in a series of studies of historic towns and suggestions for sensitive redevelopment and enhancement. These latter concerns found expression in the conservation movement of the 1960s, while the former were rediscovered in local authority design guidance in the 1970s.

MINISTERIAL ADVICE IN THE 1950s AND 1960s

As in the 1930s, modern architects became particularly disaffected with design censorship on their commissions, while such control was rarely applied to the speculative builder, and ministerial appeal evidence called attention to this. The *Architects' Journal* was moved to note that 'town planning all too often swallows the camels and strains at the gnats' (Anon 1957), a cautionary and still relevant epithet. Meanwhile, the 1959 *Bulletin of Selected Planning Appeals* (MHLG 1959) argued that it was impossible to lay down rules to define good design, and warned that control was to be 'restrained' and not to be used to 'stifle initiative or experiment in design', again advice that has persisted to the present. The 1961 Parker Morris Report made the important point that 'good layout . . . landscaping . . . and well-chosen materials . . . rather than . . . the laboured detailing of the dwelling . . . were the keys to design quality'. This was reiterated three decades later in a joint study by the House Builders Federation and the Royal Institute of British Architects (RIBA) (Davison 1990).

During the early 1960s, the central government produced a series of planning bulletins to update advice on town centre redevelopment that began to dilute the modernist, 'clean-sweep' planning originally promulgated in 1947. It began to encourage the retention of character, the wider use of development briefs (but not to control detailed design), the use of more sympathetic materials and a more human scale of development, but extensive redevelopment was still the order of the day. The 1963 Buchanan Report helped to encourage a much more radical modernism associated with urban motorways, which was echoed in the inner city and the metropolitan suburbs by high-rise council housing. The trend towards higher density and higher-rise housing was driven by government subsidies and housing manuals, urban containment policies and municipal politics. Public housing progressively differentiated itself from private sector housing, in the process stigmatizing both its tenants and modern architecture and reinforcing public prejudices against modernism. Technological failure, poor maintenance and management, and lack of investment in community facilities accelerated the decay of these estates, which continue to act as millstones to the professional reputation of architects and planners, and as easy (if false) targets for public scepticism about the values or otherwise of design controls. The high-rise office buildings of the late 1960s and early 1970s merely completed the picture of a debased and disgraced modernism that has intensified design conservatism in England.

Meanwhile, the 1965 Goss Report to the RIBA portrayed development control as more often than not an uncreative, highly bureaucratic process subject to unnecessary delays, and often administered by poor-quality staff with a dearth of design skills. This led the minister to accept the primacy of architectural judgements in Circular 28/66, while bemoaning the general lack of contextual awareness in design. Meanwhile, Lewis Keeble (1961: 172) argued that in appeal decisions the ministry 'refused to reject . . . anything which was not demonstrably horrific'. Again, all these observations have a relevance to contemporary control practice.

CONSERVATION IMPERATIVES AND MORE SENSITIVE AND PARTICIPATIVE CONTROL

The conservation movement and its impacts upon planning practice is the focus of Larkham's chapter 8, but it also occupies an important place in the development of design thinking and control practice. Not only did it consolidate the townscape 'philosophy' and methodology as the basis for control, but it also developed the notion of a more participatory form of control in which local amenity societies and interested persons ('self appointed arbiters of taste' in the words of Michael Manser, 1983) could comment upon planning applications, a practice which gradually became universal and was eventually enshrined in planning procedures. The 1967 Civic Amenities Act marked an important shift in emphasis away from the preservation of individual historic buildings towards the conservation of coherent areas of townscape, and 'from negative control to creative planning for preservation.' In conservation areas, local planning authorities were allowed to pay 'special regard . . .

Figure 10.4 A mixed use dockside development in Bristol, completed in the late 1980s, included the restoration and conversion of three listed buildings. Design control worked hard to achieve basement car parking, a riverside walkway, attractive amenity space, a landmark office building and mixed tenure housing

to such matters as materials, colour, vertical or horizontal emphasis and the grain of design' (MHLG Circular 61/68). In the first instance, many designations and much practice was purely negative and defensive, but gradually the influence of better-trained conservation officers, mostly employed by county planning authorities, began to be felt, and small budgets for enhancement and grants for rehabilitation and repair began to be used creatively to forge a more proactive approach to conservation. This, in turn, began to raise questions about the general skills and standards of design control in local planning authorities at large (Tugnutt and Robertson 1987).

THE 1970S PROPERTY BOOM: DELAY ECLIPSES DESIGN

Ironically, as conservation area designation proceeded apace, and the shift to housing rehabilitation programmes began to conserve what was left of the inner city housing stock, the 1971–3 property boom was providing a new wave of modernism in city centres. This intensified the public reaction in favour of a conservation approach and more traditional and contextual forms of development (Aldous 1975). However, the translation of such ideas into more prescriptive and effective forms of design control was discouraged by the reaction of the development industry and government to another aspect of the property boom, the swamping of local planning authority development control sections with planning applications, and the subsequent delays in their processing.

As a consequence of this dramatic rise in development control workloads, issues of planning delay, refusal rates and land availability were placed high on the planning agenda and have continued to be dominant to the present day. As the government sought to 'streamline the planning machine' in Circular 142/73, indicting design controls as a 'cause of frustration', it set in train a series of inquiries that were to harden attitudes to design control and stifle key local design initiatives. The 1973 interim report of Dobry's review of the development control system advocated waiving design control outside designated areas, and relaxing controls over architect-designed buildings, but a wave of protest reversed this recommendation in the final 1975 report where the importance to environmental quality of both lay judgements on design and of matters of detail was asserted. The government ignored the latter points, just as it largely ignored the findings of the study on *Promotion of High Standards of Architectural Design* (DoE 1974a), which bemoaned the lack of governmental architectural patronage and design research. The contrast with French government design initiatives of the period is striking (Loew 1995).

DESIGN GUIDANCE AND THE CRITIQUE OF THE STANDARDS APPROACH

One direct product of a conservation team was the Essex County Council's 1973 *Design Guide for Residential Areas*, produced to give some substance to vague, motherhood, 'high quality of design' policies in the Essex County Development Plan. This drew heavily on the 'townscape' principles of site planning, developed by Unwin, Cullen and Nairn in searching for principles for design control in small town centres, suburban arcadia and the countryside. It was remarkable for its sustained critique both of the quantitative standards approach to residential design and of the tyranny of highway standards. It provided for dramatic savings in 'land take', a rise in densities and a reduction in service costs to appeal to rural and amenity interests and developers simultaneously, and these were the keys to its widespread acceptance.

What aroused extensive criticism amongst architects, developers and the DoE was its advice on the treatment of elevations, embracing proportion, balance, unity, use

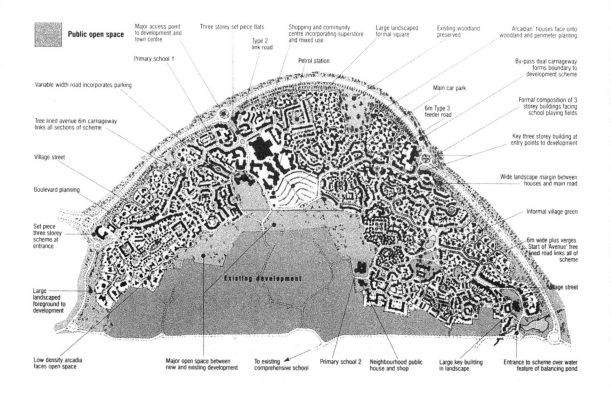

Public open space

Major access point to development and town centre

Three storey set piece flats

Type 2 link road

Shopping and community centre incorporating superstore and mixed use

Large landscaped formal square

Existing woodland preserved

'Arcadian' houses face onto woodland and perimeter planting

Primary school 1

Petrol station

By-pass dual carriageway forms boundary to development scheme

Variable width road incorporates parking

Main car park

6m Type 3 feeder road

Formal composition of 3 storey buildings facing school playing fields

Tree lined avenue 6m carriageway links all sections of scheme

Key three storey building at entry points to development

Village street

Wide landscape margin between houses and main road

Boulevard planning

Informal village green

Set piece three storey scheme at entrance

6m wide plus verges. Start of 'Avenue' tree lined road links all of scheme

Existing development

Large landscaped foreground to development

Village street

Low density arcadia faces open space

Major open space between new and existing development

To existing comprehensive school

Primary school 2

Neighbourhood public house and shop

Large key building in landscape

Entrance to scheme over water feature of balancing pond

Figure 10.5 The 1998 Essex Design Guide, retitled for 'residential and mixed use areas', created an extended vocabulary for suburban forms detailed in 13 case studies. Key features are the through streets, bus access, tree planting and coherent landscaping and adoption of sustainable design principles

of materials, roof pitches, etc. Ironically, the neo-vernacular styles that it advocated rapidly established great popularity in the market-place, and this, combined with extensive and uncritical plagiarism of the guide by numerous local authorities (a continuing problem), led to the 'Essex vernacular' spreading throughout the country. A second major attack upon the standards approach to design appeared in a study on *The Value of Standards for the External Residential Environment* (DoE 1976a). This identified the lack of coordination and meaningful integration of existing standards and recommended a far more flexible and critical way of using them, emphasizing their performance in context. Few local authorities were capable of developing such an approach, but in 1979 the London Borough of Camden developed an exemplary *Environmental Code* as an appendix to its development plan. Like neighbouring Westminster's plan, this included well-crafted design policies, but the vast majority of local planning authorities still had no statutory design policies whatsoever, a situation that was not rectified until the mid-1990s.

A design bulletin on *Residential Roads and Footpaths* (DoE 1977b) incorporated many of the refinements of road standards made by the Essex Design Guide and the new town development corporations. Gradually, the 'prairie landscapes' of suburbia gave way to much more compact cul-de-sac layouts, with housing given more vernacular revival stylings with the use of very traditional-looking materials. These held sway until the mid-1990s when sustainability considerations led to a preference for more permeable layouts for more direct pedestrian and cycle movement (see the revised 1998 edition of the Essex Design Guide), although housing consumers have yet to be convinced of the vices of the cul-de-sac.

Despite these advances, in 1977 the House of Commons Expenditure Committee launched an inquiry into development control practice to explore issues of delay and their resource costs. The House Builders' Federation (HBF), the RIBA and the DoE took strongly negative stances on design control, but planners, surveyors and national and local amenity groups all took a positive stance. However, the concerns of the HBF held sway, particularly with regard to the Essex Design Guide, which was extensively criticized for being too detailed, and the Expenditure Committee adopted a very cautious view on design control, recommending a detailed level of control only in designated areas, and suggesting that the government issue new design advice as soon as possible. This the new government duly did in Circular 22/80.

CONSERVATIVE DEREGULATION AND THE DEMISE OF DESIGN IN THE 1980s

The return of a Conservative government in 1979, committed to unfettering private enterprise and encouraging the creation of wealth, had a major impact upon the planning system. Various government initiatives sought to reduce significantly the sphere of planning control, and Circular 22/80, *Development Control Policy and Practice*, restated the general presumption in favour of development (which had been introduced in 1949) and sought to restrict the operation of aesthetic control to 'environmentally sensitive' areas. The Secretary of State for the Environment (Michael Heseltine) took an early opportunity to argue against the 'unnecessary imposition of design standards' by planners and councillors, and this view was quoted and elaborated in four key paragraphs in the circular. The by-now-familiar argument was made that aesthetics were subjective, that tastes or fashions should not be imposed on developers and that local planning authorities should 'only exceptionally control design details if the sensitive character of the area or the particular building justifies it' and should be guided by 'professionally qualified advisers'. Design guidance was useful, but was to be 'used as guidance, and not as detailed rules'. Interestingly, in Scotland a 1980 Planning Advice Note provided much more positive advice to encourage the wider use of briefs and guidance. So much of the anti-design rhetoric that was characteristic of English planning of the 1980s did not permeate north of the border, and the Scottish Office have maintained a flow of positive design advice (SOED 1991, 1994).

The mid-1980s, particularly with Nicholas Ridley as Secretary of State at the DoE, marked an all-time low in terms of the cause of design in planning practice. A series of deregulatory circulars (15/84, 16/84, 14/85, 2/87) and the introduction of a new business class created a much stronger presumption in favour of development, and made it much more risky for local planning authorities to take a tough line negotiating planning applications, particularly on matters of design. In response to evidence (subsequently contested) that appeals on design matters remained at a high level, the government reissued three of the four paragraphs of advice in Circular 22/80 as Circular 31/85, concluding with a strong warning that it would enforce the advice through the appeal process, advice that was strongly reinforced in Circular 2/87. The numbers and proportion of appeals (as a percentage of refusals) rose significantly, as did their chances of success, creating an appeal-led planning system and increasing ministerial controls over the pattern, pace and quality of development (Punter and Bell 1997). The 1987 stock market collapse and subsequent property crash gradually created a more realistic development climate, but not before extensive damage had been done to both strategic and local aspects of design control, particularly in the forms of out-of-town business parks and shopping centres and inner-area redevelopment schemes. A more aggressive approach to the pursuit of planning permissions had been developed and the Audit Commission (1992) noted the 'increasing sophistication, bullishness and articulacy' as well as gamesmanship of applicants in the late 1980s, all of which made the pursuit of design quality much more problematic.

In retrospect, it is perhaps surprising that design control was not more completely emasculated during the deregulatory climate of the 1990s. This probably reflects its continuing appeal to the other side of the conservative psyche: the desire to minimize the impact of change upon cherished townscapes and landscapes and the domestic environment of home owners. But during the mid-1980s it often seemed that only the Prince of Wales was prepared to speak up for the cause of public inputs into development/design control and for a more positive attitude to design regulation. If the notion of the Prince of Wales speaking up for the concerns of the proverbial 'man in the street' seems more than a little ridiculous, nonetheless his stance was of considerable importance in preventing the further erosion of design and conservation controls. His plea 'to respect old buildings, street plans and traditional scales . . . and not to feel guilty about a preference for facades, ornaments and soft materials' was widely echoed by lay planning committees, amenity groups and the general public in the design control process (Jencks 1990: 43).

In 1987, the Prince shifted his attention to design controls at large, and attacked the vagueness, obscurity and lack of teeth of both design and conservation advice. In a subsequent book and television programme he put forward a set of 10 commandments or principles for harmonizing development (place, hierarchy, scale, harmony, enclosure, materials, decoration, art, signs and lights, and community) (Prince of Wales 1988). These concentrated upon the external appearance of buildings, but nevertheless showed a considerable grasp of the key principles of urban design espoused by Anglo-American design writers since 1960, and he sparked an interesting debate that helped to focus the discussion on practical urban design policies (Tibbalds 1988b; Punter 1990b: Figure 2.8). Some local authorities subsequently applied versions of the 10 commandments to the design policies in their development plans.

THE EMERGENCE OF A MORE POSITIVE APPROACH TO DESIGN

One of the first to respond to the Prince's ideas was Francis Tibbalds who, as a respected urban designer and President of the Royal Town Planning Institute (RTPI) in 1988, had chosen to promote urban design as a theme of his presidential campaign (Tibbalds 1988a). Tibbalds drew extensively on *Responsive Environments* (Bentley *et al.* 1985) for his 'ten commandments' of urban design (Tibbalds, 1988b). He emphasized that design should not remain obsessed with issues of elevations, but should concentrate more upon the quality of streets and spaces and their comfort, safety and vitality. These ideas were applied in the *Birmingham Urban Design Study* (1990) which merged traditional British townscape concerns with Kevin Lynch's notions of legibility and Jane Jacobs' ideas of rediscovering the street as key aspects of design policy. This kind of analysis provided a much better basis for design briefing and the formulation of design policy than had previously existed in England.

A variety of studies of British and American control practice provided conflicting evidence about the performance of the British planning system, but began to develop a case for the clearer policy framework for design control (Delafons 1990; Wakeford 1990; DoE 1991c). Surveys of design guidance tended to confirm an English obsession with matters of detail (DoE 1991; Chapman and Larkham 1992), although these could be justified by the predominance of householder and minor commercial applications (64 per cent) in control practice. The Royal

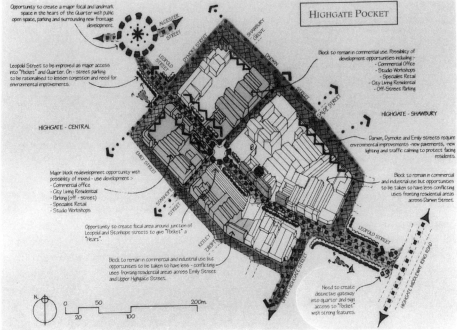

Figure 10.6 The 1990 Birmingham Urban Design Study identified inner city character areas for individual analysis. Since then, the city has been undertaking a series of Quarters Studies to identify development sites and enhancement measures and promote regeneration. The Highgate Pocket is part of the Chinese/Markets Quarter Study (1996).

Reproduced by permission of Birmingham City Council

Fine Art Commission, which has proved to be an important force for more enlightened control since 1924, advocated redrafting existing government advice to recognize design as a material consideration, to be much more positive about the pursuit of design quality and to encourage more positive design guidance (Hillman 1990).

Many of these ideas and views found favour with a new secretary of state for the Environment, Chris Patten, and his positive speeches (1990) led Francis Tibbalds and RTPI interests to draft a new circular and to lobby for new central government guidance and research on design control (RTPI 1990). Eventually, under a subsequent Secretary of State, the RTPI and the RIBA agreed a seven-point statement on design control that found its way into an annex to the Planning Policy Guidance Note 1 *General Policy and Principles*.

This restated much of the design advice in the widely reviled Circular 22/80, but was markedly more positive in tone. It unequivocally stated that the appearance of development, and its relationship to its surroundings, was a material consideration in control decisions, and it underlined the responsibility of developers for ensuring good design and the need for both sides to have 'skilled advisers'. For the first time, the importance of the spaces between buildings and of landscape design was stressed, and it was stated that development should 'result in a benefit in environmental and landscape terms'. Local planning authorities were urged to provide applicants with clear indications of their expectations, but not to be too prescriptive or detailed in these, and to encourage applicants to consult with them early in the development process, while applicants were urged to improve the illustrative material supporting their applications. While most of the caveats and restraints of Circular 22/80 remained, the important factor was that a majority of planning authorities considered that a more positive climate for design policy, guidance and intervention had been created. This impression was greatly reinforced when John Gummer became Secretary of State for the Environment in 1993.

THE PLAN-LED SYSTEM AND THE IMPORTANCE OF DESIGN POLICIES

During the 1980s, a few design-oriented local authorities, particularly the London Boroughs of Westminster and Camden, had come to the conclusion that, to give their design aspirations more influence on development, they had to formulate and enshrine them carefully in policies in their development plans. The 1990 and 1991 legislative amendments set the seal on this trend and meant that every authority in the land had to begin the task of formulating a set of design policies to cover all of their territory. Not surprisingly, many found this a daunting task and, while the RTPI pressed the central government to fund some research to support this endeavour, it was not until early 1994 that the results of this research were forthcoming (see Punter and Carmona 1997), by which time a new Secretary of State was taking a rather different approach to the promotion of design issues. As a result, the development of design policies, which remains the cornerstone of any attempts to develop a statutory basis for design control, has still not received the attention it needs from the central government and seems likely to receive only limited attention in the forthcoming good practice guide (DoE 1999).

A revised PPG 1 (1997) took on board some of the key findings of the policy research by emphasizing the importance of a broad definition of urban design, the need for character appraisal as a basis for policy formulation, the importance of responding to context in its fullest sense, the importance of spaces and a quality public domain, and the need to protect local distinctiveness and to promote sustainable, mixed-use developments that reduce the need to travel. Others may find their way into the new Good Practice Guide because they are now accepted parts of professional practice – the concept of a hierarchy of policy and guidance, the value of large-scale design strategies and area frameworks, etc. Others have been pointedly ignored, such as the more fundamental role that should be played by landscape considerations. The task with design policies, as with much else in design control, is to bring practice in the majority of local planning authorities much closer to the level and sophistication of the best, a task not easily accomplished without higher levels of design skills and more resources in control.

AFFIRMATIVE ACTIONS – THE QUALITY INITIATIVE AND URBAN DESIGN
CAMPAIGN

John Gummer became Secretary of State for the Environment in 1993. He 'came in
with a personal, passionate view about architecture, towns and urban life' (Gummer
1997) and saw the need both to win the confidence of the design professions and to
raise public consciousness about design. He was determined to take a holistic view
of design, linking it to a broad environmental agenda. There were some difficulties
persuading the DoE to abandon its longstanding agnosticism in design, but a broad
consultative 'Quality Initiative' was initiated (DoE 1994a). From this emerged a
strong sustainability theme focused on mixed-use, user-friendly, public transport
and walking/cycling, local involvement and control, design guidelines and local
identity, environmental awareness and design skills, and issues of density (especially
relating to the first two themes).

Gummer consciously used the consultation process, other speeches and pronouncements to change the whole tone of the debate about design control. He was
not about to introduce new controls on design (Gummer 1994) and he was careful to
maintain his positive attitude to the development industry. He was successful in
drawing in other bodies and professions to contribute to the debate through initiatives, research and conferences (e.g. English Partnerships 1995; RICS 1996), while
the Countryside Commission (1993, 1994) was already embarked upon the pursuit of
local distinctiveness through its village appraisal experiments.

Gummer and the DoE responded to the professional and academic lobbying for
the cause of urban design with the launch of an Urban Design Campaign in mid-
1995. Twenty-one schemes were selected and briefing/consultation/collaboration
initiatives were funded both to 'spread the word' throughout England and also to
gather experience (DoE 1995e). Studies on London's environmental quality, the
Thames Strategy and sustainable densities, design briefs, mixed use and advice on
road layouts were just some of the recent research projects which supported the
campaign and were starting to inject new ideas and agendas into design thinking
and practice (see Punter 1996).

The DoE are relying upon a commission to produce *Good Practice Guidance on
Design in the Planning System* to encapsulate the results of all this research in a digest-
ible form for all the actors in the development process. At the time of writing (May
1998) this still remains in near final draft form, a testament to the continuing ner-
vousness of central government about design advice. But the broad lineaments of its
content are clear, and consistent with the Quality Initiative in promoting urbanism
and urban design, creating places and promoting local distinctiveness, linking community control and the management of development, raising the standards of practice and developing a toolkit for urban design. The latter advocates an integrated
package of design policies (in development plans), guides, frameworks, briefs and
urban design statements, but has an ethos of the promotion of design quality and
advanced skills rather than more control per se. The Scottish Office commissioned a
similar study in June 1997, the Northern Ireland Office focused on work on road
standards, housing layout and design briefing, while the Welsh Office have merely
edited English guidance into an 11-paragraph advice note (Welsh Office 1996).

The English Good Practice Guide will be a milestone in the development of the
design dimension of planning, the first substantive government statement for 45
years and the first purpose-written advice about what is considered to be good practice. It will summarize widely agreed general design principles that have underpinned urban design teaching for more than a decade (see Bentley *et al.* 1985), and it

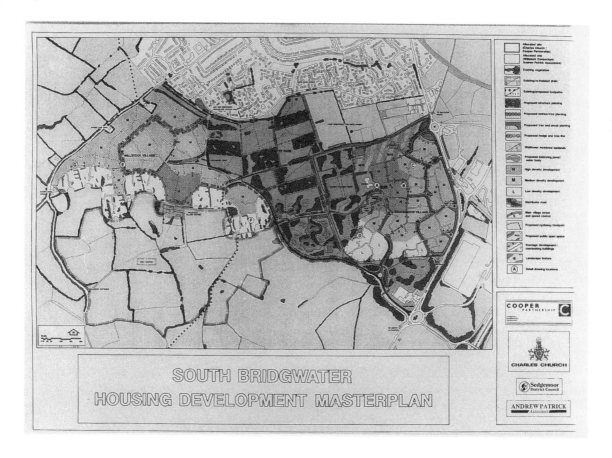

SOUTH BRIDGWATER
HOUSING DEVELOPMENT MASTERPLAN

Figure 10.7 A suburban extension master plan for South Bridgwater in Somerset, as yet unimplemented. This master plan emerged from one of the Urban Design Campaign's experiments and emphasised high quality landscaping and natural drainage, pedestrian permeable layouts and locally distinctive architecture in this Somerset Levels landscape

will elaborate the mechanisms for translating principles into policies and guidance at all scales from city-wide to individual sites. It will promote a view of design as a process in which improving design skills and developing the means of collaboration across professional, development and public interests are paramount.

NEW IMPROVED DESIGN GUIDANCE

New government guidance on design was enshrined in a revised version of PPG 1 published in 1997. This took on board the outcomes of the Quality Initiative and the aspirations of the Urban Design Campaign to provide further advances in the pursuit of design quality via the planning process. Urban design was given pride of place and its role in promoting sustainable development was emphasized. Principles of mixed use and brownfield development that minimize the need to travel and maximize the potential for public transport were enshrined elsewhere in PPG 1. Emphasis was placed on design policies based on careful assessment of the character of the locality, but these were still to 'avoid unnecessary prescription or detail', and guidance need-ed to be similarly based on character assessment and show evidence of widespread consultation. Applicants were required to provide urban design statements. Other-wise the guidance included all the strictures of the 1992 version of PPG 1 to emphasize the essential continuity of advice in this area. The continuing gaps in advice, on the details of sustainable design, on the role of landscape and practice of landscaping, and on the skills shortage, will be only partly addressed in the new Good Practice Guide.

Figure 10.8 Glasgow prides itself on high quality design (viz. City of Architecture and Design 1999) but did not feel it could refuse or even significantly improve this covered shopping centre (1996), largely because it contained John Lewis, the most sought-after department store in the UK, to anchor retail activity

NEW LABOUR AND THE URBAN DESIGN ALLIANCE

Labour MPs and ministers acknowledged the contribution that John Gummer made to the cause of design quality when they took up office in May 1997. But such was the momentum generated by Gummer's initiatives that the design professions themselves took up the design quality agenda and launched the Urban Design Alliance in December 1997. This brings the surveying, architecture, planning, landscape and engineering professions together with the Urban Design Group and the Civic Trust into a collaboration that seeks to promote the cause of urban design in environmental enhancement and urban regeneration, to raise its profile in national and local government, and to raise its skill base amongst all sectors in the design and development processes. At the time of writing, it is still developing its programme of consciousness raising and lobbying and concentrating upon approaches to the Department of the Environment, Transport and the Regions (the successor to the DoE) for a white paper on the role of urban design in regeneration and renewal (and more importantly sustainable development). Whether it can play a primary role in forging a new consensus about environmental design for sustainable development, in the process resolving some of the key issues about urban compaction, urban environmental quality, and the need for desirable locations and forms for new housing is a moot point, but clearly design issues occupy a more important position in contemporary planning practice today than at any stage over the last 50 years.

CONCLUSIONS

In this account of a half century of design control, the tensions between central government restraint and local authority initiative have been clearly evident. Not all local planning authorities experience these tensions; a large number seem content to take a minimalist line on design control by virtue of their desire for development and their priorities for job creation, their staff resources and orientation, or the aspirations and objectives of their councillors and their acceptance of existing development norms. Those which have tried to pursue a much more proactive approach on design have often encountered difficulties because they have had to transcend the potentially tight limits imposed by government circulars on plan policies, guidance and decisions. Ironically it has been the most proactive authorities, with the most committed and skilled staff, who have had their practice most contested.

Government advice has progressed substantially over the period, and there is now a much clearer and more useful definition of design that is more relevant to environmental quality in the broadest sense. There is awareness of how policy, guidance and control mechanisms fit together and the government is beginning to get to grips with what design for sustainable development might mean. But the system is essentially based upon leaving the initiative for design with the householder/developer and his/her designer, even though an ever smaller proportion of development is actually architect designed. The design considerations defined as valid by central government are extremely basic, and local authorities' room for manoeuvre seems very limited. However it must be remembered that government advice is only enforced at appeal or through plan review so that many authorities continue to negotiate with applicants as if they had a wide range of powers and were able to exert considerable influence upon design outcomes.

Beyond this, a two-tier system of control operates across the country, and some local planning authorities have gone to great lengths to ensure that large tracts of their built-up areas are covered with statutory, and failing that non-statutory, protective designations to ensure that they can operate detailed design control very widely. So, despite a strong central government line, there are dramatic variations in design control regimes across the country, just as there are dramatic variations in control regimes (refusal rates, appeal rates and speed of decisions: Audit Commission 1992).

Evaluating control outcomes
How can the contribution of control to design quality be evaluated? The effect of design control is extremely difficult to measure because much of what it achieves is invisible. This is the sum of the 11 per cent of planning permissions which are refused annually, two-thirds of which have design factors in the reasons for refusal and two-fifths of which have design as the most important reason for refusal (Punter and Bell 1997), and the 'value added' through negotiations. The Audit Commission (1992) have suggested that local planning authorities ought to be able to monitor and demonstrate the 'value added' on a regular basis, but it is difficult to measure and to attribute due to the multiplicity of actors and events in the development and design processes. Some major improvements in design come about because an architect is given more scope or has a better idea, because cost constraints are eased or a better quality product can be marketed, and it is often impossible to filter out how the local authority improved a scheme during the design process. To make a sound evaluation one needs to be able to assess what would have happened without design control, what sorts of standards householders/ developers would have set, and how much time and effort would go into the design process in its absence. Nonetheless, key observers of the development scene, like the Royal Fine Art Commission, are convinced of the positive effects of design control and of its ability to 'raise the general standard both of layout and design' (Royal Fine Art Commission 1985: 21).

One has to contrast such a view with the agnosticism expressed by the Ministry of Housing and Local Government, via Harold Macmillan in 1953, and widely echoed in central government and architectural circles ever since. Certainly, looking at the quality of the built environment approved by local planning authorities over the last half century does not immediately suggest that design control has achieved great things. In fact many public developments in the form of system-built council estates, decked office schemes, urban dual carriageways, multi-storey car parks and Arndale-type shopping schemes constitute the greatest design atrocities in the history of British urbanism, though few of these were the product of a careful, public design-control process. In any event, the lessons of the 1960s and early 1970s have been largely learned in terms of the scale, mix and quality of development and the public amenities created, and there is now a widespread view that the quality of design is slowly improving.

Planning always struggles to get the right designer working for the right developer on the right site, but it rarely achieves it, frequently leaving control as a damage-limitation exercise where mediocrity is the best that can be achieved. Worse still, the powers of design control are frequently such that it ends up actually legitimizing very poor quality design by having to approve it, and frequently it is the planners who take the blame for this rather than the developers who remain largely anonymous. As Lewis Keeble noted in 1971, 'planning is principally judged by the quality of development that receives planning permission,' and he emphasized the dilemma facing planners in this respect and the necessity for control to achieve more to win more public support for planning at large.

It is possible to judge the achievements of design control only if the constraints placed on it by central government and economic realities are fully understood. The dominance of speculative developments encourages a lowest common denominator approach to residential and commercial development. Researchers have defined the concept of 'affordable quality' to describe what consumers are prepared to pay for design (Rowley 1998), while design quality is rarely considered to add more than a few per cent to capital or rental values. Corporate or franchise architecture obeys similar rules and, worse still, assumes that consumers need an instantly recognizable shape or colour and often a vast expanse of empty car-parking out front before they will patronize the establishment. Efforts to preserve local distinctiveness seem doomed in the face of the globalization of urban form. But, at the end of the day, it is the aspirations of the developers and their willingness to employ or empower a talented designer that dictates the quality of design and development, and frankly, the British consumer has rarely placed enough value on good design to set high standards.

Improving design interventions
A vocal minority of architects have long argued that design control stifles creativity and imaginative design, and this message has been constantly reiterated by government guidance since 1953. However, the evidence that these architects have assembled has always been very weak (RIBA 1993), though undoubtedly the very existence of control causes both designers and especially developers to play safe. There remain important criticisms of the practice of design control that can be refuted only by the adoption of best practice policies and procedures. These have been articulated by architects like Moro (1958), Manser (1983) and Manser and Adam (1992), but most fully developed in an American context by Scheer and Preiser (1994). Most of these can be refuted by ensuring that design control does not focus exclusively on issues of external appearance and puts urban design concerns at the heart of its praxis; by insisting that design principles are place specific and community based and that issues of sustainability, safety and accessibility are placed

Figure 10.9 On the suburban arterials and outer edge of Britain's towns and cities it is often hard to detect any design control beyond that of the vehicle safety preoccupations of the highway engineer. Here (Cardiff Gate), a typically mundane McDonalds provides a 'gateway' to a vast expanse of 'tin sheds' adorned only by huge corporate logos. Notions of sustainable design have yet to come to grips with these developments

at the heart of the design agenda; by encouraging the exercise of architectural skills and the production of contemporary design; and by ensuring that all the above are clearly set out in well-publicized statutory policies as a basis for control. Issues of censorship and the overruling of professional expertise seem less relevant the more control focuses on issues of urban and environmental design rather than merely external appearance, but there are two criticisms that cannot be so easily refuted. The first has already been acknowledged: that, in design, control is only one mechanism for improving the quality of the built environment, albeit an important one. As John Gummer and the Urban Design Alliance recognized, the promotion of design quality is a multi-faceted task that must embrace all the actors in the process, but especially the development industry. The second criticism is that design control continues to be performed by overworked, inexperienced and underskilled staff. This remains a major barrier to quality control and is an issue that the professions and academia need to address as a matter of urgency. It is unlikely that any local planning authority is going to throw more resources at the problem, but there are now signs that a large number are seeking urban design expertise in their staff complement.

Critics of the quality of housing development have been the first to recognize that an improvement in design quality is really dependent upon the investment of more money in the development, and have come to focus upon the profits that accrue to the landowner from conversion of the land from agricultural to urban uses as the most appropriate source of these funds. Ian Davison (1990: 30) has long argued that 5 to 10 per cent of land value would reap enormous benefits to new residents and the wider community in the form of 'better design, materials and open space', while Robert Adam (1997) sees the problem as 'lucky landowners not greedy developers'. Such issues will be critical to more sustainable forms of development where better public transport, higher quality services, more accessible open space and high levels of resource and nature conservation are essential. They might be addressed in part by a tax on greenfield development, but the perversity of nationalizing development rights and then giving them back to landowners for free still needs to be properly addressed.

These issues are at the heart of a more sustainable approach to development and to questions of future urban forms and overall design quality. And if one were to define the key issue for design control over the next 50 years it would be to articulate and incorporate principles of sustainable design into its practice. Already research has suggested that the principles of sustainable design have to be articulated at the site, neighbourhood, district, city, and city region levels (Barton *et al.* 1995). The traditional practice of reactive design control has to become more proactive, more strategic and part of much larger scale thinking about sustainable patterns of development that conserve critical environmental capital, minimize the need to travel and the ability to walk and cycle, and maximize accessibility to quality public transport. Even the most basic design concepts like sustainable densities or mixed use are the subject of considerable definitional confusion and controversy and need to be subjected to detailed study and debate. But in the end, if the design dimension of planning is to be more than 'rearranging the deck chairs on the Titanic', it must incorporate the key parameters of sustainable design and be able to influence not just individual development but the whole shape, capital web, and natural resource base of our towns and cities. This is the challenge for the future.

FURTHER READING

This paper draws heavily on my own work on the history of aesthetic control which is detailed in two articles, published in 1986–7, on 'A history of aesthetic control 1909–1985'. This is updated and deepened into the sphere of design policy in Punter and Carmona (1997) *The Design Dimension of Planning*, while the control dimension is explored in a detailed case study in Punter (1990) *Design Control in Central Bristol 1940–1990*. Tugnutt and Robertson (1987) *Making Townscape: A Contextual Approach to Building in an Urban Setting* provides a fully illustrated account of many of the principles of detailed design control, while Bentley *et al.* (1985) *Responsive Environments: A Manual for Designers* contains the most accessible synthesis of urban design literature and successfully translates this into a methodology for design briefing. Barton *et al.* (1995) *Sustainable Settlements: A Guide for Planners, Designers and Developers* provides an excellent complement to Bentley and is also written as a practical manual. Scheer and Preiser (1994) *Design Review: Challenging Urban Aesthetic Control* sets an Anglo-American context for design review and provides a level of critique that surpasses anything available in Britain. Finally, the long-promised DETR (Urban Initiatives) *A Good Practice Guide for Design in the Planning System* is likely to be essential reading for practitioners, amenity interests and all students of design matters.

chapter 11

The Changing Role of the Courts in Planning

MICHAEL PURDUE

THE GROWTH OF JUDICIAL INTERVENTION

The Town and Country Planning Act 1947 was enacted at a time when the courts were very reluctant to be seen to be interfering with the administration of government in the UK. In an essay on 'The Common Law and the Constitution', Sir Stephen Sedley refers to the famous judgement of Lord Greene in *Associated Picture Houses v Wednesbury Corporation*,[1] the judgement which has given rise to the eponymous principle of *Wednesbury* unreasonableness. He describes the decision as one 'which introduces no new doctrine of law and of which the outcome exemplifies the state of torpor into which English public law had descended by 1948' (Sedley 1997). (The Wednesbury principle is that, unless the decision maker has made an error of law, the exercise of power can be overturned by the courts only if the decision is 'so unreasonable that no reasonable authority could ever come to it'.)

In the case of the town and country planning legislation, the extent of this torpor is illustrated by the paucity of court decisions on planning matters from 1947 to 1957. More important than the actual numbers of challenges is the prevailing attitude taken by the judiciary. In a number of cases[2] the House of Lords, by characterizing the ministerial powers as executive or administrative, avoided a close scrutiny of both the basis and the procedural fairness of the minister's decisions. As Sedley points out, the decision in *Franklin v Minister of Town and Country Planning*[3] is still the most notorious case of judicial deference to executive action. The case turned on whether the minister had effectively prejudged the outcome of the inquiry held into whether Stevenage should be the site of a new town. The House held quite reasonably that, in deciding whether to confirm his designation order, the minister was entitled to have a bias towards his own policy as long as he had genuinely considered the report of the inspector and the contrary arguments of the objectors. The significance of this decision is that the tenor of all the speeches was that the minister's decision was virtually unreviewable.

The (then) passivity of the judiciary towards the executive has been traced back to both the experience of the two world wars and the anxiety of the judiciary not to be seen as conservative obstructionists (De Smith *et al.* 1995: 7). In the case of the Town and Country Planning Act 1947, Grant has pointed out that the judiciary had played an important role in the writing of the three major wartime reports (Barlow, Uthwatt and Scott) on which the Act was primarily based. He therefore has argued that 'the judges clearly shared immediately after the war the common faith in the necessity for wide reaching governmental powers to achieve the efficient reconstruction of a war ravaged country' (Grant 1978a). This statement perhaps exaggerates the extent of the postwar consensus on the need for planning powers and tends to assume that the judiciary all have a common set of beliefs. Indeed, Grant himself criticizes Griffith's book *The Politics of the Judiciary* (1977) for holding that the judiciary hold a 'homogenous collection of attitudes, beliefs and principles'. Even in the early 1950s, the courts were prepared to strike down enforcement notices for very technical defects.[4] As will be seen, the only consistent trait of the role of the courts in planning cases has been the way they have disagreed among themselves as to the proper extent of review, and the variation in their approach depending upon the particular context. Nevertheless, it does seem clear that the courts in the immediate postwar years were very reluctant to be seen as doing anything which smacked of judicial sabotage of the planning legislation.

It is also significant that the only statutory right of challenge in the courts to be found in the Town and Country Planning Act 1947 related to the new development plans. It has been argued that this suggests that the draughtsman of the 1947 legislation clearly anticipated little judicial intervention (Grant 1982: 610). This is probably correct, but it is interesting that the minister steering the bill through parliament (Silkin), expressly stated that the purpose of this clause was to *limit* the vulnerability of development plans to judicial review.[5] The point is that even at this period of decline in judicial activity, the legality of development plans and other decisions by statutory bodies would be theoretically vulnerable to challenge in the courts, and there was a quite generous time limit of 6 months in which a challenge could be mounted. The clause in the bill providing for challenge in the courts therefore imposed a strict time limit of 6 weeks and precluded challenge by any other legal proceedings. (The minister also thought that the grounds on which statutory challenge could be made were more limited than for judicial review, though this has not been the way in which the courts have interpreted the wording.)

Over the last 50 years, the courts have in practice made little distinction between the grounds for bringing an application for judicial review and the express grounds on which a statutory challenge can be made. As the grounds for judicial review have been expanded, the courts have interpreted widely what amounts to acting 'outside the powers of the Act' – which is the standard formula for statutory review.

It is, therefore, rather ironic that, although the first statutory right of challenge was inserted to *restrict* the role of the courts, these provisions (in Part XII of the Town and Country Planning Act 1990 entitled *Validity*) today keep the High Court very busy. In this regard, the report of the Franks Committee in 1957 was particularly important. It was this report that recommended that there should be a statutory right of appeal on a point of law to the High Court from ministerial decisions. In the case of planning appeals, this recommendation was implemented by Section 31 of the Town and Country Planning Act 1959, which established a statutory right of challenge in the High Court against a range of decisions and orders of the minister. It is interesting to note that this new right was inserted into the bill unopposed.

The really important factors conducive to increased judicial intervention, however, were the opening up of the decision making process by the Inquiries Procedure Rules (such as the requirement that the inspector's report be published) and, in particular, the requirement imposed on both an inspector and the minister to give reasons for their decision on planning appeals, whether the decision was to uphold or reject the appeal. Both requirements were introduced as a result of recommendations on the Franks Report. As in the case of enforcement notice appeal decisions made by or on behalf of the minister, it is not so much the actual statutory right of challenge in the High Court which has encouraged legal proceedings but the fact that the openness and formality of the appeal procedures builds up a thick dossier of evidence. At the same time, 'the circumstances in which the courts have been prepared to intervene to provide for relief for unlawful administrative action have expanded in spectacular fashion' (De Smith *et al.* 1995: 3). As a result, over the last 40 years or so, judicial intervention has provided rich pickings for practising lawyers and academics. Indeed, one judge has gone so far as to state that 'one of the curiosities of planning law is that it seems to have developed its own jurisprudence of judicial review'.[6]

THE CONSTITUTIONAL BASIS FOR REVIEW AND THE MACHINERY OF CHALLENGE

The UK constitution is still fundamentally judge-made in that the cornerstone principle, the sovereignty of parliament, is not to be found in any basic document or statute but in the decisions of the courts. The paradox is that the power of parliament to make or unmake any laws (and so to abolish any common law principles) is based on the courts' recognition or acquiescence in that power. While the UK's accession to the European Community and the radical rewriting of the constitution by the Blair government[7] has meant that many important matters of constitutional law have become virtual 'no-go' areas for the Westminster parliament, the courts (with the important exception of European Community law) still deny themselves any power to rule that a provision of an Act of Parliament is either invalid or void.

In the case of administrative law, the courts have, however, used the doctrines of parliamentary sovereignty and the rule of law to assert a right to rule on whether the actions of public bodies exercising statutory powers have a proper statutory basis. Thus, as has already been explained, though there is no express statutory right to challenge the legality of a planning decision, decisions of planning authorities can be challenged in the courts by way of an application for judicial review. This remedy now has a statutory basis in Section 31 of the Supreme Court Act 1981. Nevertheless, it is still essentially a judge-made remedy in that the 1981 Act provides no guidance on what kinds of decisions can be challenged or on what grounds. In the case of grounds of review, there is ample evidence that the judiciary have developed what may be termed 'free-standing' principles of administrative justice which will give way only to clear statutory exclusion. Of course, in the field of town and country planning (which is almost entirely composed of statute) the starting point must be the statute, and much of the courts' work in reviewing the exercise of statutory powers is a matter of statutory interpretation. The important point is that although the UK courts cannot resort to a written constitution to out-trump an Act of Parliament, the judges themselves have developed fundamental principles which will only be overridden by the totally unambiguous wording of a statute.

A good example of this is the Court of Appeal decision in *R v Secretary of State for the Home Department*[8] where the statute expressly stated that the Secretary of State was not required to give reasons for refusing an application for naturalization. The majority in the Court of Appeal, while accepting that there was no need to give reasons in the light of the wording of the statute, did go on to hold that there was a duty before making the decision for the minister to give the applicant sufficient information (as to the minister's concerns) to enable him to make representations as to those concerns. The court stressed that to assume that parliament intended to allow the minister to act unfairly would be wholly inconsistent with the principles of administrative law.

There, are therefore, two distinct methods by which the High Court can be called on to review the legality of a planning decision. First, there is a statutory right to challenge the decisions of the Secretary of State (and, to a much lesser extent, decisions of local planning authorities).[9] Second, where there is no statutory right, the inherent jurisdiction of the High Court applies, and planning decisions (whether made by the Secretary of State or a local planning authority) can be challenged by way of an application for judicial review. The two procedures are normally kept distinct because, as we have seen with development plans, the Act not only provides a right of challenge, but also makes it exclusive. The reason why statutory review normally applies only to decisions of the Secretary of State is presumably because in the case of the decisions of local planning authorities there is a right to appeal to the Secretary of State.[10] Thus, in the case of planning determinations, the applicant and the applicant alone has a right of appeal. There is, therefore, not much point in the applicant directly challenging by way of judicial review a refusal by a local planning authority. In any case, the court would usually refuse such an application where there was a right of appeal. In recent years, however, there has been a surge in the use of the *application for judicial review* (AJR) by third parties to challenge the grant of planning permission. This trend brings us to the vexed question of who should have access to the courts.

ACCESS TO PLANNING JUSTICE

With both statutory review and AJR there are restrictions on who can challenge the legality of planning decisions. In the case of statutory review, the standard formula is that only *persons aggrieved* by the decision can apply, though the local planning authority usually has special right to challenge decisions made by the Secretary of State. In the case of AJR the applicant has to have *sufficient interest* to get leave,[11] and a remedy may be refused at the substantive stage if there is not sufficient interest.[12] The exact meaning of these terms has generated much case law, and the judicial decisions do reveal an interesting conflict on the role of third parties in the planning system. Thus, in *Buxton v Minister of Housing and Local Government*[13] it was held that the owner of adjoining land, whose property would be adversely affected by an application for permission to mine chalk, was not able to challenge a grant of planning permission on appeal, even though he had appeared and called evidence at the inquiry. Yet more than a decade later in *Turner v Secretary of State for the Environment*[14] another judge held that members of a local preservation society, who had objected and given evidence at an Inquiry into a planning appeal, were *persons aggrieved* and in principle had jurisdiction to challenge the minister's decision.

The crucial difference between *Buxton* and *Turner* is that in the former case the development control process was seen as essentially a two-sided contest between the applicant and the public authorities. The fact that the general public had very few specific legal rights to intervene in that process was taken to mean that parliament had not intended the general public to have any right to challenge the legality of planning decisions. A vital link was made between the statutory right to make representations and the right to ensure that the minister in considering those representations acted legally. This approach has a logical coherence, but it ignores the fact that over recent years, while the vogue for public participation may have waxed and waned, ordinary people not only look to the development control system to ensure the proper planning of the their district but consider that they should be closely involved in its administration.

The conflict between *Buxton* and *Turner* has never been formally resolved, and so in theory the point is still an open one. However, all the recent cases suggest that the courts would interpret 'person aggrieved' to include any person whose interests will be affected by the outcome of a planning decision. What is less unclear is whether the term 'person aggrieved' still excludes someone who will not be personally affected but nevertheless wishes to challenge the decision in the public interest. The outcome of that may depend on the conclusion of a similar judicial conflict as to who may use AJR to challenge decisions of local planning authorities.

In the case of AJR, courts have accepted that persons whose economic interests will be adversely affected by a grant of planning permission have 'sufficient interest' to challenge the legality of the grant by a local planning authority,[15] and it would also seem that local residents whose interests will be materially affected have standing. [16] Indeed in *R v Hammersmith and Fulham B C ex parte People Before Profit Ltd* [17] the judges went as far as to advance the equivalent of a citizen's right to ensure that applications for planning permission are determined legally when they stated:

> a person was entitled to object in a planning matter if he had a legitimate bona fide reason. He did not have to be a resident. But he was not to be an officious bystander or an officious busybody. He must have what any reasonable person would have said was a legitimate interest in being heard in objection. One could not set down elaborate and comprehensive rules about that because anyone might have a legitimate bona fide interest in places far removed from where they lived. They might be places where people went on holiday, they might be places where people went for sporting events, they might be places which people felt were so much in the public interest that they ought to have been heard about them as a citizen of the country.

However, doubt as to what is required to show sufficient interest has been caused by two recent High Court decisions which involved the challenge by local residents (who were concerned about environmental issues) of the legality of grants of permission for mining. In the *Garnett* [18] case, without giving any reasons, it was held that the applicant did not have sufficient standing. Then within a month of this, a judgment in the *Dixon*[19] case took a fundamentally different approach. In essence it was held that, at the leave stage, it is not necessary for the applicant to show any special interest over and above the generality of the public as long as there is an arguable case and the application is not an abuse of the court's time. The rationale, as with the question of who is a person aggrieved, is that ordinary citizens have a right to ensure that the planning system is not abused: it is not an exclusive game between the applicant and the local planning authority. This approach still leaves it open to the court to refuse a remedy even if they were to find the grant legally flawed, if they considered that the circumstances (including the applicant's lack of any special interest) made this inappropriate.

It is significant that, in the *Garnett* case, the view was also expressed that the applicant's chances of success on the merits were slim. It is very rare for the courts to hold that there are strong arguments that the grant of permission is illegal but then to refuse the application on grounds of standing. Over the past 50 years, the main concern of the courts has been to ensure that the planning powers are exercised legally. This question of legality itself raises difficult questions about the role of the courts and their views as to the scope of planning.

The two most crucial planks of the planning system are defined in a very open ended way. Both the definition of what can be controlled (Section 55) and the basis on which applications can be determined (Section 70) are not set out precisely but refer vaguely to *material changes of use* and *material considerations*. The courts, by their right to lay down the correct interpretation of these sections, play a pivotal role in the manner in which the system is operated. Over the last 50 years, the courts have fairly consistently adopted what can be termed a deferential or at least supervisory role. Thus, in the case of the definition of development, it has been repeatedly stated that the application of the words in the definition is a question of 'fact and degree' for planning authorities. The courts have been content to give very general guidance as to the factual circumstances that the words are *capable* of covering. Indeed, the judiciary have tended to give approval to the approaches taken in ministerial decisions, thus allowing the system to be driven by the operators. For example, the concept of the *planning unit*, which is very important in determining whether a change is material, is largely the creation not of the courts but of ministerial decisions.[20]

Of course, a planning authority cannot deliberately expand the definition just because it would be convenient to be able to control such activities. As Hough (1997: 895) has pointed out, there is a very important distinction between the decision on whether the authority has jurisdiction over the activities and the decision on whether to refuse or allow the development. However, Hough is undoubtedly correct in holding that the courts, by accepting that the question of whether a change is material can turn on whether it has planning consequences, have made the two decisions overlap. The fact that the change will have an adverse off-site impact can be used by a local planning authority both to determine as a matter of fact and degree that it is development and then to make that adverse impact the basis of a policy decision to refuse permission for the change.

In the case of the decision on the determination of a planning application, the courts were at first inclined to give a restrictive interpretation of what was capable of being a *material consideration* and to confine the term to amenity considerations. Thus, in a 1976 case[21] it was stated that 'the purpose of all town and country planning is to preserve amenities and the sensible and attractive layout of properties'. In more recent years the courts, as with the definition of development, have accepted a very wide scope to material considerations, and to include both social and economic considerations (Purdue 1989). The result is that planning permission can be legally refused because a proposed development does not contain provision for affordable housing[22] or it raises fears of crime,[23] and it can be granted because the development provides employment, or the profits generated will enable other planning advantages to be obtained.[24]

In *Tesco v Secretary of State for the Environment*[25] the House of Lords has made plain that the weight to be given to a material consideration is purely a matter of policy for the decision maker (even to the extent of deciding to give the consideration no weight at all). On the other hand, the courts seem very unsure as to their role in deciding whether a consideration, which is capable as an abstract matter of law of being material, is actually material in the particular factual circumstances. In *Bolton M. B. C. v Secretary of State for the Environment*[26] it was held that where it was alleged that there had been a failure on behalf of the decision maker to take into account a material consideration, it was for the judge to decide whether it was a matter which should have been taken into account. Yet a distinction was drawn between the matter being relevant and it being 'fundamental to the decision'. This seems to suggest that an argument could be capable of being relevant, but not relevant to the particular decision unless there was a real possibility that it would have made a difference to the actual outcome. In *Tesco* it was similarly held that 'material' meant the same as 'relevant' and it is for the courts to decide what is relevant if the matter is brought before them. All these statements leave unclear the extent to which it is for the court or the planning authority to decide whether the consideration is in the particular circumstances relevant.

This last issue was considered in another case [27] where it was suggested that:

> where the consideration in issue fell within a category or class where it was prima facie material, the question of whether it was in law material might often be difficult to decide and one of degree, and one where the court might be slow to intervene.

It was held that, although relevance was a question of law for the courts, this could depend on a question of fact which came within the jurisdiction of the decision maker – thus neatly marking out the division of labour. In a 1998 case[28] it was then held that while the impact on a private view could be material, whether it was or not depended on its necessity in the public interest; and that was an issue for the decision maker not the court to decide. This last case would seem to confuse the question of policy (as to the weight to be given to the private interest) and whether a particular private interest was a material consideration.

The need for an appropriate division of labour also applies to the issue of the application of the policies in the development plan and other relevant government policies. Sections 54A and 70 of the 1990 Act make plain that the application must be decided in accordance with the development plan except where other material considerations (which include government policies) indicate otherwise. As a result, almost all planning decisions will require careful scrutiny of those policies. This in turn will involve detailed argument as to their meaning. As Section 54A requires as a matter of law that the application be determined 'in accordance with the plan' it is arguable that it is a matter of law for the courts to decide in any particular case whether or not a proposed development conforms to the plan. Yet the interpretation and application of planning policies is not a task for which the courts are trained. Although the issue has never been finally determined, the tenor of recent decisions is that it is also primarily a matter of fact and degree for the planning authorities.[29]

In the case of government policies, early *dicta* held that the decision maker erred in law if the policies were not properly applied or understood: this appeared to suggest that it was for the courts authoritatively to interpret such policies. [30] Again, recent cases have emphasized that the courts should be slow to overturn the construction and application of planning policies. In this regard the most important statement of the law was made in *R v Derbyshire C C ex p Woods*:[31]

> If there is a dispute about the meaning of the words included in a policy document which a planning authority is bound to take into account, it is of course for the court to determine as a matter of law, what the words are capable of meaning. If the decision maker attaches a meaning to the words they are not capable of bearing, then it will have made an error of law, and it will have failed properly to understand the policy... If there is room for dispute about the breadth of the meaning the words may properly bear then there may in particular cases be material considerations of law which will

deprive a word of one of its possible shades of meaning in that case as a matter
of law.

As I have pointed out elsewhere (Purdue 1999), this approach allows for flexibility
while retaining for the courts the right to intervene when they consider it necessary.
There will be cases where the words can only have one possible meaning – in which
case, the decision maker will have erred in law by giving those words another meaning. In other cases, the words may be capable of a range of meanings, and the
relevant planning authority can choose the most appropriate in the particular policy
context.

REASONING AND RATIONALITY

It would seem to be generally accepted that, on the whole, there are more advantages than disadvantages in imposing a legal duty on decision makers to give reasons
for their decisions. Nevertheless, the courts still hold that unless there is a statutory
duty to give reasons, no general duty to do so can be implied, though the number of
exceptions to this principle is threatening to overturn the principle in practice. Planning law however is fortunate in that, since 1962, subordinate legislation has
imposed an express duty for planning authorities to give reasons. This statutory duty
is, however, not comprehensive or indeed consistent. While local planning authorities are required to state 'clearly and precisely their full reasons' for refusing permission or for imposing conditions,[32] there is no requirement on them to give reasons
full or otherwise for granting permission. There is also a duty on local planning
authorities to give reasons why they considered it expedient to issue an enforcement
notice.[33] As has already been pointed out, there is a duty imposed on the inspectors
and ministers in planning appeals to give reasons for their decisions.

The existence of a statutory duty to give reasons undoubtedly makes it easier for
legal challenges to be made in the courts. The courts provide a means of imposing a
check on the quality of decision making by requiring the reasoning process to be
spelt out and justified. In the last decade, however, there have been two House of
Lords' decisions which have had the effect of diluting the depth of this scrutiny.
The courts have for some time held that reasons must be 'proper, intelligible and
adequate'.[34] The main problem has been the standard by which to judge 'adequacy'.
First, in *Save Britain's Heritage v Secretary of State for the Environment*[35] the House of
Lords held that reasons will be considered inadequate only if the applicant has been
substantially prejudiced by the alleged failing. The important point here is that
there is no abstract standard of adequacy by which reasons are to be judged. So even
if there is a gap in the reasons, this will not result in the court quashing the decisions,
unless that gap or inadequacy has substantially prejudiced the applicant. The result
is in effect that inadequacy of reasons is not in itself an error of law. In the Court of
Appeal, it had been accepted that even if there was inadequacy of reasoning, the
court would refuse to quash it if it could be said with confidence that the inadequacy
could not conceal a flaw in the decision-making process. The important difference in
practice between the House of Lords and the Court of Appeal was therefore the test
as to prejudice. The stance of the Court of Appeal was that, once inadequacy is
shown, the burden is on the respondent to show that there is no chance of prejudice.
For the House of Lords, it is on the applicant to show that the shortcomings of the
reasons raised substantial doubt as to whether the decision was free from an error of
law.

Then in the *Bolton* case[36] it was emphasized that reasoning could be considered to be inadequate only if there was a failure to address the 'principal important contro-versial issues'. So, although the decision maker must by law consider all the *material* considerations, the reasons do not have to set out the views of the decision maker on arguments based on material considerations if they are not the principal important controversial issues. Both the *Save* and the *Bolton* decisions concerned appeals where the minister had to respond to an inspector's report; and in *MJT Securities v Secretary of State for the Environment*[37] the High Court suggested that with small inquiries (and here the reference seemed to be to decisions by inspectors – which constitute the vast majority) the reasons should refer to all the material considerations. The Court of Appeal however expressly disagreed and held that the test of adequacy did not vary depending on the size of the inquiry and the number of issues.[38]

The difference in judicial opinion in policy terms clearly derives from different views as to the balance to be drawn between burdening the decision maker and the need to ensure that all material considerations are *seen* to be regarded. Thus, in *Bolton* it was stated:

> To require [the Secretary of State] to refer to every material consideration, however significant, and to deal with every argument, however peripheral, would be to impose an unjustifiable burden.[39]

By contrast in *MJT Securities*, in the High Court, the judge submitted that:

> there could be no doubt that the development of administrative law over the last 25 years had performed an important quality control function for adminis-trative decision making. . . . . . . the need for reasons to be adequate and intelli-gible had meant that the courts provided a means of imposing a check on the quality of decision making by requiring the reasoning process to be spelt out and justified.[40]

Not surprisingly, Stephen Crow (1998: 419), the former Chief Planning Inspector, has observed that the approach taken in *MJT Securities* by the Court of Appeal 'is fortunate for practical administration' and he rejects the view that the High Court should exercise a quality control function. However, in the present author's view, the present line taken by the courts gives too much leeway to the decision maker. The Act requires (and the courts have accepted) that the decision maker *must* have regard to all the material considerations. It has been pointed out that the courts have already held that a consideration will only be material if there was a real possibility that it could make a difference to the decision. This strict test would seem to be sufficient to ensure that the writers of decision letters did not have to set out their views on peripheral and academic arguments. It is also important both on grounds of justice and of the quality of decision making that the decision maker is required to show that all the material issues have been considered. On the issue of proving substantial hardship, it does seem wrong for the courts to fuse the issue of whether the duty to give adequate reasons has been carried out and what is essentially a causation question of whether the omission has resulted in substantial hardship (Hough 1998: 625). In this respect, Section 288 distinguishes between the questions of whether there has been compliance with the relevant requirements and whether this has caused substantial hardship, and the wording suggests that there is no special burden on the applicant to prove that hardship has been caused.

HAS THE "PETTIFOGGING" STOPPED? THE ROLE OF THE COURTS IN
ENFORCEMENT

Enforcement is often described as the sharp end of planning in that in the final
analysis it requires the backing of the criminal law. This aspect results not only in the
courts being extra vigilant to ensure that all the procedures are followed but it also
involves the participation of the inferior courts who enforce the criminal law. This
essay is not the place for a detailed examination of the history and law on enforcement (the particular problems that resulted from the original provisions in the 1947
Act have already been excellently analysed by Grant, 1982: ch. 9). At the risk of
simplification there are two main problem areas.

The first area of difficulty is similar to the issues already discussed, as it arises with
the control of the High Court over enforcement appeals. The enforcement procedures are complicated, and it is very easy for local planning authorities to make
mistakes both of fact and law. The appeal to the Secretary of State gives an
opportunity for the inspector to resolve such mistakes and to carry out repair works
on the notice. The legislation provides the inspector with sweeping powers to carry
out that work as long as it will not result in injustice.[41] The courts have created
complicated and technical distinctions between errors which result in notices being
complete nullities and errors which make the notice invalid. An enforcement is
basically a nullity when it is clear from the face of the notice that the planning
authority has exceeded its powers. (The distinction is important in that a nullity
cannot be cured on appeal.) The courts have in the past made a further distinction
between invalidities which can be cured on appeal and those which are so material
that they cannot be cured and which must therefore be quashed by the courts if
challenged. It is perhaps these distinctions which led Sedley to claim that planning
has developed its own jurisprudence of judicial review since in other areas of
administrative law the courts have eschewed degrees of invalidity or nullity. Today,
cases of an enforcement notice turning out to be a complete nullity are rare but do
still occur. More significant in practical terms is the extent of the powers of amendment, and the Court of Appeal has recently refused to read in limitations on this
power. In a 1997 case,[42] it was stated that:

> The courts would not in my judgment be doing anyone a service if they were
> to write into section 176 of the 1990 Act words which are simply not there.
> ... the law had now reached the stage where the pettifogging has stopped,
> where artificial and nice distinctions understood only by lawyers no longer
> prevail and the Act can be read so that it means what it says, namely that the
> Secretary of State may correct *any* defect or error in an enforcement notice if he
> is satisfied that the correction can be made without injustice to either party to
> the planning appeal.

The second area of difficulty relates to the jurisdiction of the inferior courts in
criminal prosecutions and the problem of collateral challenge. If a party adversely
affected by an enforcement notice fails to appeal or to apply for judicial review, it
may become impossible to challenge the legality of the notice directly in the High
Court either because time has run out or challenge is excluded. The difficult question is whether the validity of the notice can be raised as a defence to criminal
prosecution for failing to comply with the notice. On the one hand, it could be very
unfair if a person could be convicted of a criminal offence when if that person had
taken legal advice and acted promptly the notice could have been quashed as

invalid. On the other hand, it is not in the public interest that the effectiveness of enforcement should be undermined by eleventh hour arguments which raise difficult legal questions of administrative law not suitable for a magistrates' court.

The House of Lords decision in *R v Wicks* [43] has now settled the issue at least with regard to enforcement notices. The only defence, based on the validity of the enforcement notice, which can be raised in the magistrates' court is that the notice is a nullity because it is clear from its face that it has not been issued in accordance with the statutory requirements. This strict approach was justified on the basis of the history and wording of the statutory scheme on enforcement notices which Lord Hoffmann said showed a consistent policy of progressively restricting the kind of issues which a person served with an enforcement notice can raise when he is prosecuted for failing to comply. [44]

The *Wicks* decision strictly only applies to enforcement notices, and it has already been distinguished with regard to breach of condition notices where there is no right of appeal. [45] There is also the problem of why there should be a distinction between enforcement notices which are nullities (where the nullity can be raised as a defence) and those which are *ultra vires* because of errors of law which do not show on the face of the notice. Nevertheless, it is clear that the present judiciary are keen to support the effectiveness of the enforcement of planning and will only intervene where there are clear errors of law resulting in unfairness.

CONCLUSION

Because of the profits at stake, the decisions of planning authorities are the subject of intensive scrutiny and litigation. In the case of Section 78 appeals, Professor Stephen Crow (1998: 429) has pointed out that between 1992 and 1997 over 500 decisions were challenged in the High Court: an average of 100 a year. Lawyers tend to consider that all this scrutiny must be to the good, and clearly it would be intolerable if there was no mechanism by which parties could ensure that planning authorities did not abuse their powers. On the other hand, Daintiff (1997: 13) has argued that the open-textured nature of the standards of judicial review creates real problems of effectiveness and efficiency. He submits that judicial review

> is seen by administrators as making it increasingly difficult to administer policies efficiently, as adding substantially to departmental costs, and sometimes as effectively destroying the substantive effect of policies, through the imposition of delay while approaches censured in judicial review are corrected.

However, it is very difficult to quantify the cost-effectiveness of judicial intervention and whether the hoped for gains in terms of justice and quality outweigh the costs. In the particular case of planning, the judges seem on the whole to be aware of the need for restraint, though the amount of discretion given to them means that inevitably their decisions must be consciously or unconsciously influenced by their own views as to the proper role of planning or the merits of a particular decisions. While the last 50 years have seen judicial intervention becoming more widespread and penetrating, there is also a constant ebb and flow as the judges seek to achieve the correct balance between fussy interference and proper supervision and control. The Human Rights Act 1998 will undoubtedly strengthen the constitutional base of the judiciary. Linked with the development of the proportionality principle, this could lead the judiciary into a greater involvement in substantive planning matters.

If this were to happen, there will be a corresponding need to strengthen the planning expertise of the courts. One possibility is the creation of what Lord Woolf (1992) has termed a 'multi-faceted tribunal' – usually referred to as an 'environmental court'. The new tribunal would have an expanded jurisdiction and would be staffed by environmental experts as well as lawyers. Such a reform would raise very difficult issues of accountability, but it would help to solve some of the problems of the legitimacy of judicial intervention which have occurred in the first 50 years of planning.

FURTHER READING

One of the best accounts of the role of the courts in planning is in Grant (1982) *Urban Planning Law* and in his article (1978a) 'Planning, politics and the judges'. The above are now rather dated but a revised edition of the former is in hand. A current analysis of the role of the judiciary in reviewing the legality of administrative action generally can be found in Sedley (1997) *The Making and Remaking of the British Constitution* and in the comprehensive but very long and expensive De Smith *et al.* (1995) *Judicial Review of Administrative Action*. For an attack on the abuse of the right of challenge in the courts, see Crow (1998) 'Challenging appeal decisions, or the use and abuse of the "toothcomb"'. The arguments for an 'environmental court' are set out in Carnwath (1992) 'Environmental enforcement: the need for a specialist court', and Woolf (1992) 'Are the judiciary environmentally myopic?'

chapter 12

Vision and Reality

Urban Social Policy

BRIAN ROBSON

INTRODUCTON

At a recent family gathering, we asked one of our grandchildren what were the best bits of her holiday in France. She replied, 'Swimming at midnight and going horse-riding on a big horse', an innocuous and not unexpected response. More unexpected and more interesting was her reaction to a visit to Chartres: 'I liked the blue stained glass windows, but I couldn't understand the pictures in them'. The vision of faith so lovingly delineated by the master craftsmen of the Middle Ages had become a fascinating blur to a child of the late twentieth century. Her perception of the beauty in those famous windows was instinctive and unprompted, but her understanding of what they conveyed was limited by an education and upbringing based on tolerance and the recognition of many faiths. It is easy enough to explain to such a child – well versed in the use of both CD-Roms and TV – the role played by those images, but much harder to explain their meaning. The suffering, hardship and torments of faith are not a natural part of the experience of the fortunate children of affluent cocooning parents.

Half a century on, much of the work of the 1945 Labour government is beginning to have the same impact, pleasant but essentially blurred. From time to time anniversaries may sharpen the focus, as with the 1998 outburst of sentiment about the establishment of the National Health Service or the 1997 recollections of the Town and Country Planning Act of 1947. We do not recall, except as a sad footnote to the demise of the industry, the nationalization of the coal mines. After the messiness of privatization, we may now view with some nostalgia the nationalization of the railways and begin to have a clearer picture as to why that was thought necessary. For the most part, however, all those efforts at state ownership are now largely seen as an unnecessary and unfortunate waste of time, effort and resource. The reasons why they were so ardently sought after and welcomed are now blurred.

That there was a fervent desire to make a better society, one which was fairer, more compassionate and more equal, has been eloquently conveyed by Peter Hennessy in his book *Never Again*:

> Never again, for me, captures the motivating impulse of the first half dozen
> years after the war – never again would there be war; never again would the
> British people be housed in slums, living off a meagre diet thanks to low
> wages or no wages at all; never again would mass unemployment blight the

lives of millions; never again would natural abilities remain dormant in the absence of educational stimulus (Hennessy 1992: 2).

But what was then clearly seen by many as the best way to achieve this ideal is now suspect. Indeed, even the ideal is now modified: equality of opportunity has become a mealy mouthed pandering to freedom of choice; the penny pinching 'care in the community', along with a mawkish concern over animals and a prurient uproar over sex abuse, reflect the degenerated compassion of contemporary society.

Unemployment has become all too integral an experience for too many families, and the rising number of homeless makes a mockery of the dream of good housing for all. Any drive towards fairness in contemporary society seems much concerned with jealousy and a desire to find somebody or something to blame for life's misfortunes, preferably with a view to getting monetary recompense.

This is perhaps too extreme a view. There is no doubt that Britain in many ways has changed for the better over the last 50 years. For the most part, people's health has improved: the housing stock is better: the average standard of living has risen; we are less insular, better informed, better educated. At least that is what we would like to think. It is a pleasing picture which does not bear too close a scrutiny for, like the stained glass windows, it encompasses many distressing stories – of faith misplaced, of faith and trust betrayed. Just as the wartime society out of which the 1945 government emerged was not one of whole-hearted cooperation and continuous effort but rather was marked by rising petty criminality and rent by deep divisions, so our present-day Britain is a society with a nasty brutal and brutish undertone; still enmeshed in the narrow confines of an outdated nationalism; with too large a minority of its population ill educated; and with a hard core of selfishness and uncouth behaviour which permeates everywhere.

This dichotomy pervades all of Britain: there is no difference in the selfishness of the well-heeled rural house owner with a vociferous antipathy to the development of greenfield sites and that of the property developer weeping crocodile tears about the exorbitant cost of developing brownfield sites. More portentous and apparently more high-minded self-centredness is reflected in the claims of Oxford and Cambridge universities that they should receive proportionately more money than other higher education institutions in order to maintain an archaic system which benefits a small number of selected young people. Similarly, the professions such as law and medicine guard themselves against criticism through their closed systems of accountability, but are never backward in claiming large shares of public money in remuneration. The current agonizing over waiting lists in hospitals has its roots in the essential selfishness of doctors who, from the outset of nationalization, managed to secure and to maintain a disastrous relationship between public and private medicine which benefits them, insurance companies and the better-off.

THE PERCEIVED OVERLAP OF SOCIAL AND URBAN PROBLEMS

These are not, of course, the aspects of the downside of modern Britain that have been much scrutinized by the media or tackled by government over the past 50 years. Instead (until recently) it has been easier to subsume everything that seems wrong as being a product of urbanism and more particularly of the 'inner city.'

Feeding on misplaced nostalgia and a supposed innate British love of the countryside, it has been easy to focus anxiety and action on that 'other' who dwells in tower blocks and sink estates. This 'other', purportedly only fit for the routine heavy labour of obsolete industries, is pinpointed as the source of rising crime, vandalism, drug culture and any other ills of modern society.

To a large extent the social tensions and social problems faced by the country have been transmuted into the problems of cities in Britain. At times, social policy and urban policy have almost become one and the same thing. We can see this inter-relationship evolving in three phases of policy in the postwar period. First was the thrust of urban planning in the two postwar decades; second the rediscovery of poverty and the start of concern about inner cities at the end of the 1960s, and third the current administration's lack of ostensible interest in urban policy *per se* and in its place its development of a range of socially directed legislation.

THE SOCIAL IMPACTS OF POSTWAR PLANNING

There was no explicitly urban social policy in the postwar years. Social legislation on health, housing, education, social welfare and fiscal issues was not specific to differ-ent types of location. The closest thing to an urban strategy was the postwar plan-ning policy of urban containment. This had a strong but covert, and perhaps unintentional, social dimension. It was, as Hall has argued (Hall *et al.* 1973), a pact between rural interests that wished to put a collar around the apparently inexorable outward expansion of towns, and the industrial cities and towns whose managers sought to erase and redevelop their Victorian legacy and yet retain their population and economic investment. The creation of the new and expanded towns and the controlled development of village expansion beyond the green belts admirably served both interests. Yet it had a marked social impact on the geography of Britain. The outward population migration was highly selective. Even though the planned movement of skilled families to the new towns was never more than a small fraction of the total outward movement, market forces ensured that it was the professional classes and the skilled artisans who moved out of the urban areas. Many of the worst housed, usually the unskilled families, were not able to move to the new towns (Heraud 1966). Despite the early aspirations to create communities that were socially mixed, indeed that were mixed geographically so that different income groups would live cheek by jowl within integrated neighbourhoods, that aim was frustrated by the workings of the housing market.

As outward migration increased, it was the unskilled who remained within the big cities from which population was decanted or voluntarily migrated. Many of the families that remained were accommodated in the social housing that was developed so massively in urban areas in the 1950s and 1960s. Only in very few of the big towns and cities did a significant professional class remain – in London, because of its size and the length of commuting which meant that a sufficient number of professionals could form secure enclaves in its inner areas; in medium-sized university towns such as Oxford and Cambridge; or even in some university contexts within large cities such as Edgbaston in Birmingham, Clifton in Bristol or The Park in Nottingham. While the outward drift of population had started well before the war, the earlier inter-war migration had largely been in the form of suburbanization, still largely encompassed within the administrative areas of most towns. It was the twin postwar forces of urban containment, with a planning regime that encouraged development beyond green belts, together with the growth of car ownership that provided a combination that stamped so firm a shape on the rural/urban social divide. Ironically, in gentrifying the rural areas, it also ensured that poverty amongst the 'indigenous' rural households became a largely unseen phenomenon.

THE HOUSING IMPACTS

The dominant element of urban social policy at this time was the pursuit of new housing. Successive administrations vied with each other to build larger numbers of houses and, during the 1950s, the tenure mix of new houses altered from predominantly public to predominantly private as the exigencies of postwar budgets gave way to the expansionary years lauded by Macmillan during his premiership in the late 1950s (Merrett and Gray 1982; Holmans 1987). For the towns, the changes led, seemingly inexorably, from the building of good quality traditional housing in large public estates to the use of industrialized construction methods and the growth of high-rise flats which reached their peak in the early 1970s (Dunleavy 1981). Such developments – universally despised today – were, when first introduced, an enormous physical improvement on the Victorian by-law terraces that they replaced. So long as the stock was new and memories of what they replaced were fresh, they not only represented improved housing conditions but they also symbolized the new post-Victorian modernist era on which the country had set its sights ever since the Festival of Britain in 1951.

Some voices of caution were raised about the impacts of high-rise living (Gittus 1976), but so long as there was an overall shortage of housing and virtually full employment they appeared a solution to the recurring crises of housing. It was only later – when the shoddiness of their construction, the costs of their communal maintenance and their inappropriateness as homes for young families grew ever more obvious – that opinion turned so dramatically against them as a solution. But the consequence of the rise and fall of high-rise housing was that the big cities (in which predominantly such flats had been built) were faced with a substantial stock of unpopular and expensive housing in which increasingly the very poor and the problem families were housed. This exacerbated, at a micro scale, the polarization between the comfortable and the uncomfortable that, at a macro scale, had emerged between town and country. After the 1970s, the expansion of refurbishment (in the form of *housing action areas* and *housing improvement areas*) and the reversion to traditional low-rise houses took centre stage. However, not only was a diminishing amount of new social housing built, but as a tenure it had come to be associated irrevocably with the poor and the inadequate (unlike its role in providing improved housing for all in the early legislation at the end of World War I).

The, doubtless unintentional, product of the planning and housing policies of the first two postwar decades was therefore a society much more marked by the geographical polarization of the comfortable and the uncomfortable, both in the divide between town and country as well as within the towns themselves.

URBAN POLICIES

A second, and surprisingly long, phase has been the development of explicit policies for 'inner' cities that started with Harold Wilson's declaration of an 'urban policy' in 1968. This has been developed piecemeal over the following 30 years. The irony is that this evolving programme came full circle; 'from social to social in three iterations'. It started, rather feebly, with an explicitly social dimension that responded to the perceived problems of Commonwealth immigration (with some of its policy instruments, such as *educational priority areas*, directed at attempts to improve inner city schooling and community life and with grants to assist those whose first language was not English). It then developed an explicitly economic dimension in the *enhanced urban programme* in 1977, partly in response to the structuralist critique of the *community development projects* (Benington 1975) and three *inner area studies* of London, Birmingham and Liverpool. It subsequently focused on physical regeneration and infrastructure under the Conservative administrations of the 1980s. It came full circle in its current third phase that has seen a growing concern for the social dimension of regeneration during the course of the 1990s.

The traditional urban programme

The initial phase during the 1960s was a rather half-hearted attempt to identify and tackle the 'residual' problem of the disadvantaged in the big cities. Many commentators (Edwards and Batley 1978) have seen the initial development of 'urban policy' in the late 1960s as a spur of the moment political reaction to the furore prompted by Enoch Powell's 'rivers of blood' speech; in response to which civil servants quickly invented some appropriate policy instruments. It had little resource and little direction. What it did introduce, however, was a raft of small-scale community led or community influenced projects (Lawless 1989). Through various of its funding regimes, it helped to transform and expand the activities of many voluntary sector bodies; and this worked hand in glove with the growing professionalization of voluntary agencies during the 1970s.

The enhanced urban programme

With the *enhanced urban programme* in 1977–8, the scale of resourcing was significantly higher and the focus of policy progressively changed, not least with the incoming Conservative administration in 1979. The concept of partnership started as the linking of central and local government in the form of joint committees to oversee the development of programmes in the seven *partnership authorities* (in Birmingham, Hackney, Islington, Lambeth, Liverpool, Manchester/Salford and Newcastle/Gateshead). This soon altered as central government came to see local authorities as part of the problem rather than a necessary part of any solution.

Hence, instead, public/private partnerships became the new focus, one that sidelined local authorities and encouraged greater involvement by developers and business interests. Many of the financial instruments introduced were explicitly aimed at providing incentives to such participation: *enterprise zones, simplified planning zones, derelict land grant, city grant* and, above all, the *urban development corporations* were all mechanisms to stimulate renewed investment by the private sector in areas from which it had withdrawn in the process of de-urbanization and de-industrialization (Robson 1988; Barnekov *et al.* 1989). Some of the welter of policy instruments of the 1980s are shown in Figure 12.1.

There was a belief, particularly marked during the 18 years of Conservative government (1979–97), that the revival of urban areas depended solely on market forces; that 'trickle down' would eventually produce work for the deprived and that no matter how poorly paid or unrewarding that work it would have beneficial social effects. Many commentators who had some experience both of academic research into urban matters and of working at the grass roots, argued that this concentration on economic policies was not having the necessary social impact (Robson 1994). The official evaluation of urban policy, long delayed in its publication, carried an unwelcome message about the uncertainties and failure of urban policy. It showed very clearly the weaknesses of the then approach to regeneration (Robson *et al.* 1994). While the analysis demonstrated that the expenditure of public resources did have relative beneficial effects on the targeted urban areas as a whole, the very worst places (typically the cores of the major conurbations) continued to deteriorate – the worst places worsened. An important part of this failure was the result of policies that were too narrowly concentrated on infrastructure and a physical bricks and mortar approach to regeneration (Turok 1992).

Of course, some policy instruments succeeded in terms of these goals. In particular, some of the urban development corporations, such as Central Manchester and Tyne and Wear, achieved considerable success in the physical regeneration of their urban development areas. They levered large sums of private investment back into areas that had been suffering from the withdrawal of such investment; they transformed the physical appearance and the economic role of their areas, even in the face of a deep property recession in the early 1990s; they created (as in Leeds) substantial numbers of new jobs; and they brought substantial numbers of residents back into the central areas of cities (DETR 1998a).

Central Manchester Development Corporation (CMDC) is an excellent example of such recolonization of central urban locations (Robson *et al.* 1998). At the outset of its life in 1988, the resident population in the designated area was only some 200, many of whom were caretakers and others who lived in the premises in which they worked. At its wind-down in 1996, the resident population had grown to over 3,000 both through the development of new housing within and on the fringes of the central business district – in Castlefield and elsewhere – and through the refurbishment of the numerous abandoned warehouses along the lines of the area's canals. Perhaps most significantly, the area's housing market had become self-sustaining. Whereas at the outset all of the developments were subsidized with public resource, at the end of the corporation's life new housing was being constructed in the area without the benefit of subsidy. A genuine new market had been created.

This and other examples of the recolonization of central areas in cities – such as Birmingham's Telford Basin and Leeds's The Calls – have become a significant marker of the turn-around of many of the big cities. The refurbishment of abandoned commercial buildings undertaken by some of the UDCs has demonstrated that there is potential to capitalize on waterfront and canal-side sites to create new largely professional enclaves of residential areas in central locations within big cities. These new residents can begin to accelerate the process of regeneration. They represent a local market for restaurants, clubs, music, theatre and shopping; and most of the developments have been accompanied by a growth in such services. For the economic prospects of cities this represents a virtuous spiral of regeneration. There is, of course, a downside. Even though many of the cities have developed middle income and low income housing developments within adjacent central areas (e.g. Hunslet Green in Leeds, or Piccadilly Village and the variety of housing association refurbishments in Manchester), the disproportionate bulk of new inner-area residents are professional and relatively high income households. Few if any benefits may flow to the existing poor communities in nearby areas. Indeed, one of the prerequisites of the design of successful central housing appears to be to emphasize physical protection and isolation from surrounding areas. They are typically fenced off, guarded enclaves that ostentatiously turn their backs on their neighbourhoods. Nevertheless, such developments have been one of the most striking and successful products of the UDC experiment.

However, what the UDCs did not do very successfully was to achieve effective linkage between the physical improvements and the new jobs created in their areas, on the one hand, and the deprived residents living in and near those inner areas, on the other. Few of the UDCs gave any priority to their local communities; those that did (such as Trafford Park's training programmes targeted at deprived areas in Old Trafford, or Tyne and Wear's establishment of links between new developments at Royal Quays and such deprived neighbouring areas as Meadowell Estate) were very

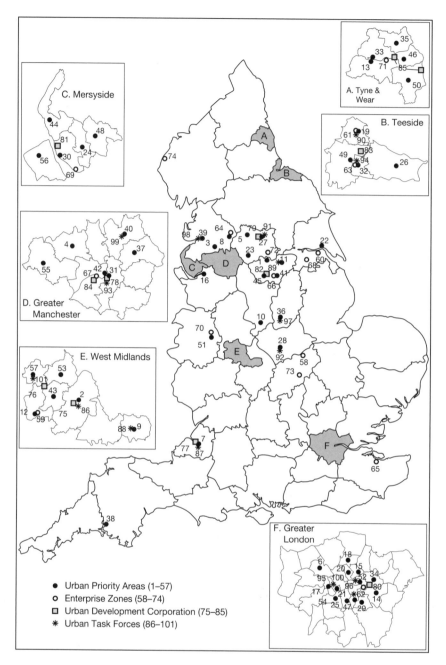

Figure 12.1 Urban
policy instruments
under Action for
Cities in the late
1980s

Legend within figure:
- ● Urban Priority Areas (1–57)
- ○ Enterprise Zones (58–74)
- ▢ Urban Development Corporation (75–85)
- ✳ Urban Task Forces (86–101)

much the exception. And for all the successes of many of the UDCs, there was a
significant minority whose achievements are difficult to trumpet, as in Bristol and
Plymouth (NAO 1997a).

COORDINATION AND PARTNERSHIP

More generally, what was apparent in the urban policies of the 1980s was both a lack
of coherence, especially in the financing of the varied and varying policies, and a
wide variation in outcomes. Helpfully, the government of the day took on board
some of the messages of the evaluations of urban policy and introduced the *single*

Key to Figure 12.1

Urban priority areas (in Action for Cities, 1987)			*Enterprise zones*
1 Barnsley	21 Kensington	40 Rochdale	58 Corby
2 Birmingham	22 Kingston-upon-	41 Rotherham	59 Dudley
3 Blackburn	Hull	42 Salford	60 Glandford
4 Bolton	23 Kirklees	43 Sandwell	61 Hartlepool
5 Bradford	24 Knowsley	44 Sefton	62 Isle of Dogs
6 Brent	25 Lambeth	45 Sheffield	63 Middlesbrough
7 Bristol	26 Langbaurgh	46 South Tyneside	64 Northeast
8 Burnley	27 Leeds	47 Southwark	Lancashire
9 Coventry	28 Leicester	48 St Helens	65 Northwest Kent
10 Derby	29 Lewisham	49 Stockton upon	66 Rotherham
11 Doncaster	30 Liverpool	Tees	67 Salford/Trafford
12 Dudley	31 Manchester	50 Sunderland	68 Scunthorpe
13 Gateshead	32 Middlesbrough	51 The Wrekin	69 Speke
14 Greenwich	33 Newcastle-upon-	52 Tower Hamlets	70 Telford
15 Hackney	Tyne	53 Walsall	71 Tyneside
16 Halton	34 Newham	54 Wandsworth	72 Wakefield
17 Hammersmith/	35 North Tyneside	55 Wigan	73 Wellingborough
Fulham	36 Nottingham	56 Wirral	74 Workington
18 Haringey	37 Oldham	57 Workington	
19 Hartlepool	38 Plymouth		
20 Islington	39 Preston		

Urban development corporations (established 1981–8)	*Urban task forces (established 1986–7)*
75 Birmingham Heartlands	86 Birmingham, Handsworth
76 Black Country	87 Bristol, St Pauls
77 Bristol	88 Coventry
78 Central Manchester	89 Doncaster
79 Leeds	90 Hartlepool
80 London Docklands	91 Leeds, Chapeltown
81 Merseyside	92 Leicester, Highfields
82 Sheffield	93 Manchester, Moss Side
83 Teesside	94 Middlesbrough, North Central
84 Trafford Park	95 North Kensington
85 Tyne and Wear	96 North Peckham
	97 Nottingham
	98 Preston
	99 Rochdale
	100 Spitalfields
	101 Wolverhampton

regeneration budget (SRB) in 1993 in an effort to introduce greater coherence into the financing of urban policy. Even though the implementation of SRB programmes has met with a mixed reception, the thrust of its approach from the early 1990s took clear account of the various criticisms directed at its predecessor policy instruments. In place of the marginalizing of local authorities, the SRB and *city challenge* gave local authorities a clear central role and, above all, both of these programmes laid emphasis on giving real substance to the concept of partnerships and of cross-agency collaboration.

City challenge and, to an even greater extent, the SRB gave bidders real incentives to establish effective partnerships across the domains of the public sector, private sector and voluntary/community sector. *City challenge* was first introduced in 1992 and, over its two rounds of competitive bidding, resulted in 31 partnerships each led by the relevant local authority and each given £37.5 million over a 5-year period to develop self-sustaining regeneration in their designated area. The programme has now ended, and the initial evaluation (Russell *et al.* 1996) argued that the programme had been a significant success. In terms of what it had delivered by the end of its third year, the partnerships had largely met or exceeded their planned outputs. Together they had levered-in over £1 billion of private resources, built or improved 40,000 houses, created or preserved over 50,000 jobs, created or improved over 1 million sq. metres of workspace, promoted over 3,000 business start-ups, and re-claimed or improved nearly 2,000 hectares of derelict land. One of the distinctive and novel features of city challenge was the emphasis it put on the management frameworks through which outputs were delivered. The other was the stress it placed on the principle of partnership.

Both of these features were equally strongly emphasized in the SRB programmes, which has produced a rapidly growing number of often quite small projects over its four rounds of bidding. Like city challenge, these were bid for on a competitive basis by partnerships that drew on public, private and community bodies. In practice, most of the partnerships were led by local authorities or by Training and Enterprise Councils. Indeed, in the early rounds of the SRB many such partnerships consisted of little more than bidding arrangements, in which the partners were as much signatories to bidding forms as active collaborators; once funding had been secured, the implementation of programmes was largely left to the local authorities who were predominantly the lead bodies in bids. It has proved difficult in practice to involve the voluntary sector – much less communities themselves – as equal partners (Macfarlane and Mabbott 1993). However, the principle of partnership working became an increasingly real feature of the delivery of programmes in the later rounds of SRB. There are now many examples of genuine collaboration in strategic management and in implementation, such as Royds in Bradford, STRIDE in South Shields, or Manor and Castle in Sheffield (DETR 1998c).

While there is widespread belief in the virtues of partnership approaches, the concept has not gone without critics (Harding 1990; Bailey *et al.* 1995). In the USA it is argued that in practice partnerships have favoured the private sector, thereby heightening the inequality of access to the control of regeneration, have undermined the democratic process, and have failed to meet public (as against private) goals. In Britain, there has been similar criticism: that partnerships are 'forced' creations prompted by government and the EU for grant-chasing purposes, that they are part of a proliferation of organizations that have brought duplication of effort and a lack of clarity about who is responsible for what, that their goals are aimed at the lowest common denominator in order to achieve consensus; and that they lack the ability to prioritize (not least over resource allocation across areas) because their constituent organizations continue to have different goals, political objectives and policy capacities. As they have proliferated, and as the range of new organizations has grown, so the ideal of better coordination associated with the partnership principle may paradoxically have grown less plausible as a result of the crowded policy environment.

However, the belief remains strongly rooted that effective partnerships improve performance and generate better value for money. This is argued on two principal grounds: that they maximize the probability of coordination across the many agen-cies that are, or ought to be, involved in regeneration; and that they enhance the sense of 'ownership' of programmes and schemes (both by agencies and by communities) and thereby make their impact more effective and more long term. They also provide a context in which charismatic leadership can give shape and direction to the goals of regenerating localities (Judd and Parkinson 1990).

To these principles of effective partnership and the stress on the delivery of outputs, SRB added a third, that of more integrated working across government departments. This was made explicit in the SRB since its budget was composed of resources drawn from over 20 existing programmes from a range of government departments (as well as DETR, these comprised the Home Office, the Department for Education and Employment (DfEE) and DTI). The essence of the funding regime therefore became that of integrating activities across the variety of elements of deprivation – housing, schooling, training, job creation, environment, policing, social welfare, probation and the like. Since SRB coincided with the establishment of integrated regional offices of government that drew together a range of arms of government, the focus on cross-departmental coordination became a recurring theme. The dilemma of departmentalism has long been a weakness of both central and local government. Earlier attempts to establish cross-cutting mechanisms (e.g. in the *city action teams* set up, with very small budgets, in some of the big cities) had had little effect. Even though departmental imperialism remains a fact of life (as seen in the battles over the budgets and powers of the English regional development agencies), there are now many more examples of closer integration in the thinking and priorities of government departments and across such agencies as Training and Enterprise Councils (TECs) and health authorities. Many of the more alert local authorities have restructured themselves by partly replacing functional service departments with more strategic or area-based departmental roles.

Such innovations have not only recognized the interconnectedness of the problems faced by deprived areas. They have also reflected the growing awareness inside government (and local authorities) that physical and economic regeneration by themselves were insufficient if the people living in deprived areas did not enjoy demonstrable benefits from the programmes. The social dimension had again entered the equation – somewhat belatedly, but none the less valuable for that.

This new thrust of policy, begun with city challenge and the SRB, has been built upon by the present administration. Integration has become what is now fashionably referred to as 'joined-up thinking'. The social dimension, with its focus on deprived households, is reflected not merely in the welcome establishment of the Social Exclusion Unit (SEU) but also in the fact that, while the government has not articulated any specific urban dimension to its policies, the New Deal and the numerous reviews and policy papers have, in effect, begun to spell out social strategies that in practice will impact strongly on deprived urban households. An example is the DETR's review of the SRB (DETR 1998b). This concluded: that a fifth round of bidding should be held; that (as in the fourth round) there should be an explicit stress on social disadvantage so that 80 per cent of its resources should be targeted to a limited number of the most deprived areas across the country; and that individual projects should be of a sufficiently large scale to ensure that strong management arrangements can be built into the delivery phase and that projects will benefit from the synergy and efficiency of size. Interestingly, a competitive principle will continue to be part of the process, in the expectation that this will produce higher quality and more innovative proposals from partnerships.

The most significant drift in policy over the two decades of urban policy has been the gradual realization that the social dimension is more than a mere add-on to policy. The SEU established by the Blair government in the autumn of 1997 is to be welcomed for firmly focusing attention away from bricks, mortar, infrastructure and

Liverpool	Leicester
Manchester	Birmingham
Newham	Sandwell
Hackney	Kingston upon Hull
Tower Hamlets	Bradford
Southwark	Norwich
Newcastle-upon-Tyne	Brighton and Hove
Middlesbrough	Bristol
Nottingham	

Figure 12.2 New deal for communities: local authorities chosen as pathfinders

economic competitiveness, and on to people. As with earlier attempts to integrate policy across departments, its remit is essentially non-departmental and it therefore reinforces the emphasis given to inter-agency and cross-departmental collaboration and partnership. How much success it will have remains to be seen. The government's failure in the Department of Social Security to progress 'thinking the unthinkable' on the issue of pensions and the apparent triumph of both bottom-line accountancy and electoral exigency looks like a return to business as usual. However, what the SEU has already achieved is a refocusing of the agenda to emphasize social deprivation. Its early reports (e.g. on truancy and on difficult housing estates) may not have developed especially novel proposals, but what they have done is to sensitize central government departments and local authorities to such issues and to encourage collaborative responses. This has been strongly reinforced by other elements of policy, not least the '*best value*' programme, and the education, health and employment *action zones*. The most recent SEU report, on difficult housing estates, is a masterly survey of the problems faces by impoverished areas (SEU 1998). It has provided the platform for the *New Deal for Communities* (DETR 1998d) under which 17 pilot neighbourhoods of up to 4,000 people will be funded to develop community-driven integrated assaults on the interconnected problems of low skill, poor employment, alienation, crime and the poverty that characterizes them.

These initiatives have begun to give force to the need to ensure inter-agency collaboration and the more effective expenditure of public resources. Their essence is a client-focused rather than a programme-focused approach, and therein lies the prospect of both a more sensitive and a more effective delivery of services. For the unemployed single-parent mother, for example, it is an administrative irrelevance that the various sources of help that she seeks are funded from different central or local authority departments. The development of services focused on her as a client must be a goal of more effective service delivery in order to deliver integrated across the board advice or help with housing, schooling, training, child care and the range of needs that face the disadvantaged.

The encouraging aspect of all this is that we seem to have learned from the long period of experimentation with urban policy. In this learning process, over a period of some three decades, the principles of coordination, balance between social and physical regeneration, partnership and quality have rightly come to dominate.

There are, however, some ambiguities in the current range of policies. One is the uncertain geographical focus to which they apply. The establishment of regional development agencies in the nine regions of England appears to sit awkwardly with an emphasis on targeting resources to a limited range of the most deprived areas. As they develop, the regional development agencies appear likely to be subject to increasing 'representative' influence in the form of the non-statutory chambers (and the possible development of statutory assemblies in due course). The temptation for them to allocate resources on a roughly equal geographical basis within each region seems likely to be one of the conundrums with which the agencies will have to grapple. Since a large fraction of their budgets is comprised of the SRB, this dilemma may apply especially forcefully to regeneration priorities. The 'ownership' of the SRB (as between DETR and its arms in the government regional offices, on the one hand, and the regional development agencies on the other) is just such an area of ambiguity. This is one of the drawbacks of the government having yet developed no explicit urban policy to emphasise the value of targeting resource to deprived urban areas.

THE RECURRING PATTERN OF DEPRIVATION

Studies of deprivation have shown a wide variety of patterns and of change in the levels of deprivation from one area to another between 1981 and 1991. However, one such study concluded:

> our evidence shows that levels of disadvantage remain high in most deprived areas and that the gap in living standards between them and other kinds of area is in some crucial respects no smaller. In the extent and depth of poverty and in death rates, many deprived areas have become worse off than ever compared with other places (Willmott 1994: 105).

Despite the very considerable improvements in urban social policy during the course of the 1990s, there is as yet still little tangible evidence that the outcomes of regeneration policies have done much to change the map of deprivation. DETR's Index of Urban Deprivation shows clearly how far economic policies have failed to 'trickle down' to the most disadvantaged areas. The original index (Robson *et al.* 1995) was based on 1991 data. It measured some dozen socioeconomic indicators of deprivation to produce a composite value such that the higher a district's score the more deprived it was. The figures showed how deprivation was concentrated on the big northern metropolitan areas, London boroughs, northern towns such as Middlesbrough, Blackburn, Hull, Doncaster, Preston and Hartlepool, and within some of the seaside resort towns such as Blackpool and Brighton. Within the most deprived 50 ranks, only Leicester, Southampton, Portsmouth, Bristol and Lincoln did not fall within these categories. None of this comes as a surprise; it mirrors the impact of de-industrialization and the flight of people and investments from the big cities and towns. What may be more depressing is that the results of the updating of the index for 1996 suggests how little the pattern changed between 1991 and 1996 (Robson *et al.* 1998), a half decade when regeneration policy was working with much clearer purpose and focus. In the 1991 index the worst four places were Liverpool, Newham, Manchester and Hackney. In the 1996 index the same four districts remained in the worst four positions and in exactly the same rank order (see Figure 12.3). Of the 10 worst places in 1996, no fewer than eight had been in the 10 ten in 1991; of the worst 50 in 1996, no fewer than 46 had been in the worst 50 in 1991. There is also some suggestion of an increasing degree of polarization between the more and less deprived places. Fewer districts in total had positive (i.e. deprived) scores in 1996 than in 1991 (309 to 316); yet more districts had scores of over 15.0 in 1996 than in 1991 (81 as against 73) and considerably fewer had scores of under 15.0 (228 to 243).

There have, however, been some relative changes in the patterns between 1991 and 1996 despite the fact that the general shape of deprivation remains much as it was. Interestingly, the changes suggest a degree of convergence across local authorities in England. The places that improved relatively were largely northern industrial cities; those that relatively deteriorated were parts of Greater London, the resort towns and many of the peripheral parts of the southeast and East Anglia. Such convergence cannot, however, be taken as an indication that the regional economies of northern and southern areas are growing more alike in terms of their competitiveness. Much of the explanation lies in unemployment figures; these have shown regional convergence during the early 1990s, which is unprecedented during a period of falling general unemployment. This arises largely from changes in labour force participation rates, since southern areas have shown the smallest falls in employment and the largest rises in labour supply, whereas the traditionally depressed areas experienced the largest falls in employment together with falls in labour supply (Green 1998).

As this chapter is being written, the shadow of recession, and certainly of increased unemployment, hovers over Britain and more particularly over some of its most deprived areas. The collapse of the Japanese economy and of the 'tiger' economies of southeast Asia has already caused severe loss of jobs on Tyneside. Whether

District	1991 Index	1996 Index	1991 Rank	1996 Rank
Liverpool	399	401	1	1
Newham	378	386	2	2
Manchester	375	363	3	3
Hackney	363	352	4	4
Knowsley	359	337	5	9
Birmingham	350	347	6	5
Sandwell	342	338	7	7
Haringey	318	315	8	13
Islington	312	322	9	10
Salford	310	266	10	23
Oldham	306	248	11	33
Middlesbrough	303	264	12	24
Tower Hamlets	303	343	13	6
Bradford	300	259	14	28
Southwark	300	337	15	8
Nottingham	300	284	16	16
Sunderland	293	269	17	21
Hull	292	261	18	26
Wolverhampton	291	259	19	27
Lambeth	290	316	20	12
Newcastle	289	280	21	19
Camden	286	282	22	17
Walsall	282	250	23	31
Blackburn	275	230	24	41
Greenwich	270	316	25	11
Gateshead	268	246	26	35
Sheffield	267	261	27	25
South Tyneside	267	237	28	38
Lewisham	265	294	29	14
Coventry	263	235	30	40

Figure 12.3 District rankings from the 1991 and 1996 Index of Deprivation

Note: Of the 354 English districts, only those ranked 1–30 in 1991 are shown. Higher scores indicate greater deprivation. Districts whose rank is higher for 1996 than 1991 have deteriorated relatively; those with lower ranks have relatively improved

the Asian presence will hold firm in south Wales and other revived areas is uncertain. The departure of Siemens from a relatively new investment (again in the Newcastle region) was hedged about with explanations that did not completely answer the suspicion that such firms might prefer to keep their European investment within the single currency.

The danger is that if the Labour government is blown off course by a full-blown recession – that potent symbol of market forces – it has little to fall back on. Having tried to sell itself as capitalism with a smiling face, its warm words about social priorities seem to lack a sense of drive and purpose. This may be because, unlike the intake of 1945, the present Labour party is, with few exceptions, the product of 'comfortable' Britain. Professional origins have become standard amongst members of parliament since it is seen as a career rather than a public service. There is no powerful expression, as there was in 1945, that there are wrongs to be righted. Rather the concept is that the rider of the national horse has a gentler pair of hands and that the smartly applied dig of the heels and the tighter rein will never be applied even when needed.

Yet, the continuing evidence of social polarization and of high levels of deprivation in most of our big cities suggests that there are wrongs to be righted. The vision of 1945 was of a fairer society. For the end of the millennium, a compelling vision might be to ensure that we avoid creating a lost generation amongst the young men of inner city areas. De-industrialization, the loss of semi-skilled and unskilled jobs and the growth of the female workforce have meant that, for large numbers of young men, the prospects of joining the mainstream of society are bleak. By their teenage years, many young males are ill educated, functionally inept, socialized into crime and disorder, and with low self-esteem. The damage that they do to the social order of innumerable housing estates is immense (Campbell 1993). Does this not suggest that a vision for the present administration should be to channel resources to address such needs? For example, it has been clear for some time that intervention in early childhood can have a beneficial effect, especially for children who are living in households that are deprived or have other difficulties. The Head Start programme in the United States has been called 'a 25 year-old bi-partisan billion dollar success story' (Zigler and Muenchow 1992: 211). Despite some reservations in the initial stages of the programme, recent research has shown positive outcomes for well-designed, well-targeted, well-funded projects, most notably the High/Scope Ypsilanti, Michigan, Perry Pre-School Project (Audit Commission 1996). The research shows the benefits of money spent on such a programme in terms of reducing crime, and suggests that money would be better spent on pre-school projects than, for example, on prisons (Donahue and Siegelman, 1998).

As long ago as 1926, Bertrand Russell argued that it was a disaster to axe the nursery school provision established by the 1918 Education Act in order to maintain Britain's military might:

> To serve this end our children are condemned to disease and misery and unawakened intelligence from which multitudes could be saved by the same sum being spent on nursery schools . . . the nursery school, if it became universal, could in one generation remove the profound differences in education which divide the classes, could produce a population all enjoying the mental and physical development which is now confined to the most fortunate and could remove the terrible deadweight of disease and stupidity, and malevolence which now makes progress so difficult (Russell 1926: 181).

The present minister for higher education started her career with a cool analysis of the problems and needs for early education and expressed the view that, when this is achieved, 'every child will improve his chances of having a fair start' (Blackstone 1971: 169). That did not happen: instead, long drawn-out arguments about the alternatives of play or learning, education or care, and private or public provision, resulted in a mish-mash of provision ranging from the state-funded local authority nursery, through the middle-class backed pre-school playgroups, to a wide variety of private provision – good, bad and indifferent. By 1993, the situation in Britain was described as chaotic and inadequate, especially when contrasted with other developed countries:

> Instead of comprehensive, multi-functional, affordable provision, the UK muddles on instead of investing in its future citizens, helping them early in their lives to learn how to learn ... there is a fragmenting of services with different affiliations and philosophies (David 1993: 153).

The Audit's Commission's 1996 report *Counting to Five* showed that this remained the case despite (or because of) the introduction of vouchers for nursery education. The present government has said there should be places for all four year-olds whose parents want them, and that the target should be to achieve this goal for three year-olds. However, no extra funding has been allocated, and local authorities are supposed to make provision from existing funds except where there is a pioneering centre of excellence that may draw on other monies. A worthwhile millennium investment into which to put public funds would be a coherent national nursery system with special provision for those who, *pace* Hennessy, may 'never again' enjoy continuous work, or 'never again' have a continuous prosperous stable family existence. It might require higher taxes: it could certainly use more lottery money. In this context, one of the most promising of the government's many 'zonal' initiatives is the Home Office's Sure Start programme which aims to target resources to help poor families with very young children.

Opinion polls suggest that people in Britain understand that there is a need for a tougher attitude towards social policy and that it may be costly in personal terms: witness the majority approval in opinion polls that ask about attitudes to higher taxes hypothecated to improve education, health, etc. That is the vision: there is a marvellous sense of self-satisfaction when such opinions are reported. Reality, alas, seems somewhat different. The vote for a change of government in 1997 seems to have been less a desire for a change of practice than for a change of style and personality. Certainly the politicians would appear to think so as they back off from hard choices that might affect the votes of the comfortable majority. Politically, they are probably right. In the secrecy of the contemporary ballot box, the vision of a better society is blurred by the compelling urge to satisfy individual needs and desires. Is that the final reality of parliamentary democracy?

FURTHER READING

Useful essays on the issues facing the reform of the welfare state are to be found in Glennerster and Hills (1998) *The State of Welfare*. An overview of recent information on income and wealth in the UK can be found in the two volumes of the Joseph Rowntree Foundation (1995) *Inquiry into Income and Wealth*. The spatial patterns of poverty are interpreted most authoritatively by Green (1994) *The Geography of Poverty and Wealth*. There are many accounts of the grim circumstances endured by those living in difficult estates. The most graphic is Campbell (1993) *Goliath: Britain's Dangerous Places*, which looks at the breakdown of social order and the changing roles of men and women in the lives of families and local communities. The 1998 report from the SEU *Bringing Britain Together: A National Strategy for Neighbourhood Renewal* offers a recent account of the problems faced by such estates.

The evolution of social (and other) policy is excellently covered in Peter Hennessy (1992). There is a huge literature on housing policy: see the references given in Balchin's chapter in this volume.

On the development of specific urban policy, the early approaches are well discussed in Edwards and Batley (1978) *The Politics of Positive Discrimination: An Evaluation of the Urban Programme 1967–77*. The switch to privatization is well covered (with trans-Atlantic comparisons) in Barnekov *et al.* (1989). *Privatism and Urban Policy in Britain and the United States* and by Deakin and Edwards (1993) *The Enterprise Culture and the Inner Cities*.

To keep up-to-date with current policy and policy instruments it is well worth browsing the websites of government departments which can be accessed via www.open.gov.uk or, for DETR's urban regeneration programmes, at www.regeneration.detr.gov.uk.

chapter 13

Public Participation in Planning

YVONNE RYDIN

INTRODUCTON

Public participation has been a consistent preoccupation of the planning system: is there enough, is it the right sort, has sufficient account been taken of it? This chapter reviews the historical development of public participation within planning over the postwar period, using specific examples of planning practice. It distinguishes five periods: early experience of the postwar planning system; the publication of the Skeffington report; the reality of expanded participation in the 1970s; the Thatcherite emphasis on speed and efficiency; and the 1990s context of new urban governance and Local Agenda 21. In each period, counter-pressures to the prevailing trend are noted, both various community movements and protest actions and the impact of measures to ensure probity in local governance practice. The final section examines some key themes concerning public participation, notably the extent to which the concern with procedures obscures some more fundamental problems of collective action and collective decision making.

EARLY EXPERIENCES OF PUBLIC PARTICIPATION

The 1947 Town and Country Planning Act was, in many ways, a daring piece of legislation, replacing the piecemeal approach of the prewar period with a comprehensive vision of planning for every part of Britain. The learning curve for planners involved in plan preparation during a period of rapid peripheral development and numerous urban redevelopment schemes was a steep one. It is perhaps surprising that public participation preoccupied them at all, but a degree of liaison with communities affected by planning decisions and development schemes was a consistent thread. This liaison essentially took the form of providing information to, and of engaging in limited consultation with, the public.

An early example is provided by the exhibition of *A Plan for Hornsey* organized by the Borough Council in June 1945. This presented the town plan for the borough, prepared under prewar legislation but very much in the spirit of postwar reconstruction and planning. The exhibition was held in Hornsey Gas Company showrooms in the main shopping centre for a period of 11 days from 10 a.m. to 8 p.m. The accompanying booklet provided an indication of the attitude of the local authority towards public involvement. It clearly stated that the town plan was 'our plan of an ideal borough', but the council were now posing the question 'is it yours?': 'That is why we are holding this Exhibition, for we wish not only to show you our schemes for planning and housing, but to learn your views and invite your criticism'. However, the booklet made it clear that the contents of the exhibition were 'based on sound and practical principles'; it is not clear how public criticism could counter such a claim to solid planning expertise.

This exhibition both presaged the experience of the postwar planning system and harked back to older, early twentieth century ideas on planning. The very idea of an exhibition echoes the call of Patrick Geddes (1905) for a new 'civics', an interdisciplinary approach to studying urban life and improving it through planning, which would involve the public in pageants, exhibitions and similar events. Geddes' aim was to reinvigorate public debate and culture around urban issues. It is doubtful whether the exhibition in the Hornsey Gas Company showrooms would have fulfilled his vision. As occurs so often in the history of public participation in planning, practice can readily be found wanting by comparison with an ideal. The Hornsey case also shows how (limited) participation at one stage in the planning process does not necessarily prevent conflict at a later stage. For, amongst the extensive discussion of kitchen layouts and council-promoted flowerbeds, there was a proposal for redesigning the road layout of the borough and creating a network of new ring roads and major through roads; some of these never proceeded any further, but the plans for widening the A1 Archway road to the west of the borough was to become one of the major planning battles of the 1970s, with vociferous public protest and disrupted public inquires (Tyme 1978).

THE SKEFFINGTON REPORT

By the end of the 1960s, the pressures of development had continued for almost two decades, and there was growing resistance to both the scale of development permitted and the quality of the built environment that was resulting. There was a widespread sense that the prevailing form of interaction with the public over land-use planning matters was insufficient. But, as Cullingworth argues (1990: 374), the main impetus for an important series of policy statements in the late 1960s came from central government, not the grassroots. The Labour government was broadly sympathetic to more participation, and the civil service was highly enthusiastic, seeing it as an opportunity to dispose of 'a crushing burden of casework' (cited in *op. cit.*). Public participation was seen as an essential element in devolving more planning work down to the local government level, while maintaining support for planning decisions.

A series of central government policy initiatives promoted the concept of participation. In 1965, the Planning Advisory Group report recommended that local authorities should be required to provide opportunities for detailed comments, representations and objections on draft plans, and also to take them into account. The resulting 1967 white paper stressed that an effective and up-to-date planning system must ensure full public participation, and the 1968 planning act required local authorities to inform the minister about the steps they had taken on public consultation and the response they had received. At the same time, the Skeffington Committee was appointed to consider 'the best methods, including publicity, of securing the participation of the public at the formative stage in the making of development plans for their area'. Their 1969 report *People and Plans* remains a central reference point for considering public participation.

The report was based on the principle that it 'matters to us all that we should know that we can influence the shape of our community'. The Skeffington model emphasized the importance of all members of the public joining in planning decisions; participation was 'the act of sharing in the formulation of policies and proposals'. The public were to be informed, consulted and actively involved through surveys and 'other activities'. Planners were charged with actively consulting the public at all stages of the planning process and not just at one discrete moment. Particular emphasis was given to the possibility of setting up community forums as vehicles for facilitating such consultation and appointing a specialist officer, a community development officer, to encourage participation, stimulate discussion and act as a conduit for people's views to the local authority. Public participation was seen as a 'good thing' in its own right, but it was also justified in terms of making the planning process smoother and less contentious. However, while the public were to be more involved in the preparation of plans, the actual completion of those plans remained with the planners: 'the completion of plans – the setting into statutory form of the proposals and decisions – is a task demanding the highest standards of professional skill and must be undertaken by the professional staff of the local planning authority'.

While there was considerable central government interest in promoting participation, this was in the context of a general shift away from the traditional deferential attitude to government, in which consultation of the public was a privilege, towards a more critical and questioning attitude, which implied demands for more involvement in decision making as of right. It was also against a backdrop of many instances of the wilful disregard of communities during the era of slum clearance and comprehensive redevelopment in the 1960s. Dennis (1972: 28) describes the procedural changes as arising from the combination of the 'growing public disesteem' for planning and the ever more ambitious role that planners were taking on. His own account of planning in Sunderland during 1965–9 is a devastating critique of the treatment of a local community by a local authority which effectively blighted an area by its plans for slum clearance, and failed totally to communicate with the residents, let alone take their views into account.

The calls for more formal public participation, therefore, shaded into a demand for a more participatory form of democracy at the local level, with 'the public' or, more realistically, specific 'communities' jointly undertaking policy deliberations with local government (Illsley and McCarthy 1996). It is telling that one of the most widely cited academic references on public participation also arises from this time (though from North America). Arnstein's 'ladder' of public participation (1969) has eight rungs with 'manipulation' and 'therapy' at the bottom, 'information', 'consultation' and 'placation' denoting various degrees of tokenism, and 'partnership', 'delegated power' and 'citizen control' representing degrees of citizen power (Figure

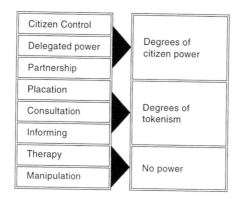

Figure 13.1
Arnstein's ladder of
participation

13.1). Achieving the higher rungs of the ladder was seen as inherently preferable. In this view, increased participation is about changing the nature of the local planning process, not just ensuring legitimacy for its policy decisions and planning outcomes. Thus, by the late 1960s, a tension was already evident between those who saw participation as a way of making local authority planning more effective and those who sought to change planning more fundamentally.

THE REALITY OF PUBLIC PARTICIPATION IN THE 1970S

The Skeffington Committee recommendations did strike a chord with some local authorities, but their implementation through central government legislation and advice resulted in a very much watered down regime of publicity and consultation on development plans and planning decisions. The result was, not surprisingly, a very limited degree of public involvement or, more cynically, apathy. The Skeffington proposal for community forums proved naïve, with such forums becoming simply a channel of communication – often one-way communication from the local authority inviting representations on its proposals. Such forums tended not to offer up positive suggestions or engage in any proactive campaigning; this was left to grassroots groups which did not have the officially sanctioned status of a community forum: 'Generally, Skeffington-type consultative groups have suffered the fate of incorporation into local authority procedures, unable to take an independent critical line' (Brindley *et al.* 1996: 90). Such community forums have also been widely used as a means of establishing contact with black and ethnic minority groups, but, as Thomas and Krishnarayan point out (1994: 1905), 'it carries with it real risks of tokenism when other policy processes remain impervious to significant influence'. The shortcomings of Skeffington identified early on by Levin and Donnison (1969: 478) proved to be accurate: 'the committee assume too readily that the conventions of a Quaker meeting can be adopted in the commercial, political, professional and racial rough-house in which planning decisions are actually made'.

The problems of achieving public participation were exacerbated by the reforms of the 1968 Town and Country Planning Act which instituted a two-tier system of development plans, the more strategic structure plan and the more detailed local plan (see Davies, chapter 4). These changes to the development plan system generated confusion among the general public and increased the need for public participation by having two levels of plan. In practice it led to more public interest being displayed in relation to the detailed local plan rather than the more abstract structure plan. The problems of the this system were then multiplied by the local government reforms of the early 1970s which instituted a two-tier system of local government across Britain (see Davies, chapter 4). This opened up the potential for considerable conflict between local authorities and thereby absorbed many planning resources – resources which could have been expended on developing better relations with local communities.

The nature of public participation on development plans in the 1970s can be conveyed by some examples of planning practice in this area. The formulaic approach to involving the public is demonstrated by the process surrounding the Waltham Forest Borough Plan (1978) where the legitimacy of the participation exercise was based on the statutory requirements of planning legislation, rather than on any broader political vision. This consultation took place in two stages: on the Report of Survey and 'Options' stage, and on the preferred Draft Plan. The first stage comprised:

- consultation by the circulation of papers to local organizations, statutory bodies and other local authorities followed up by a series of five meetings;
- general publicity through local newspapers and a newspaper-format pamphlet;
- a questionnaire distributed with the pamphlet to all households in the borough, of which 1,100 responses were received;
- a commissioned survey comprising 582 interviews.

In relation to the proposals for the town centre, the following methods were added:

- a public exhibition held in a vacant council shop in the high street, which was visited by 2,500 people;
- three public meetings which together attracted 370 people;
- six commissioned group discussions.

A similar range of methods was used again at the second, draft plan stage. The second questionnaire produced only 539 responses, plus another 410 on the town centre proposals; the travelling, library-based exhibition attracted 2,454 visitors while the town centre exhibition attracted 2,186 people. A public meeting on the town centre was attended by 60 members of the public. The report on consultation expressed some disappointment at the low level of response, particularly at the second stage. However, in evaluating the effectiveness of the public consultation, the borough noted that 'the publicity techniques adopted effectively satisfied the council's twin aims of publicizing the existence of the plan and ensuring that the public were given the opportunity to comment on the plan'. In effect they had done all that could be expected of them.

But as significant as the seeking of public involvement was the borough's response to that involvement. The report chose to deal with public comment in an 'attack-and-response' mode. Comments were listed, mainly in tabular form, and the council response was set alongside it, the latter usually taking up much more space than the original comment. Clearly the intention was to be seen to be taking the comments seriously, but the effect was to close off discussion, with the borough having the final word. This was not a dialogue. The borough had to decide what weight to give to public comment:

> The views expressed in the course of consultation on the draft plan are one, albeit important, factor which must be taken into account in reaching a decision as to whether to amend the plan, but the response is not all powerful and it is important to recognise what it means. The number of people and organisations commenting on even the most contentious issues is very low and cannot be said to represent more than a tiny proportion of the people likely to be affected by the action proposed.

The borough concluded that the 'value of the response is to provide an indication of the strength of feeling about particular policies and proposals. This is but one element contributing to the decision making.' The decision making and the power remained with the local authority and this was legitimated by the imperfect form of pluralism that the public participation methods evoked.

Waltham Forest clearly did try hard to get the public to participate and expended considerable resources in the attempt. Other local authorities took the procedural requirements as a norm rather than a minimum and faced criticism from within the local community for doing so. In 1977, Croydon decided to prepare a non-statutory borough plan as a link between the Greater London Development Plan and the statutory district plans to be prepared for parts of the borough. A discussion document *Tomorrow's Croydon* was published in 1979 and a 6-week consultation period set. Consultation involved: distributing the document to 191 organizations, of whom 76 responded; distributing 18,000 copies of a handbill to the public; and some publicity in the local newspaper. The borough's *Report on Public Consultation* (Croydon London Borough 1979) records:

> There were certain points common to the introductory remarks of a large number of organisations. Most common was the regret that the limited consultation period had curtailed the consultation and discussion felt necessary to produce a properly considered and representative reply.... Other general comments about the nature of the borough plan which were frequently voiced were that ... more planning should be based on the needs of peoples and communities.

In response to the limitations of formal consultation exercises on development plans, some planning authorities did attempt a more innovative and proactive approach. Leicester City Council, for example, took the relatively unusual step in 1975 of issuing a substantial booklet for the general public on *Planning for Leicester*. Supported by substantial advertising, it was issued free and intended, not primarily as an account of the council's planning proposals, but as a guide to the planning process and planning procedures in Leicester.

> In their dealings with the public ... the [planning] committee have become conscious that their duties and functions are not always easily understood ... nor are their limitations. It was felt that a booklet of this nature would make some contribution to rectifying the situation.

This was a form of planning education intended as a precursor to formal consultation on district plans. In this it was fulfilling one of the Skeffington aims, that public participation would have an educational dimension: 'the continuity of debate which is implicit in the participation process can itself be educative for both the planner and the public'.

The Leicester document also recognized that this formal consultation had not always been a satisfactory experience in the past. The council claimed that: 'the importance of this booklet lies in the fact that it represents the beginning of a new era'. In this new era, the public would understand the nature of planners' work, and

> [The planning committee will] be aware continuously of the feelings and wishes of the people of Leicester. . . . Comments and criticisms are welcomed on all aspects of the committee's work. They are sympathetically received and properly considered before a decision is reached. Planning in Leicester is rapidly becoming planning for Leicester.

But this was not, it should be noted 'planning *by* Leicester' as many community activists were increasingly demanding. The foreword by the chairman of the planning committee made clear the legal and political reality, that public opinion matters and that planners go to considerable lengths to discover what that public opinion is on planning issues, but the council is in the position of decision maker: '*Your* views will help *us* to make such judgement in the most informed way' (my emphasis).

At the same time as formal public participation was being focused on procedures surrounding plan preparation, dissatisfaction with specific projects and development control decisions was generating much more vocal opposition in many localities. The disjunction between the dry formality of official consultation exercises and the often vocal and emotional attempts to influence specific cases was emblematic of public participation in the early 1970s. These conflicts focused particularly on redevelopment schemes and road-building (Tyme 1978). Smith (1981: 16) identifies five reasons for the failure of public participation in this period:

- the issue of the delegation of power to participants was not confronted;
- people were not consulted on issues they wished to discuss;
- the methods used were not suitable for meaningful involvement;
- the organization and structure of local authorities made it virtually impossible to develop a coherent view;
- both the council and the public had unrealistic expectations of what could be achieved.

He concludes that in terms 'of the increasing open government and public participation in local government decision making, the 1970s were a decade of missed opportunity for community work'.

An example of this type of conflict is provided by the proposed redevelopment of Tolmers Square in London (Wates 1976). Housing problems had been identified in this area by the local authority (Camden) in the 1960s, and there were proposals for clearance and redevelopment. As was common practice at that time, the council did not attempt any public consultation. In 1973, however, the local residents, largely tenants, began to organize themselves. They set up the Tolmers Village Association and, with the assistance of planning students, developed their own plans for the area. The association sought to pressure the borough to use their compulsory purchase powers to facilitate these development plans. This was successful only to the extent that some community-based development went ahead. But, though community action had been partly effective in changing council plans, this did not amount to the exercise of citizen power by which some within the local community were judging it.

It was not only working-class communities who were disillusioned with their treatment by local planning; middle-class amenity groups also resented it. In *The Fight for Bristol*, the Bristol Civic Society tells of 'how a local community fought not only against insensitive planning but against what increasingly was seen as the undemocratic character of the planning system' (Priest and Cobb 1980: 9). It refers to a map of inner and outer ring roads for Bristol as a 'planners' dream thwarted by public protest'. In practice, this protest was organized by a Bristol Planning Group which 'contained a much wider range of skills than was then, or even now, available to the city's planning department'! Through the 1970s, this group used the formal procedures of public participation to challenge road and redevelopment schemes and achieved many successes. But in contrast to the experiences of working-class communities outlined above, in Bristol the protesters achieved a new mode of cooperation with the planners. The authors point in particular to 'the arrival of younger men in the planning office, ready and willing to talk to the amenity lobby'. This incorporation of selected interests within the planning system provided a different context for public participation in later decades.

THE IMPACT OF THATCHERISM

The impact of Thatcherism on the planning system has been well documented (Brindley *et al.* 1996; Thornley 1991). There was a concerted attempt to limit the constraints that planning placed on market activities, notably by reducing the importance of the development plan as compared to market criteria, such as demand for and commercial profitability of the development. In pursuit of this goal, specific spatial areas were removed from the routine operation of the planning system, including urban development corporation areas, enterprise zones and special planning zones. Much attention was focused inwards on the operation of the planning system within the local authority. There was an emphasis on speeding up plan making and planning decisions in pursuit of 'better' planning authority 'performance'. As Thomas (1996) has noted, these changes had severe implications for public participation in planning. In particular, quicker planning processes left less time for public participation.

These changes did not prevent vocal attempts by local communities to influence the changing shape of their built environments. Rather, the more market-oriented form of planning led to considerable protest about the scale and location of development from many affected communities. Local protest groups continued to use formal and informal means to challenge specific development proposals, ranging from involvement in the set consultation procedures to various modes of direct action (Short *et al.* 1986). A surprising feature to many commentators was the extent of protest from within the electoral heartland of the Conservative government. The local reaction to proposals for relaxing greenbelt restrictions in the early 1980s was sufficiently electorally threatening to the Conservative government for a proposed DoE circular to be dropped (Elson 1986). This was mirrored in opposition by Conservative-controlled local government to Conservative central government policies (Barlow 1995). Thus, local authorities, as well as local residents, fought the Secretary of State's modifications to the Berkshire structure plan which required substantial additional development. A parallel protest movement arose in opposition to the Conservative government's attempt to find disposal sites for low-level nuclear waste (Blowers 1995).

The position of communities within Labour-controlled local authorities was rather different during this period, because of the general context of conflict between central and local government and the particular antipathy of the Conservative government to urban Labour councils. Some local authorities, within the limits of the legal requirements, sought to be more responsive in their consultation on development plans. In the foreword to the Greenwich 1986 local plan, the planning chairperson stressed that 'as a result of what you said, various parts of the plan have now changed'. It was further explained that the plan was being put on deposit 'so that you can check if you are satisfied with the changes that have been made. If not, you can object . . . . We shall discuss your objection with you and try to find a solution.'

Many Labour councils of a 'New Left' persuasion went further and sought to develop new modes of engagement with their local communities; decentralization strategies became more common, and many sought to 'empower' their local electorate more directly (Boddy and Fudge 1984; Burns *et al.* 1994). The aim was to develop an alternative model of local socialism, given the dominance of a New Right government at the national level. These empowering strategies were not restricted to planning, but ranged across the spectrum of local authority activity. Indeed, many of the most significant developments were in forging a new relationship with local communities over service delivery.

There were a few attempts to develop a more distinctively participatory form of planning practice, known as 'popular planning'. This describes planning *by* the local community and not just planning *for* that community or even *with* that community; the aim is the transfer of decision-making powers to the community level. However, the success rate for popular planning has not been good. In the London Docklands, the removal of a substantial area of land from the planning control of the local authorities and into the remit of an urban development corporation effectively removed all public participation opportunities. The influence of the local communities was totally dependent on the attitude of the corporation, which in the early days preferred promotion of development to any engagement with local people. With the support of the Popular Planning Unit of the Greater London Council, the community in the Poplar district of Docklands prepared their own plan for the area, in opposition to corporation plans for the London Docklands Airport, but the development corporation refused to recognize the plan and it was never accorded any status within the planning process.

By contrast, Coin Street has been heralded as *the* success story of popular planning. In the South Bank area of London a plan prepared in collaboration with the local community was eventually implemented. This led to the successful provision of local needs housing in an area of high land values and commercial pressures for office development. The central factors were the support of the local authorities involved, the ability of the local community to adopt a number of more or less confrontational roles in the planning process through the use of a number of different community organizations, and the 'window of opportunity' offered by a downturn in the development cycle which relieved the pressure for high-value development for a short space of time. However, the transformation of a community into community developers has created its own problems and, over time, tensions have developed within the group over the direction of the scheme. The conflict between the community and the planning authority has been transformed into a conflict within the community (Brindley *et al.* 1996).

PUBLIC PARTICIPATION IN THE 1990S

The broad continuity in public participation procedures over several decades resulted by the 1990s in some evidence of social learning among both the public and planning authorities. Research by Murdoch *et al.* (1996) has found that structure plans are no longer seen as abstract and overly strategic, thereby deterring public involvement. A variety of groups now engage with the plan-making process, as well as with consideration of individual development proposals. But the emphasis in the 1980s on the need for efficiency in the service delivery of the planning system was also carried through to the early 1990s. In particular, plan making was streamlined so that local authorities had to consult only on outline or strategic proposals rather than on the full draft plan; and more use of written representations at local plan public inquiries was also encouraged. As Thomas (1994) points out, these changes reduced the influence of those less familiar with the formal procedures. Hull and Vigar (1996) also note that this streamlined plan-preparation process facilitated the involvement of developers and other vested interests in public local inquiries but was likely to result in little engagement from the public and voluntary organizations. Furthermore, Murdoch *et al.* (1996) found that lengthy consultation periods did not appreciably alter the development allocations contained in structure plans, since these were decided early in the structure plan review process, justified by reference to central government advice and obscured in a pseudo-technical language of forecasts

and land availability. This is confirmed by Hull and Vigar, who argue that a techno-
cratic style of argumentation and the use of forums such as public inquiries may limit
public participation to professional organizations: local authorities, developers and
their representatives, government agencies and national environmental groups.
Interestingly, Murdoch *et al.* also note that initial development allocations
avoided those areas which proved later in the consultation process to have very vocal
anti-development constituencies.

Elsewhere, some local authorities sought to learn from past experience and
develop more meaningful ways of engaging with their communities (Figure 13.2).
Illsey and McCarthy (1996) describe the example of community planning in Dundee which, over a decade, moved towards a greater recognition of the value of better
community relations. They detail the use of 'planning for real' exercises and the
shift away from the old style 'prepare, reveal, defend' strategy. They also point to
the lessons of the Dundee experience: there is a need to enhance the capacity of
local people and to build strong community networks which include a representative
and accountable community structure. A range of opportunities to accommodate
different levels of involvement is needed, and an explicit set of objectives should be
set to allow monitoring of planning outcomes. Public participation here is not so
much about the procedures that the council should adopt, or their enthusiasm for the
project, but rather about building the community institutions through which the
public would participate.

One problem is that the 'community' identified by the planning authority – usually the population within the geographical area for which a plan is being prepared –
may not fit with the sense of community as experienced by residents. Indeed, the
emphasis on residents who live in the same spatial area and are assumed to share
interests and aspirations may not capture the other communities of interest and
values that people may belong to – based on work, educational and leisure facilities
or ideological outlook.

More broadly, the 1990s have seen a shift towards a new urban governance, in
which the emphasis is on bringing together a range of 'stakeholders' to build local
policy and to forge the conditions for action on that policy. The limitations of relying
on local government actors alone to implement policy effectively are increasingly
recognized and, therefore, at the same time that local government procedures are
being streamlined, the development of forums involving local government alongside

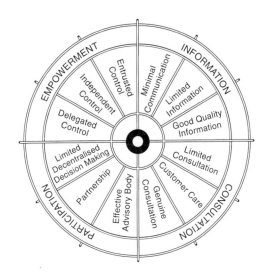

Figure 13.2 South
Lanarkshire's wheel
of participation

other organizations is increasingly common. This holds out opportunities for greater public participation but, given that the rationale for many of these forums is enhancing the power to take action on policy, it is business interests rather than community organizations who are often accorded precedence within the new urban governance (Stewart and Stoker 1995).

A more explicit concern with public participation has resulted from the re-emerging environmental agenda of the 1990s. At the Rio Summit in 1992, a manifesto for sustainable development was adopted. Known as Agenda 21, this included specific reference to the role of local authorities and, indeed, many of the measures discussed elsewhere in the document require local level action. This has given rise to a Local Agenda 21 process (LA21) seeking to implement sustainable development at the scale of the locality (Lafferty and Eckerberg 1997). LA21 has several dimensions. It is partly about securing improvements in local environmental quality through a range of policies; partly about achieving a holistic approach by integrating policy approaches in different sectors; and partly about securing greater public involvement in and identification with the goal of sustainable development.

Many commentators have emphasized the nature of LA21 as a process concerned with changing the nature of local politics. Greater participation by the public is, therefore, seen as an indicator of success in LA21. To this end, there has been experimentation with new mechanisms for achieving that participation: citizens' juries, community visioning and more 'planning for real' exercises (Jacobs 1997). The aim is to overcome the identified problems of past practice. The public inquiry may appear very transparent with the public presentation of 'evidence' and cross-examination, but these can be unsuited to the kind of questioning of expertise that many members of the public wish to engage in (Hull and Vigar 1996). Thomas and Krishnarayan (1994: 1899) point out that 'bureaucratic procedures which ignore the cultures or outlooks of ethnic minorities can, in practice, discriminate against these minorities'.

The emphasis on public involvement within LA21 arises because change towards sustainability is to be achieved not only by government action but also by alterations in individual behaviour. Furthermore, the sustainable development agenda itself has a political dimension emphasizing community empowerment (Brundtland Report 1987). Thus, environmental indicators are used not only as a measure of the successful implementation of local government policy but also as a tool for communication and a means of achieving a 'genuinely active local democracy' (Macnaghten and Jacobs 1997). This implies a more dialogic model of the environmental policy process, a model which is currently inhibited, according to research by Macnaghten and Jacobs, by a lack of public trust in government and a sense of powerlessness. The problems of public participation in the past thus return to constrain moves towards a more participatory mode in the present. There is also the problem of varying local government interest in moving towards a more participatory form of local democracy.

Young (1996) has found four different strategies adopted in LA21 processes (1996): the top down strategy keeps control in the local authorities' hands; the limited dialogue strategy allows for more discussion but only on an agenda set by the local authority; the 'Yes ... but' strategy opens up broader discussion but closes it down when decisions have to be taken; and the bottom-up strategy represents the relatively rare case of community-based decision making. Young suggests community decision making may be considered acceptable only where no significant resource allocation is involved.

Another potential constraint on public participation in the 1990s comes from the shifts toward an audit culture (Power 1997). Public bodies are now required to demonstrate that they have acted with probity (Nolan 1997). Over local planning stands the shadow, not only of community protests ignored but also of corruption in highly publicized cases. For these reasons, there is a new emphasis on high standards of public life and on leaving a clear 'paper trail' to show that procedures have been followed. This again throws public participation back into the realm of formal bureaucracy rather than the more informal and uncertain world of community empowerment and consensus building. Yet, as Innes (1996) details, the internal drama of consensus building forums denies the ready identification of a decision with a particular actor or even with a particular commonly held rationale; the dynamics of these forums are often more complex and contradictory – more like real life than the bureaucratic ideal! While probity is, of course, to be welcomed, there may be dangers for the new participatory approaches in the current way in which probity is being ensured.

PUBLIC PARTICIPATION AND COLLECTIVE DECISION MAKING

This account of public participation in planning has shown that there has been a consistent concern with engaging the public in planning decision making. It has also shown repeated evidence of dissatisfaction with the way in which participation has been sought, often measuring planning practice against an ideal of community empowerment and direct grass-roots involvement in that decision making. In much of the discussion on public participation, particularly that arising from specific community experiences, there is a profound distrust of planners and the way in which they relate to the public. There is a fear that participation can be used in many ways: 'to divert, frustrate and manipulate' (Smith and Jones 1981). However, there is clearly among most planners a genuine desire to engage with the public and to develop policies and proposals which command local support, and a resulting attention to developing new methods for improving the quality of the relationship between planners and the public. This is currently given theoretical expression through Patsy Healey's collaborative planning (1997) which seeks to use the concepts and frameworks of Giddens' structuration approach and Habermas' communicative rationality to present a model of planning in which stakeholders are brought together to 'shape places' jointly and build a consensus for local planning.

But all the goodwill of planners will not resolve the underlying central issue of where the locus of decision making should be and who should exercise power within planning. The tendency of the community-based literature is to argue for community or citizen empowerment, and to take decentralized popular planning as the ideal. But it is worthwhile ending this chapter with a questioning of this ideal. The fact that many of the demands for community empowerment result from extreme dissatisfaction with an example of local planning by the public sector (whether public sector development or the planning of private sector development) does not of itself mean that such empowerment should be the generalized model for planning practice.

There are two reasons for suggesting caution in the demands we place on public participation. The first relates to the problems of engaging the public in planning decision making. Low levels of participation are generally taken as an indicator of a failed participation exercise. Some argue that the fact that a large proportion of the population are not involved does not mean that they could not become so if activated by skilled agencies (Mabileau *et al.* 1989). However, the collective action problem in planning may be more entrenched. This was quite clearly identified in a report on public participation in Waltham Forest (1978) where it is noted that a disproportionate number of respondents lived near sites proposed for development. By contrast, those likely to benefit were under-represented 'because they cannot readily identify themselves'. Participation is always likely to be skewed *towards* groups who will bear or benefit from an identifiable and significant impact of the policy and can overcome the disincentives to collective action by organizing to campaign on the basis of those impacts; and *away* from those groups who comprise a large number of people bearing a more uncertain or less significant impact, for whom the costs of organization will outweigh the likely benefits of campaigning and participation. To this must be added those who actively do not wish to be involved in public participation, but regard it as a burden rather than a benefit of citizenship. There may be those who regard public participation as a form of social activity. Research by Parry and Moyser (1989) notes that those who are already locally active, involved in existing social groups and with a large network of local contacts are those most likely to participate in policy making. But for many others, the best kind of planning is one which does not necessitate public involvement.

The second reason is that planning decisions are a form of collective decision making. This is not the same as decision making by the local community since that represents only a subset of the broader social collectivity. Planning purely by the local community can be justified only if no other claims on that local space are recognized. What of the need for preserving environmental public goods which extend beyond the local space? What if the local community do not recognize the need to preserve a local space of biodiversity value? What of human rights which should be uniformly recognized across all spaces? What if the local community chooses to exclude people on the basis of race or some other prejudice? What of the need to place facilities that society as a whole requires? What if local opposition to low-level nuclear waste facilities results in less geographically sound or environmentally optimal sites being chosen? Some may claim that proper information and persuasion will result in local communities taking the 'right' decision in each case, but this may not necessarily be so. It is at least worth considering whether there is not a role for the state taking decisions even against the wishes expressed through public participation. It may be that there are many classes of planning decision which can be left to the local community, even without the involvement of local planners, and others where collective decision making by the state is justified. The rational choice approach points out that people often have insufficient incentive to become fully informed on an issue; perhaps community participation should be limited to those cases where there *is* sufficient incentive?

The real issue here is over the legitimacy of the planning system and its robustness in the face of criticism. The 'prepare, reveal, defend' strategy that planners have adopted may not have proved acceptable in the past, but the most appropriate response may not be to abrogate the role of the planner. The New Labour government is currently looking at ways of 'modernizing' local government (DETR 1998g) to build up the legitimacy of local government as a whole. In relation to the planning system, what may be needed is a strengthening of the public's ability to attack planners' decisions. Rather than hoping that all planning decisions can be consensual or taken by the community, would it not be more realistic to consider the institutions by which challenges can be mounted to planning decisions and the legitimacy of the process by which such challenges are finally decided on? As the above discussion has made clear, there are doubts about many of the existing institutions, such as public local inquiries. The role of central government in acting as 'poacher' and 'gamekeeper' by deciding on planning applications in which it has an interest has also provoked disquiet in the past. McAuslan (1980) analyses these instances as part of a broader conflict within the planning system between the ideology of the public interest and the ideology of public participation, a conflict in which participation is usually the loser.

There may be a need for new institutions operating at local and regional or even national levels to consider challenges to planning decisions more effectively and fairly. This may involve ceding a new status to groups outside the state. McAuslan (1980: 261) also points out that the 'tendency for outside pressure groups to become over-dependent on the goodwill of the bureaucracy that they are meant to be scrutinising is enhanced by the absence . . . of any legislation or judicial decisions which give specific standing or rights of consultation to such groups.' The new urban governance of planning should involve different roles for planners, groups *and* the public. Within this system of governance, support for the planning system and its outcomes is as likely to arise from the extent to which the public feel that grievances have been adequately dealt with, as the quantum amount of public involvement in planning forums.

ACKNOWLEDGEMENTS

I would like to thank Andy Thornley and Mark Pennington for their helpful comments on an earlier draft.

FURTHER READING

The most thorough examination of the treatment of public participation within the planning system is to be found in McAuslan (1980) *The Ideologies of Planning Law*. Thomas (1996) 'Public participation in planning' discusses public participation in relation to democratic theory (including Arnstein's ladder) as well as considering national policy in the 1990s and the range of participation strategies. Gyford (1994) 'Politics and planning in London' includes a broad account of public participation. For a more direct flavour of the language of public participation, the reader is recommended to contrast the liberalism (and optimism) of the Skeffington Report (1969) with the radicalism (and disappointment) of Wates (1976) *The Battle for Tolmers Square* or the anger (and disappointment) of Dennis (1972) *Public Participation and Planners' Blight*.

chapter 14

Transport Planning

PAUL TRUELOVE

THE FIRST POSTWAR PLANS

Whilst the legislators of the 1940s may have had a clear vision of the planning system they believed was needed in Britain, that vision did not include any conception of the huge rise in car ownership that was to take place. Even so, plans of the 1940s did provide for additional roadspace; and the need to bring order to urban transport networks was evidenced, for example, by the ring-road proposals contained in plans produced by Abercrombie and by the relief roads for places such as Oxford proposed by Thomas Sharp (1953). These new roads would bring additional capacity to the network, but the pioneer planners had no traffic survey information at their disposal and, in any case, postwar fuel shortages would have rendered any such surveys futile. The planners had to rely on their vision, although many ideas that still have currency had already been expounded. Thus, the idea of segregating pedestrians from vehicular traffic had been spelt out by Alker Tripp (1942). The 1945 Nicholas plan for Manchester included a giant new railway terminus, Trinity station, in recognition of the lack of integration implicit in having the city centre served by four major termini.

We are accustomed now to make international comparisons when attempting to forecast changes, but no analogies were drawn between the high prewar car ownership levels in the USA, and what might take place in postwar Europe. Contemporary history had a far stronger influence upon policy. Thus, the newly created British Rail embarked upon a programme of steam locomotive building rather than on more efficient diesel locomotives: it would have been most unwise to base traction policy on a system making use of imported fuel, which would be vulnerable in time of war.

The original town maps of the 1950s showed the primary routes, but did little to anticipate any changes. At a more local scale, the development plans did establish

Year	Vehicles Licensed (thousands)
1950	3,970
1960	8,512
1970	13,548
1980	19,199
1990	24,673

Figure 14.1 Motor vehicles licensed, 1950–90

Source: Transport Statistics Great Britain

the idea that development proposals needed to have parking provided to a set stand-ard. Ever since, parking provision has been the subject of standard conditions attached to permissions to develop. The purpose of such a condition has changed over time. By the 1960s, it changed from one of requiring reluctant developers to include parking to serve their city office blocks, to one limiting developers as to how much they could include.

Whilst the lasting legacy for transport policy of the development plans has been limited in scope, the legacy from some of the early new towns has been much more impressive. Stevenage in particular has provided a model. The first town centre pedestrian precinct could be created here without the opposition from the estab-lished shopkeepers who impeded the introduction of pedestrian shopping streets elsewhere. The arrangement of shops on three sides of a square, with a bus station on the fourth side, and parking and delivery access behind the shops, has in general format been widely imitated. Less extensively copied until recently has been the inclusion of segregated cycleways as an integral part of the traffic network.

The comprehensive development area plans of the early 1960s sometimes showed town centre bypasses, but the proposals were not the product of any systematic traffic forecasts, and they bore little relationship to possible resource availability. Even so, once proposals for town-centre relief roads gained some official status, the proposals often proved durable and came to form the basis of schemes constructed a decade or so later, often in combination with the pedestrianization of the superseded High Street (DoT 1995).

THE BUCHANAN REPORT

The Buchanan Report (1963) was a visionary document in anticipating possible consequences of the growth in car ownership, yet it failed miserably to anticipate the dispersal that has taken place since then. The report advocated the systematic adop-tion of road hierarchies, and the horizontal or vertical separation of pedestrians from traffic. The task of implementing proposals in the Buchanan report did not fall neatly into the departmental empires of borough engineers or planning officers, and so there was no single agency solely charged with, say, the introduction of vertical segregation in city centres. The only mechanism available was through the devel-opment control process. There remain today a few monuments to the attempt to introduce pedestrian deck circulation within cities, but rarely was urban redevelop-ment on such a scale that the first floor level ever became the natural level for pedestrian circulation.

Outside city centres, the cornerstone of the Buchanan proposals was the estab-lishment of a road hierarchy and the creation of environmental areas free from extraneous traffic. This could lead to housing layouts in which some dwellings could be reached only by quite indirect and inconveniently tortuous routes. This concept could be set in place only for quite large development schemes, and local planners had much more influence over their housing department than over private develop-ers. The unfortunate consequence of this was to make some local authority housing schemes physically isolated – as with Hulme in Manchester and Castle Vale in Birmingham. The 'environmental area' almost defined the ghetto. More positively, the concept of the environmental area has survived and subsequently evolved into the more generally applicable concept of traffic calming.

The Buchanan report came after the designation of Cumbernauld, a Scottish new town planned to accommodate free car movement, but rather too late to be a general influence upon new town plans. However, Runcorn (designated as a new town in

1964) represents an early attempt to come to grips with the problems of rising car ownership (Ling 1967). The housing 'villages' excluded all through traffic, and the roads were planned in a neat hierarchy ranging from urban motorway to local access road. The most impressive innovation was that the town layout attempted to favour public transport by linking each local centre directly by a segregated busway. The original plan envisaged the then fashionable monorail, but perhaps fortunately, financial stringency dictated that the vehicle actually used was a traditional bus, which was not confined to the segregated right of way and could divert away to serve, for example, peripheral industrial estates.

In one respect, the Runcorn new town road layout did not recognize one major consequence of rising car ownership. Like the first generation of new towns, Runcorn was expected to be self contained, with local jobs for all the residents. The urban motorway was designed as a figure of eight loop, with the town centre in the middle. In fact, 30 per cent of the workforce found jobs outside Runcorn, and an equal proportion of the jobs in Runcorn were filled by in-commuters. The loop form of the motorway was therefore inappropriate and not wholly completed. A better link towards Warrington was substituted.

It was not only in new towns that town planners were having an influence on fixed-track public transport proposals, even though the initial impetus came from other agencies, bus companies, or developers holding the rights for new technologies. In the 1960s, major cities were considering new forms of public transport, usually rail based, since buses were thought to be inescapably enmeshed in general traffic congestion. The implementation of the Runcorn busway came too late to influence this view, and only in the late 1990s were serious attempts made to give buses systematic priorities in established cities. The Manchester Rapid Transit Study (De Leuw 1967) compared different fixed-track systems, from innovatory monorails to conventional metro. The role of the town planners in the evaluation was to compare environmental impacts of the proposed elevated structures. They concluded that the environmental impacts of the elevated structures required were broadly comparable and all were unacceptable. This was very influential, for it meant that new systems would have to be in cutting or underground, and this carried

Figure 14.2
Segregated Busway,
Runcorn new town

huge cost penalties. Cost benefit analysis, carried out as part of the conurbation transportation study, showed the rapid transit proposal to have no overwhelming superiority and the project faltered. The movement towards new fixed-track public transport in Britain recovered only with the idea of Light Rapid Transit in the 1980s.

EARLY STEPS TOWARDS INTEGRATED TRANSPORT PLANNING

A consequence of the Buchanan report was a substantial growth of research on future transport infrastructure. Recently developed American techniques of transport modelling were applied to forecast how travellers would use hypothetical transport networks, and then the newly developed techniques of cost benefit analysis were applied to assist in determining which policies to pursue. With such methodologies, the process became basically one of testing networks, and if the best networks were not adopted, then the best plan could not emerge. Most of the road schemes tested came from the trunk road programme of the Ministry of Transport, together with some locally proposed bypasses and town-centre relief roads. The public transport proposals contained some of the new ideas, but they also included proposals for upgrading local rail services. Under cost benefit analysis, few road proposals were altered but, interestingly, the upgrading of existing rail services generally showed up as a better buy than investing in expensive new systems. The overall conclusions of the studies, to spend some money on road building and some on upgrading existing rail infrastructure (called a balanced transportation plan), met the British penchant for compromise, giving something for both the road and the public transport lobbies. The recommendation for rail upgrading, common to the Merseyside, Manchester and other studies, and coming at about 1970 was timely, for in 1968 conurbation passenger transport authorities had been set up and had yet to establish their presence.

The 1968 Transport Act was far reaching and ambitious. It included measures to support socially necessary railways financially, to divert freight from road to rail, and to create *passenger transport authorities* (PTAs). That these authorities still exist, albeit with reduced powers, is remarkable given the political changes since 1968. The intention was to create authorities with conurbation-wide responsibilities for public transport, at a time when there was no coordination between bus and rail services and no conurbation-wide local authority. The PTAs drew members and funding from the constituent local authorities prior to the creation of the metropolitan county councils in 1974, and they were able to survive the abolition of these councils in 1986. Their operation led to a better use of suburban rail lines, which British Rail had neglected to exploit to the full.

By 1960, land-use planning in the form of 1947 Act development plans, approved and revised on a five-yearly cycle at best, proved to be unable to keep up with changes in the scale and pace of urban and rural development. The proposals of the Planning Advisory Group (1965) attempted to link the development plan process into local policy making. Strategies would be set out in broad brush structure plans, without the precise land use boundaries used on the former development plans, with more detailed local plans for areas of rapid change. However, the transport components of the new structure plans that resulted in the 1970s drew largely upon plans prepared by other agencies. The rail network had by now stabilized and, under the 1974 Railways Act, British Rail was given a public service obligation to maintain services broadly as they existed in 1974; major road proposals came from central government.

Outside the cities, the motorway network was developing rapidly, but major road proposals came under increasingly hostile scrutiny. An early indication of this came in the Greater London Development Plan Inquiry (1973) which started in 1970. The plan provided for a system of new orbital motorways, the innermost of which, Ringway 1, required extensive property acquisition. The inquiry coincided with the opening of a stretch of the A40 urban motorway, Westway. This new road provided dramatic evidence of the scale and intrusiveness of new urban roads. The inquiry questioned the extent of the new road provision, but recommended the inclusion of the innermost Ringway. It was considered that this would provide significant environmental gains from the diversion of traffic from less suitable existing roads. In the event, the London Labour Party adopted an anti-motorway stance, and subsequently won the 1973 Greater London Council elections (Hall 1980).

During the years following the publication of the Buchanan report, when the mood was that car ownership growth necessitated redevelopment on a massive scale, a few urban motorways were built. Mancunian Way (Manchester) and the Aston Expressway (Birmingham) did not traverse environmentally sensitive areas populated by articulate and competent objectors. Birmingham's inner ring road, completed at about the same time, had had its origins in the 1930s or before, and was well on the way to implementation as a piece of municipal betterment in the city's tradition, before its side effects were considered. Other cities such as Glasgow continued for some years with motorway building, abetted by the central government funding for proposals claimed to assist in economic regeneration. In general, these new urban roads were exceptions.

Quite early, the House of Commons Expenditure Committee (1973) was advocating a major effort to improve public transport and to discourage the use of the private car. Twenty-five years later, those objectives became the conventional wisdom. Substantial achievements on the ground remain isolated rather than general. Other cities followed London in curtailing road building plans. In historic cities such as Oxford and York, long-standing road proposals were abandoned in favour of usually nebulous car restraint or public transport development strategies. The reaction against inter-urban road building came later and, in the early 1970s, the inter-urban

Figure 14.3 Westway demonstration 1970

Source: Times Newspapers Ltd (Harris)

motorway network was developing rapidly. There had been few objectors to the first such motorways. At the opening of the Preston bypass in 1958 (now part of the M6) there were no apologies. The new road was a matter of national pride. The objectives for early motorways had been narrowly defined. The M1, which had first appeared as a line on a map before the second world war, was built to relieve the A5, the main traffic artery to the west midlands, which in villages such as Markyate Street was only 4.3 m wide. There was no thought as to whether there was any duplication or overlap with the role of the West Coast Main Line railway or whether Milton Keynes was a suitable site for a new city.

In the mid-1970s, the objections first made against urban motorways began to be raised against inter-urban road proposals. The real chance for influencing the detail of motorway proposals was at the public consultation stage, but the forum for hearing of objections was the public inquiry. The inquiry was ostensibly a local inquiry into local objections, and the inspector at the inquiry into the proposed M42 refused to allow cross-examination about the traffic forecasts justifying the scheme, on the basis that the motorway was part of a nationally agreed programme. Objectors therefore felt that the public inquiry had no real effect, other than as a vent for popular anger, and they began to disrupt inquiries. In 1976, the inquiry into the proposed Aire Valley trunk road, a scheme still alive in a different guise, was indefinitely adjourned (Tyme 1978).

One of the unresolved problems of the past 50 years of transport planning has been that of providing the public with a voice in major decisions on projects with long-term implications for the wider environment. It is impossible to build nuclear power stations, new airports and motorways without environmental impacts. Dissatisfaction with the inquiry into a proposed fifth terminal at Heathrow Airport echoes dissatisfaction with the public inquiry process voiced over 20 years earlier on in connection with the third London airport (Roskill Report 1971) and the Stansted airport inquiries (Banister 1994). More than a generation separate John Tyme, who orchestrated the Aire Valley road protests, from Swampy the direct action digger, protesting about the Newbury bypass in 1997. Even so, their actions had a common basis, stemming from a frustration with the process of making the major policy decisions. It is possible to envisage procedural improvements. An inquiry process that clearly had two stages, one concerned with the principle of the development and the second with the detail, would have advantages. Better compensation for people adversely affected would help. Even so, the basic problem remains beyond the scope of procedural improvements, raising fundamental questions as to how a country is governed. Whilst the existing system leaves protesters dissatisfied, there is no doubt that the action of extreme protesters has played a part in moulding mainstream attitudes. In the early 1970s, government attitudes to rural motorways had not evolved beyond a belief in their modernity and their economically beneficial effects, voiced when the first motorways opened.

The economic benefits of road construction remained unquestioned for some time, but in 1977 the Advisory Committee on Trunk Road Assessment questioned the importance of roads for economic growth. They argued that, in a developed economy, transport costs form only a very small percentage of total product costs, and that companies in remote regions may be protected by their isolation from the competition of companies that enjoy greater economies of scale. It took until the late 1990s before this thinking reached government. However, in the early 1970s the reasons for rural roadbuilding were unquestioned.

TRANSPORT POLICIES AND PROGRAMMES

While motorways and trunk roads were the responsibility of the central government, local road proposals came from county highway schemes. Implementation of these proceeded through the Transport Policies and Programmes (TPPs) of 1974 onwards. These TPPs just predated the first structure plans and provided a system for local authorities to produce a budget for transport schemes, apparently quite separately from the strategies set out in the structure plans afterwards. What the structure plans did provide was a policy context for major development applications. If the structure plan contained a policy statement that the county would not permit major developments in rural areas where the roads were inadequate, then that statement would be of value at any planning appeal. Perhaps structure plans would inevitably appear to have a secondary role in transport projects, because structure plans were not linked to a budget. TPPs may have promoted a greater level of integration within the transport sector, but they did nothing to promote integration between transport and land-use planning. Integration was the watchword, but achievements were small scale.

The TPPs were intended to represent a break from the past, when central government grants for local transport projects were a patchwork of miscellaneous measures. Under the new system, it was intended that a local authority should each year set its own priorities for expenditure on new roads, public transport and road maintenance, and bid for a *transport supplementary grant* (TSG) to cover a percentage of all these (DoE 1973b). In theory, if a council wished to spend money on revenue support for public transport rather than on capital works, it would be able to do so. In practice, local authorities which made proposals that were not in accordance with the views of the central government of the day were threatened with loss of grant. Defiance could be costly, although for many years South Yorkshire managed to maintain its cheap fares policy.

From their inception, TPPs were not comprehensive in their scope. In the early years, the main problem was simply the progressive squeezing of the level of TSG, with schemes receding into the future year by year and with money for little other than road maintenance. The long-run effect of this has been that road maintenance has suffered, for of course it is a soft target when local authorities have to economize, and the school roof is leaking. The argument that local authorities should be able to determine their own spending priorities could have been used to merge money for major local road schemes into the block grant that local authorities receive; but this did not happen. Not until the 1990s did the TPP receive a new lease of life when the local authorities in the west midlands proposed to submit to the Department of Transport a package bid, presenting the priorities of the whole group. However, by this time much of the finance for road infrastructure was coming from quite different sources, because of the work of urban development corporations, and money from the European Union, mostly from the regional development fund.

URBAN DEVELOPMENT CORPORATIONS

Following the election of a conservative government in 1979, integration ceased to be the watchword, and curbing public sector expenditure became a major priority. In the 1980s, the aims of policy integration expressed by the Planning Advisory Group had been overtaken by the more pressing concerns of urban regeneration, and the changing political climate meant that this concern stimulated ad hoc initiatives such as enterprise zones and urban development corporations. These developments made it harder to coordinate land use and transport plans (Truelove 1994). Thus the Merry Hill shopping centre (Tym 1993) was built in an area with totally inadequate roads.

The urban development corporations actively promoted new infrastructure. It was the London Docklands Development Corporation (LDDC), set up in 1980, that provided the model. The objective of the LDDC was to regenerate a part of east London that had become derelict. Because of its location close to the City, the land was potentially extremely valuable. However, there was no private sector interest in promoting such redevelopment, because of the poor access, both by road and by rail. In 1982 the decision was made by the LDDC to build the Docklands Light Railway. The success of this venture, justified at the time by putting a presumed value upon each job created in the Docklands, may be judged by the fact that since its opening the line has been extended from Tower Gateway to Bank, and in 1998 under the Thames to Lewisham. A more significant measure of success is the scale of development that was triggered by the new lines.

Away from London, it is unlikely that such a spectacular transformation could be achieved in areas of severe industrial decline. Nevertheless, it was true that without adequate access, new industry would not be attracted to sites where old heavy industry had declined, such as the Don Valley near Sheffield, or the Black Country. If companies had the choice between locating on a business park on a greenfield site on the periphery of a conurbation, near an orbital motorway, and a brownfield site of uncertain stability and pollution in an old congested industrial area, then there was no contest. In the 1980s, there was no question of government controls over industrial location. To be successful in regenerating the local economy, the UDCs had to improve access, and this meant building new roads.

By the 1990s, the UDCs were the biggest spenders on new road construction in the conurbations, building their own 'spine roads' to open up land for development, but locating these with little regard to the wider transport priorities of the public bodies such as passenger transport authorities. A road designed to provide good access to redevelopment sites also improved conditions for commuters, and in a small way contributed towards increased car dependence. Where the new spine road

Figure 14.4
Docklands Light
Railway

was in the same travel corridor as a PTA sponsored new light rail route, as occurred in the Black Country, then the new road would have the effect of reducing congestion for cars and buses alike, and hence reducing the patronage on the new light-rail system.

Funding for the UDCs, including that for transport infrastructure, came from the DoE, not from the Department of Transport. The UDCs had powers of compulsory purchase, where this was necessary to foster regeneration. In the 1980s, the movement towards massive new shopping centres was in full swing. A UDC could have used its land assembly powers to acquire land for such major traffic generators around existing local railway stations or proposed Light Rapid Transport (LRT) stops in its area. In the event this did not usually happen, and Meadowhall near Sheffield is the only really large new shopping centre to have good rail and LRT access. The creation of single purpose agencies with the sole purpose of fostering regeneration has been shown to be effective in job creation terms in Docklands and elsewhere, but the price has been greater difficulties in linking land use and planning policies.

Integration between transport and land-use planning was further hampered by the deregulation of local bus services in 1986. Long-distance coach travel had already been deregulated in 1981. At first there had been some competition, with some extraordinarily low fares. For a time it was possible to travel by coach from Birmingham to London for £1. This did not last. National Express retains a dominant position, challenged only on a small number of routes such as to the London airports. After the deregulation of local public transport, the situation did not stabilize as quickly, nor were the implications for land-use planning quickly apparent.

With the deregulation of urban public transport, the PTAs lost their role as coordinators of all forms of local public transport. They retained their role as sponsors of local rail services, and were at the forefront of proposals for new rail-based schemes. The problems that the metro schemes of the 1960s were intended to solve had not gone away. The stumbling block had been the cost. From about 1988, as many as 40 towns and cities saw LRT as a means of obtaining the benefits of a rail-based system at a much lower cost. There had been no change in city centre infrastructure, but the crucial difference was that it was now believed that modern light rail vehicles were acceptable on city streets. Expensive tunnelling could be avoided. Light rail vehicles, unlike trains, could accelerate and brake sharply and turn sharp corners. They could climb steep gradients and required lighter less expensive structures such as bridges. Moreover they could use existing railway tracks. None of this was particularly revolutionary: modern trams had been in use for many years on mainland Europe. This sudden burst of enthusiasm resulted in many plans, but in very few achievements. The basic difficulty was in choice of route. Those routes where there was the necessary very strong corridor of demand were difficult to fit into existing suburbs without property demolition. Routes where construction was feasible, say along abandoned railway right of way, were often not corridors of heavy travel demand. The happy exception was in Manchester, where two radial rail routes on well-established commuter routes to Altrincham and to Bury were in need of re-equipment and could be linked by a short on-street section across the centre of Manchester. Elsewhere, implementation never took place, or failed to live up to expectations, as in Sheffield.

Figure 14.5
Manchester Light
Rapid Transit

ATTEMPTS TO REGULATE DISPERSAL

With ever-rising car ownership, congestion continued to have its effects of making traditional centres less attractive. Two out of three households owned cars in 1992, and virtually all these used a car for a weekly shopping trip. Until the issue in the mid 1990s of updated versions of planning policy guidance notes on town centres (PPG 6) and transport (PPG 13), the major retailers continued to migrate to peripheral sites largely unhindered by planning constraints.

These new policy guidelines marked a change from previous *laissez faire* policies, whereby planning permission could be refused only if the application would cause 'demonstrable harm to matters of acknowledged importance' (DoE 1984), and were intended to advise local planning authorities as to how to respond to applications for major shopping and housing developments. These developments should be located where public transport was available. It is doubtful whether the authors of the guidelines envisaged that car owners would suddenly change their preferred mode of transport, but application of the guidance should reduce in some degree the total dependence upon a single mode of transport. More prosaically, it should ensure that the carless minority was not hampered by the migration of shopping facilities to somewhere beyond reach. The trouble is that public transport is provided where bus operators see it as likely to be profitable and not where planning authorities deem it to be needed. The effectiveness of planning conditions requiring public transport provision remains to be seen.

The further problem was simply the extent to which dispersal of shopping centres to peripheral sites had already taken place. After all, it had been almost impossible to prove that a new centre would cause demonstrable harm to established shopping areas in traditional centres accessible by public transport. Since the issue of PPG 13 in 1994, the pace of construction of new centres has slowed. The inertia in the planning system is great, and there are still a few that opened in 1998, such as the

Trafford Centre at Dumplington, which includes the centre of Manchester within its catchment area.

The change in government attitudes towards the growth in car ownership has evolved slowly, shaped by a number of political concerns. Concern about the decline of town centres, and the self defeating effects of road building, were coupled with a greater consciousness of the effects of pollution, not just in Los Angeles and Santiago, but also on the ordinary high streets of England. The 1989 *Roads for Prosperity* white paper (note the title!) saw a continued need for more and wider inter-urban motorways, but later proposals were on a much smaller scale than required to accommodate forecast traffic increases made at the same time. The general public was becoming aware that new roads generated new traffic, most obviously from observing the very rapid pace at which the M25 became overloaded. Increasingly, critics of the road building programme were urging an end to the 'predict and provide' approach implicit in the Department of Transport calculations, and eventually the government asked the Standing Advisory Committee on Trunk Road Assessment (SACTRA) to advise as to the significance of generated traffic. The method used to evaluate new road proposals, called COBA, a contraction of cost benefit analysis, had remained little changed for over 25 years. A value was ascribed to travel time savings with and without the proposal under investigation, and these benefits were set against the costs of the scheme. The list of costs and benefits included within COBA was quite extensive, including, for example, savings in accident costs as well as benefits to commercial traffic. No allowance was made for generated traffic.

To be fair to the departmental view, the question of the effects of new roads generating new traffic is not quite as simple as the popular view of the M25 might imply. Perhaps the additional traffic is not the result of the new road, but the result of new developments that have received planning permission close to that road. If a new road were uncrowded, and additional traffic used it, this increased the benefits rather than detracting from them. However, SACTRA (1994) pointed out that if a new road was full to capacity, then the effect of any extra generated traffic would be to slow traffic down, and the time savings that form the main benefits under COBA would simply not be obtained. The economic case for the new road would be undermined.

Against a background of increasing concern about the roads policy, and of rising public expenditure, the conservative government cut the road building programme in the mid-1990s (DoT 1994). Further cuts were made following the change in government in 1997. However, one important scheme escaped both sets of cuts: the Birmingham Northern Relief Road (BNRR). In one sense this was a conventional proposal: it would provide an alternative route to a highly congested stretch of the M6 through Walsall. However, for the Conservative government it was to be a showpiece for the Private Finance Initiative (PFI). For some years, the Conservative government had sought ways of bringing private finance to help fund public projects, to reduce the public sector borrowing requirement. When an extension to the Docklands Light Railway from Tower Gateway to Bank had been proposed, the LDDC had obtained a £70 million contribution from the developers Olympia and York, who saw the extension as essential to obtaining city-centre office rental values from their development at Canary Wharf. This had been on an ad hoc basis, but the government wished to develop the idea of private sector contributions on a more systematic basis, and this the PFI was intended to achieve. From 1992, all government departments had to consider whether the PFI could be applied to their major projects. The proposed BNRR was intended to attract private sector interest by being built as a toll road. It thus escaped Conservative cuts, because the project would not require public funding, and the government wished to demonstrate its big idea. Explanations as to why it survived the rapid review by the incoming Labour government must be more speculative. However, if new road building is in general to be curtailed, then inevitably some form of demand management or road pricing must eventually be introduced. Plainly, this will be difficult politically, and progress towards it is possible only on a step by step basis. Tolling on the Dartford and Severn bridges is already accepted. Tolling on the BNRR would form one step towards making the public accustomed to the idea of paying for road space.

The role of the PFI in fostering public transport projects has not spread rapidly, because of the limited opportunities for making a profit. However, private sector contributions have been a condition for government backing for LRT schemes. Here though, one senses that companies have made a token capital contribution that will subtract little from the profits to be made on vehicle supply or construction contracts for the project. By the mid-1990s, Light Rapid Transit schemes were no longer seen as a panacea for city transport ills. The success of the Manchester Metrolink, largely routed along previously electrified suburban railways with an established clientele, was not emulated in Sheffield.

One very costly public transport project has gone ahead under the PFI, and that is the extension of the Docklands Light Railway to Lewisham, designed, constructed and maintained by a private company. Here there is an obvious potential market. There are already people in Kent and southeast London who commute to Docklands by way of central London. The original intention was that the builders would be paid by the operators, on the basis of the ridership and daily availability of the new line (i.e. the company would take the full commercial risk of the venture). The final agreement provided that, for the first 10 years of their franchise, the company would be paid solely on the basis of the availability of the line for trains and that thereafter they would be paid on a basis that included the ridership. In this way the government could claim a success for the PFI, and the company could recover most of its outlay in the first 10 years, through the front-end loading of the finances.

Away from the glamorous capital intensive projects, the main development in the 1990s has been the growing role of package bids for Transport Supplementary Grant, with local authorities putting in joint proposals, for bus showcase routes, cycleways and traffic calming, often with virtually no local road building schemes.

The relatively slow progress made in providing bus lanes and bus only roads, since the time of their adoption in Runcorn new town must be attributable, in part at least, to the fact that they are not glamorous projects. Yet their potential remains enormous. A bus segregated from general traffic can obtain operating speeds comparable with LRT. Even as bus priorities are approaching centre stage in urban transport, many of the measures proposed for bus showcase routes seem timid, with little definite action to prevent their obstruction by cars moving or parked. Almost certainly, bus only roads will require some new construction, at the worst junctions. What does not seem necessary, unless perhaps to add a little high-tech glamour, is any bus guidance system. Implementation of a guided busway in Leeds in 1997 has at least emphasized the value of systematic priorities. There is also the indirect benefit of reduced enforcement problems in keeping cars out of the guideway. In general, however, if the vehicle needs a driver, he/she may as well steer the vehicle.

The role of cycle routes now has general recognition and a place in TPP documents, but the value of their adoption will vary greatly from place to place, from essential in Cambridge to little more than a politically correct token in cities such as Birmingham where only 2 per cent of the workforce cycle to work, and where some provisions for cyclists jointly with pedestrians at junctions slow cyclists down.

Perhaps of greater benefit to cyclists has been the spread of area traffic calming, following the basic recognition that a pedestrian hit by a vehicle at 40 mph will probably be killed, whereas a pedestrian hit by a vehicle at 20 mph will probably survive.

The widespread adoption of traffic calming measures illustrates a further process at work during the 1990s, and that is the transfer of transport planning ideas between countries. Speed bumps may now be seen in cities throughout the developed world. On the whole, Britain is a net importer of ideas about traffic calming, with the lead being taken by countries such as Holland, where the idea of grouping dwellings around cul-de-sac yards, within which traffic can circulate only very slowly, is more firmly established (Hass-Klau *et al.* 1992). The job of educating drivers is a harder task than designing road layouts, and the major feature of some traffic calming plans is the proliferation of signs. Despite a popular backlash against some of the more bizarre attributes of traffic calming schemes, such schemes are the most prevalent manifestation of the activities of transport planners in the 1990s.

REGULATING THE DEMAND FOR CAR TRAVEL

Reviewing changes over the past twenty years, it is apparent that we now have a land use pattern that results in a much higher level of car dependency than necessary, fuelled by planning permissions that left dispersal largely unchecked until the early 1990s. The changes that have taken place would be almost impossible to reverse and indeed this might not be desirable. This rather gloomy record acts as something of a deterrent to anyone attempting to suggest a future role for land use planners in influencing transport plans.

There is little doubt that demand management will become an increasingly important feature of transport plans, for many types of journey (Button 1998), including local travel within cities, inter-urban movement on motorways, and travel within national parks. It is equally clear that the implementation of demand management is sensitive politically. The only definite step taken by central government has been a commitment to increase the tax on petrol year on year. Even this measure may be at risk from the countryside lobby, though there is now not much difference between the average journey to work length of country people and city commuters. Thus it seems that it will not be town planners who are decisive in any national strategic plan to regulate road use through, say, motorway tolls.

What central government has done is to encourage local authorities that new legal powers could be made available for local traffic-restraint strategies. Locally based initiatives could be the major source of innovation in demand management. If one looks at past innovations, such as the pedestrianization of shopping streets, the initiative came locally. In the case of pedestrianization, the instigator was Alfie Wood, the planning officer for Norwich. Only subsequently was legal authority to pedestrianize streets for environmental purposes incorporated into national legislation, the 1971 Planning Act. It is within historic towns, which are completely unsuited to heavy traffic, yet retain a strong magnetism for shopping, tourism, housing and employment, that demand management precedents are most likely to be set and achieve perceptible benefits to the public.

The problem with demand management is not any shortage of ideas about why or how to do it. The problem is one of political feasibility. The ideas behind demand management have been the subject of professional interest for more than half the 50 years from 1947. Professor Smeed had reported on techniques of road pricing as early as 1964. In 1967, a Ministry of Transport report *Better Use of Town Roads* was the

Figure 14.6
Pedestrianization in
Norwich

first of a long series of documents considering and advocating regulatory measures such as area licensing. The matter was considered by the panel of the Greater London Development Plan inquiry. There was an early abortive trial of demand management in the Nottingham zone and collar scheme of 1975. Some conurbation transportation studies, for example in the west midlands, recommended limits to the total provision of car parking within city centres. None of these plans endured, partly because of public hostility and also out of fear for the continued viability of city centres in the face of new competing out-of-town centres. Nevertheless, the incremental expansion of pedestrian areas and wider use of bus lanes in cities such as Oxford and York have functioned as *de facto* demand management measures. Plans for improving the local environment in Westminster and at Trafalgar Square rely upon some reduction in road capacity. Such schemes do give a clue as to future progress, for it is apparent that schemes capable of incremental introduction stand a much greater chance of success than those requiring some radical change from the status quo.

As in the case of traffic calming, progress in adopting explicit demand management policies in Britain will be influenced by examples abroad, and there are considerable variations among our neighbours. The number and size of town centre pedestrian zones in Germany is far greater than in Britain. Out-of-town shopping has developed less than in France, where there is a history of the use of tolls to fund motorway construction. It is an incremental and therefore a politically feasible step, to vary the charge, making it higher at busier times, for example on the AI autoroute towards Paris on a Sunday evening, and lower at quiet times. In Germany, which shares the British tradition of toll-free motorways, imposition of road tolls has been fiercely opposed. Even so, electronic payment for the use of *autobahnen* by heavy commercial traffic is being developed. At a more local level, the example of cordon tolls for Bergen, Trondheim and Oslo suggest how payment for road use may become accepted, initially to raise funds for infrastructure, but also to regulate demand.

Fifty years ago, planners could not have envisaged the scale of transport changes that have taken place. Our position is little different, in that it is hard to envisage the possible effects of telecommunications developments. One advantage that we do have is that we have much better information about transport policies being tried in other countries. Some of the most basic and familiar problems have not been solved. The car remains the single most desirable consumer durable. Future plans will be some combination of adaptation of land uses to accommodate car use, and some adaptation of public attitudes to accept less than total car dependence. The free market preference for dispersed, car-accessible sites will ensure that there will be no shortage of work for planners seeking to protect the human qualities of our towns and countryside for the next 50 years.

FURTHER READING

Before the 1960s, transport was not seen as of overwhelming importance in the production of plans, so most information has to be gathered from a range of planning books or plans with a wider coverage. *Cities in Flood: The Problems of Urban Growth* by Self (1957) is characteristic of this type.

The Buchanan Report, *Traffic in Towns* (1963) remains of central importance, flawed mainly by a lack of anticipation about dispersal. The report was received enthusiastically, and many plans of the 1960s claimed to follow its principles. John Adams was among the first to speak out against the 'predict and provide culture' in his *Transport Planning Vision and Practice* (1981). A good general history of the motorway programme up to 1980 is to be found in Starkie (1982) *The Motorway Age*. An alternative view is to be found in Tyme (1978) *Motorways versus Democracy*. The attempts at improving public transport infrastructure are recorded in Simpson (1987) *Planning and Public Transport in Great Britain, France and West Germany*. The 1980s was a decade of deregulation and reducing public expenditure. *Transport Deregulation* (1991), edited by Button and Pitfield, sets UK deregulation in its international context.

In *Transport Planning* (1994) Banister provides an overall update of transport planning history, including an account of the role of transport in fostering renewal in areas such as UDCs. Measures attempting to regulate dispersal, embodied in PPGs 6 and 13, are too recent to have produced an impact in policy or publications. The 1994 Linacre lecture by Goodwin well summarizes the evolution of ideas about the need to limit demand for car travel.

Two reports of the Royal Commission on Environmental Pollution deal thoroughly with several important transport issues: the 18th report (1994) *Transport and the Environment* and the 20th report (1997) *Transport and the Environment: Developments Since 1994*.

chapter 15

New Towns

URLAN WANNOP

INTRODUCTION

One in 25 of all dwellings constructed in the UK between 1945 and 1991 were built in 32 new towns developed by government agencies. The New Towns Acts in 1946 for Great Britain and in 1965 for Northern Ireland provided the legislative framework for a programme which lasted for 50 years until the last development corporations were wound up in 1996. The combined populations of the new towns had expanded by 1.4 million up to 1991. Targets for expansion aggregated to over 2 million at their peak, but a third of the planned growth did not take place. Their experiences varied widely as individual new towns attempted to fulfil the various and changing roles expected of them.

New towns were sometimes accused of having damaged social and economic conditions in the inner cities but, with official projections for up to 5 million extra households in England over the years 1995–2016, a revived programme for the early twenty-first century has become a possibility.

THE POLICY AND POLITICAL CONTEXT

The 50 years of a government programme of new towns derived from a voluntary movement of the same duration. Ebenezer Howard's book *Tomorrow: A Peaceful Path to Real Reform*, published in 1898, sketched a model new town which was subsequently crystallized in the garden cities of Letchworth (1903) and Welwyn (1919). Seeking an alternative to the insanitary, congested, polluted and deprived living conditions of the conurbations, voluntarism sustained the new towns movement until the housing acts of 1919 and 1921 enabled public acquisition and loan aid to develop garden cities (Hardy 1991: 145). However, although metropolitan decentralization and suburbanization was now well underway, no government initiative to launch new towns followed in the interwar years.

The second world war and the wide ranging plans for physical and social reconstruction which it generated resulted in a commitment to a public programme of new towns. Abercrombie's *Greater London Plan 1944* aimed to relieve overcrowding significantly while redeveloping outworn and war-damaged housing. The plan proposed to redistribute over a million people in 10 years, of whom 386,000 would be housed in new estates and towns within Greater London, 383,000 would move to eight new satellite towns outside the green belt, and 264,000 were expected to move well beyond the metropolitan area. Abercrombie and Matthew's *Clyde Valley Regional Plan 1946* similarly proposed a ring of new towns around Glasgow to relieve the even more intense housing problems of Clydeside.

A report by a new towns committee chaired by Lord Reith published just prior to the New Towns Bill spelled out the ways in which the new towns could be developed as 'self-contained and balanced communities for work and living', but it was the legacy of war damage, together with longstanding problems of slums and overcrowding that dominated the case for new towns.

As a start to rehousing two-fifths of evacuating Londoners in new towns, Stevenage was approved in 1946 against fierce local and Conservative parliamentary opposition. Stevenage Development Corporation had built only 20 houses by the end of 1950, however, tempering ambitions that new towns might be completed in only 10 years. East Kilbride was also launched to assist Glasgow with its desperate housing problems, although this was not immediately accepted by the city. Plans were less advanced elsewhere. There was no agreement as to how and where Manchester, Merseyside and Birmingham might rehouse their people. Sheffield, Leeds, Hull, Bristol, Plymouth and other major cities were also unsettled about their strategies.

In addition to Stevenage and East Kilbride, Newton Aycliffe, Crawley, Harlow and Hemel Hempstead were designated within a year of the 1946 Act. Also, there began a 30 year dispute between government departments over regional rehousing strategy and industrial location policy. It was unacceptable to industry ministers that new towns rehousing Londoners should attract employers at the expense of the development areas. But with an improved economic context by 1950, the programme was extended to include Welwyn and Hatfield, Basildon and Bracknell. Cwmbran was established to be a focus for industrial growth in south Wales, Corby to help a doubling of its steelworks, Peterlee for the Durham coalfield, and Glenrothes to support an expected new pit and Fife's economy.

The rush to designate new towns ended in 1950. The Conservative government elected in 1951 might have abandoned the programme but for its promise to build more houses each year than the Labour government. The financing of the programme concerned the Chancellor of the Exchequer, however. While the cost of new dwellings was indispensable to metropolitan renewal and had to be met somewhere, the new towns required extra investment in services and facilities and also seemed likely to go further and further into debt. It was also feared that the new towns might consume a third of all annual national investment in factory building.

Arguments within government persisted on costs, the scope to rehouse overcrowded city dwellers in high-density urban renewal, the difficulty of dampening industrial growth in Greater London, and the threat of the new towns diverting jobs from more needy regions. When finally accepted (in 1954) the new towns programme was consolidated as a major social and economic strategy for a further 20 years. A steady programme was to be continued, with annual reviews of the implications of general industrial policy and the rate of housebuilding, preventing housing running ahead of industrial growth, inducing firms to the development areas whenever possible and ensuring that London new towns drew industry from Greater London.

By 1954, the London new towns had already achieved over a third of their then targeted population growth of 281,300, whereas new towns elsewhere had achieved barely a fifth of their then combined targeted growth of 160,390. Yet, from 1955 to 1964 seven additional new towns were launched by the Conservative government;

**New Towns of the
United Kingdom
1946–1996**

O   Overspill

□   Overspill and regional
     growth

☆   Housing for economic
     development

△   Reducing long-distance
     travel-to-work

Glenrothes ☆
Cumbernald O
                □ Livingston
            O East Kilbride
            O Stonehouse
☆
Irvine

□ Londonderry
Antrim and □
Ballymena

Craigavon □

Washington □
Peterlee ☆
Newton Aycliffe ☆

O Central Lancashire
O Skelmersdale
    O Warrington
    O Runcorn

O Dawley/Telford   O Peterborough
☆ Newtown   ☆ Corby
Redditch O   O Northampton
        Milton Keynes O
            O Stevenage
        Welwyn O
            O   O Harlow
Cwmbran ☆ Hemel Hempstead O Hatfield O Basildon
                    O Bracknell

                    O Crawley

Figure 15.1 Map of
new towns of the UK
1946–96

and from 1966 and 1970 the Labour government added seven more. By 1970, the
capacity for growth in the London new towns had trebled to 918,300 and for new
towns elsewhere it had quadrupled to 942,800. Three new towns had been established also in Northern Ireland with a growth capacity of 153,500. West Yorkshire was
now alone amongst British conurbations in having no new town.

By the late 1950s, London's new towns were promising satisfactory financial
returns, and Glasgow's initial opposition to East Kilbride had been replaced by a
willingness to make a financial contribution for households who by moving to Cumbernauld would reduce the pressure for rehousing in the city. The purposes of the
new towns were further diversifying. Up to 1960, 'overspill' of overcrowded metropolitan populations and replacement of their unfit housing was the main purpose.
After 1960, other purposes became more frequent, as when new towns became
favoured as growth poles for the self-sustaining regeneration of outlying regional
economies.

In Scotland, new towns had relatively more objectives and wider acceptance in

Principal purpose	Population				
	At designation	Initial target	First revision	Final revision	1991 estimate
Overspill					
London					
1946 Stevenage	7,000	60,000	105,000		81,200
1947 Crawley	9,000	50,000	80,000		87,200
1947 Harlow	4,500	60,000	80,000	90,000	73,800
1947 Hemel Hempstead	21,200	60,000	80,000		79,000
1948 Hatfield	8,500	25,000			29,000
1948 Welwyn Garden City	18,500	50,000			41,000
1949 Basildon	25,000	50,000	86,000	140,000	157,700
1949 Bracknell	5,000	25,000	60,000		51,300
1967 Milton Keynes	40,000	250,000	180,000		148,000
1967 Peterborough	81,000	188,000	160,000		137,900
1968 Northampton	133,000	230,000	180,000		184,000
North West					
1961 Skelmersdale	10,000	80,000			41,800
1964 Runcorn	28,500	100,000			68,900
1968 Warrington	124,000	205,000	170,000		159,000
1970 Central Lancashire	235,000	321,500	258,000		255,200
West Midlands					
1964 Redditch	32,000	90,000			79,700
1968 Dawley/Telford	70,000	220,000			120,000
Clydeside					
1947 East Kilbride	2,500	45,000	50,000	82,500	69,800
1955 Cumbernauld	3,500	50,000	70,000		50,900
1973 Stonehouse	7,500	35,000			7,500
Overspill and regional growth					
Scotland					
1962 Livingston	2,063	70,000			43,300
Northern					
1964 Washington	20,000	80,000			61,200
Northern Ireland					
1965 Craigavon	61,700	180,000			78,500
1966 Antrim and Ballymena	32,500	100,000			100,160
1969 Londonderry	82,000	94,500			81,000
Housing for economic development					
East Midlands					
1950 Corby	15,700	40,000	55,000		47,100
North					
1947 Newton Aycliffe	60	10,000	20,000	45,000	24,700
1948 Peterlee	200	30,000			22,000
Scotland					
1948 Glenrothes	1,150	32,000	55,000		38,500
1966 Irvine	34,600	95,000			55,600
Wales					
1967 Newton	5,500	11,000			11,000
Reducing long-distance travel-to-work					
Wales					
1949 Cwmbran	12,000	35,000	55,000		49,000
Total	1,132,973	2,904,000	3,004,500	3,126,000	2,534,960

Figure 15.2 New town designation dates and population targets

government than in England. In the 1950s, East Kilbride and Cumbernauld aimed to support the postwar housing drive to replace the unfit slums of Glasgow and north Lanarkshire. In the 1960s, Glenrothes, Livingston and Irvine were declared 'growth areas' by which the fading manufacturing economy of central Scotland could be renewed. After the 1970s, previous ambitions for the new towns were tempered, and their socio-political role was accentuated in the 1980s as they pioneered the sale of public rented housing and extended private home ownership.

THE PROGRAMME DISTORTED

There was a particular inflexibility in the expanded Scottish programme, to which Irvine and Livingston were added in the 1960s and Stonehouse in the 1970s. Expansion rested on the wholly unfulfilled 1963 projection of an increase of a million in Scotland's population by 1981. It was not foreseen that Glasgow's historic problem of congestion would change in the 1970s to one of a surplus of vacant land; nor was it foreseen that so many households would choose private rather than public housing. And there was excessive faith in new towns as economic growth poles creating added value to regional economies.

The distorting expansion of the national programme in the mid-1960s was stimulated particularly by government alarm at a projected one-third increase in UK population by the year 2000. A national strategy for urban growth was now thought appropriate rather than an accumulation of regionally based plans. To a list of sub-regions already being searched for locations for new towns, the estuarine areas of Humberside, Deeside, Tayside, the Solway Firth and Severnside were added as possibilities for growth.

The new towns programme was now expected to provide about 365,000 houses in the 15 years up to 1981, of which about a third would be private. Doubling of capital expenditure on new towns was in prospect for the 5 years from 1967 so, whatever its urgency, some rephasing of the expanded programme was considered essential by the Treasury. There was a choice between fewer towns at a faster rate and more towns at a slower rate. Officials advised that even if the whole programme went

Figure 15.3
Stonehouse: Regional growth point. The retreat of the new town; roadside sign abandoned following Stonehouse's termination in 1976

ahead, there would be shortfall of a quarter of a million in provision for Londoners up to 1981.

Ministers decided that the programme must maintain momentum, but industry ministers were still concerned that the London new towns were growing at the expense of other areas of the country and might be helping to overheat the economy of southeast England. Because the London new towns were generating more jobs by expansion of their established industry and by commercial and public services, it was argued that their inflow of new industries might now be restrained in favour of the development areas of the UK.

Not until the late 1960s was it really accepted that not all new towns were equally capable of generating employment. Changing economic conditions were becoming apparent and policy was adjusted to allow all new and expanded towns to match their population and employment growth. Dawley, established in 1963, was finding it difficult to let its houses because insufficient employment was transferring from Birmingham. Nonetheless, despite its difficulties, Dawley was recast in 1968 as Telford, with an expanded area and an increased target for population growth. But there were now signs that the tide was turning for the new towns. National population growth had suddenly faltered.

The most significant sign of changing circumstances came from London, where unexpectedly large numbers of people were leaving without the aid of new towns. Greater London's population was projected in 1968 to be at least 700,000 fewer in 1981 than anticipated only 2 years before, when 660,000 people had been thought to need rehousing in new towns and town expansion schemes. A reduced projection of overspill was decided upon, and the proposal of a new town at Ipswich was abandoned.

After almost 10 years in preparation, a shadow national urban strategy emerged in the form of an interdepartmental study of *Long Term Population Distribution in Great Britain* (DoE 1971a). It was confirmed that demand for urban growth had much reduced; 600,000 people had already been accommodated in new and expanded towns, and a further one million could be accommodated between 1969 and 1981. The programme was now expected to be largely completed in 1981, when all new towns should have substantially achieved their targets except for Milton Keynes, Telford, Central Lancashire, Livingston and Irvine.

The ambitions of the new towns programme in England peaked around 1970, when the Central Lancashire new town was designated. By then, four new-town development corporations had already been dissolved and their assets transferred to the Commission for the New Towns. The last new town to be launched was Stonehouse in Scotland, designated in 1973 to help maintain the output of new houses for Glaswegians. Having built only 96 houses, it was terminated in 1976 by a process of regional planning (West Central Scotland Plan Team 1974) similar to that which had earlier instigated so many new towns. After just 10 years, all new towns in Northern Ireland were terminated in 1973, and a proposed Welsh new town for Cardiff people and jobs for the Valleys at Llantrisant was abandoned in 1974. It was now clear that the capacity for growth of several established new towns had been inflated far beyond their real potential.

THE FADING OF THE PROGRAMME

Poor progress in urban renewal and social problems in inner cities brought a change from tolerance to scepticism towards new towns under the Labour government elected in 1974. Following a review in 1977, the target growth of six of the most

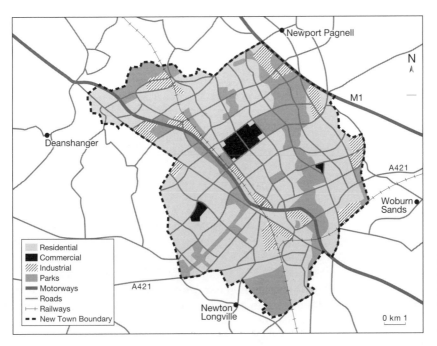

Figure 15.4 Master Plan for Milton Keynes 1970. A new town for the car-borne future. *The Planning Exchange, Glasgow*

recently started new towns was severely reduced, and all other new town expansion proposals stopped. A cut of 150,000 was made from the collective targets for London's new towns of Peterborough, Northampton and Milton Keynes. Over 100,000 was cut from the projected combined growth of Warrington and Central Lancashire. Winding up of a further eight new town corporations was arranged. At this stage, the UK new town targets as finally revised amounted to an overall planned population growth of 1,993,000 (Figure 15.5).

Scottish new towns were distinctive in their imposed role as flagships in the government's aim to restructure the economy of central Scotland. However, they always provided relatively more headlines on job creation than actual jobs: only one in six of jobs in new manufacturing firms in Scotland arose in the new towns, and only one in twenty of jobs in expanding firms. The strength of the new towns was in attracting inward investment: employment in new manufacturing enterprises was created at over three times the rate of other areas of Scotland where industrial and advance factories were similarly available (Henderson 1984: 296). But their manufacturing emphasis made new town economies highly vulnerable in periods of national recession, and the more so as the towns matured (Wannop 1985: 87). This effect of progressive ageing of manufacturing economies was shared by new towns throughout Britain (Fothergill *et al.* 1983: 254).

Town expansion schemes, based on cooperation between local authorities with Treasury financing, were initially seen as a possibly cheaper alternative to the new towns. Sixty schemes were arranged in England, and an equal number in Scotland. Satisfactory joint financing was hard to agree, particularly among small town partners short on both resources and confidence to proceed with major urban development. Some 60,000 houses were completed in expanded towns in England, of which two-thirds were for Londoners. New towns had produced twice as many houses when town development expired. Only Swindon and Basingstoke expanded to significant size. Local agreements on town development schemes were almost absent outside

	London new towns	Elsewhere in UK
1954	301,300	160,390
1959	301,300	221,890
1970	945,300	1,291,730
1977	797,300	1,195,730

Figure 15.5 New town population growth targets

the southeast, except in Scotland, where 9,000 houses had been provided for Glasgow by 1970.

LONG-TERM OWNERSHIP OF ASSETS

The New Towns Act of 1946 did not provide for the long-term ownership of the assets accumulated by the development corporations. Not until 1959 was it decided that a Commission for the New Towns should be established to manage and eventually dispose of these assets. The commission was a landlord with extensive and scattered estates and a social conscience, simultaneously excluding local authorities from local management and capturing for the Treasury a maximum return on its investment. The handover of English and Welsh new towns to the commission began with Hemel Hempstead and Crawley in 1962.

The Labour government of the late 1960s might have taken the opportunity to abolish the commission in favour of 'real democratic self-government', as its election manifesto had promised. It did not. Nor did Labour governments in the 1970s. A survey for government (Cullingworth and Karn 1968) had confirmed the extensive interest of tenants in buying their houses. But although the Conservative government of 1970 introduced discounts of up to 20 per cent on sales of new town houses, it was only from 1972 that home ownership for tenants become financially attractive when there was a switch from a housing subsidy through low rents to a selective household subsidy in the form of rebates (Aldridge 1979: 98). Privatization of the new towns was now slowly under way.

The commission was laggard in capitalizing on its portfolio of property in the 1970s. It progressively compiled a healthy financial surplus. But neither Labour nor Conservative policy favoured wholesale transfer to local authority management and ownership. Not until the Conservative government of the 1980s did sales and private building in the new towns amount to a rush to home ownership under new direction in the commission, greatly accelerating the disposal of its managed assets. The last development corporations in England and Wales gave way to the commission in 1982. Its property holdings were so extensive that, in 1995, it still held 17,000 acres of land, in addition to its managed holdings of buildings of various kinds. In its 34 years of operation, the commission raised £2.5 billion by asset sales. Anticipating its closure in 1998, the commission expected to pass on 11,000 acres of land to some other government agency.

THE SOCIAL AND ECONOMIC IMPACT OF THE NEW TOWNS

Allegations that the new towns might be damaging the social and economic health of metropolitan Britain emerged in the 1960s. The strategic problem of the inner cities was no longer seen primarily as one of moving overcrowded households from slums and polluted air. Poor educational achievement and social deprivation now had higher political profile. By the early 1970s, some conurbations had moved from a problem of urban land shortage to one of vacant and derelict land. Critics argued that new towns did not help the most needy from inner cities and drew away their jobs, wasting resources at a time of low national population and economic growth. The principal criticisms of the new towns form a useful basis for reviewing their record:

Did they damage social change in the cities?
Did they damage the economies of the cities?
Did they satisfactorily contribute to regional economic growth?
Did they satisfactorily contribute to the life and opportunities of their residents?

SOCIAL CHANGE IN THE CITIES

It was clear, by 1961, that London's new towns were not drawing a proportionate share of the lowest and the highest social classes from the capital (Heraud 1968: 56). The proportion of skilled manual workers in inner London's population shrank from 30.6 per cent in 1966 to 26.3 per cent in 1971, being a group particularly affected by redevelopment and the attractions of the new industries in the new towns. Development corporations let houses to workers matching the needs of incoming employers, rather than to the poorest in need of rehousing from London's slums. Housing managers in the new towns preferred tenants who paid rents on time and cared for their houses. Announcing in 1976 that the problems of the inner cities were now to be the focus of strategic policy, the government acknowledged that the new towns were not primarily culpable: 'For example, of the 140,000 who moved from the conurbation of Merseyside between 1966 and 1971 only 11.4 per cent moved to new towns' (DoE 1976f). Yet, the 1991 census showed that severe problems of illness, unemployment, significantly high proportions of elderly persons, and overcrowding remained markedly greater in inner parts of London and other metropolitan areas, from which recent movers had been preponderantly of the least deprived (DoE 1996b).

However, data suggest that the new towns did not seriously exacerbate inner-city problems of poverty and social exclusion. The proportion of people in social classes IV and V in 1991 was actually lower in inner London (18.5 per cent) than in new town districts (20.0 per cent), although in the other six principal English metropolitan cities it was higher (22.9 per cent).

Lone-parent households were particularly numerous in the large cities, but the absolute majority of the most deprived do not and never have lived in the inner cities. Inner London and the six principal metropolitan cities had rapidly increasing proportions of people in social classes I and II by 1991, when any previous effect of polarization of the new towns seemed to have been much reduced. Skilled manual employment in the inner cities was lost more by industrial restructuring than by decentralization to new towns or by any selective recruitment of the key workers employers sought to attract. Although Parr (1993: 232) suggests that the new and expanded towns inevitably strengthened the trend to metropolitan deconcentration in the UK, they probably acted only at the margin. Glasgow had a net loss of 22 per cent by migration of population in the period 1961–71, whereas Liverpool and Manchester (whose new towns had had much less time to attract migrants) lost more. Up to 1986, the lifetime growth of population in London's 11 new towns (including Milton Keynes, Peterborough and Northampton) amounted to 606,300, when their containing area of the Greater South East Region outside Greater London had grown by 3,266,200 since only 1961 (Hall 1989: 23). Thus, since their foundation, the new towns had housed less than a fifth of the growth of the southeast region beyond London's green belt.

Southeast England was a region of overall population growth, of course, unlike the west of Scotland, whose three new towns contributed a larger proportionate share of growth in the region beyond the older urban areas of the Clydeside conurbation. East Kilbride, Cumbernauld and Irvine grew by some 135,700 by 1991, while their containing regional commuting area had grown by some 237,000 since 1951. However, because there was such a high net loss of population by emigration from the west of Scotland, only a fifth of the exodus of Glaswegians in the 1960s was associated with formal overspill schemes (Farmer and Smith 1975: 158).

ECONOMIC CHANGE IN THE CITIES

Even as the new towns became a bogey to inner city policy in the 1960s, evidence was emerging that they were not the most significant of the trends harming metropolitan employment opportunities. Jobs transferring to the new towns were only a minority of those establishing there, and most firms leaving metropolitan Britain did not relocate to new towns. Only 32 per cent of employment moving out of London in the period 1945–65 may have located in new towns (South East Joint Planning Team 1971: 133). Subsequently, it was estimated that 44 per cent of London's total loss of manufacturing employment for the period 1966–74 was due to factory closures, 11 per cent to unplanned moves, 9 per cent to transfers to the assisted areas and only 7 per cent to London's new towns (Dennis 1978: 72). Altogether, only 1,312 jobs in Glasgow's new towns in 1968 were in firms which had transferred from the city, and fewer than 4 per cent of manufacturing workers in Cumbernauld and 8 per cent in East Kilbride worked for employers who had moved from Glasgow since 1958.

Closure of firms *in situ* has been the prime feature of 50 years of industrial change in the inner cities; 22,000 manufacturing jobs disappeared through closures in Glasgow in the decade 1958–68, while barely a fifth of the 5,000 which decentralized settled in the neighbouring new towns. As elsewhere, all this was in a period when the city was encouraging firms to leave Glasgow. Over the longer period 1960–78, still only a fifth of Clydeside's loss of manufacturing employment may have been due to the diversionary effect of the new towns (Fothergill *et al.* 1983: 258). The new towns were probably more in competition with one another for employment than with the inner cities and with older urban areas in industrial decline.

REGIONAL ECONOMIC GROWTH

When criticized for leaching industries and jobs from the conurbations, new town corporations argued that they generated industrial growth for their region which the older cities had become incapable of doing. This neglected the weak attraction of the new towns for office firms who generally preferred the cities, and for many new towns the defence was as exaggerated as the criticism. New towns were particularly favourable environments, but they were not the only places in the regions to which new industries could or did move. There was a natural trend of deconcentration in the USA and western Europe. By the 1960s, the manufacturing economy of Greater London was decentralizing to a high degree and shifting towards high technology production; the southeast region's economic wealth and activity was spreading in both range and geographical distribution. The new towns were particularly well organized and located to share in the growth, but they were neither the cause of it nor the major contributors.

Moves of firms to northern England and Scotland much accelerated in the 1960s. Employment in Glenrothes tripled in 5 years, and in Aycliffe it nearly doubled by comparison with the previous decade (Thomas 1969: 811). This growth encouraged the government to hope that further new towns might become growth points to revive the economy of declining older industrial areas. But the growth points had very uneven success. They disappointed in Northern Ireland. In Scotland, Livingston was relatively successful, but a promising wave of industrial attraction by Irvine's local authority council broke almost simultaneously with the establishment of the development corporation in 1966. Thomas (1969: 942) suggested that the 'economic success' of the new towns was due to their exceptional package of good housing, good environment and available premises. Once established, however, new town industries may not have performed distinctively. Henderson (1984: 315) found that the disproportionately large share of industry drawn to the Scottish new towns subsequently flourished no more than did new industries elsewhere.

From 1960 to 1978, there was a 26 per cent growth in manufacturing jobs in the new towns, but after 1974 most of their advantages in manufacturing location were lost (Fothergill *et al.* 1983: 253, 259). Yet, in 1990 more than half of the top urban areas in the country for high-tech employment were new towns (Begg 1991: 968). By comparison with ten other distinctive types of urban and rural district in England, new town districts showed the strongest employment growth in the country over the years 1981–91 (DoE 1996b). Jobs for both males and females grew when male jobs were being comprehensively lost in urban areas. The decade's growth in male unemployment in the new towns as a whole was exceptionally slight. New town districts were amongst those with the largest proportionate increases in jobs in production and in public and private services.

Yet, far from being self-contained, new towns were frequently integrated with their regional economies to an exceptional degree. In 1966, 54 per cent of the employed residents of Cumbernauld and 40 per cent of those of East Kilbride

Figure 15.6 Dell Computers – Bracknell 1995 – high-technology industry in southeast England's belt of sunrise industries. *The Planning Exchange, Glasgow*

worked elsewhere. Incoming workers were also numerous, with 52 per cent of jobs in Cumbernauld and 38 per cent of those in East Kilbride being daily occupied by residents of other places. Twenty-five years later, 44 per cent of Cumbernauld's employed residents and 38 per cent of East Kilbride's still left their district to work. Only four new town districts actually provided as many jobs in 1991 as there were economically active persons living there. Gatwick Airport gave Crawley an exceptional excess of available jobs, while Peterborough and Northampton were built on the economic strength of established county towns. Elsewhere, the proportion of jobs to economically active residents of new town districts was only 65 per cent in Cumbernauld, 70 per cent in Livingston and 71 per cent in Central Lancashire, all highly dependent upon work provided elsewhere.

THE RESIDENTS AND THEIR OPPORTUNITIES

The new towns overwhelmingly attracted the young. Corporations managed their stock of houses to maximize the growth of industrial employers, who preferred younger workers. But not all households moved to new towns primarily for the jobs they could offer. Thomas (1969: 840) suggests that the new towns added an extra dimension to the housing market of the 1950s and 1960s, providing for young aspiring families unable to find suitable privately rented housing in their native cities at an affordable price. A social survey of Cumbernauld in 1967 found that 45 per cent of respondents had been most attracted to the new town by the opportunity of better housing; less than half as many were drawn by the availability of a job.

Residents of the new towns took some risk in the high dependency on manufacturing industry and relatively highly skilled work. The benefits of this showed in good times, but the costs came particularly in the severe economic recession of the early 1980s, when unemployment in the new towns rose more steeply than in the conurbations. Amongst all types of district in England, the new towns had almost the highest proportion of households with two or more at work in 1991 and almost

Figure 15.7 Aerial view of Milton Keynes Central Station – its umbilical cord to London, the mainline railway to London and the major offices relocated from the capital. *The Planning Exchange, Glasgow*

the lowest proportion with none employed. But although development corporations commonly boasted of low unemployment rates, this reflected the scarcity of unskilled residents more than any innate resilience of their local economies.

As they matured, the new towns became capable of greater self-sufficiency, but this did not lead universally to increased self-containment. The 1991 census showed that new towns within commuting range of conurbations remained dormitories for high proportions of their employed residents, a tendency probably encouraged by the sale of rented houses and the growth of owner occupation in the 1980s. In 1979, as many as 95 per cent of dwellings built in East Kilbride were rented by tenants of the corporation, but by 1991 the corporation had sold 54 per cent of all its residential property.

Between 1981 and 1991, the new town districts grew at half the rate of the 1970s. They had become rather stable with a markedly low net turnover of households by migration. No longer so extremely youthful in 1991, they were firmly converging on the average for inner London and the metropolitan cities for their proportions of people of pensionable age and under 15. The proportion of economically active people of working age was rising, whereas in other kinds of district it was falling. Continuation of the 1981–91 trend to 2001 would leave the new towns with relatively fewer aged under 15 than in inner London or the principal metropolitan cities.

New town residents in 1991 had a relatively low attraction to higher education. There were below the national average of 17 year olds staying on in full-time education, and similarly with 30–44 year olds obtaining a degree or diploma. There was still a relatively low proportion of heads of household in social classes I or II, and the low proportion in social classes IV and V was shrinking more slowly than in London and the rest of metropolitan England.

The new towns did not start with uniform social status nor converge on it. Their different natures reflected the extent to which the towns were built on a large established base of private houses, and the social context of their regional roles. Harlow and central Milton Keynes did not quite reach 50 per cent of home ownership in 1991, and Peterlee, Skelmersdale and Newton Aycliffe barely exceeded this. Bracknell, Crawley and Hemel Hempstead were prominent amongst the often commuter-dependent towns in which home ownership had advanced furthest.

Migrants to the new towns were preponderantly white. While 21 per cent of Birmingham's population in 1991 were from ethnic groups other than white, in Redditch and Dawley there were fewer than 4 and 3 per cent, respectively.

The social character of many new towns was already fixed by 1960, when development corporations responded to government enquiry about difficulties in attracting senior executives and 'potential community leaders' by saying that senior people in industry did not wish to live beside their workers, did not care for a pioneering life or to live on top of their work, and considered commuting costs immaterial. Some corporations disagreed with the inference that communities could be led only by senior industrial executives.

Treasury pressure for an increase in owner occupation in the new towns persisted from the 1950s, but there was little action. In 1967, the Labour government set the objective that English new towns started since 1961 should plan for 50 per cent owner occupation overall, with the same proportion to be achieved in current programmes in older new towns. The targets were supported by a government commissioned study (Cullingworth and Karn 1968), which confirmed the ineffectiveness of current procedures to meet them. It was shown that sales of rented dwellings at discounts could be profitable for the Treasury because rents were themselves

Figure 15.8 Public
realm – Rented
development
corporation houses in
Cumbernauld 1962 –
the ordered
landscape of
centralized public
management
*Cumbernauld
Development
Corporation*

Figure 15.9 Private
realm – Houses
acquired for owner
occupation in
Cumbernauld 1998 –
features of
individuality and
defensible space
superimposed after
privatization of
previously rented
houses

uneconomic. By the 1970s, the number of owner occupiers was growing much more quickly than the number of tenants in maturing towns such as Bracknell, Basildon and Aycliffe, but it was the government's drive in the 1980s to spread the 'right-to-buy' that brought most progress. New towns were an exceptional source of tenants aspiring to house ownership in privatized Britain. East Kilbride's 24 per cent of dwellings in owner occupation in 1981 rose to 69 per cent in 1995. The 72 per cent of owner occupiers in Cumbernauld in 1995 was almost double the rate of 10 years before.

THE COST OF NEW TOWNS

From the outset, the Treasury was familiarly and properly querulous about the price of new towns, where house construction costs may have reasonably compared to those elsewhere, but involved high capital investment in the provision of infrastructure and new services. The Conservative government of the early 1950s concluded that heavy initial infrastructural investment in the first towns made it better to complete than to curtail them. Although the alternative of expanded towns was relatively cheap, it promised less return to the Treasury. Despite their high burden of initial investment costs, the new towns might yield long-term income. So further new towns were added to the programme in the 1960s, although substantial capacity for growth remained in those which were incomplete.

By 1962, nine of the twelve new towns in England and Wales had reached a surplus on their general revenue accounts, but all twelve were still net borrowers after housing subsidies had been discounted. When possible expansions of Peterborough, Northampton and Ipswich were considered in the 1960s, fresh appraisals calculated that costs per dwelling in established new towns varied by up to 50 per cent. It proved impossible to devise 'standard' costs since circumstances varied greatly among towns. The Treasury continued to question the high standards in housing, facilities and environmental conditions which development corporations expected to provide. Although the programme's overall impetus could not be halted, an interdepartmental committee set out to compare costs for wholly new towns, town development schemes, urban renewal and peripheral growth of well-established urban areas.

The study focus widened until it exploded, whereupon the work was put out to an academic consultant whose report (Stone 1973) was submitted in 1967, suggesting that wholly new towns were cheaper than town expansion projects. The Treasury could not accept the conclusions, and a further working group was set up on the regional, economic and financial implications of new towns up to the early 1980s. The report reiterated familiar conclusions about the likelihood that new towns cost more in initial capital expenditure, but that much of the cost would have to be met elsewhere if not in a new town. No long-term strategy emerged from the report.

The new towns programme was never fully coordinated within the machinery of government. The House of Commons Expenditure Committee (1975: xxxiii) was dissatisfied that development corporations had to press for public facilities across a range of government departments. The responsible minister depended on the support of colleagues in obtaining significant investment for the towns in education and health, as well as in highways and transport. The Scottish new towns perhaps benefited relatively by the compactness of Scottish Office management and by the dispersal to them of selected government offices bringing otherwise rare white collar employment.

Although the first generation of new towns moved into aggregate revenue surplus by 1961 (Sorensen 1993: 300), none of the later generations would have done so but for the concluding cancellation of large amounts of their debt. The Commission for the New Towns assessed in 1993 that government investment in the new towns had amounted to £4 billion, whereas since the start of the 1980s the commission had realised £2 billion in asset sales and retained £1.7 billion's worth. However,

Sorensen's analysis suggested that government's total investment in the English new towns up to 1993 had been £7.6 billion but, after deducting returns to government and the value of remaining assets, the net cost was around £3.3 billion.

APPRAISAL

The new towns were pioneering governmental initiatives in urban change, but they were less a unified 'programme' than the sum of various projects of differing purpose and success. Parts were added to the programme irregularly; some intended additions never arrived; and many of the parts became distorted. Aldridge (1979: 57) spoke of a 'programme without a policy', but she concluded that despite regressive decisions about owner occupied housing and private finance, the weaknesses of the

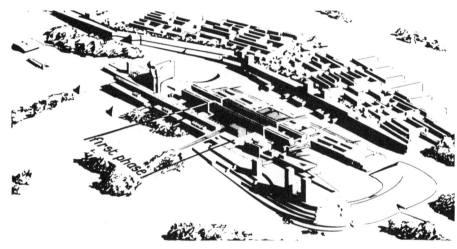

Figure 15.10 The conceptualized town centre for Cumbernauld 1962 – as originally designed, the multi-level concept anticipated that the centre would serve 70,000 residents of the new town and many more from a wider subregional catchment area. *Cumbernauld Development Corporation*

Figure 15.11 Town centre of Cumbernauld 1998 – The multi-level centre was halted and partly demolished after its first phase, curbed by Treasury restraints, a population stabilized 30 years later at only 50,000 residents, and by the anticipated retailing trend to ground level superstores surrounded by extensive car parks

new towns were due more to lack of resources and of resolve in government than to defective conception.

In the 20 years following 1945, only programmes of publicly constructed and managed rented dwellings could have as rapidly rehoused as many overcrowded or entrapped city residents as was the case. Too few households could afford private housing. Local authorities could not alone have met all the needs. But as rising numbers of metropolitan dwellers became able to meet their aspirations for private housing, they did so predominantly in suburban estates and a host of small town and village expansions. So, after the 1960s, there was considerable waste of the potential of the new town programme to provide for higher and more sustainable living standards, better protection of green belts and the countryside, and a more comfortable environment. It was the potential of the new towns intended as economic growth centres which was least fulfilled.

In the lifetimes of their corporations, the individual maximum targets for population growth of the new towns totalled 2,239,000, although by 1991 actual combined growth had reached only 1,402,000. By 1991, the London new towns had grown by 717,400 or 90 per cent of their collective targeted growth; they finally settled at 797,300. All the other new towns in the UK had grown, by 1971, by 684,587, or only 57 per cent of their collective target for growth which finally settled at 1,195,000 (Figure 15.5).

The new towns had an impetus to self-perpetuation. The career interests of their staff and corporations propelled them as much as most governments. They also had notable political value. In the 1950s they were essential to the government's promise to accelerate housebuilding. In the early 1960s they became 'economic growth poles' for regeneration in regions where political difficulties were acute. In the 1970s, cutting back on the programme was a means of earning political credit for the new emphasis on policy for the inner cities. Even in the 1980s, the shrinking programme still served political purposes, helping to promote the 'right to buy' housing policy of the Conservative government and to realize assets by extensive sales of public property.

Physical living standards in the new towns were undoubtedly favoured, politically and financially. Whatever the early and occasional shortages of schools, shops and some social facilities, the standards of roads, houses, greenery and public infrastructure in the new towns were higher than commonly achieved in either council or private areas of new development. Higher standards were repeatedly challenged by the Treasury, but persisted due to pressures from highly skilled and ambitious staff in the corporations, from articulate general managers and from their chairmen. By 1960, politicians had found new town dwellers to be mobile politically as well as physically. The aspirations which had brought residents to the new towns tended to make them also floating voters, whose allegiance could be cultivated by judicious policies.

In a world perspective, the UK new towns seemed relatively modest urban initiatives by the 1990s. It took 50 years for the population of 32 new towns in the UK to swell by 1.4 million, but only 10 years for seven new towns in the New Territories of Hong Kong to grow as much. Shenzhen, in China and abutting the New Territories of Hong Kong, grew by some 3 million in its first 20 years.

After 50 years, the new towns had lost much of their social, political and economic distinctiveness. Newness lay very far behind in the case of the most mature of them. For some, however, a rejuvenation seemed possible in the early years of the twenty-first century. The projected demand for new houses between 1991 and 2016 in southeast England in particular was indisputably enough to justify more new towns, and already by 1998 a major expansion of Stevenage had been approved by government. The private sector had offered several sites for privately developed new towns: Tillingham Hall in Essex (1986), Foxley Wood in Hampshire (1988) and Stone Bassett in Oxfordshire (1989). All were refused planning permission.

The institution of regional development corporations in 1998 offered the possibility of new mechanisms to instigate new or expanded towns. Regional conferences of local planning authorities persisted in preferring localized accretion of yet more houses to what were once small established towns and villages but had often become swollen suburbs. The issue was being raised through the South East Regional Planning Forum (SERPLAN) for strategic examination in 1998, but in other regions the possibilities for new towns were neglected. Thus, new visions like those of the 1940s and 1960s were spurned. But the new towns of the concluding 50 years of the twentieth century had sufficiently fulfilled those earlier visions to justify the shaping of a new vision of urban Britain for the first 50 years of the twenty-first century.

FURTHER READING

Literature on the new towns flourished up to the 1970s, thinning subsequently as development corporations expired and new towns in their maturity became of progressively less academic interest. Historically, Ebenezer Howard's *Tomorrow: A Peaceful Path to Real Reform* (1898) is an important document. Reprinted several times under its better known title *Garden Cities of Tomorrow*, the most easily accessible edition (published in 1946 and again in 1965) usefully contains additional contributions from Frederic Osborn and Lewis Mumford. Hardy (1991) *From Garden Cities to New Towns* covers the history of the vital involvement of the Town and Country Planning Association from Howard to the government's adoption of the new town programme in 1946.

A brilliant review of the wider context of planning history is given by Hall (1988) *Cities of Tomorrow*. Osborn and Whittick, *The New Towns: The Answer to Megalopolis* (1969), provide a detailed picture of individual new towns in the late 1960s. A highly readable account by an author who was a senior civil servant who participated in the programme is Schaffer (1970) *The New Town Story*: this has the value of being written by a participator in that story. The 'official history' of environmental planning has a volume on *New Towns Policy* by Cullingworth (1979) which provides a detailed blow-by-blow account of the inside Whitehall history up to the end of the 1960s. Much of the factual material in this chapter is from this source. Many of the new towns have produced their own largely hagiographical histories. In comparison, Aldridge (1979) presents a critique of *The British New Towns: A Programme without a Policy*. Sad to say, there is little that is up to date.

The outstanding source of material is the two CD-ROM disk set *The New Towns Record* compiled by The Planning Exchange (Tontine House, 8 Gordon Street, Glasgow G1 3PL) on behalf of the Commission for the New Towns, The Scottish Office Industry Department and the Department of Industry for Northern Ireland. The disks contain overviews on the new towns of England, Scotland, Wales and Northern Ireland, together with data on each, including many interviews with key participants in their development as well as with local residents. Maps and photographs are profuse. There are commissioned articles on physical, social and economic aspects of new town history. An extensive bibliography of new town material is included, and the full text of many regional and all master plans is reproduced, for example the *Greater London Plan 1944*, the *Clyde Valley Plan 1946*, master plans for Warrington, Skelmersdale, Northampton, etc. The full text of several significant books is contained including Howard, Cullingworth, Schaffer (referred to above) and Self (1972) *New Towns: The British Experience*. Also reproduced are the texts of the New Towns Acts together with all the annual reports of the development corporations and the Commission for the New Towns.

chapter 16

Public–Private Partnerships

STEPHEN V. WARD

INTRODUCTON

During the 1980s and 1990s, 'partnership' has became one of the most overused words in the language of governance, not least in the various policy arenas that comprise urban planning. Not surprisingly, the attraction of the term has depended partly on its vague and elastic meaning. Even the most cursory review of its use over the last two decades reveals widely varying mixes of public, private and voluntary agencies, operating at different spatial scales and levels of intensity. The most consistent feature has, however, been the existence of some kind of collaborative arrangement between public and private sectors. This dominant understanding of partnership largely entered planning discourse in the 1980s, as British policy began to be influenced by the American model of urban regeneration.

This American model seemed to have been built on local 'growth coalitions', or partnerships, of city halls and private business and development interests. To most British observers, accustomed to the widely understood norms of postwar planning, the approach was striking in its novelty. It seemed to be an alternative to British planning's established roles as controller of private development and promoter of public development. Planners could now promote private development, assuming a role which was both more sensitive to the creative forces of enterprise and less demanding of public expenditure. As such it chimed in nicely with the norms of 1980s' Thatcherism and the new Labourism of the 1990s. Actually, however, the approach was less novel than commonly supposed. Certainly the principles of partnership had not previously been applied to the run-down dock and industrial areas of the inner cities. Yet the broad approach showed far more continuities with traditional postwar urban planning regimes than are usually acknowledged. This chapter chronicles the largely ignored story of public–private partnership under the 1947 Act system. It shows that, far from constituting a fundamental remaking of planning, recent changes have merely given greater importance to themes long established in postwar planning action.

The chapter is structured thematically around three major spatial arenas of partnership activity. These are central-area commercial redevelopment, large-scale development of housing and new communities on green-field sites, and the more recent, better known (and therefore more briefly described) concerns with urban regeneration in the inner cities. This approach also has a very strong chronological dimension to it, however. Thus, an initial concern with central areas from the mid-1940s became very widespread during the 1950s and 1960s. By this time we can see attempts to extend partnerships into greenfield development during the 1960s and 1970s and to the inner cities from the late 1970s. Reflecting the varied nature of partnerships, examples will be used to add detail to the discussion. The final section offers a few critical thoughts on partnerships.

PARTNERSHIPS IN CENTRAL AREA REDEVELOPMENT

Origins

The roots of public–private partnerships go back to the extensive wartime destruction in the centres of many towns and cities, mainly in 1940–1 (Hasegawa 1992). Property values in such areas fell precipitately. Any spontaneous moves to redevelop were discouraged by wartime controls on building materials supply, labour and finance. In these circumstances there was widespread acceptance that government, local and central, would have to play a key role in re-establishing confidence in these areas (Ward 1994: 80). Unprecedented general powers soon followed to achieve this, initially under the 1944 Town and Country Planning ('blitz and blight') Act. Local planning authorities were now able to designate, acquire, replan and promote the rebuilding of extensive redevelopment areas. The 1947 Act strengthened such acquisition and replanning powers even further, allowing the designation of comprehensive development areas (CDAs).

Previously it had been almost unknown for local authorities to be so deeply implicated in the land markets of their central commercial areas. Since Victorian times local authorities had promoted some redevelopment of central streets under local legislation. But many places had no recent experience of this and nowhere had it ever been on the scale now being contemplated. The Ministry of Town and Country Planning, formed in 1943, quickly recognized the need for coherent advice about how towns and cities were to approach redevelopment. Two groups of technical experts were appointed to prepare policy guidance. The deliberations of these groups, initially circulated only informally, eventually formed the bases of two policy advice documents published in 1947 (MTCP 1947a, 1947b).

Despite the continuing fragility of central urban land markets, especially in blitzed cities, which automatically gave the major role to planners and local authorities, the task of redevelopment was conceived as one of partnership. The term itself featured in wartime and early postwar deliberations. Yet, as often happened subsequently, different meanings were attached to the term. The first Minister of Town and Country Planning, W. S. Morrison, had from the outset defined reconstruction as a 'partnership' between local and central governments.[1] But alongside this essentially statist view there quickly grew a recognition that the municipal relationship with private development capital might turn out to be even more important.

Thus, the Report of the Advisory Panel on the Reconstruction of City Centres, completed in August 1944, stated that 'the development of a site should properly involve a partnership between the ground lessor [i.e. the local authority], who provides the capital for the land, and the building lessee, who provides the capital for the erection of the buildings'.[1]

In February 1946, the Central Advisory Committee on Estate Development and Management was even more explicit:

> The contract between the Local Authority and developers should be strictly
> defined and exist as a background to their relationship. But the spirit rather

British Planning

than the letter of the contract between them should govern their dealings with each other. Their relationship should be that of partners in a joint undertaking, it should be personal and it should be human.[2]

By 1947, therefore, a concept of planning based on local authority partnership with, rather than merely control of, developers was already forming. It is, however, important to recognize that, for the moment at least, this public–private partnership was a very unequal one. It was not just that wartime changes and controls had made private development virtually impossible. The truth was that, even before 1939, commercial development activity had operated in a far more fragmented way than was soon to become usual (Scott 1996: 48). Before the war, most buildings in central areas, and particularly shops, had been developed by their principal occupiers.

The city centre planners of the early postwar years naturally, therefore, expected to be dealing with a large number of developers concerned principally with creating buildings for their own occupation. They entirely failed to foresee the extraordinary growth of specialist commercial property developers capable of redeveloping large tracts of central area land and letting shop units to final occupiers. Within 15 years, the business of central area redevelopment had entirely changed. By the early 1960s, Britain had the world's largest and most highly organized private commercial property development companies (Grebler 1964: 116).

Early partnerships

The end of wartime controls and rationing during the 1950s and the strength of the postwar consumer boom were important in producing this change (Marriott 1967; Scott 1996). So too was the comparative ease with which insurance companies and, increasingly, pension funds could fund property development. Human factors also played their part, including the often dazzling entrepreneurialism of individual developers and the already high quality of professional expertise in commercial property. Last, but certainly not least, were the partnership central area redevelopment opportunities created by the new planning system. By thinking big and assembling large areas for redevelopment, planners were automatically encouraging developers to operate on a comparable scale.

Naturally, it took a little while before this truth fully dawned on the newly emergent group of commercial developers. Its full implications only became obvious from the mid-1950s onwards as the commercial development boom mounted. Yet the potential had been building since the end of the war. It was in the worst of the blitzed cities – Plymouth, Exeter, Hull, Swansea – that the new pattern emerged from 1949. The first of the new breed of specialist commercial developers was Ravenseft (originally Ravensfield). Properties began to take on blocks of central area shopping development in these cities, on municipal land bought under the 1944 or 1947 Acts (Marriott 1967: 72). Typically consisting of 30–40 shop units, such pioneering partnership developments were small compared to what came later. Already though, they were on a much larger scale than had ever been undertaken before. Designs and detailed planning were negotiated between Ravenseft and the city officials.

For a few years, Ravenseft had the field almost to themselves. Some cities, especially Coventry, acted themselves as commercial developers (though even they were in negotiation with Ravenseft by the early 1950s) (Tiratsoo 1990). A few insurance companies also tried their hands as developer-partners of local authorities in these early days, but then settled for more 'arm's-length' involvement in long-term financing. As always, some of the big retailers also acted independently. But Ravenseft's

Figure 16.1
(opposite)
Advertisements
aimed at local
authority planning
departments, issued
in late 1960s/early
1970s by leading
developers in
shopping centres

Source:
Ravenseft,
Hammerson, Second
Covent Garden and
Laing

reputation spread quickly on the local government grapevine. By 1954, as the development potential of blitzed cities was beginning to diminish, Ravenseft moved into another lucrative arena (Marriott 1969: 80). It began developing the shopping centres of the new towns at Harlow, Aycliffe, Peterlee and East Kilbride, in partnership this time with their development corporations.

All this, it should be stressed, occurred under the original financial provisions of the 1947 Town and Country Planning Act. The conventional narrative, grown bardic with years of telling, that the Act's 100 per cent development charge on land value increases effectively strangled the private development impulse, was scarcely consistent with Ravenseft's extraordinary rise. The truth was that the company's highly profitable partnership activity was not affected in any direct way by the development charge. Under the 1947 Act, local authorities, who invariably owned the land upon which Ravenseft acted as developers, were exempted from the development charge. They were liable for payments in lieu, but these were calculated on large redevelopment areas as a whole. It was assumed (rather naively in the event) that land value increases on parts of these areas would often be offset by declines as congested commercial districts were redeveloped over wider areas (MTCP 1948: 66).

Partnerships after 1954

Postwar shortages of building materials and the continuance of the wartime building licensing system, introduced as part of wartime rationing and not removed until 1954, were probably the major deterrents to more general imitation. Yet there was also a good deal of caution within the property world about Ravenseft's mode of operation. The initial perception had been that the firm had committed itself to paying inflated ground rents. In fact, the opposite was true. As rationing gradually gave way to a consumer boom in the early 1950s, the returns they secured from retail rentals in the shop-hungry blitzed cities and new towns soon brought handsome profits.

By the mid-1950s, the prospects for private development generally had become much stronger under a Conservative Government committed to setting the developers free (Ward 1994: 122; Scott 1996: 133). The ending, in 1953–4, of the development charge, building licences and the last remnants of wartime rationing opened the floodgates. These changes encouraged more specialist commercial developers to enter the field. Not all these operated in partnership with local authorities, however. Relieved of the need to secure building licences and able now to acquire sites for redevelopment without fear of development charges, many office developers eschewed entirely any concept of partnership with local authorities. Theirs was more the relationship of poacher to the planner's gamekeeper, seeking whatever loopholes there were in the regulatory system of planning.

Paradoxically, though, the concept of partnership also gained. Towns and cities without significant war damage now became fertile terrain for partnership developments. The new incentives to developers themselves to buy redevelopment sites meant they could approach local authorities with something more than just their ground rent bids. It became more common for developers to take the initiative in land assembly. They then looked to local authorities to apply comprehensive development area powers to complete the process (MHLG 1962: 6), or developers might come up with a parcel of backland that extended the area of an existing CDA. In return for the local authority giving them a lease on the whole area, developers would usually hand over their own freeholds to the local authority. Occasionally CDA purchases were entirely funded by developers.

In general, partnerships with office developers were less common than with shop developers because office blocks could be built speculatively on relatively small sites (Marriott 1969: 82). Some areas, such as the southern part of the heavily blitzed Barbican area of the City of London, were, however, designated as CDAs and leased off in comparable fashion for office development during the later 1950s. Of longer term interest, though, were speculative office developments on sites assembled privately, without use of CDA powers, where the developers were contributing to the provision of facilities which would normally be provided out of public funds. The term 'planning gain' was not yet in use but the practice was certainly apparent by about 1960.

The best documented case is of London's Euston Centre (Marriott 1969: 181). This was developed by Joe Levy's Stock Conversion company in the early 1960s on land privately assembled since the late 1950s. The London County Council planners gave full cooperation. They remained silent about the complex and heavily disguised acquisition process that was underway and about Levy's intentions for a massive commercial development. (Until the 1959 Town and Country Planning Act, there was no requirement to inform property owners of planning applications relating to their property.) Nor did they invoke CDA powers which would have been the usual response a decade earlier. In return Stock Conversion gave them land needed for a major road widening (and was allowed to develop the remaining area more intensively as a result).

It became more difficult to replicate this approach after the 1959 Act, which had the effect of increasing private acquisition costs. But it showed how what, in the 1970s, would come to be called 'planning gain' offered another variant of public–private partnership, where public land acquisition powers were not a significant factor and where the developers, in consequence, were more dominant. At this stage, however, this was certainly not the typical form of partnership. Rather it was the new cohort of specialist retail developers such as Hammerson, Arndale, Laing, Town and City and Murrayfield (along with Ravenseft), still relying to some extent on local authorities exercising CDA powers, who represented the most common form of partnership.[3]

Yet these developers now wielded rather more influence over detailed planning than in the early postwar schemes. Often they would approach local authorities with a well-advanced proposal for a new central shopping area. Sometimes a planning consultant was used by the local authority, albeit paid for by the developers. Always, though, the developers had to win the trust of leading local council members and officials. Figures such as Sam Chippendale of Arndale, Fred Maynard of Ravenseft or Frank Price of Murrayfield (the latter a Labour alderman on Birmingham City Council) became well known in local government circles. To echo the words of the 1946 Report quoted earlier, they provided the 'personal' and 'human' dimensions to the partnerships.

Ministerial guidance

There had been very little central guidance about these partnerships since 1947. The truth was that until 1961, the Ministry of Housing and Local Government (which was the successor to the Ministry of Town and Country Planning) had little clear idea as to the way these partnerships were evolving. In that year, its officials began formulating some ground rules. The minister, Henry Brooke, was encouraging smaller authorities, many only just gaining delegated planning powers under the 1958 Local Government Act, to promote town centre redevelopments on the pattern of the bigger towns and cities. Individual cases of partnership practice in

Figure 16.2 An example of the personal and human relationship of partnership – Sam Chippendale of Arndale points out details of one of the earliest partnership shopping precinct developments at Jarrow, Tyneside, to Richard Crossman (right) and the town's mayor

these bigger authorities, especially in the northwest, were also beginning to worry officials as to whether developers were becoming too dominant.[4] Meanwhile growing awareness of rapidly increasing car numbers strengthened arguments for a stronger planning approach in the central areas.

The outcome was two guidance booklets, *Town Centres – Approach to Renewal* (1962) and *Town Centres – Cost and Control of Development* (1963). Written largely by John Delafons, a rising star then in the Urban Planning section of MHLG, both booklets endorsed partnership as the founding principle of central area renewal. As he commented to a fellow official in June 1961, during the drafting of the first: 'the meatiest bit, as far as policy goes, is the section on balance of public and private participation.'[5]

The second was more explicit in trying to avoid some of the worst consequences of the partnership approach. It asserted some of the original principles of public interest and tried not to give the developers too easy a ride. Again in Delafons' own comments to colleagues:

> The bulletin will not be entirely welcome to the development companies, since they do not like competitive tendering and the "developers' brief" is a fairly exacting system. Several have said that they prefer to work with the local authority from the start and often purport to act as the authority's "consultants". Some authorities accept this arrangement somewhat too naively. This bulletin advocates a proper working relationship but keeps the public and private interests separate.[6]

The problems were thus recognized and addressed, but policy guidance alone could not solve them. The big developers were already strongly placed in the partnership deals which they were striking with even the biggest cities. The 1960s and 1970s brought ever more ambitious central area redevelopments. Enclosed shopping precincts, pioneered by Laing's dreary scheme for the Bull Ring in Birmingham, appeared in large numbers from 1964 (Darlow 1972; Holliday 1973). The 1970s brought even more gigantic partnership shopping schemes. These included the Arndale Centres in Luton and Manchester, the latter comprising 1.2 million square feet of retailing space in the very heart of the city.

As the physical scale of these partnership developments grew, there came also ever greater subtleties in the public–private relationship. When local authorities realized just how much profit they had given to developers and their backers in the early years by agreeing low long-term ground rents, ever more complex agreements began to evolve. In the 1970s, some local authorities were also taking a direct stake in the equity of developments, partly also to ensure that these long-term returns were not lost.

PARTNERSHIPS IN MAJOR GREENFIELD DEVELOPMENTS

Political interest in the 1960s

By the mid-1960s, the long-term character of public–private partnerships in central area renewal had largely been formed. In contrast to the important changes that took place in the financial arrangements of the developers themselves, the developer–local authority relationship changed comparatively little. The main story of partnership became one of trying to apply the concept elsewhere.

An early sign of this desire came in November 1961 when the Parliamentary Secretary to the MHLG, Lord Jellicoe, penned a short note to the Permanent Secretary, the redoubtable Dame Evelyn Sharp, following a social encounter with one of the leading commercial developers of the period:

> I had a look at Cumbernauld New Town a week or so ago, and I happened to tell Mr Charles Clore, with whom I was shooting the following day, how interesting I found it.[7]

Clore also had a look and answered politely, prompting Jellicoe to wonder whether MHLG could capitalize on this interest:

> I wonder whether there is not more scope for enlisting the co-operation of the major development companies in the whole field of housing, of the redevelopment of 'twilight' areas, of central area urban renewal, and of town expansion and new town schemes. I have certainly got the impression from a number of casual conversations that the big boys may be starting to think that over the next decade or two office development may not offer the only profitable field for the investment of their resources[7]

It will be clear that Jellicoe was out of touch with what had actually been happening in central areas and new towns. Yet it was his evident desire for a larger role for public–private partnership which was important. Though nothing new actually came from his note, it was indicative of a recurrent theme amongst the political leaders of the ministry in the 1960s. During his much recorded tenure of the ministerial office in 1964–6, for example, Richard Crossman actively cultivated several leading developers, trying to involve them in the new Labour government's housing programme (Crossman 1975). Amongst them was Harry Hyams, the youngest and most financially successful of the early 1960s' London office developers. Again nothing came of this, reflecting a combination of political and official unease and Hyams' less than wholehearted interest.

Other hands did prove willing to join with public agencies, however. During the 1960s several of the major private builders played an important role in redeveloping former slum areas (Dunleavy 1981). But their role was that of contractors to local authorities rather than developers. In fact, the growing popularity of package deal arrangements for industrialized building systems actually made their relationship more like that of a partner. As in central area renewal, normal competitive tendering was rare. A few contractors were dominant; and bemused (and sometimes bribed) local councillors and officials frequently allowed them to design and build with very little public control. The results, initially greeted as a bold approach to urban renewal, in time often proved to be abysmal and occasionally catastrophic. However, we cannot truthfully lay these failures at the door of partnership. The difference between these and true partnership arrangements was that no private capital was actually being invested in the package deal contracts.

The major attempt to promote public–private partnerships more generally in the 1960s came with the Labour government's Land Commission (White Paper 1965). This was established in 1967 (and abolished in 1971). The intention was that the Commission would play a key role in acquiring undeveloped land, then selling it on to developers at development value. It would, however, be able to grant concessions to private developers who fulfilled publicly desired objectives, for example with respect to housing provision. In practice, none of these laudable objectives came to pass, largely because local authorities never trusted the new body (and because the Conservatives vowed to abolish it at the first opportunity).

Partnership approaches to town expansion in the 1960s
Despite this failure at the strategic level, local initiatives in the 1960s did occasionally produce public–private partnerships of the kind the Land Commission had seemed to promise more generally. Two of the most interesting, albeit surprisingly unstudied, were promoted by Northumberland County Council from the late 1950s (DoE 1972c: 31; Byrne 1989). These were the quasi-new towns of Killingworth and Cramlington which effectively received central approval in November 1960 and March 1963, respectively. Of the two Cramlington was the more ambitious project. It involved an area of over 6,000 acres and a projected growth in resident population from 5,200 to 62,000 by the late 1980s (which has broadly been achieved). Killingworth by contrast covered just 760 acres with a target population of 18,000.

In statutory terms both were CDAs, with the county using the enhanced planning and land acquisition powers which applied in such areas. Because both were to house overspill population from Tyneside, they also received central financial assistance for their council housing. The general level of public investment was, however, much lower than in contemporary statutory new towns. Private developers played a much bigger role than was then common in the new towns proper. This was particularly so in Cramlington where William Leech, a major Tyneside speculative house-builder, from the outset secured very large landholdings and was soon joined by another Tyneside builder, John T. Bell. These holdings remained largely in their ownership and provided the sites for the vast majority of new houses. The two builders also established a subsidiary company to develop a shopping centre.

Only just over a third of Cramlington's total area was made subject to compulsory purchase powers under the CDA designation (though most was in the event acquired by agreement). This portion was used mainly for public sector housing, built by the district council, and industrial estates, which were developed by the county council and the Board of Trade. Infrastructure was provided directly by county and district councils and the two private builders. The latter also made a per acre developed land financial contribution to the district council's development costs, as did the county council. Leech and Bell also conveyed land for public sector housing and infrastructure at cost rather than at development value. From the outset the nature of public–private financial relationships was determined by formal agreements. The public–private partnership at Killingworth was a much simpler affair. The whole area was brought under council ownership and then subsequently disposed of parcel by parcel to private developers or the local housing authority. The infrastructure was predominantly provided by the county, its cost recouped in the disposal price of development land.

These two ventures have attracted some criticism. Cramlington, for example, has developed much more as a dormitory settlement than was originally intended. This was because the private housing was largely sold to commuters. Nor was shopping provision of sufficient quality to challenge the reliance on Tyneside's centres. Both these points may be seen as deriving in part from the unusually close involvement of private developers. But against this the locally orchestrated partnership model had arguably had advantages for all parties over the more heavy-handed alternative of a development corporation under new towns legislation.

Yet the CDA partnership was not an approach to greenfield development that was widely followed. The most ambitious attempt came in 1964–5, in the wake of *The South East Study* (MHLG 1964). Buckinghamshire County Council[8] tried to promote a CDA to develop a new city of 250,000 in the north of the county (Cullingworth 1979: 228). The mechanism of development was to be broadly similar to the two local partnership new towns in Northumberland. The ministry did not, however, believe that the necessary level of private sector interest would be forthcoming. Accordingly it turned down the CDA and designated Milton Keynes as a new town in 1967.

Growing interest in the 1970s
Within a few years, however, the public expenditure consequences of this kind of action became unacceptable. *The Strategic Plan for the South East*, approved by the Heath Conservative government in 1971, made it clear that large quantities of housing were needed in greenfield locations. Instead of further new town designations, however, there was now more interest in exploring public–private partnerships to facilitate major greenfield housing development. Thus, in November 1971 a DoE Working Party on Local Authority/Private Enterprise Partnership Schemes was appointed (DoE 1972c). The following April, the DOE announced a special loan sanction allocation of £80 million, allowing local authorities to acquire land for private housing.

In part, these initiatives were also a response to the abolition of the Land Commission which, as noted, had been evolving a partnership approach to development before its demise. One of the earliest (and most unusual) housing development partnerships of the 1970s, the Buckingham Borough Development Company,[9] came about specifically for this reason (DOE 1972: 39). It was founded by local legislation in March 1971 as a joint company owned by Buckinghamshire County Council and Buckingham Town Council (after 1974, Aylesbury Vale District Council). The intention (largely fulfilled) was that the company would take over the agreed role of the Land Commission, acquiring land for development and promoting the town's expansion from under 5,000 to 15,000. Land was acquired by agreement, with the powerful incentive that the original landowners would ultimately receive 75 per cent of the increased development value of the land, after infrastructure costs had been paid. The 25 per cent remaining with the company was used to improve Buckingham's facilities.

Ultimately the company proved very successful, not only in simple housing terms but also in playing a central role in establishing the private University of Buckingham. However, its reliance on the private development process made it vulnerable to the collapse and slow recovery of the property market after 1973. It was perhaps this and the need for special legislation which limited its wider emulation. Some local authorities were able to establish joint private companies without special legislation, however. The ancient city of Norwich for example, used rights defined in its original city charter to form a small joint company, Colegate Developments Ltd, with a local developer, also in 1971 (DoE 1972c: 58).

More traditional partnership mechanisms also continued. Despite its intended replacement by the action area under the 1968 Town and Country Planning Act, reports of the death of the CDA turned out to be exaggerated, or at least premature. Because structure plans were so long delayed, old-style CDAs continued to form the basis of public–private partnerships in some areas. Much the most notable of those for housing and town development begun in the 1970s was that at South Woodham Ferrers in Essex (Neale 1984). The intention was to create a new country town of about 17,500 from an existing village of about 4,500. This entailed a CDA of some

Figure 16.3 South Woodham Ferrers – an important example of public – private partnership to facilitate large-scale greenfield development, based on use of the comprehensive development area

Source: Essex County Council Planning Department

1,300 acres, including the existing settlement, approved in September 1974. Since the area had originally been promoted as a plotland development in the years before 1914, there were many individual land titles in the CDA, many with unknown owners (Hardy and Ward, 1984: 220). A purely private-land assembly process would therefore have been extremely difficult.

Infrastructure, schools and most recreational facilities were provided by local authorities, mainly the county council. Several different developers provided the housing on land sold to reflect development value. The earliest land disposals were on a joint risk licensing system that deferred payments until the houses actually sold. Once the pump had been primed, however, subsequent disposals were on a freehold basis. Throughout, however, a distinctive feature was the use of restrictive covenants to reinforce planning controls. This brought a high degree of design control and made South Woodham Ferrers an exemplar for the Essex Design Guide which had appeared in 1973. These principles were also reflected in the town centre, developed in several phases as the population grew.

A third approach to partnership in greenfield housing developments involved planning agreements. These were not new and had been common, for a wide variety of purposes, before 1939. The centralist impulse which underlay the planning reforms of the 1940s curbed their use, however, making them subject to ministerial approval. This requirement was dropped in the subsequent reforms of the 1960s. By the early 1970s, the potential of such agreements (under Section 52 of the consolidatory 1971 Town and Country Planning Act) was beginning to be recognized. The 1972 DOE Working Party on Partnership Schemes was enthusiastic about the scope for using so-called positive agreements (DOE 1972: 13, 32). These typically involved developers agreeing to fund infrastructure or providing land for public purposes. Rather like the example of the Euston Centre quoted earlier, such an approach effectively formed the basis of a privately led development partnership.

The most ambitious use of the planning agreement partnership in housing and town development came at Lower Earley in Berkshire near Reading (Healey *et al.* 1982; Short *et al.* 1986). Over 6,000 private sector houses with a shopping centre and other community facilities were built between 1977 and the early 1990s. Rather like South Woodham Ferrers, its origins lay in *The Strategic Plan for the South East*, which identified a major growth area in the vicinity of Reading. Yet the extent of pre-existing developer ownership of land precluded any need for a CDA or action area approach.[10] The bulk of the 1,018 acres of Lower Earley were owned by a smaller, regionally based housebuilder (Pye), a major national housebuilder (Bovis) and the University of Reading. Following a planning study commissioned by the developers, a planning application was submitted in 1974, forming the basis for lengthy negotiations.[11]

In 1977, when the application was finally approved, local authorities and developers concurrently signed a planning agreement. This stipulated that 8 per cent of the selling price of the houses would be given to the local authorities (mainly the county council) to fund roads and other public facilities. No payments would, however, be made until about a third of the houses were completed, so that there were heavy 'front-end' costs for the county. Land for open spaces was also given to the district council and guaranteed options to purchase all school sites to the county council. In practice the agreement worked reasonably well. The sale of much of Pye's landholdings to many other housing developers certainly strained the partnership, however, making it difficult to secure the original planning intentions.

Figure 16.4 Lower Earley shows another approach to partnership based on a planning agreement where the hand of developers was stronger because they already held much of the land

Developments since the 1980s

Fuller discussion of planning agreements more generally can be found in chapter 5 (Grant). Here we can note that the wholesale retreat from public expenditure after the mid-1970s and especially the 1980s provided increasing scope for their use, even in small developments. The most important attempt to use the approach on a large scale in the 1980s, promoted by Consortium Developments Ltd, an organization representing the major national speculative housebuilders, was an abject failure, however (Hebbert 1992). The extent of private initiative which its proposed 'new country towns' represented went beyond any common ground of agreement with local planning objectives.

Another important change of the 1980s was the progressive abandonment of council housebuilding. This made social or affordable housing provision an import-ant item in local authority negotiations with private housing developers. The 1988 Housing Act completed this process by redefining the local authority housing role as an 'enabler' rather than a provider. This enabling role encouraged more partnership arrangements with private developers and housing associations (Fraser 1991). Although planning agreements were used, the arrangements often harked back to the old CDA partnerships, where the local authority provided housing sites. As always, this gave it a greater say in the final development, but increasingly now also who would live in the houses and rents or selling prices.

The most ambitious early use of this approach has been Leeds Partnership Homes (LPH), formed by Leeds City Council and five housing associations. Amongst other things, the city in 1991 gave 90 per cent of its housing land, valued at £33 million and sufficient for over 2,000 dwellings, to LPH. Most of the land was for affordable rental housing by housing associations. Some more attractive sites were, however, sold to the private sector, and private development was undertaken on a shared profit basis with LPH. The proceeds of such dealings with the private sector would then be used to cross-subsidize the rental housing.

PARTNERSHIP AND URBAN REGENERATION

There have been many other arrangements of this broad kind. Except for the grow-ing concern with tenancy and affordability, however, these recent developments are no more than elaborations of basic partnership forms that had been used in green-field housing developments for at least two decades. From 1977, the main arena of innovation in partnerships shifted to areas of urban regeneration, largely in the inner cities (the setting, in fact, for much of the work of LPH and its equivalents elsewhere).

Space allows consideration of only a few salient points in this story, which is integral to the development of inner city policy and has been very fully described elsewhere (e.g. Barnekov *et al.* 1989; Lewis 1992). The most fundamental point is that the inner city had always been the most unpromising terrain for partnerships with developers because the possibilities of securing attractive profits from development had seemed so remote. As far back as 1961, ministry officials responding to Lord Jellicoe's initiative had recognized the impracticality of involving private developers in what were then called 'twilight' areas.

The first attempt to develop partnerships for inner city areas seemed to accept this traditional view. Thus, the GEAR (Glasgow Eastern Area Renewal) project, established in 1976, and the English inner area partnerships conceived in 1977–8, were essentially partnerships of public sector agencies. Already the Conservative opposition was calling for approaches that brought in more private investment. In government from 1979, their political rhetoric was of 'rolling back the frontiers of the state' but the reality was an approach which mixed public and private resources. Thus, many of the enterprise zones, designated under the 1980 Local Government, Planning and Land Act, were actually on local authority-owned land. The other major innovation of this Act, urban development corporations, also deployed exceptionally strong public powers and major public investment by the corporations to draw in private investors (Imrie and Thomas 1993).

There was also a growing interest in many of the older cities of the USA which, if the promotional spin was to be believed, were coming back almost from the dead. Underpinning this 'rebirth' was a new pattern of urban politics based on public–private partnerships and 'growth coalitions' of business and political leaders (Fosler and Berger 1982; Ward 1998: 186). The pattern began to become noticeable during the 1970s as the principal exemplar cities, Boston and Baltimore, unveiled the impressive fruits of these partnerships in former run-down areas. There was also a growing official interest within the British DoE in the American *urban development action grant* (UDAG) (Barnekov *et al.* 1989: 7). This had been introduced in 1977 to encourage private developers to invest in unpromising locations. Essentially it allowed public funds to be used where the likely costs of a development project exceeded returns. The intention was that private sector had to put up the bulk of the funding, with public funds used to leverage (in the US term) the maximum private funding. Effectively, therefore, UDAG created a funding formula that necessitated some degree of partnership.

It took new political imperatives, however, to bring this interest in UDAG to fruition in Britain. In May 1981, following serious urban riots in several inner city areas, Mrs Thatcher's first Environment Secretary, Michael Heseltine, tried to forge an instant growth coalition. His approach was a little less gentlemanly than Jellicoe's shooting party encounter with Clore 20 years before. It involved taking 30 of the country's top development financial managers on a bus tour of inner Liverpool (Heseltine 1987: 140). Their response was not directly to unlock the millions Heseltine had clearly hoped for, but to second some of their staff to develop ideas. One such (that we may strongly suspect actually originated with DOE officials) was a British version of UDAG (Barnekov *et al.* 1989: 184). Such was the prevailing climate of the early 1980s, however, that ideas apparently honed in the marketplace enjoyed more credibility than those coming merely from civil servants. The British *urban development grant* duly appeared in 1982, with a version for larger projects, *urban regeneration grant*, following in 1987. The two were merged together as *city grant* in 1988.

By the late 1980s, these grants were typically securing four times as much private as public investment. They played an important role in spreading the gospel of partnership to even the most recalcitrant of Labour local authorities. By this time, though, virtually all local authorities and central government were singing from the same hymn sheet. It had become common to quote the 'leverage ratio' almost as a virility symbol of local partnerships. At the peak of the late 1980s property boom some of the urban development corporations (e.g. London Docklands, Trafford and Sheffield) were boasting ratios as much as 1 to 12 or more, though there was great variation. Even at this very favourable moment, Merseyside could only manage a ratio of 1 to 1.2. Over the first decade of its existence, its ratio was a desultory 1 to 0.23.

By the early 1990s, however, politicians began to recognize that such financial measurements of the effectiveness of partnership arrangements were perhaps a little too crude. In part, this was because the property slump was depressing the expectations of leverage. Yet there was a widening acknowledgement that an impressively large leverage ratio often did nothing for social problems or community alienation. When *city challenge* was launched in 1991, Michael Heseltine, again in the DoE, looked for a better quality of partnership, embracing voluntary and community groups (Bailey *et al.* 1995). The same spirit pervaded the formation of the English Partnerships development agency in 1993 and the creation of a unified *single regeneration budget* in 1994.

Yet, within these refinements, the essentially bilateral nature of the partnerships remains dominant, where public interest objectives can be combined with developer profits. At present, there seems no likelihood of the partnership approach being superseded. It now seems to permeate all aspects of public policy. Under the Private Finance Initiative (PFI), public–private partnerships were encouraged in the latter stages of the Major Conservative government to introduce private funding into public services that were politically impossible to privatize. This approach has actually intensified under the Blair Labour government. Labour's first Secretary of State for Environment, Transport and the Regions, John Prescott, has been particularly zealous, mainly in promoting major transport projects. In such a climate of thinking the future of the many other manifestations of partnership in planning, for example in housing, town development, urban regeneration and conservation, seems assured.

FINAL THOUGHTS

The foundations of partnership may then be traced back to the very origins of the 1947 Act system. We have shown that such arrangements were confined initially to commercial development, but that they gradually spread to greenfield housing and town development, urban regeneration and other aspects. Across all of these, several broad and partially overlapping categories of public–private partnership may be identified. The two most common forms, those based on public assembly/ownership of development land or on planning agreements, have grown directly from the exercise of normal planning powers. Much more unusual have been various joint company arrangements which permit more unorthodox dealings with developers. All these types have, however, been associated with situations where developers could, even without partnership arrangements, expect to generate profits. Typically, however, public–private partnerships have enhanced this profitability by effectively granting monopoly development rights to specific developers and by lubricating the development process in various ways.

There are some important differences where fundamental profitability has been more dubious, notably in developments involving lower value land uses in urban

Figure 16.5 Hulme Regeneration Ltd was established under City Challenge as a partnership of local and central government, private sector and other agencies. Its role has been to redevelop the Hulme area, removing derelict council housing and replacing it with a mixture of social and private housing, recreational and community facilities and business premises

regeneration areas. Here, direct financial subsidies have become an important additional bargaining tool in making partnership arrangements. Because central government has tended to be the source of such direct subsidies, they have also become an important way of promoting partnerships as a matter of general policy. Hitherto, despite central guidance and policing, the making of partnership arrangements was much more of a local option.

Within each of these broad types of partnership, there exist many further possibilities of variation. It is therefore difficult to draw anything but the most general of conclusions about the value of public–private partnerships. Clearly, it is in their nature to create privileged positions for the particular private interests which are parties to the arrangements. Once formed, they also create a tendency for the locus of decision making to shift partially out of the public arena. The exercise of the normal regulatory functions of planning may be partly pre-empted by the special relationship of partnership. These points raise important questions about public accountability and, in some cases, the probity of such arrangements. It is clear too that partnerships often work to the disadvantage of interests (e.g. community groups or businesses competing with the chosen private partners) which are excluded or under-represented in the partnership. Yet such losses in accountability and inclusivity may be compensated for by the overall benefits of partnership. Much depends on the 'price' exacted for the privileged position granted to the private partners.

Inevitably perhaps, the balance sheet is mixed. The early years of central area renewal brought undistinguished physical results and, in many cases, huge profits for the developers with only rather modest financial returns to public landlords. In major town expansions, the needs of the private development process have often compromised the achievement of public planning objectives. This has been especially so where planning agreements form the basis of the partnership, in other words where private interests are more dominant. Where the public hand has been stronger, the results have generally been more impressive. In urban regeneration, by contrast, it is clear that in the 1980s much public funding was used to underpin private profits in preference to meeting community needs.

More recent attempts to make partnerships more inclusive of community and other interests have been encouraging. Given contemporary political realities, the present conceptions of partnership, provided they are properly policed, may be the least worst way to address the development and planning needs of our cities. Yet private developer participation in these partnerships by definition depends on their seeing opportunities for profits. Harnessing this motive to cross-subsidize publicly necessary projects, particularly those that will never be profitable, remains a laudable goal that is still too rarely being achieved, however. This remains as the main challenge for public–private partnership in the early twenty-first century.

ACKNOWLEDGEMENTS

I am grateful for advice, comments and information provided by my colleagues, Roy Darke and Peter Edwards, and Richard Winter of Buckinghamshire County Council. Naturally, any errors of fact or interpretation are my own. Thanks also to Rob Woodward for assistance with the illustrations.

FURTHER READING

Until recently, practically nothing of any length has been written on the concept of partnership in Britain. On partnerships in relationship to town and city centre renewal, Marriott (1969) *The Property Boom* (also available in other editions) is a uniquely vivid portrait of developers, with some reference to the relationship to planning. Scott (1996) *The Property Masters: A History of the British Commercial Property Sector* is a more recent historical account of the commercial property development industry by an academic business historian. Neither, unfortunately, devote very much attention to partnership. The two reports on central areas produced by the Ministry of Town and Country Planning: MTCP(1947a) and (1947b) are a little more helpful. More valuable still are the MHLG two planning bulletins: *Town Centres – Approach to Renewal* (1962) and *Town Centres – Cost and Control of Development* (1963).

The collection of case studies edited by Holliday (1973) *City Centre Redevelopment*, gives a good sense of the planning side of commercial redevelopment, especially in the late 1960s and 1970s.

For the growth of partnerships to promote major housing and town developments on greenfield sites, the 1972 DoE Working Group Report *Local Authority / Private Enterprise Partnership Schemes*, though little known, is absolutely indispensable. Neale's study of *South Woodham Ferrers* (1984) gives a good sense of the planning advantages of a partnership approach in such circumstances. Hebbert (1992) 'The British garden city – metamorphosis', though not exactly focused on this topic, also provides an instructive read. Finally, the reader is spoiled for choice in relation to the current engagement with partnerships. Useful recent reviews are Bailey *et al.* (1995) *Partnership Agencies in British Urban Policy* and, on social housing, Fraser (1991) *Working Together in the 1990s*. Lewis (1992) *Inner City Regeneration* and Barnekov *et al.* (1989) *Privatism and Urban Policy* are particularly valuable for their sceptical and well-informed discussions.

chapter 17

Environmental Planning

CHRISTOPHER WOOD

INTRODUCTION

The UK planning system developed in part to counter the parlous environmental conditions existing in Britain's major towns and cities in the nineteenth century. Since its earliest years, it has had a continuing but changing relationship with environmental protection. This relationship can be likened to a pendulum in which planning swings irregularly away from and then back towards its environmental roots.

This chapter first describes why planning controls over pollution and other environmental problems are essential and, in the final analysis, inevitable. It then describes the environmental origins of the statutory UK planning system and how these were forgotten over time. The next section discusses the dormant state of environmental planning during the first two decades following the enactment of the Town and Country Planning Act (1948–67). The succeeding section chronicles the gradual swing back towards interest in environmental planning during the period 1968–87. The penultimate section describes the full swing of the environmental planning pendulum during the last decade.

In each of these sections, relevant legislation, government advice, the planning literature and planning practice are summarized. Finally, conclusions are drawn about the role of environmental issues in British planning, and the need for the system to adapt to future environmental challenges.

PLANNING AND POLLUTION CONTROL

The prevalence of pollution is succinctly summarized in an EC report (CEC 1979: 49): 'almost all human activities make some impact on the natural environment and almost all industrial processes which transform natural resources into products for man's use give rise to some pollution'. Furthermore, many planning mistakes have been made in the past: 'too much economic activity has taken place in the wrong place, using environmentally unsuitable technologies. The consequence has often been a choice between accepting pollution as a necessary evil or paying very large sums for its elimination'. It is generally accepted that pollution prevention is better than cure and, in the phrase that Royston (1979) has popularized, 'pollution prevention pays'.

Needless to say, the intention to prevent does not always preclude the necessity to cure. However carefully considered, prospective controls cannot always anticipate either changes in technology or future trends in production, which may result in unexpected pollution levels, or changes in public attitudes, which may lead to the decreasing acceptability of once-tolerated levels. Similarly, it must be remembered that achieving pollution control compliance in the first instance is no guarantee that it will continue indefinitely. Consequently, most countries adopt a two-pronged, mutually reinforcing, approach to pollution control. Holdgate (1979: 202) has summarized this as being:

1   through a land use planning or development control process in which the distribution of sources of pollution is adjusted so as to be compatible with other priority land uses, and so that pollution from new development is constrained from the outset;

2   through controls, operated by various official agencies or voluntarily within industries, limiting existing sources of pollution and ensuring that new sources comply with conditions imposed when they are built.

Land-use planning controls are primarily preventive (prospective or anticipatory) whereas technical and other (e.g. housekeeping) source controls can be both preventive and retrospective.

Local planning authorities determine the nature and location of new development. Because pollution originates as waste from production and consumption activities, one of the key variables in pollution control – the geographical point at which additional waste is created – is determined once the location of these activities has been established. Therefore, because of their control over land use, planning authorities exercise an important influence on the spatial origin of wastes and consequently upon pollution levels and their distribution. Planning authorities are undoubtedly the principal controlling authorities in deciding the location of the pollution process, whether they recognize this or not. Apart from their control over *direct* pollution sources, planning authorities determine the location of seemingly relatively non-polluting development (such as sports stadia, commercial buildings and shopping centres). These may be *indirect* pollution sources as the large numbers of motor vehicles travelling to and from them emit significant quantities of air pollutants.

Planning authorities also have a crucial role in controlling the damage arising from the resulting pollution, since they control the nature and location of receptors. In other words, apart from protecting the environment around a proposed new source of pollution, authorities can control damage from an existing source of pollution by determining the nature of new developments close to it. This may be achieved either through the granting or withholding of planning permission (e.g. refusal of housing close to an oil refinery) or by the attachment of conditions (e.g. that a school building be constructed so as to be separated by its playing fields from a major air-pollution source).

There are, of course, two stages in the planning process, the preparation of a plan and its implementation in the form of decisions on the use of specific areas of land. All the controls mentioned above can be exercised in the absence of an overall land-use plan. However, the potential role of the land-use planner in ameliorating pollution is not restricted either to attempting to ensure that the best anticipatory controls are imposed when development is permitted or to preventing such development. Rather, it extends to planning the future use of land to reduce pollution by the preparation of implementable plans.

A further role must be mentioned. Apart from their plan making and development controls, planning authorities are in a unique position – as a focus for consultation on both plan making and land use decision taking – to play a central coordinating role in the control of pollution. Experience in the USA, which may be characterized as having weak land-use planning restrictions and strong pollution controls, indicates that discretionary political land-use decisions over pollution sources and receptors are as inevitable as pollution itself (Wood 1989).

ENVIRONMENTAL ORIGINS OF THE UK PLANNING SYSTEM

Engels' famous description of Manchester in the mid-nineteenth century demonstrates forcefully the unsustainable nature of the unplanned explosion of Britain's cities during the industrial revolution:

> In a rather deep hole, in a curve of the Medlock and surrounded on all four sides by tall factories and high embankments, covered with buildings, stand two groups of about two hundred cottages, built chiefly back to back, in which live about 4,000 human beings, most of them Irish. The cottages are old, dirty, and of the smallest sort, the streets uneven, fallen into ruts and in part without drains or pavement; masses of refuse, offal and sickening filth lie among standing pools in all directions: the atmosphere is poisoned by the effluvia from these, and laden and darkened by the smoke of a dozen tall factory chimneys (Engels 1845: 98).

Air pollution, water pollution and waste disposal problems, along with appalling ventilation, and dreadful, inadequately accessed housing, were important progenitors of early town planning legislation. The Public Health Act 1875 provided local authorities with the powers to make and enforce building by-laws to control the height, structure and layout of buildings and the width of streets. Other action was taken to improve the supply of pure water and the removal of waste matter.

Apart from the Public Health Act 1875, the Rivers Pollution Prevention Act 1876 and the Alkali Act 1863 (the world's first industrial air-pollution control legislation, extended in 1906) provided rudimentary pollution control powers. Notwithstanding these, the rivers and the air remained polluted. One of the arguments advanced for garden cities by the influential Ebenezer Howard (1898: 47) was that, in existing towns

> the sunlight is being more and more shut out, while the air is so vitiated that the fine public buildings, like the sparrows, rapidly become covered with soot, and the very statues are in despair.

By contrast, the new towns would be healthy places 'bright and fair, wholesome and beautiful'.

The Housing, Town Planning, etc., Act 1909 was intended, *inter alia* to improve the physical health of the populace to secure ' the home healthy'. As Ashworth has stated 'town planning . . . could be represented as a logical extension, in accordance with changing aims and conditions, of earlier legislation concerned with housing and public health' (Ashworth 1954: 181). Notwithstanding its antecedents, however, other planning legislation passed before the 1947 Act did little to extend the powers available under the Public Health Act 1875. Indeed, the relationship between public health and town planning appears to have been largely forgotten during later years of this first British planning era. Certainly, complaints about the aesthetics of by-law housing often overlooked its sanitation objectives. No environmental protection legislation of significance was passed during this period apart from the consolidation of the Public Health Act in 1936.

With a few honourable exceptions, the planning literature of the period paid scant attention to pollution and to the planner's role in its control. Without mentioning the word 'pollution', the need to locate certain industries away from housing because of the noise, dust and smell generated was recognized by Adshead in 1923. A few years later, planners were encouraged to consider the effect of industry and the design of sewage disposal systems so as to minimize water pollution (Adams 1932). McAllister and McAllister (1941) commenced their book on town planning with a quotation about noise and foul air, but they made no further reference to pollution.

Somewhat surprisingly, certain early postwar plans laid considerable emphasis on pollution. That for Manchester (1945) indicated that river pollution was to be mitigated by reducing the density of development, and hence storm overflows, and by building new relief sewers. The 1946 Middlesbrough survey and plan contained a lengthy and virtually unique section on air pollution, describing a special survey of the problem, its influence on planning, and pollution control methods. It recommended that no housing should remain in the areas most affected by pollution and that hospitals and other sensitive land uses should be relocated in cleaner parts of the town. Abercrombie's famous Greater London plan (1945) referred to pollution only in relation to smoke from electricity generating stations.

ENVIRONMENTAL PLANNING IN ABEYANCE: 1948–67

The enactment of the Town and Country Planning Act 1947, which this book celebrates, did not presage a resurgence in environmental planning. The period 1948–67 was not one in which interest in the environment was strong, in the UK or elsewhere. There was one notable exception: the furore stirred up by the London smog of 1952 which led directly to the Clean Air Act 1956. Other legislation was enacted, with less fanfare, relating to river pollution, radioactive substances, oil pollution, litter, noise and waste disposal. This was an era in which pollution of the different environmental media was controlled separately, where it was controlled at all. Legislation often addressed only part of the problem, was based on ad hoc decision making and a philosophy of diluting and dispersing pollutants. It frequently presented polluters with loopholes: this was a period in which permission to construct a nuclear power station could be given without a public enquiry.

The two main Orders made under the Town and Country Planning Act 1947 were both relevant to the control of pollution. Air pollution and, to a lesser extent, noise arising from different industrial uses of land were taken into account in the distinction made between light, general and special industrial buildings in the *Use Classes Order*. Thus, a light industrial building was:

> an industrial building . . . in which the processes carried on or the machinery installed are such as could be carried on or installed in any residential area without detriment to the amenity of that area by reason of noise, vibration, smell, fumes, smoke, soot, ash, dust or grit.

Special industrial buildings, which included all works registrable under the Alkali etc Works Orders, were grouped according to the character of the offence likely to arise from the process, in order to ensure that the local planning authority was able to control changes of use which might give rise to pollution. The *General Development*

Order contained provisions relating to water pollution. Where development consisted of works in a river, refining or storing oils, the deposit of refuse, or the treatment or disposal of sewage, the local planning authority was required to consult the relevant river authority before determining the application.

There were no circulars issued during this period which provided advice to planning authorities about the control of pollution. However, the problem was better recognized in planning textbooks than before the war. As well as mentioning noise and water pollution, Myles Wright (1948) urged the use of planning conditions as a method of controlling smoke emissions. The Association for Planning and Regional Reconstruction (1950) devoted a section to air pollution, emphasizing its importance in siting such industries as gas production. The desirability of separating airports and industry from housing on noise grounds was also stressed. Logie (1952) reviewed the noise, the smell, dust and other atmospheric pollutants and the water pollution arising from different industries and produced a table of nuisances. The dangers of siting factories in valleys, the need for control of grit emissions and the need to locate industries with regard to the prevailing wind were stated. Powdrill (1961) recognized that vibration, noise and smell affected the environment. The importance of atmospheric pollution in planning surveys was stressed by Jackson (1963), the siting of land uses with respect to pollution being seen as a planning function. Noise and smoke were regarded by Abercrombie (1967) as matters requiring (unspecified) planning action. Many books, however, continued to neglect pollution, including the first (1964) and second (1967) editions of Cullingworth's text.

The same was true of the planning journals. Almost nothing on the topic was published. It was greatly to the credit of John Graham, the chief public health inspector of Manchester, that he was one of the first authors to stress the relationship between planning and air pollution. He argued that the attainment of clean air 'requires the combined efforts of many at national and local levels but in particular of public health and planning officers' (Graham 1957).

Unsurprisingly, in the absence of official encouragement in legislation, regulations or circulars, few development plans mentioned pollution. However, the Glasgow City Council plan (1960) dealt with air pollution, river and canal pollution and the reclamation of derelict land in the first review of its plan. Pollution problems from motor vehicles and oil burning were envisaged, and a planning measure – redevelopment – was seen as one of the methods of controlling smoke pollution. The London County Council plan (1962) omitted any reference to the problem, although the analysis section of their earlier plan (1951) emphasized air pollution, referring to smoke abatement, gas washing and cleaning, district heating, the siting of industrial uses to the leeward of residential areas, and the use of buffer zones as control measures.

As might have been anticipated from the earlier plans, the Middlesbrough report of survey (1952) referred to air pollution from industry, the clearance of old housing close to industry and the question of river pollution from sewage effluents, stating that 'strong economic arguments will be required to justify the expense that would be involved' in treating sewage. The approved written statement – the statutory document – did not touch upon pollution, however. Pollution control was obviously not an officially relevant planning matter.

This lack of official interest in pollution control extended to the new town planning of the period. The various new town reports devoted at most one or two paragraphs to pollution and tended only to refer to the existence of particular local problems without explaining how they could be overcome by planning methods. The lack of concern about pollution in these reports was the more disappointing because new town planning offered unrivalled opportunities for an effective contribution to pollution control.

The regional planning studies undertaken in the 1960s tended to pay varying attention to the pollution problem, some completely ignoring it. Probably because of the higher pollution levels prevailing in the north of the country, the northern councils showed more concern than others. The *North West Study* (Department of Economic Affairs 1965) devoted several paragraphs to the problems of dereliction and smoke pollution, detailing the use of planning conditions to prevent the former and smoke control orders to control the latter. In the fullest treatment of the subject, the Yorkshire and Humberside Economic Planning Council report *A Review of Yorkshire and Humberside* (1966) recognized derelict land, atmospheric pollution and water pollution as serious problems and described their incidence in a number of sections. It advocated careful planning of new chemical industry to avoid polluting residential areas and the use of development control, including planning conditions, to control land pollution.

It was unusual for pollution to be considered in planning decisions during the period, and it is very clear that liaison between planning and public health departments was not all that it might have been. Where pollution was an important issue, its significance was usually disguised by planning jargon. Graham (1957), for example, quoted a Manchester Corporation planning refusal (which, he explained, was made solely on pollution control grounds): 'the proposed development would be detrimental to the amenities of the neighbourhood and amenity, and convenience would not be secured by permitting the proposed development'. Nevertheless, the planning pendulum was about to swing back towards environmental protection.

REVIVING INTEREST IN ENVIRONMENTAL PLANNING: 1968–87

The emergence of modern environmentalism can probably be dated from the publication of *Silent Spring* (Carson 1962). Hardin's classic essay 'the tragedy of the commons' appeared in 1968, the US National Environmental Policy Act (with its early phraseology about inter-generational equity) came into effect in 1970, and *The Limits to Growth* appeared in 1972 (Meadows *et al*). This urgent American interest in the environment influenced the organization of the first major international United Nations conference on the environment in Stockholm in 1972. Many more were to follow. The next two decades witnessed oscillations in public interest (and consequently in environmental planning) but each swing towards environmental concern, and especially that which greeted the publication of the Brundtland Commission's report *Our Common Future* (1987), exceeded the previous ones.

This period saw the formation of the Department of the Environment in 1970, the setting up of the Royal Commission on Environmental Pollution (RCEP) and the passing of significant environmental protection legislation. The seminal Control of Pollution Act 1974, which followed a revision of the Clean Air Act in 1968, and the Deposit of Poisonous Wastes Act 1972, brought legislative control over pollution of several media together for the first time. Britain's accession to the EC in 1972 at the same time as the environment officially became a European issue was a further factor in the growth of environmental concern (Bell 1997). Local government reform in England and Wales in 1974 left new local authorities with more professional staff and much better equipped to resolve local environmental pollution problems than had previously been the case.

It has been argued (Miller 1990) that one of the reasons that the UK planning system escaped extensive dismantling during the deregulatory phase of the

Thatcher administrations of the mid-1980s was that it remained a useful and flexible mechanism through which a number of environmental policies could be implemented. Even such doctrinaire manifestations as enterprise zones and (to a lesser extent) simplified planning zones were designed and designated to ensure that quasi-planning powers could continue to be used to protect the environment (Wood and Hooper 1989).

The 1968 planning act required local planning authorities, in preparing a structure plan, to formulate 'policy and general proposals in respect of the development and other use of land in that area (including measures for the improvement of the physical environment and the management of traffic)'. Similar, but non-obligatory, provisions applied to the preparation of local plans. In a memorandum on structure plan preparation, the DoE (1971b) stressed the importance of pollution control: 'proposals should be related to the need to combat and prevent pollution, even though responsibility and specific action in this field will often be for other bodies than the local planning authority'. This advice was expanded in a later version of the memorandum:

> The term 'physical environment' should be interpreted as including not only policies to protect an environment regarded as being of a high quality and policies for improving a poor environment (e.g. derelict land reclamation schemes), but also land use policies designed to minimise non-visual intrusions such as noise, smell and dirt. The authority should show in the reasoned justification:
>
> (a) how environmental considerations have been taken into account in the formulation of their policies: and
> (b) the relationship of the policy and general proposals to other measures for reducing water and air pollution and noise (DoE 1977c).

New versions of the *Use Classes Order* and the *General Development Order* reiterated (and in the latter case extended) the obligations of local planning authorities in relation to the control of pollution from certain types of development.

For the first time, a number of central government circulars dealing with planning control of water pollution, noise pollution, air pollution and land pollution were issued. A draft circular on planning and clean air (DoE 1972b), which was sent to all local planning authorities (LPAs) for consultation (though never formally released) recommended that LPAs obtain advice from environmental health officers and the Alkali Inspectorate in development control decisions where air pollution was a factor. It advised against the use of planning conditions designed to secure greater control of processes controlled by the Alkali Inspectorate. This was to prove a recurrent theme in government advice over the years.

A circular on planning and noise (DoE 1973a) gave specific advice about planning measures for dealing with aircraft, traffic and industrial noise in both plan making and development control. It could leave LPAs in no doubt that theirs were the only effective noise pollution control powers, something which remains largely true today. A circular on waste disposal (DoE 1976e) emphasized that control of pollution previously practised through the use of planning conditions should now be arranged through the more specific and flexible waste disposal licenses required by the Control of Pollution Act 1974. This was an example of the planning system abandoning its position as an environmental long-stop as more specific powers became available. Other circulars dealt with planning applications relating to hazardous industry (and for development adjacent to existing hazardous industry) (DoE 1972a), with noise abatement zones as an adjunct to pre-existing planning powers for controlling noise and with the use of the planning system to prevent odour nuisance (DoE 1976c).

However, a circular issued in 1977 can be interpreted as effectively requiring LPAs to reduce the relative importance of pollution in making decisions in order to give priority to industry:

> The need to take all possible steps to assist industry in no way obviates the need for vigilance where there may be health and safety hazards or pollution problems. It is important that in such cases planning authorities should work in close liaison with those responsible for pollution control and the disposal of waste. Planning authorities are reminded however that they should exercise care in considering the use of conditional planning permission ... planning conditions should not be imposed in an attempt to deal with problems which are the subject of controls under separate environmental legislation, whether the controlling authority belongs to central or local government (DoE 1977d).

This circular marked the beginning of a period in which, in effect, the potential of the planning system to assist in pollution control was played down rather than receiving the emphasis it had briefly enjoyed.

In 1980, the new Conservative government stressed the importance of giving priority to industrial development and granting permission for small-scale commercial or industrial activities wherever possible, while not neglecting 'health and safety standards, noise, smell or other pollution problems' (DoE 1980). It went on seemingly to contradict the strictures in the earlier circular about the use of planning conditions to control pollution:

> Where there are planning objections it will often be possible to meet them to a sufficient degree by attaching conditions to the permission or by the use of agreements under Section 52 of the Town and Country Planning Act 1971 rather than by refusing the application. Such opportunities should be taken.

This emphasis on the use of planning conditions and agreements rather than refusal was not intended to extend to conditions overlapping the specific historic air pollution controls over registered works. This was something that the influential Royal Commission on Environmental Pollution had emphasized in its 1976 report:

> If the planning authority ... consider that an unacceptable amount of pollution is likely to be emitted from a proposed plant when the Alkali Inspectorate's requirements have been met their sanction should be refusal of planning permission not the imposition of planning conditions designed to control emissions.

A chapter devoted to 'planning and pollution' undoubtedly ensured that the strengths and weaknesses of planning controls over pollution would be widely and well understood. While they recognized that LPAs had to weigh many factors other than pollution in reaching decisions, they criticized the planning system. 'Our concern is not that pollution is not always given top priority; it is that it is often dealt with inadequately, and sometimes forgotten altogether, in the planning process'. They felt that part of the problem arose from a lack of guidance and advice, and they recommended a number of steps to rectify the situation, including various mandatory consultations (e.g. with the Alkali Inspectorate).

Pollution issues began to appear more frequently in the planning literature during this period. Cullingworth (1972) extended the treatment of dereliction in earlier editions of his textbook to provide a thorough treatment of domestic smoke emissions, vehicle emissions and noise, though he gave little insight into the planner's role in controlling pollutants. Solesbury's (1974) book on policy planning suggested an ambitious environmental protection programme taking its context from structure plans. Kimber and Richardson (1974) provided some insight into the practicalities of utilizing planning controls over pollution sources. Wood's book on town planning and pollution control (1976) reviewed the state of the embryonic subject and gave various examples of the integration of pollution control into plan making and development control practice. Miller and Wood (1983) continued the theme by presenting a number of detailed case studies of air, water, land and noise pollution control. A limited number of articles about planning and pollution control (and environmental planning more generally) appeared during this period (Williams 1973; Payne and Brough 1981; Wood 1986). Towards the end of the period, an increasing number of books and articles about environmental impact assessment (EIA) began to appear (Lee and Wood 1978; Clark *et al.* 1980; Tomlinson 1986). The control of pollution by planning techniques was but one element of the broadening approach to environmental planning represented by EIA.

The best treatment of pollution problems in regional and subregional planning studies during this period was in the *Strategic Plan for the North West* (DoE 1974c), the *Coventry–Solihull–Warwickshire Subregional Strategy* (Warwickshire County Council 1971) and the *West Central Scotland Plan* (1974). It is clear that, in general, the later planning studies considered pollution problems to a greater extent than the earlier ones, but many still gave only cursory acknowledgement to pollution control. Attention was characteristically confined to locating major new urban developments, whether industrial or residential, away from existing sources and receptors, and at sites where dispersion of air pollution was likely to be good. Reclamation of derelict land and restoration of areas after mineral working were also regarded as planning problems worthy of comment. The Warrington New Town report (Austin-Smith/ Lord Partnership 1969) contained an excellent discussion of pollution, only surpassed by the best treatment in regional and subregional studies.

Real advances were made in the treatment of pollution issues in a number of structure plans (and, to a lesser extent, in local plans) during this period. The Cheshire Structure Plan (1977) and the Teesside Structure Plan (1974) provided two examples of good practice. In comparison with the regional, subregional and new town studies and with the old-style development plans which preceded them, structure plans demonstrated: a much greater grasp of air, land, water and noise pollution problems; recognition of planning powers in the control of pollution; appreciation of the roles of planning in pollution control; and awareness of planning techniques for controlling pollution.

There can be no doubt that pollution was considered in many development control decisions taken by LPAs and in inquiries into these and 'called-in' decisions during the period. One decision to permit construction of a new village close to the largest oil refining complex in the country was described by the chairperson of the Cheshire Structure Plan Examination in Public in 1977 as 'the height of folly'. In an apt reference to the origins of environmental planning, he added that it perpetuated 'the worst effects of the industrial revolution of 150 years ago' (DoE 1978).

It is clear that pollution was a much more important factor in development control during this period than previously. Pollution grounds could stand as the sole reason for refusing planning permission for development if the situation was sufficiently bad. Certainly, the language employed at public inquiries changed from general 'injury to amenity' to more specific reference to the pollution problem arising, although central government continued to couch its conclusions in terms of 'amenity'.

RE-EMERGENCE OF ENVIRONMENTAL PLANNING SINCE 1988

The planning system has undoubtedly rediscovered its environmental origins during the last decade. There has been significant environmental legislation, a flurry of relevant government circulars and planning policy guidance notes, and a flowering of books and articles on environmental planning. Research on environmental planning has burgeoned and environmental planning training has advanced considerably. Mrs Thatcher's remarkable conversion to the environmental cause in 1988 heightened awareness. Rising affluence and concomitant public concern and the escalating requirements of European legislation have been inter-related drivers of this rebirth. In addition, as the RCEP (1998) has pointed out:

* there has also been a great growth in the number and importance of international conventions relating to the environment, at both global and regional scale;
* formal techniques have been used increasingly to aid decision-making;
* the influence of environmental non-governmental organisations has grown.

As a result of these factors, the environment has become a high-profile political issue during the period, and parliamentary environmental committees have become commensurately influential.

The Environmental Protection Act 1990 and the Environment Act 1995 together represent the most significant pollution control legislation to date. For the first time, there exists a single body, the Environment Agency, charged with administering standard-based integrated pollution control of land, water and most air pollution. Other major environmental legislation included the Water Act 1989, the Clean Air Act 1993 and the Noise and Statutory Nuisance Act 1993 (Bell 1997).

The need for planning control did not diminish, however, as the Environment Agency (1997) emphasized:

> Although the Environment Agency operates within an extensive regulatory framework, it must be recognised that our *actual* controls in respect of development are limited. The Agency is therefore dependent upon effective planning legislation to ensure the protection of the environment and to prevent future problems arising as a result of development.

The Town and Country Planning Act 1990 was supplemented by the Planning (Hazardous Substances) Act 1990. The Planning and Compensation Act 1991 not only required development plans to be given much greater emphasis in determining planning applications but also required the preparation of waste local plans. The *Use Classes Order 1987* maintained the definition of light industry, which has now been employed throughout the half-century of UK statutory planning. The *General Development Procedure Order 1995* consolidated the list of consultations which LPAs must initiate. This has expanded substantially over the years and now includes, for example, development within 250 metres of land which has been used for the deposit of refuse or waste, and development within a notified hazardous substance area.

The European Directive on EIA came into effect in 1988 and was implemented principally through the planning system. EIA required pollution control (and ecological, historical, landscape and cultural) issues to be given greater emphasis in certain planning decisions. Inevitably, LPAs and non-governmental agencies started to demand informal EIAs for other types of development. EIA gave a huge fillip to environmental planning, bringing it to the consciousness of central government, local authorities and researchers and resulting in explosive growth in the number of environmental planners employed in consultancies.

Central government responded to this further swing of the pendulum by issuing several circulars on planning and environmental control. These included circulars on EIA (DoE 1988), on water treatment infrastructure (DoE 1991a), on hazardous substances (DoE 1992f), on derelict land (DETR 1998h) and on waste disposal (DoE 1994e). The 1972 draft circular on planning and clean air (DoE 1972b) was finally published (in much modified form) a quarter of a century later as *Air Quality and Land Use Planning* (DETR 1997a). It reiterated the requirement that LPAs should 'include in their development plans policies for the improvement of the environment and . . . have regard to environmental considerations when formulating plan policies and proposals'. It explained the relevance of the UK National Air Quality Strategy which laid down health-based air quality standards and air quality objectives and stated that: 'all local authorities will be expected to have regard to national air quality objectives when preparing development plans'.

The circular stated that air quality could be a material consideration in planning decisions. While it re-emphasized the importance of not duplicating controls imposed under more specific legislation (e.g. the Environmental Protection Act 1990), it stressed the importance of air quality considerations: 'Where the impact of development is likely to be significant in air quality terms, then, provided the impact relates to the use and amenity of land, the planning application may be refused or the impact mitigated by the imposing of conditions'. The phrase 'the use and amenity of land' is likely to prove a fruitful basis for debate at planning inquiries and in the courts.

Planning policy guidance notes dealt with, *inter alia*, renewable energy (DoE 1993b), pollution control (DoE 1994g) and transport (DoE 1994i). PPG 24, on noise, set down levels for different types of noise as a basis for making development control decisions (DoE 1994h). PPG 12 recommended that the environmental appraisal of development plans be carried out (DoE 1992a). In addition, numerous mineral policy guidance notes were issued.

Central government also issued several unprecedented best practice guides on aspects of environmental planning. These included advice on EIA (DoE 1995c) and on the environmental appraisal of development plans (DoE 1993a). It commissioned several environmental planning research projects on, for example, pollution and waste management (DoE 1992d), climate change (DoE 1992e), hazardous substances consents (DoE 1994f) and derelict land prevention (DoE 1995a). Numerous other funded and unfunded research projects on environmental planning were undertaken during this period. Environmental planning training both in core and specialized studies in planning schools and in short courses improved markedly during the period (RTPI 1997).

The RCEP continued to research environmental topics and to produce influential reports, several of which had important implications for the planning system. In particular, its 1988 report on *Best Practicable Environmental Option* pointed the way towards integrated pollution control, emphasized the importance of LPA involvement and introduced the concept of the 'precautionary principle', seized upon by some LPAs as a reason for refusing planning permission. Its 1994 report on *Transport and the Environment* contained numerous recommendations relating to the role of town and country planning in limiting vehicular traffic.

The 1990 white paper *This Common Inheritance* reviewed the state of the whole of the UK physical environment, made numerous commitments and stressed the role of land use planning in environmental protection:

> In considering whether to grant planning permission for a particular develop-
> ment, a local authority must consider all the effects, including potential pollu-
> tion: permission should not be granted if that might expose people to danger.

In the 1994 white paper *Sustainable Development: the UK Strategy* it was stressed that: 'the planning system is a key instrument in delivering land use and development compatible with the aims of sustainable development'. To this end, development plans had to take account of environmental considerations. The environmental appraisal of development plans was intended to ensure that this was done satisfactorily (DoE 1993a). The 1998 white paper *A New Deal for Transport* on the future of transport policy re-emphasized the need for LPAs to use their powers to reduce traffic flows.

In comparison to the sparse literature on environmental planning in earlier periods, numerous books were published during this period. Selman (1992), Blowers (1993), Glasson *et al.* (1994), Haughton and Hunter (1994) and the RTPI (1996) were some of the better known examples. Cullingworth and Nadin (1997) and Rydin (1993 and 1998) all contained chapters on planning and the environment.

The number of journal articles dealing with environmental planning increased exponentially. It is symptomatic that *Planning Outlook* was relaunched as the *Journal of Environmental Planning and Management* (following the early lead of the *Journal of Planning and Property Law* which became the *Journal of Planning and Environment Law*). Examples of the genre are Slater *et al.* (1994), Graham (1996), Bond (1997), Owens (1997) and Scott *et al.* (1998).

The 1982 United Nations Conference on Environment and Development in Rio de Janeiro spawned not only a national commitment to sustainable development (white paper 1994) but a series of local Agenda 21 strategies (Local Government Management Board 1993). Some of these strategies, which dealt with all aspects of the environment in a local authority area, were prepared with the active participation of town planners and some were not. The publications of the UK Round Table on Sustainable Development (e.g. 1996) were another influence on planning practice.

Given the welter of legislation, instruction, guidance and literature on air, water, noise and land pollution, wastes, hazards and energy use, it is not surprising that environmental planning practice has advanced markedly during the period. A development plan without environmental protection policies is now as rare as one containing such policies was during the 1948–67 period. For example, the Bedfordshire Structure Plan (1994) stressed the need for the EIA of certain types of proposal and was itself subjected to a rigorous environmental appraisal. The Congleton Local Plan (1992) contained policies on waste disposal, dereliction, pollution and hazard control. The Bury Unitary Development Plan (1993) devoted 22 pages to the environment and included energy conservation as well as pollution control policies.

Under the post-1991 plan-led regime, decisions on planning applications must be determined in accordance with the development plan unless material considerations indicate otherwise. Pollution may be a material consideration in planning decisions. In marked contrast to the planning decision mentioned by Graham during the period

1948–67, Bath and North East Somerset Council gave damage to nearby buildings arising from air pollution from shoppers' vehicles as the only ground for refusing planning permission for a supermarket in Bath. Following an appeal, the public inquiry inspector considered that five matters, including air pollution, were relevant. The Secretary of State was 'satisfied that air quality should properly be regarded as a material consideration for the purposes of his decision' (Government Office for the South West 1997). He considered three air pollution factors to be relevant – damage to health, failure to reduce mileage travelled and damage to listed World Heritage Site buildings. He was, however, unconvinced on all three counts and allowed the appeal.

While LPAs may still find it difficult to defend such decisions at an inquiry, applicants do not always appeal. Where permission is granted, conditions relating to pollution control are sometimes attached. Many of these may strictly exceed their legal powers and developers may either adhere to them or ignore them, in which case LPAs may decide not to attempt to enforce them. There appear to be a substantial number of successful bluffs, however, with developers being content to fulfil pollution control conditions which may not be legally defensible. Practice still appears to vary considerably from the over-cautious to the incautious.

Decisions likely to result in serious pollution problems are still sufficiently numerous to suggest that the scope for planning abatement of pollution in development control is not fully being used. There appear to be three reasons for this. The first is continuing uncertainty about the precise legal standing of planning powers to control pollution. The second is the attitude of elected representatives who sometimes ignore planners' advice and who may tend to relegate pollution problems in comparison to other planning matters unless they are forcefully reminded of their importance by their constituents or by influential non-governmental organizations. The third is the cost of pollution abatement, whether it be in terms of money, numbers of jobs lost, numbers of houses foregone or some other calculable political disbenefit.

CONCLUSIONS

Town planning emerged as one response to the environmental problems created by the industrial revolution. For many years, the statutory planning system created by the 1947 Act virtually ignored its environmental origins. Gradually, environmental protection began to resurface and has emerged as one of the most important objectives of the planning system today. Certainly the weight attributed to environmental considerations in plan making and development control decisions has increased very substantially and is likely to increase further. The planning pendulum has swung firmly back to its environmental origins.

The nature of environmental challenges faced by the planning system has, of course, changed. Previously, stationary sources were the main cause of air pollution, water pollution and much noise pollution. Transport has become one of the chief culprits and the increased use of chemicals in industry, in the home and in agriculture has also led to new and dispersed pollution problems. Other challenges are likely to emerge in the future.

The nature of environmental control has also changed away from ad hoc decision making towards the use of standards and integrated pollution control. Changes to the EIA process in 1999 tightened and broadened the range of projects subject to EIA, thus further extending the types of environmental impacts considered in many planning decisions. Sustainability issues are likely to continue to increase in importance.

The planning system has adapted to these changes though many planners may have found the process testing. Town planning will need to continue to respond to the demands which society places upon it to protect the environment. Of the many steps that could be taken, linking Local Agenda 21 processes more closely to statutory planning is but one. Another is to reflect the universal desire for greater participation in environmental decision making by permitting third party rights of appeal against planning permission for certain types of potentially damaging development. Further research and training are also needed. Whatever the changes necessary, it is clear that, notwithstanding the strengthening of UK pollution control powers, the continued involvement of LPAs in environmental control is inevitable, whichever way the pendulum swings in the future.

FURTHER READING

Cullingworth and Nadin (12th edition,1997) *Town and Country Planning in the UK* provide an extensive guide to further reading on the environment. Wood (1976) *Town Planning and Pollution Control* and (1989) *Planning Pollution Prevention*, and Miller and Wood (1983) *Planning and Pollution* review the literature on planning and pollution control and provide various case study examples of practice. Several important white papers mentioned in the text, including *This Common Inheritance* (1990), *Sustainable Development: The UK Strategy* (1994) and *A New Deal for Transport* (1998) provide an overview of government environmental policy. The various reports of the Royal Commission on Environmental Pollution (e.g. RCEP 1994 and 1997) provide well researched and informative accounts of various pollution and planning issues.

Planning Policy Guidance Notes are statements of government policy (but one has to take care to get the latest version): *Planning and Pollution Control* (PPG 23, 1994) provides an excellent (if slightly dated) overview while *Planning and Noise* (PPG 24, 1994) covers planning controls over noise. Planning controls over air pollution are the subject of a circular on *Air Quality and Land Use Planning* (DETR 1997a). Glasson *et al.* (1994) provide a useful *Introduction to Environmental Impact Assessment*, Haughton and Hunter (1994) deal with *Sustainable Cities*, and Selman (1992) reviews *Environmental Planning* more generally.

chapter 18

An American Perspective on UK Planning

DAVID L. CALLIES

INTRODUCTION

It is not for nothing that the relationship between the UK and the USA has been described as two peoples divided by a common language. Urban planning and the policy behind it is no exception. While there are many similarities between the USA and UK – public/private development agreements, attempts at streamlining the process of development approval, convergence of planning gain and land development conditions, emergence of development-free areas, use of enterprise zones – these similarities are comparatively technical. In the larger sense, the differences continue to be substantial. There is no national plan in the USA, precious little in the way of regional plans and, lacking a central review of any kind, scattered local plans of indifferent quality and specificity. Despite movement in each others' direction, UK development takes place largely by permit and permission, whereas much US development is permitted as of right. Although the movement in the UK has waned, there is nothing in the USA to compare to the experiment in publicly funded new towns. While the extraction of planning gain is increasing in the UK, it is a long way from the US practice of exacting land and fees from private development. There is no compensation for loss of development potential caused by land development regulations or refusal of planning permission in the UK, whereas recent US court decisions provide for compensation to a landowner for regulation which goes 'too far'. There appears to be less institutionalized public participation, particularly at the local government level, in the UK than in the USA, where hearings and interventions by 'interested parties' proliferate and often stifle projects based purely on local concerns rather than regional ones. National and regional (state) parks are virtually all publicly owned in the USA, whereas such parks are largely privately owned but publicly regulated in the UK.

GOVERNMENT AND INSTITUTIONS: A BRIEF COMPARISON

It is difficult to deal with the similarities and differences in planning between the USA and the UK without some brief commentary on the differences in governmental structure and theory of the locus of power. First and most obviously, the UK is (so far) a unitary state. England, Scotland, Wales and Northern Ireland are still largely governed by a single central government made up of parliament, parliamentary ministers of the party in power and, symbolically at least, a monarch. While different statutory schemes sometimes apply to the principal components of the kingdom (including planning laws) this does not alter the essential unitary character of the state. Parliament is regarded as supreme, with the ability to create and abolish local governments limited only by political expediency. There is no written constitution. Even the nation's highest court is composed of law lords who are also entitled to sit in the parliamentary upper house.

The USA, for all the apparent power of the national government in Washington, is a federation of states. The state is the principal unit of government and the ultimate repository of sovereignty. The states created the national government by means of a constitutional convention, and that federal government must trace every exercise of power to that document. It is, therefore, a constitution of grant, not of limitation. The states have all the power not delegated to the national government, to which they can both add and subtract by means of amendments to the federal constitution. States can do anything governmentally (through legislatures) which was not delegated to the national government in the federal constitution nor prohibited by a popularly promulgated state constitution. As implicit from the foregoing, such state constitutions are popular documents of restraint and not of grant.

Lastly, an entirely separate federal judiciary, headed by a Supreme Court, decides issues of constitutional interpretation, including when land has been taken inappropriately by government either through compulsory purchase or by regulation, both of which require public purpose and compensation.

These differences between the USA and the UK have profound implications for land-use planning and control. First, since land-use control is regarded as an exercise of the police power and since only the states have such power, it is the states that exercise mandatory planning and land use controls, often by delegating a portion of that power to local government through planning and zoning enabling statutes. What power the national government has over the use of land comes about either through adjuncts to legislation passed pursuant to the Constitution's Commerce Clause (ceding to the national government authority over interstate commerce), such as the Clean Air Act, or through conditions attached to federal grants for state participants in various federal projects, such as the Coastal Zone Management Act.

This is in sharp contrast to the exercise in the UK of plenary planning and development control power through acts of parliament, and the creation of central departments responsible for land-use planning. Lastly, the UK is influenced by relevant policies of the EU, particularly with regard to environmental issues (which have become increasingly relevant to planning).

THE PLAN AS GUIDELINE/THE PLAN AS LAW

The British system of land-use control is closely tied to its extensive system of planning. While there may not be a formal national plan, national planning objectives are accomplished by central 'guidance' which has to be taken into account locally. The Planning and Compensation Act 1991 represents a notable change in the planning framework. First, the central government has made it clear that development control should be more directly in accord with local plans. Second, structure plans no longer require the approval of the central government, though they have to have regard to central planning guidance documents.

The result appears to be a shift to a more legalistic treatment of local plans in applications for planning permission. This mirrors experimentation of the same sort in many US jurisdictions, though generally the plan – usually labelled a *comprehensive plan* to which land-use controls such as zoning are in theory to conform – is more of a guidance document. Evidence of such shift in the USA is language in state zoning enabling legislation and city charters requiring specific conformance or concurrence between such plans and zoning ordinances. These often require that no permit for development be granted unless it accords with the applicable detailed development plan. Whether this is altogether a good thing is another matter. Certainly the plan becomes a crucial document in the development permitting process. On the other hand, if the plan is so detailed, what need of any other land use control mechanism such as zoning? At least one major US city has come to such a conclusion and is in the process of turning its short, map-detailed development plans into lengthy guidance documents instead. Meanwhile, courts faced with disharmony in those jurisdictions in which conformance is required have had no difficulty in upholding denial of land development approval which is not in accordance with the applicable plan.

PLANNING PERMISSION VS DEVELOPMENT RIGHTS

The other half of the planning equation is, of course, development control. At least since the 1947 planning act, most land development, at whatever intensity, requires local government permission on a case-by-case basis. With the exception of certain special zones and classes established by central government order (discussed in the following section) there is no development permitted as of right. This is in sharp contrast to American practice where whole classes of development are permitted as of right, depending upon the relevant zone classification in local zoning ordinances. What is required in the UK is *planning permission* from the local planning authority. Moreover, the UK system provides for no substantive court appeal for denial of such planning permission. The rationale for such a system is the nationalization of development rights and values (discussed by Grant in chapter 5).

From the perspective of preventing development which is not in accordance with applicable plans or some other concept of appropriateness, it is hard to imagine a more effective system. Virtually nothing is permitted without governmental permission, and there are plenty of plans and other guidance documents around to ensure no shortage of criteria concerning what is not permitted. Of course, there is no guarantee whatsoever that development will proceed in the face of such restriction. Positive planning has always been the Achilles heel in the UK system. But while it is relatively easy to halt development which is deemed inappropriate, it is extremely difficult to require 'appropriate' development to take place. If a regulation is sufficiently draconian, land development by the private sector simply grinds to a halt altogether.

This is in sharp contrast to land development regulation in much of the USA.[1] Indeed, much land development permission in states like Texas and Oklahoma can be accomplished by means of review for building permit (and zoning conformance) in two to three months, since most land development is permitted as of right, depending upon the zoning applicable to the subject property. Moreover, much of the land in the USA is subject to no planning control or land use regulation whatsoever. It is not simply happenstance, of course, that much of this relaxed form of zoning (or its lack altogether) occurs in western, midwestern and southwestern states where private property rights are jealously guarded and where the states are predominantly rural in nature. Since there is virtually no national system either of planning or zoning,[2] states are by and large free to deal with land development regulations under that aspect of their sovereign authority known as the police power in any way they choose, so long as the regulation does not effect a 'regulatory taking'. No state has created a system like the one in the UK requiring planning permission for all material development and, though some cities like Honolulu and Irvine

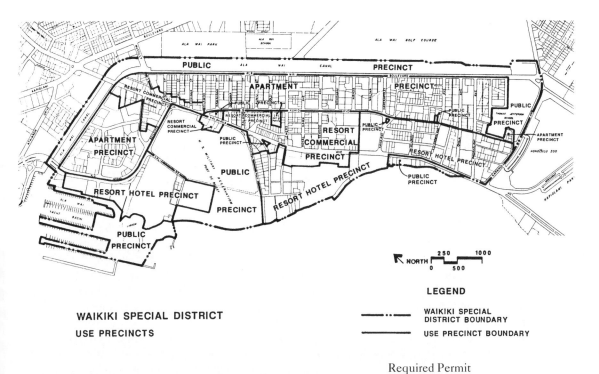

WAIKIKI SPECIAL DISTRICT

USE PRECINCTS

LEGEND

— ·· — WAIKIKI SPECIAL DISTRICT BOUNDARY

——— USE PRECINCT BOUNDARY

	Required Permit
Signs	Exempt
Tree removal over six inches in diameter	Minor
Detached dwellings and duplex units and accessory structures	Exempt
Grading and stockpiling	Exempt
Major modification, alteration, repair or addition to historic structures	Major
Minor modification, alteration, repair or addition to historic structures	Minor
Major exterior repair, alteration or addition to nonhistoric structures	Minor
Minor exterior repair, alteration or additions to nonhistoric structures, which does not adversely change the character or appearance of the structure	Exempt
Interior repairs, alterations and renovations so all structures	Exempt
Demolition of historic structures	Major
Demolition of nonhistoric structures	Exempt
Fences and walls	Exempt
Streetscape improvements, including street furniture, light fixtures, sidewalk paving, bus shelters and other elements in public rights-of-way	Minor
Major above-grade infrastructure improvements not covered elsewhere, including new roadways, road widenings, new substations, new parks and significant improvements to existing parks	Minor
Minor above-grade infrastructure improvements not covered elsewhere; all below-grade infrastructure improvements; and all emergency and routine repair and maintenance work	Exempt
New buildings not covered above	Major

Figure 18.1 Waikiki special district plan

(California) incorporate a development permission system in their zoning codes, these are quite exceptional.

ZONES: EXCEPTION TO THE PLANNING PERMISSION DOCTRINE

Clearly, development as of right is something of a rarity in UK, but that may be changing. On the other hand, development by permission only in the USA has been something of a rarity, but now that may be changing as well. The two systems may be moving in each others' direction but if so, the pace is glacial. Local zoning still represents the principal form of land-use control in the USA, although conformance or concurrence with a comprehensive plan is a requirement which is growing. Nevertheless, there is an increasing tendency to write new local zoning ordinances with additional planning requirements (such as site plan and other reviews).

However, the UK system does allow a limited range of developments according to various 'use classes' and 'general development orders'. To this needs now be added the powers to establish enterprise zones (EZs) and simplified planning zones (SPZs) – which, though currently dormant, still remain in the legislation. Prepared by selected local authorities, and subject to approval by the Secretary of State, EZs are designed to attract business and industry to formerly derelict land by offering a series of tax breaks and financial incentives, coupled with simplified planning controls and freedom from the need to conform to local plans. The 32 EZs have for the most part developed successfully, but there is considerable debate over whether that is simply because of the package of incentives offered (notably the 10 year exemption from property taxes and the sometimes extensive publicly funded infrastructure that has enhanced the development potential of the zones). Sometimes, the EZ is part and parcel of a larger redevelopment scheme or effort, so that much of the development would probably have occurred anyway (though not necessarily in the same place). The US counterparts are pale comparisons in terms of incentives, and accordingly have not been demonstrably as successful, though they are becoming popular once again. Philosophically, there is a niggling problem with the notion that if an area is sufficiently depressed, sound planning and financial considerations are out of the window. This is, of course, pretty common redevelopment philosophy on the ground that any economic improvement is better than a derelict site.

The SPZ is a local equivalent to a development order made by the Secretary of State. Its hallmark is advance approval of a variety of uses without the need to seek planning permission. Either the SPZ lists a series of uses to be permitted, or all is permitted and certain uses are excluded. There are only a dozen such zones in UK, in part because of the relatively cumbersome process of establishing them. They do not appear to offer much advantage over the normal planning system. The SPZ is closely akin to the zoning district classification in the typical US zoning ordinance, where all listed uses are permitted as of right and no further permissions besides a building permit (or, in the event of a large housing development, subdivision approval) is necessary. Such a system, of course, is directly counter to the whole approach of the British town planning system. Some jurisdictions in the USA are moving away from permitted development in such zones without at least some discretionary approval process. While this makes a certain amount of planning sense, it is highly intrusive with respect to cherished American rights in private property.

PLANNING GAIN AND LAND DEVELOPMENT CONDITIONS

The imposition of land development conditions imposed by local government for development permits or permissions is common in both countries. The debate over the fairness of such conditions is much the same as are the practical aspects and the inherent problems. The applicable law, however, appears to be somewhat different.

Local planning authorities in the UK often impose requirements for public facilities such as highways as conditions attached to planning permission for development. The issue – as in the USA – is the extent of such conditions and whether they are reasonably related to a planning consideration. Thus, for example, providing a new highway lane might well be an appropriate condition for permission to construct a new supermarket on the ground that traffic will increase substantially, particularly if the proposed supermarket will be constructed on a greenfield site. It is not, however, an appropriate condition for a small shop atop a subway stop in an urban redevelopment zone, either because there is no additional road traffic to be generated or because a highway lane is wildly disproportionate to whatever modest increase in road traffic would result from the shop. Much the same analysis would apply in the USA, with the first being a matter of the connection of the proposed public facility to the land-use problems generated by the proposed development (rational or essential *nexus*) and the second a matter of *proportionality*.

The legal standards imposed by the courts are, however, somewhat different. British courts appear to grant local authorities considerably more leeway in deciding what is a material planning consideration, whereas the US Supreme Court has laid down rather strict *nexus* and *proportionality* standards (particularly the latter). Moreover, there is national guidance in the UK on the matter of land development conditions [3] but none whatsoever in the USA and precious little in the way of statutory guidance from the individual states.

The problems, however, are the same. Locally imposed conditions may be applied (some would say often are) against the will of the developer in order to secure approval. Even when the condition is improper if not illegal, the landowner/developer will often forego a challenge in order to avoid the delay (and the alienation of the local authority) which an appeal would entail. (Developers regard this as a form of extortion.) Of equal concern is the potential for 'purchasing' permissions by means of such conditions in situations where sound land planning would dictate denial. It is one thing to alleviate problems which a project may generate by making contributions to ameliorative public facilities, but quite another to purchase such permissions by means of marginally related 'community benefits'.

TAKINGS AND COMPENSATION

The power to implement plans by acquiring public facility sites and right-of-ways which serve or encourage development is a critical part of plan implementation in both countries. Here the two systems are virtually identical. Most governments at every level have the power to acquire land and other property by compulsory purchase either as a natural attribute of sovereignty or by statutory delegation. The limitation as to public use or necessity for the taking appears to be broadly construed, and fair or just compensation for what is 'taken' is virtually guaranteed by statute (UK) or constitution (USA).

The power of local planning authorities to grant or deny planning permission clearly affects the implementation of plans and planning decisions in the UK, just as the power to downzone or refuse applications for rezoning and special permits affects the ability to implement comprehensive plans in the USA. Here, however, the systems are decidedly different. In the USA, a land-use regulation which leaves no economically beneficial use of the restricted property may be challenged by the landowner as the equivalent of compulsory purchase (so-called *inverse condemnation*) for which government must pay compensation. The same is true if a regulation greatly reduces the value of a landowner's property, substantially interfering with reasonable, investment-backed expectations. In the UK, by comparison, the general rule is that such regulations cannot 'take' property, and there are no substantive grounds for appealing the denial of planning permission, regardless of the economic consequences. This is a direct result of the nationalization of land development rights in 1947, though the fund from which payments were made for the loss of development rights has since lapsed.

The result is that, in the UK, there is an ability to implement local land-use plans without concern over the economic effect of limits on land use. Thus, for example, greenbelt and national park designations include a vast acreage of private land in which virtually all development and many uses of land are sharply curtailed, yet there is no possibility of claims against government for 'regulatory taking'. Contrast this with the success of David Lucas who successfully sought compensation through inverse condemnation from the State of South Carolina when his beachfront lots were rendered undevelopable by the state's shoreline protection statute (Roberts and Shearer 1992).

NEW TOWNS

New towns are the subject of Wannop's chapter. This is not a subject that would figure in a text on American planning. There is nothing in the USA to compare with this public, governmental experiment in town formation. To the extent that implementation of such concentration and dispersal from older central cities occurs at all, the private sector does it. Largely residential enclaves come to mind, such as Reston and Columbia in the east, Irvine and Kapolei in the west, and Celebration in the south. Kapolei in particular implements a medium-range development plan and a longer-range general plan for the island of Oahu to disperse population and commercial and residential development to a 'second city'. Decades in the planning, the 'city' consists of residential villages around a loose core of office and commercial and governmental development together with a huge and so far undeveloped site for a state university campus. Though the development is private (indeed all the land is under one ownership), it does implement a detailed local land-use plan every bit as comprehensive as that of a British new town, but the pace of development and dispersion from the central urban centre of Honolulu is far more deliberate.

PRESERVING OPEN SPACE

Dispersal of population and industry by establishing government new towns is certainly one way to preserve open space around cities, but private development does not necessarily follow government initiative. The British planning system, which deprives an owner of most economic use of land, is in part responsible for the ability of local and national government to prevent material development on vast swathes of land in the UK, both surrounding major cities like London and Glasgow (green belts) and in rural areas (national parks).

This ability to preserve 'the countryside' takes several forms. Perhaps the internationally most famous is the green belt. Not a park, not a nature designation, not publicly owned, the green belt is primarily a planning policy and designation for virtual non-development. There are 19 in Britain, covering 1.5 million hectares in England and 155,000 hectares in Scotland. Green belts had their genesis as a response to increased housing development around central cities, coupled with a desire to preserve agriculture and other open space uses and amenities. Of course, this results in leapfrog development beyond the green belt, as well as increased use of so-called 'derelict' land closer to and within cities. The key to the green belt is national policy support through a series of planning policy guidelines, to which local authorities must have regard in deciding applications for planning permission – and which they themselves, and their electors, are keen to protect. By all accounts, the green belt policy has been effective in preserving the countryside and controlling, if not containing, urban growth. In the USA, there have been only sporadic attempts at similar green belt policy at the local government level (such as Petaluma, California) and at the state level (as in the Oregon statewide land-use control system). There is, of course, no such national policy.

As in the USA, the UK has a number of national parks. These are run by independent national park authorities, while in the USA, the National Park Service is responsible. Thus the planning and use of these parks are arguably more centralized than in the UK. National parks typically suffer from some conflict between the goals of conserving and enhancing wildlife and natural beauty and promoting opportunities for their understanding and enjoyment by the public. A relatively recent change in the UK is the shift of responsibility for the national parks from local government to individual national park authorities. As conflicts between permitted development and national park preservation goals in the USA often demonstrate, there is a need for relatively independent and basically conservation-driven judgement on planning matters. This is particularly true in Britain where most of the land in the national parks is in private hands.

Only in coastal areas has the UK purchased relatively large portions of scenic property (mainly by the National Trust). Virtually all national park land in the USA, by comparison, is publicly (usually federally) owned, as compared to, say, state parks like the huge Adirondack Park in New York, where land holdings are more or less evenly split between public and private owners, with many towns and villages within its borders. It took separate state legislation in the 1970s to provide a vehicle for resolving planning, use and development conflicts. Some would say that this has been successful only in part.

The UK uses a series of lesser designations available only occasionally in the USA, on a state-by-state basis. Among these are sites of special scientific interest (SSSIs), areas of outstanding natural beauty (AONBs) and heritage coasts. SSSIs alone number over 6,000 and cover some 8 per cent of the land area. Add to these 333 national nature reserves and 487 local nature reserves and one has, with the national parks, a countryside preservation programme of impressive proportions. Local planning authorities must take special notice of the restrictions on the various classifications before permitting development of any sort. There is nothing remotely similar in the USA. However, vast portions of the western USA are owned outright by the federal government and held as national forests and seashores as well as national parks. These are managed and planned by the US Forest Service which permits a host of relatively (though increasingly controversial) non-intensive uses such as grazing and timber harvesting.

All these devices and designations, along with national parks, are used most frequently to preserve the best parts of Britain's extensive seacoast. As in the USA, the conflict in the coastal areas is between conservation and development. The coast is attractive not only for recreation and tourism, but also for certain industrial uses. Coastal areas are ideal for resort and recreational development from hotels to holiday accommodations in the form of condominium apartments and holiday cottages both for seasonal and retirement use. In the UK, add caravans. In the USA, with the exception of a few national seaside areas and parks, conservation takes place at the state and local government level under the auspices of the national Coastal Zone Management Act, to which most coastal states do (but need not) subscribe in order to obtain federal management plan funds and a level of control over federal activities in the coastal zone. State or local governments, depending upon the option chosen by the state, develop a coastal management plan defining the coastal zone (seaward as well as landward) and setting up, by statute and/or local ordinance, a coastal protection programme providing for both conservation and development. Usually, some sort of special permit process is required in addition to whatever other controls – local zoning and so forth – apply. There is, therefore, more overlap than in the UK system which appears to rely on local authorities taking into consideration the purpose and requirements of the various designations noted above.

TRANSPORTATION PLANNING AND DEVELOPMENT

The place of transportation infrastructure in the planning scheme of things has two principal parts: its role in encouraging and shaping the form and pace of land development, and its impacts on the land itself. As to the former, there is little that is more effective than roads and highways as a means of fostering development. This factor is, of course, evident in the British planning and construction of motorways, ringroads and the like. Driven by a relatively unanticipated explosion in the ownership and use of the private automobile, major programmes of roadbuilding soon replaced the previous reliance on public transportation (particularly buses and trains) in the UK, to an extent unequalled in the USA. In the USA, the growth in such use had as its principal effect the demise of the inter-urban light-rail transportation systems that were becoming popular. The heavy rail network in the USA never did come close to that in more-compact Britain and, although track in use declined by about 50 per cent, this was not nearly so significant from a planning perspective. The easier it was to get to the cities of the UK, the more they turned into conurbations. Oddly, there appears to have been little attention paid to this critical link between development planning and transportation planning until comparatively recently. Today, there is considerable public concern over the role of such transportation planning, and as a result, it appears that most major roadbuilding schemes have ground to a halt, with dozens of road schemes withdrawn and some programmed new routes abandoned.

The second major issue associated with major roadbuilding is the effect on the environment through which the road passes. New roads around or between cities must perforce cut through 'the countryside'. The new policies deflecting roadbuilding resources away from motorways and trunk roads and towards such as town bypasses and improvement of congested segments specifically state the need to preserve countryside and to avoid or mitigate environmental disadvantages.

Much of the same desire to preserve the countryside is evident in US literature and practice. Perhaps the most famous is the dismantling of the Embarcadero freeway in San Francisco, largely to eliminate the urban blight associated with elevated freeways, but there are other instances of highway projects being successfully modified, if not eliminated, for broad planning and environmental objectives.

Of course, given the central nature of both UK planning, funding and construction of transportation infrastructure, once a public decision is made to limit certain aspects of that infrastructure, it is carried out through the planning, funding and other implementation mechanisms of the central government. This aspect of centralization is, as noted earlier in this chapter, unlike the federal system in the USA in which each state has its own department of transportation. Nevertheless the results, at least with respect to major transportation projects, are similar. Although the USA lacks a national transportation plan, the so-called freeway network linking large parts of the country for commercial as well as 'residential' transportation purposes coupled with the perceived need to provide rapid transportation of military vehicles in time of national emergency, has become a virtual icon in transportation construction and policy in the USA at least since shortly after World War II. These 'federal aid' highways are just that: connecting, bypass and trunk roads constructed principally with federal money collected from taxes paid on petroleum and from long-distance freight hauliers using such highways and roads.

Where the federal government chooses to spend transportation dollars dictates the place, pace and scope of virtually all major roadbuilding in the USA, and state transportation planning reflects the federal conditions attached to these massive influxes of federal money. Nowhere is this more evident (and the noticeable shift to urban transportation projects such as rapid transit systems) than in the Intermodal Surface Transportation Efficiency Act of 1991(ISTEA) and its recently passed re-authorization, the Transportation Equity Act for the 21st Century of 1998 (TEA-21). Fully 60 per cent of the over $100 billion package is earmarked for other than national highway system construction and maintenance projects, including bridge construction and reconstruction, mass transit and community benefits. Planning continues to be a major hallmark and requirement for the receiving and using of these funds.

PUBLIC PARTICIPATION

Public participation in planning and land development in both the USA and the UK has been robust. It has, however, taken different forms. In the UK, the central government has held major 'public inquiries' into the planning and implementation of projects of national significance, such as a new airport for London and major nuclear power generating facilities. These have extended over many months (sometimes years) and generated huge volumes of testimony. There is no analogue in the USA.

In the USA, however, both planning and development decisions at the state and local level are submitted to the ubiquitous initiative and referendum process by which proposals are submitted to the relevant electorate for popular vote. In the many states which permit (by constitution, statute or common law) such ballot-box decision making, there are significant restrictions. Thus, for example, only so-called 'legislative' actions such as rezonings and ordinance or statutory text amendments are subject to either initiative or referendum. Judicial and quasi-judicial or administrative decisions, such as the consideration of coastal zone development or building permits, are not.

Beyond these significant differences, public participation is quite similar in each country. Citizens have the right to attend and make public comment upon plans and planning decisions. Under each system, the right is generally to be heard, hopefully influencing the decision in the political area, rather than to participate as a direct stakeholder with power to affect, let alone veto, a government planning or development outcome. In both countries, it appears that the price of public participation is delay – sometimes extraordinary delay – in the planning and land development process.

The problems are also the same, though it appears that critical comment and recognition may be greater in the UK (except for the environmental impact statement process in the USA which has rarely stopped, but often delayed, public projects such as highways for years at a time). 'Too much' public participation adds significant costs to plans and development projects, occasionally stopping them. This is often one of the goals of organized 'citizen' participation through groups such as the Sierra Club and Earth First in the USA, and the Council for the Protection of Rural England and Friends of the Earth in the UK. Rather than participate in the process as part of an interested public, the goal is often to have a major role in, if not a veto over, planning and other public decisions. This has been rightly criticized as a misuse of citizen participation, particularly in countries like the USA and UK where the ultimate decision makers are elected representatives in the first place. It is, moreover, a troublesome thought that a vocal and aroused local citizenry could exercise too much influence over a planning or development decision taken with regional concerns, such as the location of a wastewater treatment plant, a half-way house or a prison. The so-called NIMBY syndrome, coupled with not-so-subtle discrimination based on race, ethnicity or economic class, is easily masked by too much majoritarian tyranny into which public participation can easily degenerate.

CONCLUDING REMARKS

The lynchpin of the UK system continues to be a combination of the need for local government planning permission for most land development, and the reference by local government to plans in deciding whether to grant such permission. While some classes and areas of development are permitted as of right, the effect on the system as a whole does not appear to be significant. Also, plans are increasingly important in the granting of planning permission. If one is going to have such unlimited power over private land use, then increased reliance on published plans is a positive, if not an essential, feature.

It is, therefore, still easy for government in the UK to deny planning permission for development without legal repercussions. In particular, the US doctrine of regulatory taking, requiring compensation under the fifth Amendment to the US Constitution for a regulation which 'takes' property rights, has no British counterpart. This, in turn, makes it relatively easy to restrict development on private land for the preservation of agricultural land, open space, green belts and seacoasts. The British appear to accept these restrictions on private property with considerably more equanimity than most Americans who are happy to preserve these values, so long as it does not mean restricting their own property.

It should also make it easier to exact land development conditions through the doctrine of planning gain, always provided such conditions are truly related to problems caused by the relevant development and are not simply a local government wish-list of unrelated community benefits. The nexus/proportionality theories resulting from US Constitutional law are worth reviewing in this context. All community facilities ought not to be borne on the backs of the land development community.

That said, the siting and provision of public facilities can have a considerable effect on land development, and needs to be closely integrated with land planning, as the experience in both US and UK transportation planning and development demonstrates. While the UK is more up front about at least attempting national transportation planning, there is quite a lot of the same in the USA through conditions attached to federal grants for highway construction. Both countries need to do better in evaluating the effects of major transportation decisions (such as motorways and highways) on both the countryside through which transportation corridors pass and the 'destinations' which they serve.

Lastly, there is a need throughout the planning system to ensure an adequate measure of public participation, if plans are increasingly to assume critical significance in land development decisions such as the granting of planning permission and the siting of public facilities. This does not necessarily mean that the general public should have a veto over such plans. Moreover, care must be taken to prevent organized, vocal groups – whether local or national – from disproportionately affecting plans and planning decisions which should be made in a regional and national context.

FURTHER READING

For the British reader, the best introduction to US planning is Wakeford (1990) *American Development Control: Parallels and Paradoxes from an English Perspective*. Another comparative study is Cullingworth (1993) *The Political Culture of Planning*, especially Part V, 'American planning in comparative Perspective'. A broader analysis is Vogel (1986) *National Styles of Regulation: Environmental Policy in Great Britain and the United States*. Another interesting, though dated, analysis is Clawson and Hall (1973) *Planning and Urban Growth: An Anglo-American Comparison*.

For a detailed (and amusing) exploration of the waywardness of US zoning, see Babcock (1966) *The Zoning Game* and its sequel Babcock and Siemon (1990) *The Zoning Game Revisited*. A wider treatment of about the same vintage from a British perspective is Delafons (1969) *Land Use Controls in the United States*. A good picture of land use controls from a state and regional perspective is given in Buchsbaum and Smith (1993) *State and Regional Comprehensive Planning* and Kelly (1993) *Managing Community Growth*.

There are numerous books on the 'taking' issue. Particularly up to date are Callies (1996) *Takings*, Laitos (1998) *The Law of Property Rights Protection* and Meltz *et al.* (1999) *The Takings Issue*.

Planning gain (impact fees) in the USA is dealt with usefully in Freilich and Bushek (1995) *Exactions, Impact Fees and Dedications* which includes 'Paying for growth and planning gain: an Anglo-American comparison of development conditions, impact fees, and development agreements' by Callies and Grant (also published in *Urban Lawyer (1991)* 23: 221–48). See also Nicholas, *et al.* (1991) *A Practitioner's Guide to Development Impact Fees*.

The impact of the ballot box on decision making is documented in Caves (1992) *Land Use Planning: The Ballot Box Revolution*.

postscript[1]

British Planning:

Positive or Reluctant?

BARRY CULLINGWORTH

A major implicit assumption of postwar planning policy was that, within a stable social and economic system, the main concerns would be the redistribution of economic activity ('the balanced distribution of industry') and of populations (especially to new and expanded towns beyond the green belt). Little demographic and social change was anticipated (despite major changes in educational opportunity, health services and social security). In fact, of course, the changes have been so extensive as to transform the context within which the planning system operates and the tasks on which it should be engaged. Over the postwar years, the population has increased (from 46 to 60 million), households have multiplied even more dramatically (with large increases predicted), while traffic has exceeded all forecasts (from 2.5 to 27 million vehicles). There are many such indicators of change. They play havoc with carefully crafted plans and can (within an equally unpredictable political framework) give rise to demands for changes in the character and purpose of plans.

Given these changes, it might have been expected that the planning system would have been subjected to intensive review. Incredibly, in line with a lack of concern for the workings (as distinct from the procedures) of the system, the overall effects have received no assessment since Peter Hall's team produced the 1973 study of *The Containment of Urban England*. It is clear, however, that whatever the effects have been, the philosophies of containment and redistribution have remained central. In the 1940s, these philosophies were translated into policies for restraining urban growth and channelling development forces into new and expanded towns. These policies were never adequately implemented, and much development has taken place in locations which were decided upon by political bargaining. The position has worsened as land requirements for a more affluent and mobile society have increased – while the less affluent have been sidelined. Support for containment policies has never wavered, but redistribution policies have been under attack since the first new town was proposed for Stevenage; and they have become increasingly strident.

Looking back on this over the 50 years, several major issues stand out. What started as a political fight by counties to protect their agricultural borders against intrusion by the big city housebuilders (public and private) has grown into a more broadly based, populist opposition to building anywhere in the countryside. The support given to green belts has grown into an effective bulwark of suburbanites against 'urban sprawl' – given a higher, positive transformation into 'environmental quality' and now 'sustainability'. New property and development interests have arisen which are attuned to, and benefit from, the planning system. Housebuilders may complain about the restrictions on land supply, but only those who are unsuccessful in acquiring land on which development is eventually permitted have cause for complaint: the lucky ones (who tend to be the larger builders who can operate land banks, purchase options and such like) reap rich rewards. In terms of political arithmetic however, these are greatly outnumbered by the hugely increased number of owner occupiers with an equity interest in the status quo. Similarly with the high stakes in the out-of-town retailing market: the profits to be gained as a result of the restriction on their number gives a premium to successful contenders. All this has also encouraged 'planning gain' – a new variant in the long saga of attempts to devise a workable system of community participation in land value profits.

Thus the planning system has spawned new markets which involve public and private interests, a large degree of uncertainty, and a high level of profits for the winners. Though the development values issue is not high on any political agenda, it underlies some of the basic difficulties facing the planning system. Planning will be severely constrained by public expenditure problems until something akin to the so-called 'financial provisions' of the 1947 Act are resuscitated. Popular proposals currently range from a proposed tax on greenfield sites to the financing of development on brownfield sites. Grant argues (in chapter 5) for a rationalization of planning gain – which has the great advantage of being politically possible.

Arguably, the most important land use planning issue facing all postwar governments has been accommodating new urban development (increasingly intertwined with – and now dominated by – transport issues). The new towns were a bold and effective mechanism for this though, given the scale of the programme and its premature demise, they could never make the total contribution of which they were capable. Instead, much development has leapfrogged green belts and other urban planning fences. As a result, cross-country commuting has increased greatly. Moreover, given the dispersed nature of the development, much of it cannot be served by public transport. This is one important component of the transport problem which successive governments have been afraid to tackle. The tragedy is that by postponing any major attempt to deal with it, the problem has become far more complex.

LOCAL CHOICE

Much of the difficulty stems from the opposition to urban development in locations which have positive planning advantages. It was increased by the Conservative policy of 'local choice' clearly set out by Chris Patten during his brief tenure as Secretary of State for the Environment:

> While there is undoubtedly a continuing need for more houses, there are choices about the way we meet that need. One of the functions of the planning system is to help us identify those choices, and make them sensibly. What is more, many of the important choices are decisions which can and should be made locally, to reflect the values which local communities place on their surroundings. If the planning system works properly at the local level, there is less need for the central government decision taking – by me or by my inspectors – which can so easily appear to the local community to attach too little weight to their views (Patten 1989).

This may be good politics, but it is abysmal planning. Decisions on the location of major developments are not matters for local choice: they are regional or national issues. (Given the inadequacy of regional decision taking, it currently has to be the central government that has to decide.) As with many of the early new towns, local inhabitants will object most strongly to what looks (and perhaps is) a desecration of their local environment.

The Conservative government was particularly apprehensive (and timid) on the locations of new developments, since so much opposition came from their own supporters. They discovered that the planning system, rather than being regarded as a bureaucratic imposition, was seen as a strong line of defence against change. Green belts, the restraint of urban growth, and the protection of the countryside attract extensive support; not so the promotion of new settlements, or even the establishment of park and ride facilities on the urban fringe. In the British planning system, change is something to be resisted, rather than facilitated or even accepted.

New forms of protectionism have emerged with alliances of old-style preservationists concerned with local issues of environmental defence, and new-style environmentalists concerned with wider issues of environmental quality and 'sustainability'. These are powerful forces, as the Conservative government discovered when it attempted, in the mid-1980s, to foster a more market-led planning policy in outer suburbia. Its mistake was in ignoring suburban supporters who would be affected by a market-oriented decision on the location of housing development. A draft circular on housing land was interpreted in the shires as heralding a relaxation of green-belt controls, thus threatening the quality of local environments. The resulting outcry led to a redrafting of the circular to make it clear that no such relaxation was intended (Elson 1986). This experience influenced reactions to the increasing pressure from housebuilders to be allowed to develop new settlements – the term presumably carrying more homely connotations than 'new towns'. Owing to the vociferous (local) public opposition, all were rebuffed.

NEW SETTLEMENTS

What followed was a period in which the official stance was acceptance of new settlements in principle and rejection in practice. A restrained praise was voiced for a limited number of new settlements 'especially when the developer meets all of the local infrastructure costs and the need for community facilities'. This acceptance of the principle (of 'well-conceived schemes in appropriate locations') was accompanied by a succession of refusals (Breheny *et al.* 1993: 56). Among the official reasons for rejecting proposals for new settlements was an emphasis on the importance of local support. This was initially expressed in terms of 'local environmental concerns', but increasingly it focused on the necessity of new settlements being subjected to the full development plan processes, and its attendant political pressures. Under the emerging regional planning guidance system (and whatever develops from that), proposals for major developments will presumably be settled in principle within the framework of a regional strategy. How this will work out remains to be seen.

As an aid to determining appropriate forms of development, the DoE commissioned study of *Alternative Development Patterns: New Settlements* (Breheny *et al.* 1993) which, in addition to a technical appraisal of various forms of development, unequivocally stated that 'unless much tougher containment policies are introduced – at the same time when concerns are being expressed over urban intensification – it is inevitable that significant greenfield/village development will take place in the

UK'. The analysis of the differing types of development did not go very far in demonstrating the superiority of any one type of development over another.[2] This is not surprising: *general* issues of urban form are of limited practical value since the real problems are not general but site-specific. The advantages and disadvantages of particular development forms vary according to the features of alternative sites and their location in a specific subregion (and, with larger developments, perhaps the wider region as well). They will vary also according to the size, character and purpose of the development, its transportation links and potentialities, and its present and future relationships with the surrounding areas.

In the meantime, development proceeds (or not) on particular sites for which builders seek planning permission. This 'non-planning' approach is checked by a process which contains one or more of the elements of strong local opposition, public inquiries and ministerial decisions. Somewhere buried in this process there may be some vestige of planning policy, but it is a hit-or-miss affair. Certainly, it is a far cry from 'positive planning' or ensuring that the right development goes ahead at the right place at the right time!

LAND USE AND TRANSPORT

Crucial to the siting of a development are the existing and potential transportation facilities. It is extraordinary that this elementary point has to be constantly reiterated, and is so frequently ignored. However, land use planning and transport planning inhabit separate worlds of organization, responsibility, finance and implementation – though recent pronouncements, consultations and white papers show that there are good intentions in this area.

The lack of integration (or even relationship) between the two is fatal to much of the contemporary planning scene. At the risk of labouring the point, consider the extent to which development is precluded on urban fringe sites and encouraged further out into the countryside. This is so common that illustrations are hardly necessary, but a DoE study on *Reducing the Need to Travel through Land Use and Transport Planning* (1995f) is particularly revealing of the problem and the lack of adequate response. The study includes an account of the failure of the Oxfordshire 'settlement strategy' which concentrates development in selected county towns beyond the Oxford green belt, thereby facilitating the provision of public transport. However, a study of travel patterns of the new residents in three of these towns (Bicester, Didcot and Witney) revealed 'high travel distances, high levels of car use, little use of public transport, and almost 90 percent of employed residents travelling to work outside the town'. By contrast, a new housing estate on the edge of Oxford has far less car travel: the public transport system provides a better alternative. The DoE report laconically comments that 'these conclusions suggest that local authorities will need to consider carefully the regional dimension of location planning, and the transport policies applied in individual settlements'. Indeed!

The difficulty of devising and implementing transport policies is discussed by Truelove in chapter 14. That this is not a party political matter is demonstrated by the travails of the Labour government in failing (at least so far) to decide what should be done. Road charging is the economists' preference, but the indications are that charges would have to be very substantial if they are to make much impact. The very fact that motorists are prepared to suffer the agonies of congestion shows that the private car has enormous attractions. In any case, traffic grows to fill available space, and 'as you price some traffic out, other traffic will be attracted by lower journey times'.[3] This is the same argument that the Ministry of Transport resisted for so many years: that roads actually attract traffic. Anthony Downs has elaborated an elegant theory on this which he terms 'triple convergence'. This is based on the simple fact that since every driver seeks the easiest route, the cumulative result is a convergence on that route. If it then becomes overcrowded, some drivers will switch to an alternative route which has become relatively less crowded. These switches continue until there is an equilibrium situation (which, like any human equilibrium, is not stable – conditions constantly change). On this theory, building a new road or widening an existing one will have a 'triple convergence'; first, motorists will switch from other routes to the new one ('spatial convergence'); second, some motorists who avoided the peak hours will travel at the more convenient peak hour ('time convergence'); third, travellers who had used public transport will switch to driving since the new road now makes the journey faster.[4] Though the current reluctance to build new or improved roads does more for the management of public expenditure than it does for transport, it has a rationale which points to the use of other instruments, such as the development of public transport, and restrictions on car usage, particularly by way of parking controls. In the long run, much could be done by establishing a better relationship between land use and transport planning. Transport is a means of getting to places: it is the location of places, and their relationship to the means of access which is the crucial point.

Though much public controversy focuses on the location of residential development (and, of course, out-of-town shopping centres), far too little attention is given to the location of firms. In my home area of south Cambridgeshire, there is intense opposition to housing developments (currently largely taking place in the necklace of villages around Cambridge). Yet these same villages have accepted science parks, business parks and research parks which create the jobs which give rise to the housing need which is opposed (a point made in the report on housing from the Select Committee[5]). Similarly, but less dramatically, the rural economy is bolstered by a proliferation of small industrial estates and warehousing (particularly in old hangars and barns). A proposal for a private new town near Cambridge on the site of an old barracks has attracted strong opposition, while a few miles away planning permission has been given for the development of a former airfield as another research park and a leisure centre. None of this is to say that these developments are unnecessary, but it is impossible to see any semblance of a plan which integrates land uses and the transportation which these engender.

PUBLIC AND PRIVATE INTERESTS IN PLANNING

The British planning system provides no third-party legal rights, but it guarantees something much more effective: procedural and political avenues to prevent development. The latest popular planning acronym (like NIMBY, an American import) is BANANA: Build Absolutely Nothing Anywhere Near Anything. It is used with a wry smile, but its widespread applicability is unquestionable. The 'local choice' slogan raised this almost to a matter of high principle.

Politicians face a hard time these days, and the dice are loaded against them in supporting development which 'local choice' opposes. There is no easy solution, as successive governments have learned. Even the elaboration of a planning policy is beset with difficulties, as official *planning policy guidance* publications demonstrate. These emanate from a desire to provide a policy framework, but this is difficult to devise. It must be drafted in such a way as to be applicable to a multiplicity of widely differing circumstances. Even if this can be achieved with sufficiently bland language, there is an inevitable uncertainty in forecasting the comparative effects of different courses of action. Will better car parking make a town more or less attractive? Will a bypass improve traffic conditions in a congested area, or will it simply allow a different pattern of congestion? Will a large new development be better than several small ones? Moreover, as is demonstrated repeatedly at public inquiries, differing interests can 'cherry pick' from the 24 PPGs to show how well their arguments meet the official guidance. Arguments for and against development in villages can be equally supported. While 'the overall strategy . . . should be to allocate the maximum number of houses to existing larger urban areas' (PPG 13), the building of houses in villages can help to sustain the local services which are necessary for their economic survival (PPG 7).

At this level of abstraction, almost anything can be in conformity with 'planning guidance'. The issues require to be addressed in the context of specific areas in particular regions within the framework of a regional plan. It is here that the absence of a regional tier of government is so regrettable. Fortunately, there are indications that this may emerge as a result of the establishment of the government offices for the regions, the 'standing conferences' of local authorities, the regional development agencies and the EC planning initiatives. The whole of England is now covered by *regional planning guidance*, and a consultation paper has been issued on *The Future of Regional Guidance* (DETR 1998f). The latter provides some explicit criticism of the inadequacy of the present system of regional planning guidance, and an indication that, together with the promised *integrated transport policy*, major reform is in the air. Together with the recent changes to the constitution of the UK, there are grounds for optimism, despite previous experience.[6]

POSITIVE PLANNING

Given a workable framework for regional planning (easier said than done), one can hope that planning will give a lead, rather than acting as an umpire among opposing sides in planning disputes. The planning system should be an initiator of land use planning and programmes for coordinated development. Currently, plans are devised essentially to restrict: they contain little that is of a proactive nature. They form a framework for reacting to proposals put forward by individual development interests. The result is that there is inadequate investment particularly in places such as the inner city. Private investment is simply not profitable without public policy support, particularly in assembling areas for large-scale development. There are well established powers for this, but public resources have not been forthcoming. That the impasse can be broken is illustrated by the examples given by Ward in his discussion (in chapter 16) of public–private partnerships

The logic of positive planning shows itself in many ways. Thus, the role of environmental assessment on the planning system could change its focus from the evaluation of individual planning applications into a procedure for selecting the most appropriate sites for development. To quote PPG 23 (*Planning and Pollution Control*) an environmental statement 'should include an outline discussion of the main alternatives studied by the developer and an indication of the reasons for choosing the development proposed'. Even clearer is the policy set out in *Making Waste Work* (DoE 1995g). This not only gives local authorities the responsibility of preventing the development of waste facilities in undesirable locations, but gives them the positive role of 'ensuring that there is adequate scope for the provision of the right facilities in the right place'. (The wording recalls the language of 1944.) There is a logic in positive planning which is inherent in the concept.

This is not to say that positive planning is easy: on the contrary it is extraordinarily difficult. So many matters have to be considered; and these can be elusive, complex and conflicting. Action is restricted by the limitations imposed by the existing pattern of development, by inadequate resources, by political barriers and by the sheer impossibility of forecasting the future; but we can do a lot better than we are doing.[7]

Notes

chapter 1: Introduction and Overview

1. Including Ward in this volume, and Delafons, J. (1998) 'Reforming the British planning system, 1964–1965 – The Planning Advisory Group and the genesis of the planning act of 1968', *Planning Perspectives* 13: 373–87.

2. In fact, there was considerable support within the 1951 Conservative government for retaining the 1947 scheme in an amended form, and it was clear that the 1953–4 solution was 'inherently unstable'. It certainly was, and they had to amend it in 1959. Anyone interested in ploughing through the detailed story is referred to vol 4 of the official history of *Environmental Planning 1939–1969* (Cullingworth 1981).

3. This might be a view distorted by personal experience as a member of the West Midlands Economic Planning Council.

4. The description was the title of a 1979 report by the Outer Circle Policy Unit with the Council for Science and the Council of Justice: *The Big Public Inquiry: A Proposed New Procedure for the Impartial Investigation of Projects with Major National Implications*. It would be useful if this could now be reprinted.

chapter 4: The Planning System and the Development Plan

References from Ministry of Town and Country Planning files, 1943–48, in the Public Record Office

1. *Town and Country Planning Act: Plans or Schemes of the Future*, memorandum by G.L. Pepler, Plans Division, 6 January 1944 (HLG71/1259).

2. *Note on Main Outline of a Planning System, Memorandum No. 2*, by Legislative Division, August 1943 (HLG71/1259).

3. *The Process of National Planning, Memorandum 3*, by the Legislative Division, November 1943 (HLG71/1638).

4. *Technical Considerations of Outline Plans*, minute by K. S. Dodd, Chief Regional Planning Officer, 29 December 1943 (HLG71/1638).

5. Manuscript note by the Minister on a Memorandum to him from 'G W' (Sir Geoffrey Whiskard, Permanent Secretary), 18 February 1944 (HLG71/1638).

6. *Outline of a Proposed System of Planning for the Future*, by Blaise Gillie, expressing the general line of thought of the Plans Division, 22 January 1944 (HLG71/1638).

7. *A Technical Examination of the Model Clauses of June 1939 in the Light of Subsequent Developments and Prospective Legislation*, memorandum by K. S. Dodd, Chief Regional Planning Officer, on setting up a Committee on the Model Clauses, chaired by G. T. Pound, 11 January 1944 (HLG71/232).

8. *Notes of a Meeting on the 'Pound Committee' Reports*, memorandum by E. S. Hill, Legislative Division, 13 June 1945 (HLG71/236).

9. *The New Planning System, Provisions Regards Planning Standards*, memorandum by E. S. Hill, Legislative Division, 16 January 1946 (HLG71/231).

10. *The Planning Code*, memorandum by A. M. Jenkins, 23 January 1948 (HLG71/24).

chapter 5: Compensation and Betterment

1. In the Committee's view, implementation of the 1932 Act had been hindered by the liability of authorities to compensate for values which:.

   (i) had not been lost at all but had shifted to other sites where development was to be permitted under the scheme (or 'shifting values'); or
   (ii) were purely speculative in the sense that valuations for compensation purposes were assuming a higher level of development probability on a site by site basis than was true overall, by including each time a speculative element (or 'floating value').

2. In the 1944 white paper *The Control of Land Use* it was argued that the Uthwatt proposals would be inequitable as between owners of developed and undeveloped land, would be administratively complex and would be harsh on those whose established land investments would be lost.

3. Of these, the principal cases were those within the Third Schedule to the Act, which in effect protected the financial value of certain development expectations, such as the right to extend a building by up to 10 per cent. These measures were eventually repealed by the Planning and Compensation Act 1991. The other main instrument was the purchase notice, which allowed a landowner to require an authority to acquire his land if it was left without a 'reasonably beneficial use'. These provisions remain in force, but have in practice been made largely irrelevant because of the tenor of the policy advice issued by Government (DOE Circular 13/83, *Purchase Notices*) and upheld by the courts (see, e.g. *Colley v Canterbury City Council*, Court of Appeal, 28 July, 1998).

4. In *Westminster City Council v Great Portland Estates Ltd* [1981] AC 636.

5. This process, known as 'enabling development' was specifically upheld by the Court of Appeal in relation to the redevelopment proposals for the Royal Opera House Covent Garden in *R v Westminster City Council, ex p Monahan* [1989] JPL 107, where the only reasons for allowing a significant element of commercial development at the site was to cross-subsidize the opera house scheme.

6. *Earl Fitzwilliam's Wentworth Estate Co Ltd. v. M.H.L.G.* [1952] AC 362.

7. Although capital gains tax continues today to apply to land, and hence to betterment, it is not a differential tax and in practice it is difficult to assess the extent to which it succeeds in taxing betterment, because of the generous 'roll forward' allowances which secure mitigation of the tax where capital released from one business is rolled forward into a new business.

8. Hansard: vol 657 HC Debs. col. 979 (9 April 1962).

9. See, e.g. *R v South Northamptonshire District Council, ex p Crest Homes Ltd* [1995] JPL 200; *R v Plymouth City Council ex parte Plymouth and South Devon Co-operative Society Ltd* (1993) 67 P & CR 78.

10. *Tesco Stores Ltd v Secretary of State for the Environment* [1995] 2 All ER 636.

chapter 9: British Planning in its European Context

1. The terms *European Union* and *European Community* are often used interchangeably. Strictly speaking, *European Union* embraces all three pillars of the Union – the European Community, Common Foreign and Security Policy, and Justice and Home Affairs. However, the *European Community* is by far the main part of the Union, including all legislative and common policies. The second and third pillars are agreements in the Treaty on European Union (Maastricht Treaty) to seek more intensive cooperation on an intergovernmental basis. In practice, the term 'Union' has been widely adopted to describe all activities since the Maastricht Treaty.

2. *Agenda 2000* proposed that negotiations on accession should start with Hungary, Poland, Estonia, the Czech Republic and Slovenia. The Commission had previously recommended that negotiations should be opened with Cyprus. Switzerland has also made an application, and Malta has recently renewed its application on accession.

chapter 11: The Changing Role of the Courts in Planning

1. [1948] KB 223.

2. Robinson v Minister of Town and Country Planning [1947] KB 702; Johnson & Co (Builders) v Minister of Health [1947] 2 ALL E R 395.

3. Franklin v Minister of Town and Country Planning [1948] AC 87.

4. See East Riding C.C. v Park Estate (Bridlington) Ltd (1956) 6 P & C R 231.

5. Hansard, HC Debates vol 437, col 1335, 13 May 1947.

6. Mr Justice Sedley in R v Teeside Development Corporation ex p Morrison [1998] JPL 23 at 39.

7. I am referring here particularly to the Scotland Act 1988, the Governance of Wales Act 1998, and Human Rights Act 1998.

8. [1997] 1 ALL E R 228.

9. Town and Country Planning Act 1990, sections 284–92.

10. It is significant in this regard that now that most development plan approvals are made by local planning authorities, it is the decision of the local planning authorities which are being challenged under section 287.

11. See section 31(3) of the Supreme Court Act 1980, and Rule 3(7) of the Rules of the Supreme Court.

12. Indeed, in the House of Lords decision in Inland Revenue Commissioners v National Federation of Self Employed and Small Businesses Limited [1882] AC 617, it was generally accepted by their lordships that leave should only be refused on grounds of standing where the applicant is an obvious busybody, and it would be an abuse of process to allow the applicant to proceed.

13. Buxton v Minister of Housing and Local Government [1961] 1 QB 278.

14. Turner v Secretary of State for the Environment [1973] 28 P & C R 123.

15. See R v Canterbury Council ex p Springimage Ltd [1993] JPL 58.

16. See Covent Garden Community Association Ltd v Greater London Council [1981] JPL 183.

17. [1981] JPL 869 at 870.

18. See R v North Somerset DC ex p Garnett [1997] JPL 1015.

19. See R v Somerset C.C. ex p Richard Dixon [1997] JPL 1030.

20. The *planning unit* determines the area of land which must be considered in determining whether a material change in the use of land has taken place.

21. Copeland Borough Council v Secretary of State for the Environment (1976) 31 P & C R 403.

22. See Mitchell v Secretary of State for the Environment [1994] 2 PLR 1030, and E.C.C. Construction v Secretary of State for the Environment [1995] JPL 322.

23. See West Midlands Probation Committee v Secretary of State for the Environment [1998] JPL 388.

24. See R v Westminster City Council ex p Monahan [1990] 1 QB 87 (the Covent Garden case).

25. Tesco v Secretary of State for the Environment [1995] 1 WLR 759.

26. [1991] 6 P & C R 343.

27. Fairclough Homes Ltd v Secretary of State for the Environment [1992] JPL 247 at 251.

28. Wood-Robinson v Secretary of State for the Environment [1998] JPL 976.

29. See City of Edinburgh Council v Secretary of State for Scotland [1998] JPL 224, and R v Leominster D.C. ex p Pothecary [1998] JPL 335.

30. See Surrey Heath B.C. v Secretary of State for the Environment(1986) 53 P & C R 428.

31. [1997] JPL 958 at 967.

32. See Article 22(1)(a) of the General Development Procedure Order 1995.

33. See Regulation 3 of the Town and Country Planning (Enforcement Notices and Appeals) Regulation 1991.

34. See Westminster City Council v Great Portland Estates plc [1984] AC 661.

35. [1991] 2 ALL E R 10.

36. [1995] JPL 1043.

37. [1997] JPL 43.

38. See [1998] JPL at 144.

39. [1995] JPL 1043 at 1046.

40. [1997] JPL 43 at 48.

41. See section 176 (1) of the Town and Country Planning Act 1990.

42. Hammond v Secretary of State for the Environment [1997] JPL 724 at 732.

43. R v Wicks [1997] JPL 1049.

44. ibid [1997] JPL 1049 at 1063.

45. Dilieto v London Borough of Ealing [1998] PLCR 212.

chapter 16: Public–Private Partnerships

1. (Public Record Office) HLG 88/15 Ministry of Town and Country Planning Advisory Panel on Reconstruction of City Centres: Comments on Report 1944–5, p 4.

2. (Public Record Office) HLG 88/6 Ministry of Town and Country Planning Central Advisory Committee on Estate Development and Management: Report as signed by Committee 1946, p 32.

3. Arndale Property Trust Ltd (undated, *c.* 1965) *Arndale in Partnership*, Bradford: Arndale P.T.

4. (Public Record Office) HLG 136/42 The Balance to be Struck Between Public and Private Participation in the Redevelopment of Central Areas: Preparation of Note on Departmental Policy.

5. (Public Record Office) HLG 136/20 Town Centres – Approach to Renewal, Planning Bulletin No.1, Delafons – Sylvester-Evans 25.9.61.

6. (Public Record Office) HLG 136/22 Town Centres – Cost and Control of Development, Planning Bulletin No.3, Delafons – Sylvester-Evans and Pugh 3.5.63.

7. (Public Record Office) HLG 136/143 Encouragement of Private Enterprise to Participate in Redevelopment of Town Centres, Twilight Areas and Town Expansion – Departmental Meeting, 22.11.61 (Points Raised by Parly Sec), Jellicoe – Sharp, 10.11.61.

8. Buckinghamshire County Council (undated, *c.* 1965) North Bucks New City: CDA and Designation Parts I and II, Buckingham County Council.

9. Buckingham Borough Development Co Ltd (1981) Buckingham Town Expansion, Buckingham: BBDCL (typescript).

10. Barton Willmore and Partners (1973) Lower Earley: A Comprehensive Plan for the Development of Lower Earley, Reading: BWP.

11. Wokingham District Council (1977) Lower Earley Development Brief, Wokingham DC.

chapter 18: An American Perspective on UK Planning

1. Exceptions are such states as California and Hawaii, where costs associated with the increasingly permit-only development of land have helped drive housing prices to the highest levels in the USA.

2. With the exception of minimal development control associated with national environmental laws such as the Clean Air Act and the Clean Water Act, and certain resource protection statutes (adherence to which is voluntary) such as the Coastal Zone Management Act.

3. DOE *Planning Obligations* (Circular 1/97), London: HMSO.

Postscript

1. This postscript draws freely on previous publications, including Cullingworth (1997a) and (1997b) and Cullingworth and Nadin (1997).

2. It did, however, carefully avoid making the mass of assumptions which flawed an earlier study by the National Institute of Economic and Social Research (Stone 1973; Cullingworth 1979: 473).

3. Anthony Fowkes, quote in 'Commuting Survey', *The Economist*, 5 March 1998, p. 25.

4. Downs first set out his theory in a 1962 article: 'The law of peak-hour expressway convergence', *Traffic Quarterly* 16: 393–409. See the lengthier, and more accessible, 1992 book *Stuck in Traffic* (Washington, DC: Brookings Institution, and Cambridge, MA: Lincoln Institute of Land Policy). This summary is taken from Cullingworth and Nadin (1997) and my *Planning in the USA*, which discusses American transportation policies.

5. *Tenth Report from the Environment, Transport and Regional Affairs Committee, Session 1997–98, on Housing* (HC 495-I), London: TSO.

6. See Wannop, U. and Cherry, G. E. (1994) 'The development of regional planning in the United Kingdom', *Planning Perspectives* 9: 29–60.

7. The highly relevant *Sociable Cities: The Legacy of Ebenezer Howard* by Peter Hall and Colin Ward, Chichester: Wiley, 1998) was published after this essay was written.

References

Note: Readers who are familiar with Her Majesty's Stationery Office must now become accustomed to its successor: The Stationery Office (TSO)

Abercrombie. P. (1945) *Greater London Plan 1944*, London: HMSO.

Abercrombie, P. (1967) *Town and Country Planning*, Oxford: Oxford University Press.

Abercrombie, P. and Matthew, R. (1949) *Clyde Valley Regional Plan 1946*, Edinburgh: HMSO.

ACTRA (Advisory Committee on Trunk Road Assessment) (1977), *Report*, London: HMSO.

Adam, R. (1997) *Good Design in Speculative Housing; the Consumer, the Developer, the Architect and the Planner: Whose Design is Good?*, Royal Fine Art Commission Seminar, London (mimeo).

Adams, J (1981) *Transport Planning Vision and Practice*, London: Routledge & Kegan Paul.

Adams, T. (1932) *Recent Advances in Town Planning*, London: Churchill.

Adams, W. M. (1996) *Future Nature: A Vision for Conservation*, London: Earthscan.

Adshead, S. D. (1923) *Town Planning and Town Development*, London: Methuen.

Albrechts, L. *et al.* (1988) *Regional Policy at the Crossroads*, London: Jessica Kingsley.

Alden, J. and Boland, P. (eds) (1996) *Regional Development Strategies: A European Perspective*, London: Jessica Kingsley.

Aldous, T. (1975) *Goodbye Britain*, London: Sidgwick & Jackson.

Aldridge, H. R. (1915) *The Case for Town Planning*, London: National Housing and Town Planning Council.

Aldridge, M. (1979) *The British New Towns: A Programme without a Policy*, London: Routledge and Kegan Paul.

Allanson, P. and Whitby, M. C. (1996) *The Rural Economy and the British Countryside*, London: Earthscan.

Amery, C. (1995) 'The ministry of sloth?', *Perspectives on Architecture* 12: 26–9.

Anon (1957) 'A high street keeps in keeping' (editorial), *Architects' Journal* 126: 774.

Armstrong, H. and Taylor, J. (1993) *Regional Economics and Policy* (2nd edn), New York: Harvester Wheatsheaf.

Arnstein, S. (1969) 'A ladder of citizen participation', *Journal of the American Institute of Planners* 35: 216–24.

Artobolevskii, S. S. (1996) *Regional Policy in Europe*, London: Jessica Kingsley.

Ashworth, G. J. (1994) 'From history to heritage: from heritage to identity: in search of concepts and models', in Ashworth, G. J. and Larkham, P. J. (eds) *Building A New Heritage: Tourism, Culture and Identity in the New Europe*, London: Routledge.

Ashworth, W. (1954) *The Genesis of Modern British Town Planning*, London: Routledge & Kegan Paul.

Association for Planning and Regional Reconstruction (1950) *Town and Country Planning Textbook*, London: Architectural Press.

Atkinson, R. and Moon, G. (1994) *Urban Policy in Britain: The City, The State and the Market*, London: Macmillan.

Audit Commission (1992) *Building in Quality: A Study of Development Control*, London: HMSO.

Audit Commission (1996) *Under-Fives Count: A Management Handbook on the Education of Children under Five*, London: HMSO.

Audit Commission (1998) *Building in Quality: A Review*, London: Audit Commission Publications.

Austin-Smith / Lord Partnership (1969) *Warrington New Town*, Warrington New Town Development Corporation.

Babcock, R. F. (1966) *The Zoning Game*, Madison: University of Wisconsin Press.

Babcock, R. F. and Siemon, C. L. (1990) *The Zoning Game Revisited*, Cambridge, MA: Lincoln Institute of Land Policy.

Bachtler, J. and Turok, I. (eds) (1997) *The Coherence of EU Regional Policy: Contrasting Perspectives on the Structural Funds*, London: Jessica Kingsley.

Bailey, N. and Robertson, D. (1994) *Scotland's Housing Renewal Programme – A National or Local Policy?*, Paper presented at the Conference of the European Network for Housing Research, Glasgow.

Bailey, N., Barker, A. and MacDonald, K. (1995) *Partnership Agencies in British Urban Policy*, London: UCL Press.

Baker, M. (1998) 'Planning for the English regions: a review of the secretary of state's regional planning guidance', *Planning Practice and Research* 13: 153–69.

Balchin, P. N. (1979) *Housing Improvement and Social Inequality*, Farnborough, Hants: Saxon House.

Balchin, P. N. (1990) *Regional Policy in Britain: The North–South Divide*, London: Paul Chapman.

Balchin, P. N. (1995) *Housing Policy: An Introduction* (3rd edn), London: Routledge.

Balchin, P. N. (ed.) (1996) *Housing Policy in Europe*, London: Routledge.

Balchin, P. N. and Rhoden, M. (eds) (1997) *Housing: The Essential Foundations*, London: Routledge.

Ball, M. (1983) *Housing Policy and Economic Power*, London: Methuen.

Banister, D. (1994) *Transport Planning*, London: Spon.

Barber, S. and Millns, T. (1993) *Building the New Europe: The Role of Local Authorities in the UK*, London: Association of County Councils.

Barlow, J. (1995) *Public Participation in Urban Development: The European Experience*, London: Policy Studies Institute.

Barlow Report (1940) *Report of the Royal Commission on the Distribution of the Industrial Population* (Cmd 6153), London: HMSO.

Barnekov, T., Boyle, R., and Rich, D. (1989) *Privatism and Urban Policy in Britain and the United States*, New York: Oxford University Press.

Barrett, H. and Larkham, P. J. (1994) *Disguising Development: Façadism in City Centres*, Research Paper 11, Faculty of the Built Environment, University of Central England, Birmingham.

Barton, H., Davis, G. and Guise, R. (1995) *Sustainable Settlements: A Guide for Planners, Designers and Developers*, Luton: Local Government Management Board.

Bastrup-Birk, H. and Doucet, P. (1997) 'European spatial planning from the heart', *Built Environment* 23: 307–14.

Bath City Council (1993) *The Conservation Area of Bath*, Bath City Council.

Bedfordshire County Council (1994) *Bedfordshire Structure Plan 2011: Consultation Draft*, Bedford: Bedfordshire CC.

Begg, I. (1991) 'High technology location and urban areas of Great Britain: developments in the 1980s', *Urban Studies* 28: 961–81.

Bell, S. (1997) *Environmental Law*, London: Blackstone.

Benington, J. (1975) *Local Government Becomes Big Business*, London: Community Development Project Information Unit.

Bentley, I. (1990) 'Ecological urban design', *Architects' Journal* 192 (24): 69–71.

Bentley, I. *et al.* (1985) *Responsive Environments: A Manual for Designers*, London: Architectural Press.

Binney, M. (1984) *Our Vanishing Heritage*, London: Arlington.

Birmingham City Council (Tibbalds, Colbourne and Karski) (1990) *Birmingham Urban Design Study*, City of Birmingham Planning Department.

Bishop, K., Phillips, A. and Warren, L. M. (1997) 'Protected areas for the future: models from the past', *Journal of Environmental Planning and Management* 40: 81–110.

Blackman, T. (1995) *Urban Policy in Practice*, London: Routledge.

Blackstone, T. (1971) *A Fair Start: Provision of Pre-School Education*, London: Allen Lane Penguin Books.

Blowers, A. (ed) (1993) *Planning for a Sustainable Environment*, London: Earthscan.

Blowers, A. (1995) 'Nuclear waste disposal: a technical problem in search of a political solution', in T. Gray (ed) *UK Environmental Policy in the 1990s*, London: Macmillan.

Blunden, J. and Curry, N. (1989) *A People's Charter? Forty Years of the National Parks and Access to the Countryside Act 1949*, London: HMSO.

Boddy, M. and Fudge, C. (1984) *Local Socialism*, London: Macmillan.

Boelhouwer, P. (1991) *Convergence or Divergence in the General Housing Policy in Seven European Countries*, Paper presented at the Conference on the European Network for Housing Research, Oslo.

Bond, A. J. (1997) 'Environmental assessment and planning: a chronology of development in England and Wales', *Journal of Environmental Planning and Management* 40: 261–71.

Booth, P. (1989) 'How effective is zoning on the control of development?', *Environment and Planning B: Planning and Design* 16: 401–15.

Booth, P. (1996) *Controlling Development: Certainty and Discretion in Europe, the USA and Hong Kong*, London: UCL Press.

Booth, P. (1998a) 'Sheffield and its golden frame: the greening of an industrial city', in Mercier, G. and Bèthemont, J. (eds.) *La Ville en Quête de la Nature*, Septentrion, Sillery, Quebec, 99–115.

Booth, P. (1998b) *From Regulation to Discretion: The Evolution of Development Control in the British Planning System 1909–1947*, Paper presented to the 8th International Planning History Conference, Sydney.

Booth, P. and Stafford, T. (1994) 'Revisions and modifications: the effects of change in French *plans d'occupation des sols*', *Environment and Planning B: Planning and Design* 21: 305–322.

Borchardt, K. (1995) *European Integration: The Origins and Growth of the European Community* (4th edn), Luxembourg: Office for the Official Publications of the European Community.

Bowers, J. and Cheshire, P. (1983) *Agriculture, the Countryside, and Land Use: An Economic Critique*, London: Methuen.

Boyer, M. C. (1983) *Dreaming the Rational City*, Cambridge, MA: MIT Press.

Brainsby, M. and Carter, H. (1997) 'Shimizu: part I – the implications for listed building control' and 'Shimizu: part II – the implications for conservation area controls', *Journal of Planning and Environment Law* 1997: 503–10, 603–10.

Bramley, G. (1989) *Land Supply, Planning, and Private Housebuilding*, Bristol: School for Advanced Urban Studies, University of Bristol.

Bramley, G. and Watkins, C. (1996) *Steering the Housing Market: New Building and the Changing Planning System*, Bristol: Policy Press.

Bramley, G., Bartlett, W. and Lambert, C. (1995) *Planning, the Market and Private Housebuilding*, London: UCL Press.

Bramley, G., Munro, M. and Lancaster, S. (1997) *The Economic Determinants of Household Formation: A Literature Review*, London: DETR.

Breheny, M., Gent, T. and Lock, D. (1993) *Alternative Development Patterns: New Settlements* (DoE), London: HMSO.

Brindley, T., Rydin, Y. and Stoker, G. (1996) *Remaking Planning: The Politics of Urban Change* (2nd edn), London: Routledge.

Bristow, M. R. (1992) *The Origins of the Singapore Land Use Planning System*, Occasional Paper 32, Department of Planning and Landscape, University of Manchester.

Brown, A. J. (1972) *The Framework of Regional Economics in the United Kingdom*, Cambridge: Cambridge University Press.

Brundtland Report (1987) (World Commission on Environment and Development) *Our Common Future*, Oxford: Oxford University Press.

Brunivels, P. and Rodrigues, D (1989) *Investing in Enterprise: A Comprehensive Guide to Inner City Regeneration and Urban Renewal*, Oxford: Blackwell.

Bruton, M. and Nicholson, D. (1987), *Local Planning in Practice*, London: Hutchinson.

Buchanan Report (1963) *Traffic in Towns*, London: HMSO.

Buchsbaum, P. A. and Smith, L. J. (eds) (1993) *State and Regional Comprehensive Planning*, Chicago: American Bar Association.

Bull, D. (1980) 'The anti-discretion movement in Britain: fact or phantom', *Journal of Social Welfare Law* 3 (March), 65–84.

Burns, D., Hambleton, R. and Hoggett, P. (1994) *The Politics of Decentralisation: Revitalising Local Democracy*, London: Macmillan.

Bury Metropolitan Borough Council (1993) *Bury Unitary Development Plan: Deposit Plan*, Bury: Bury MBC.

Button, K. J. (ed.) (1998) *Road Pricing, Traffic Congestion, and the Environment: Issues of Efficiency and Social Feasibility*, Northampton, MA: Edward Elgar.

Button, K. J. and Pitfield, D. (eds) (1991) *Transport Deregulation: An International Movement*, London: Macmillan.

Byrne, D. (1989) *Beyond the Inner City*, Milton Keynes: Open University Press.

Callies, D. L. (ed.) (1996) *Takings*, Chicago: American Bar Association.

Callies, D. L. and Grant, M. (1991) 'Paying for growth and planning gain: an Anglo-American comparison of development conditions, impact fees, and development agreements', *Urban Lawyer* 23: 221–48 [also in Freilich and Bushek (1995) *Exactions, Impact Fees and Dedications*].

Camden, London Borough of (1979) *A Plan for Camden: The Environmental Code*, London Borough of Camden.

Cameron, G. C. (1974) 'Regional economic policy in the United Kingdom', in Hansen, N. M. (ed.) *Public Policy and Regional Economic Development: The Experience of Nine Western Countries*, Cambridge, MA: Ballinger.

Campbell, B. (1993) *Goliath: Britain's Dangerous Places*, London: Methuen.

Campbell, L. H., Avery, M., Donald, P., Evans, A. D., Green, R. E. and Wilson, J. D. (1997) *A Review of the Indirect Effects of Pesticides on Birds*, JNCC Report 227, Peterborough: Joint Nature Conservation Committee.

Carnwath, R. (1992) 'Environmental enforcement: the need for a specialist court', *Journal of Planning and Environment Law* 1992: 799–808.

Carson, R. (1962) *Silent Spring*, New York: Houghton Mifflin.

Caves, R. W. (1992) *Land Use Planning: The Ballot Box Revolution*, Newbury Park, CA: Sage.

CEC (1979) *State of the Environment: Second Report*, Luxembourg: Office for the Official Publications of the EC.

CEC (1990) *Green Paper on the Urban Environment: Communication from the Commission to the Council and Parliament* [COM (90) 218 final], Brussels.

CEC (1991) *Europe 2000: Outlook for the Development of the Community's Territory*, Luxembourg: Office for the Official Publications of the EC.

CEC (1994) *Europe 2000+ – Cooperation for European Territorial Development*, Luxembourg: Office for the Official Publications of the EC.

CEC (1995) *The Prospective Development of the Northern Seaboard* (Regional Development Studies 18), Luxembourg: Office for the Official Publications of the EC.

CEC (1996a) *First Report on Economic and Social Cohesion: Preliminary Edition*, Luxembourg: Office for the Official Publications of the EC.

CEC (1996b) *Study of Prospects in the Atlantic Regions* (Regional Development Studies 8), Luxembourg: Office for the Official Publications of the EC.

CEC (1996c) *Prospects for the Development of the Central and Capital Cities and Regions* (Regional Development Studies 22), Luxembourg: Office for the Official Publications of the EC.

CEC (1996d) *European Sustainable Cities Final Report* (EC Expert Group on the Urban Environment), Luxembourg: Office for the Official Publications of the EC.

CEC (1997a) *European Spatial Development Perspective, First Official Draft Presented at the Informal Meeting of Ministers Responsible for Spatial Planning in the Member States of the European Union, Noordwijk, June 1997*, Luxembourg: Office for the Official Publications of the EC.

CEC (1997b) *The EU Compendium of Spatial Planning Systems and Policies* (Regional Development Studies 28), Luxembourg: Office for the Official Publications of the EC.

CEC (1998) *Completed Draft of the European Spatial Development Perspective* Luxembourg: Office for the Official Publications of the EC.

Champion, A. (1994) 'Population change and migration in Britain since 1981: evidence for continuing deconcentration', *Environment and Planning A* 26: 1501–20.

Champion, T. (1996) 'Protecting the monuments: archaeological legislation from the 1882 Act to PPG 16', in Hunter, M. (ed.) *Preserving the Past: The Rise of Heritage in Modern Britain*, Stroud: Sutton.

Chapman, D. and Larkham, P. J. (1992) *Discovering the Art of Relationship: Urban Design, Aesthetic Control and Design Guidance*, Research Paper 9, Faculty of the Built Environment, Birmingham Polytechnic.

Cherry, G. E. (1974) *The Evolution of British Town Planning*, Leighton Buzzard: Leonard Hill.

Cherry, G. E. (1996) *Town Planning in Britain Since 1900*, Oxford: Blackwell.

Cherry, G. E. and Rogers, A. W. (1996) *Rural Change and Planning: England and Wales in the Twentieth Century*, London: Spon.

Cheshire County Council (1977) *Cheshire Structure Plan: Written Statement*, Chester: Cheshire CC.

Cheshire, P. (1985) 'The environmental implications of European agricultural support policies' in Baldock, D. and Condor, D. (eds) *Can the CAP Fit The Environment?*, London: Institute for European Environmental Policy.

Chisholm, M. (1995) *Britain on the Edge of Europe*, London: Routledge.

Clark, B. D., Bisset, R. and Wathern, P. (1980) *Environmental Impact Assessment: A Bibliography with Abstracts*, London: Mansell.

Clawson, M. and Hall, P. (1973) *Planning and Urban Growth: An Anglo-American Comparison*, Baltimore: Johns Hopkins University Press.

Cocks, R. (1998) 'The mysterious origin of the law for conservation', *Journal of Planning and Environment Law* 1998: 203–9.

Committee on Spatial Development (1994) *Principles for European Spatial Development Policy*, Paper adopted by the Informal Meeting of Ministers of Spatial Planning, September 1994, Leipzig.

Congleton Borough Council (1992) *Congleton Local Plan: Consultation Draft*, Congleton: Congleton BC.

Coombes, M. (1994) 'The regional policy maps – plus ça change, plus la même chose?', *Town and Country Planning* 63: 20–2.

Corkindale, J. (1998) *Reforming Land Use Planning: Property Rights Approaches*, London: Institute of Economic Affairs.

Couch, C. (1990) *Urban Renewal Theory and Practice*, London: Macmillan.

Council of Europe (1983) *European Regional/Spatial Planning Charter* (Torremolinos Charter) Strasbourg: CoE.

Countryside Commission (1976) *The Lake District Upland Management Experiment* (CCP 93) (with Lake District Special Planning Board), London: CC.

Countryside Commission (1986) 'What is really happening to the landscape?', *Countryside Commission News* 23: 4–5.

Countryside Commission (1993) *Design in the Countryside* (CCP 418).

Countryside Commission (1994) *Design in the Countryside Experiments*, Cheltenham: CC.

Countryside Commission (1996) *Village Design: Making Local Character Count in New Development: Guidance to Local Communities*, Cheltenham: CC.

Countryside Commission (1998a) *Countryside Stewardship: Monitoring and Evaluation of the Pilot Scheme 1991–1996* (Research Note 3), Cheltenham: CC.

Countryside Commission (1998b) *Countryside Planning Statement*, Cheltenham: CC.

Countryside Commission (1998c) *Agricultural Landscapes: A Third Look* (CCP 521), Cheltenham: CC.

Countryside Commission (1998d) *The New Agency – A Prospectus*, Cheltenham, CC.

Countryside Commission (1998e) *Planning for Countryside Quality – Policy Statement*, Cheltenham: CC.

Countryside Commission and English Nature (1996) *The Character of England: Landscape, Wildlife and Natural Features*, Cheltenham: C.C. and Peterborough: English Nature.

Cox, G. and Lowe, P. (1983) 'A battle not the war: the politics of the Wildlife and Countryside Act', in Gilg, A. (ed.) *Countryside Planning Yearbook 1983*, Norwich: Geo Books.

Cox, G., Lowe, P. and Winter, M. (1988) 'Private rights and public responsibilties: the prospects for agricultural and environmental controls', *Journal of Rural Studies* 4: 323–37.

Craig, P. and de Búrca, G. (1995) *EC Law, Text, Cases and Materials*, Oxford: Clarendon.

Cross, D. T. and Bristow, M. R. (eds) (1983) *English Structure Planning: A Commentary on Procedure and Practice in the Seventies*, London: Pion.

Crossman, R. H. S. (1975) *The Diaries of a Cabinet Minister: vol 1: 1964–66*, London: Hamish Hamilton and Jonathan Cape.

Crow, S. (1996) 'Development control: the child that grew up in the cold', *Planning Perspectives* 11: 399–411.

Crow, S. (1998) 'Challenging appeal decisions, or the use and abuse of the "toothcomb"', *Journal of Planning and Environment Law* 1998: 419–31.

Croydon London Borough (1979) *Tomorrow's Croydon*, LB Croydon.

Cullen, G. (1961) *Townscape*, London: Architectural Press.

Cullingworth, J. B. (1972) *Town and Country Planning in Britain* (4th edn), London: Allen and Unwin.

Cullingworth, J. B. (1975) *Environmental Planning 1939–1969, vol 1: Reconstruction and Land Use Planning 1939–1947*, London: HMSO.

Cullingworth, J. B. (1979) *Environmental Planning 1939–1969, vol 3: New Towns Policy*, London: HMSO.

Cullingworth, J.B. (1980) *Environmental Planning 1939–1969, vol 4: Land Values, Compensation and Betterment*, London: HMSO.

Cullingworth, J. B. (1990) *Town and Country Planning in Britain* (10th edn), London: Unwin Hyman.

Cullingworth, J. B (1993) *The Political Culture of Planning: American Land Use Planning in Comparative Perspective*, New York: Routledge.

Cullingworth, J. B. (1997a) 'British land-use planning: a failure to cope with change?', *Urban Studies* 34: 945–60.

Cullingworth, J. B. (1997b) 'Fifty years of the 1947 Act' and 'Planning policy – time for change', *Town and Country Planning* 66: 130, 156–7.

Cullingworth, J. B. and Karn, V. A. (1968) *The Ownership and Management of Housing in the New Towns*, London: HMSO.

Cullingworth, J. B. and Nadin, V. (1997) *Town and Country Planning in the UK* (12th edn), London: Routledge.

Curry, N. (1994) *Countryside Recreation, Access and Land Use Planning*, London: Spon.

Curry, N. (1997) 'Enjoyment of the countryside', *Town and Country Planning* 66: 131–3.

Daintiff, T. (1997) *Constitutional Implications of Executive Self-Regulation: The New Administrative Law*, London: Institute of Advanced Legal Studies.

Damesick, P. J. (1987a) 'The changing economic context for regional development in the United Kingdom', in Damesick, P. J. and Wood, P. A. *Regional Problems, Problem Regions and Public Policy in the United Kingdom*, Oxford: Clarendon.

Damesick, P. J. (1987b) 'Regional economic change since the 1960s', in Damesick, P. J. and Wood, P. A. *Regional Problems, Problem Regions and Public Policy in the United Kingdom*, Oxford: Clarendon.

Damesick, P. J. and Wood, P. A. (1987) *Regional Problems, Problem Regions and Public Policy in the United Kingdom*, Oxford: Clarendon.

Darlow, C. (1972) *Enclosed Shopping Centres*, London: Architectural Press.

David, T. (ed.) (1993) *Educational Provision for our Youngest Children: A European Perspective*, London: Paul Chapman.

Davidson, J. and Wibberley, G. (1977) *Planning and the Rural Environment*, Oxford: Pergamon.

Davidson, S. (1998) 'Spinning the wheel of empowerment', *Planning* 3 (April), 14–15.

Davies, H. W. E. (1980) 'The relevance of development control', *Town Planning Review* 51: 5–17.

Davies, H. W. E. (1993) 'Towards a European planning system?' *Planning Practice and Research* 9: 63–9.

Davies, H. W. E. and Gosling, J. A., with Hsia, M. T. (1994) *The Impact of the European Community on Land Use Planning in the UK*, London: RTPI.

Davies, H. W. E., Edwards, D. and Rowley, A. R. (1986) 'The relationship between development plans, development control and appeals', *The Planner* 72(10): 11–15.

Davies, H. W. E., Edwards, D., Hooper, A. J. and Punter, J. V. (1989) *Planning Control in Western Europe*, London: HMSO.

Davis, K. C. (1969) *Discretionary Justice: A Preliminary Inquiry*, Baton Rouge: Louisiana State University Press.

Davison, I. (1990) *Good Design in Housing*, London: House Builders Federation and the Royal Institute of British Architects.

Deakin, N. and Edwards, J. (1993) *The Enterprise Culture and the Inner Cities*, Oxford: Oxford University Press.

Delafons, J. (1969) *Land Use Controls in the United States*, Cambridge, MA: MIT Press.

Delafons, J. (1990) *Aesthetic Control: A Report on Methods Used in the USA to Control the Design of Buildings*, Monograph 41, Institute of Urban and Regional Development, University of California, Berkeley.

Delafons, J. (1997a) *Politics and Preservation: A Policy History of the Built Heritage 1882–1996* London: Spon.

Delafons, J. (1997b) 'Sustainable conservation', *Built Environment* 23: 111–120.

Delafons, J. (1998), 'Reforming the British planning system, 1964–1965 – The Planning Advisory Group and the genesis of the planning act of 1968', *Planning Perspectives* 13: 373–87.

De Leuw, Cather and Partners, *Manchester Rapid Transit Study*, Manchester: Manchester City Transport.

Dennis, N. (1972) *Public Participation and Planners' Blight*, London: Faber.

Dennis, R. (1978) 'The decline of manufacturing employment in Greater London: 1966–74', *Urban Studies* 15: 63–73.

Department of Economic Affairs (1965) *The North West Study*, London: HMSO.

Department of National Heritage (1996) *Protecting our Heritage: A Consultation Document on the Built Heritage of England and Wales*, London: DNH.

Department of the Environment, see DoE.

Department of the Environment, Transport and the Regions, see DETR.

Department of Transport, see DoT.

De Smith, S., Woolf, H., and Jowell, J. (1995) *Judicial Review of Administrative Action* (4th edn), London: Sweet and Maxwell.

DETR (1997a) *Air Quality and Land Use Planning*, London: TSO.

DETR (1997b) *Mitigation Measures in Environmental Statements*, London: DETR.

DETR (1998a) *Urban Development Corporations: Performance and Good Practice*, London: TSO.

DETR (1998b) *Regeneration Programmes – The Way Forward, Discussion Paper*, London: DETR.

DETR (1998c) *Community-Based Regeneration Initiatives: A Working Paper*, London: DETR.

DETR (1998d) *New Deal for Communities: Phase I Proposals*, London: DETR.

DETR (1998e) *Access to the Open Countryside in England and Wales: A Consultation Paper*, London: DETR.

DETR (1998f) *The Future of Regional Planning Guidance: Consultation Paper*, London: DETR.

DETR (1998g) *Modernising Local Government* (Cm 4014), London: HMSO.

DETR (1998h) *Prevention of Dereliction through the Planning System* (Circular 2/98), London: TSO.

DETR (1998i) *Sites of Special Scientific Interest: Better Protection and Management: Consultation Paper*, London: DETR.

DETR (1998j) *Planning and Affordable Housing* (Circular 6/98), London: TSO.

DETR (1999, forthcoming) *A Good Practice Guide for Design in the Planning System*, London: TSO.

Diamond, D. R. and Spence, N. A. (1983) *Regional Policy Evaluation: A Methodological Review and the Scottish Example*, Aldershot: Gower.

Dinan, D. (1999) *Ever Closer Union?: An Introduction to the European Community*, London: Macmillan.

Dobry Report (1973) *Review of the Development Control System: Interim Report*, London: HMSO.

Dobry Report (1975) *Review of the Development Control System: Final Report*, London: HMSO.

DoE (1971a) *Long Term Population Distribution in Great Britain: A Study – Report by an Inter-Departmental Study Group*, London: HMSO (reprinted in Cullingworth, J. B. *Problems of an Urban Society, vol 3: Planning for Change*, London: Allen & Unwin, 1973).

DoE (1971b) *Memorandum on Part I of the Town and Country Planning Act 1968* (Circular 44/71), London: HMSO.

DoE (1972a) *Development Involving the Use or Storage in Bulk of Hazardous Materials* (Circular 1/72), London: HMSO.

DoE (1972b) *Draft Circular on Planning and Clean Air*, London: DoE.

DoE (1972c) *Report of the Working Party on Local Authority/Private Enterprise Partnership Schemes*, London: HMSO.

DoE (1973a) *Planning and Noise* (Circular 10/73), London: HMSO.

DoE (1973b) *Local Transport Grants* (Circular 104/73), London: HMSO.

DoE (1974a) *Promotion of High Standards of Architectural Design* (Matthew Skillington Report), London: DoE.

DoE (1974b), *Structure Plans* (Circular 98/74), London: HMSO.

DoE (1974c) *Strategic Plan for the North West*, London: HMSO.

DoE (1975) *What is our Heritage?* London: HMSO.

DoE (1976a) *The Value of Standards for the External Residential Environment*, London: DoE.

DoE (1976b) *Design Guidance Survey*, London: DoE.

DoE (1976c) *Control of Pollution Act 1974 – Implementation of Part II: Noise* (Circular 2/76), London: HMSO.

DoE (1976d) *Control of Smells from the Animal Waste Processing Industry* (Circular 43/76), London: HMSO.

DoE (1976e) *Control of Pollution Act 1974: (Waste on Land) Disposal Licences* (Circular 55/76), London: HMSO.

DoE (1976f) *Inner Urban Policy* (Press Release 835), London: Department of the Environment.

DoE (1977a) *Housing Policy: A Consultative Document* (Cmnd 6851), London: HMSO.

DoE (1977b) *Residential Roads and Footpaths* (Design Bulletin 32), London: HMSO.

DoE (1977c) *Memorandum on Structure and Local Plans* (Circular 55/77), London: HMSO.

DoE (1977d) *Local Government and the Industrial Strategy* (Circular 71/77), London: HMSO.

DoE (1978) *Examination in Public of the Structure Plan for Cheshire: Transcript of the Proceedings, Tuesday 22 November 1977*, Manchester: DoE North West Regional Office.

DoE (1980) *Development Control: Policy and Practice* (Circular 22/80), London: HMSO.

DoE (1981) *Organisation of Ancient Monuments and Historic Buildings in England: A Consultation Paper*, London: DoE.

DoE (1983) *Draft Circular on Good Design and Development Control* (mimeo), London: DoE.

DoE (1984) *Land for Housing* (Circular 15/84), London: HMSO.

DoE (1985a) *Development and Employment* (Circular 14/85), London: HMSO.

DoE (1985b) *Aesthetic Control* (Circular 31/85), London: HMSO.

DoE (1986) *The Future of Development Plans, A Consultation Paper*, London: DoE.

DoE (1987) *Historic Buildings and Conservation Areas: Policy and Procedures* (Circular 8/87), London: HMSO.

DoE (1988) *Environmental Assessment* (Circular 15/88), London: HMSO.

DoE (1989) *Landfill Sites: Development Control* (Circular 17/89), London: HMSO.

DoE (1990a) *Archaeology and Planning* (PPG 16), London: HMSO.

DoE (1990b) *Area Renewal, Unfitness, Slum Clearance and Enforcement Action* (Circular 6/90), London: HMSO.

DoE (1991a) *Water Industry Investment: Planning Considerations* (Circular 17/91), London: HMSO.

DoE (1991b) *Planning and Affordable Housing* (Circular 7/91), London: HMSO.

DoE (1991c) *Time for Design: Monitoring the Initiative*, London: HMSO.

DoE (1992/1997), *General Policy and Principles* (PPG 1), London: HMSO.

DoE (1992a) *Planning Policy Guidance: Development Plans and Regional Planning Guidance* (PPG 12) London: HMSO.

DoE (1992b) *Development Plans: A Good Practice Guide*, London: HMSO.

DoE (1992c) *Housing* (PPG 3) (revised), London: HMSO.

DoE (1992d) *Planning, Pollution and Waste Management*, London: HMSO.

DoE (1992e) *Land Use Planning Policy and Climate Change*, London: HMSO.

DoE (1992f) *Planning Controls for Hazardous Substances* (Circular 11/92), London: HMSO.

DoE (1993a) *Environmental Appraisal of Development Plans: A Good Practice Guide*, London: HMSO.

DoE (1993b) *Renewable Energy* (PPG 22), London: HMSO.

DoE (1994a) *Quality in Town and Country: A Discussion Document*, London: DoE.

DoE (1994b) *Quality in Town and Country: Discussion of Responses to the Discussion Document*, London: DoE.

DoE (1994c) *Planning and the Historic Environment* (PPG 15), London: HMSO.

DoE (1994d) *Regional Planning Guidance for the South East* (RPG 9), London: HMSO.

DoE (1994e) *Environmental Protection Act 1990, Part II, Waste Management Licensing, The Framework Directive on Waste* (Circular 11/94), London: HMSO.

DoE (1994f) *Hazardous Substances Consents: A Review of the Operation of Statutory Planning Controls over Hazardous Substances*, London: HMSO.

DoE (1994g) *Planning and Pollution Control* (PPG 23), London: HMSO.

DoE (1994h) *Planning and Noise* (PPG 24), London: HMSO.

DoE (1994i) *Transport* (PPG 13), London: HMSO.

DoE (1995a) *Derelict Land Prevention and the Planning System*, London: HMSO.

DoE (1995b) *General Development Order Consolidation 1995* (Circular 9/95), London: HMSO.

DoE (1995c) *Preparation of Environmental Statements for Planning Projects that Require Environmental Assessment: A Good Practice Guide*, London: HMSO.

DoE (1995d) *Projections of Households in England to 2016*, London: HMSO.

DoE (1995e) *Quality in Town and Country: Urban Design Campaign*, London: DoE.

DoE (1995f) *Planning Policy Guidance 13: A Guide to Better Practice: Reducing the Need to Travel through Land Use and Transport Planning*, London: HMSO.

DoE (1995g) *Making Waste Work: A Strategy for Sustainable Waste Management in England and Wales* (Cm 3040), London: HMSO.

DoE (1996a) *Planning and Affordable Housing* (Circular 13/96), London: HMSO.

DoE (1996b) *Urban Trends in England: Latest Evidence from the 1991 Census*, Housing and Society Research Group, University of Newcastle Upon Tyne, London: HMSO.

DoE (1997a) *The Countryside: Environmental Quality and Economic and Social Development* (PPG 7), London: HMSO.

DoE (1997b) *Planning Obligations* (Circular 1/97), London: HMSO.

Donahue, J. J. and Siegelman, P. (1998) 'Allocating resources among prisons and social programs in the battle v crime', *Journal of Legal Studies* 27: 1–43.

DoT (1993) *Transport Policies and Programmes (package bids)*, London: HMSO.

DoT (1994) *Trunk Roads in England: 1994 Review*, London: HMSO.

DoT (1995) *Better Places through Bypasses: Report of the Bypass Demonstration Project*, London: HMSO.

Downs, A. (1962) 'The law of peak-hour expressway convergence', *Traffic Quarterly* 16: 393–409.

Downs, A. (1972) 'Up and down with ecology: the issue-attention cycle', *The Public Interest* 28 (Summer): 38–50.

Downs, A. (1992) *Stuck in Traffic: Coping with Peak-hour Traffic Congestion*, Washington DC: Brookings Institution, and Cambridge, MA: Lincoln Institute of Land Policy.

Dudley Report (1944) *The Design of Dwellings*, Central Housing Advisory Committee, London: HMSO.

Dunleavy, P. (1981) *The Politics of Mass Housing in Britain 1945–75: A Study of Corporate Power and Professional Influence in the Welfare State*, Oxford: Clarendon Press.

Dwyer, J. and Hodge, I. (1996) *Countryside in Trust: Land Management by Conservation, Amenity and Recreation Organisations*, Chichester: Wiley.

Eccles, C. (1990) *The Rose Theatre*, London: Hern.

Edwards, G. and Spence, D. (1997) *The European Commission* (2nd edn), London: Catermill International.

Edwards. J. and Batley, R. (1978) *The Politics of Positive Discrimination: An Evaluation of the Urban Programme 1967–77*, London: Tavistock.

Elson, M. (1986) *Green Belts*, London: Heinemann.

Elson, M., Walker, S. and Macdonald, R. (1993) *The Effectiveness of Green Belts* (DoE), London: HMSO.

Elson, M., Steenberg, C. and Mendham, N. (1996) *Green Belts and Affordable Housing: Can We Have Both?*, Bristol: Policy Press.

Engels, F. (1845) *The Condition of the Working Class in England* (reprinted 1987, Penguin: Harmondsworth).

English Heritage (1995) *Conservation Area Practice Guidance Note* (2nd edition), London: English Heritage.

English Heritage (1996) *The Monuments Protection Programme 1986–90*, London: English Heritage.

English Heritage (1997a) *Conservation Area Appraisal*, London: English Heritage.

English Heritage (1997b) *Sustaining the Historic Environment: New Perspectives on the Future*, London: English Heritage.

English Partnerships (1995) *Time for Design: Good Practice in Building Landscape and Urban Design*, London: EP.

Environment Agency (1997) *Liaison with Local Planning Authorities*, London: EA.

Essex County Council (1973) *A Design Guide for Residential Areas*, Chelmsford: Essex County Council.

Essex Planning Officers Association (1998) *The Essex Design Guide for Residential and Mixed Use Areas*, Chelmsford: Essex County Council.

Evans, A. W. (1988) *No Room! No Room! The Costs of the British Town and Country Planning System*, London: Institute of Economic Affairs.

Evans, A. W. (1991) 'Rabbit hutches on postage stamps: planning, development and political economy', *Urban Studies* 28: 853–70.

Faludi, A. and Zonneveld, W. (1997) 'Shaping Europe: The ESDP', *Built Environment* 23: 257- 66.

Farmer, E. and Smith, R (1975) 'Overspill theory: a metropolitan case study', *Urban Studies* 12: 151–68.

Fit, J. and Kragt, R. (1994) 'The long road to European spatial planning: a matter of patience and mission', *Tijdschrift voor Economische en Sociale Geografie* 85: 461–5.

Fordham, R. (1993) 'Why planning gain is not a tax on land betterment', *Planning* no. 1014, 16 April 1993.

Forrest, R., Murie, A. and Williams, P. (1990) *Home Ownership: Differentiation and Fragmentation*, London: Unwin Hyman.

Forsyth, C. (1996) 'Of fig leaves and fairy tales: the ultra vires doctrine, the sovereignty of parliament and judicial review', *Cambridge Law Journal* 55: 122–40.

Fosler, R. S. and Berger, R. A. (eds) (1982) *Public-Private Partnership in American Cities*, Lexington: Heath.

Fothergill, S. and Gudgin, G. (1982) *Unequal Growth: Urban and Regional Employment Change in the UK*, London: Heinemann.

Fothergill, S. and Guy, N. (1990) *Retreat from the Regions: Corporate Change and the Closure of Factories*, London: Jessica Kingsley.

Fothergill, S., Kitson, M. and Monk, S. (1983) 'The impact of the new and expanded towns programmes on industrial location in Britain', *Regional Studies* 17: 251–60.

Fowler, P. (1989) 'Heritage: a post-modern perspective', in Uzzell, D. L. (ed.) *Heritage Interpretation: The Natural and Built Environment*, London: Belhaven.

Franks Report (1957) *Report of the Committee on Administrative Tribunals and Inquiries* (Cmnd 218), London: HMSO.

Fraser, R. (1991) *Working Together in the 1990s*, London: Institute of Housing.

Freilich, R. H. and Bushek, D. W. (eds) (1995) *Exactions, Impact Fees and Dedications*, Chicago: American Bar Association.

Gaze, J. (1998) *Figures in a Landscape: A History of the National Trust*, London: Barrie & Jackson.

Geddes, P. (1905) *Civics as Applied Sociology*, reprinted in Meller, H. (ed) *The Ideal City*, Leicester University Press.

Gibb, K. and Munro, M. (1991) *Housing Finance in the UK*, Basingstoke: Macmillan.

Gillie, F. B. and Hughes, P. L. (1950) *Some Principles of Land Planning*, Liverpool: Liverpool University Press.

Gittus, E. (1976) *Flats, Families and the Under-Fives*, London: Routledge and Kegan Paul.

Glasgow City Council (1960) *First Quinquennial Review: Survey Report*, Glasgow: Glasgow CC.

Glasson, B. and Booth, P. (1992) 'Negotiation and delay in the development control process', *Town Planning Review* 63: 63–78.

Glasson, J., Therivel, R. and Chadwick, A. (1994) *Introduction to Environmental Impact Assessment*, London: UCL Press.

Glennerster, H. and Hills (eds) (1998) *The State of Welfare*, Oxford: Oxford University Press.

Goodchild, B. (1994) 'Housing design, urban form and sustainable development', *Town Planning Review* 65:143–57.

Goodwin, P. B. (1994) *Traffic Growth and the Dynamics of Sustainable Transport Policies*, (Linacre Lecture) Transport Studies Unit, Oxford.

Goss, A. (1965) *The Architect and Town Planning*, London: Royal Institute of British Architects.

Government Office for the South West (1997) *Land at Kensington Bus Depot, London Road, Bath: Appeal by Safeway Stores plc* (APP/FO114/A/95/255444), Bristol: GOSW.

Gowers Report (1950) *Report of the Committee on Houses of Outstanding Historic or Architectural Interest*, London: HMSO.

Graham, J. (1957) 'Clean air: the relationship between land use planning and air pollution', *Journal of the Town Planning Institute* 43: 166–73.

Graham, T. (1996) 'PPG 23 and the duplication of controls', *Journal of Planning and Environment Law* 1996: 816–20.

Grant, M. (1976) 'The Community Land Act: an overview', *Journal of Planning Law* 1976: 614-26, 675-90, 732-48.

Grant, M. (1978a) 'Planning, politics and the Judges', *Journal of Planning Law* 1978:512–23.

Grant, M. (1978b) 'Community land?', *Journal of Planning Law* 1978: 669-84.

Grant, M. (1979) 'Britain's Community Land Act: a post-mortem', *Urban Law and Policy* 2: 359–73.

Grant, M (1982) *Urban Planning Law*, London: Sweet & Maxwell.

Grant, M. (1986) 'Planning and land taxation: Development Land Tax and beyond', *Journal of Planning and Environment Law* 1986: 92–106.

Grant, M. (1991) 'Betterment again? The planning balance in the 1990s', *Journal of Planning and Environment Law Occasional Paper* 18, London: Sweet & Maxwell.

Grant, M. (1992) 'Planning law and the British planning system', *Town Planning Review* 63: 3–12.

Grant, M. (1994) 'Planning permission for sale?' *Current Problems in Property Law: Blundell Memorial Lectures* 71–89.

Grant, M. (1996) *Permitted Development* (2nd edn), London: Sweet & Maxwell.

Graves, P. and Ross, S. (1991) 'Conservation areas: a presumption to preserve', *Estates Gazette* 913: 108–10.

Greater London Development Plan: Report of the Panel of Inquiry (1973), London: HMSO.

Grebler, L. (1964) *Urban Renewal in European Countries: Its Emergence and Potentials*, Philadelphia: University of Pennsylvania Press.

Green, A. (1994) *The Geography of Poverty and Wealth*, Warwick: University of Warwick.

Green, A. (1998) 'The changing geography of non-employment in Britain', In Lawless, P., Martin, R., and Hardy, S. (eds) *Unemployment and Social Exclusion: Landscapes of Labour Inequality*, London: Jessica Kingsley.

Greenwich London Borough (1986) *The People's Plan*, LB Greenwich.

Griffith, J. A. G. (1977) *The Politics of the Judiciary*, London: Fontana.

Gummer, J. (1994) 'Quality in town and country' (speech), London: DoE.

Gummer, J. (1997) Personal interview by John Punter, (at the House of Commons), July.

Gyford, J. (1994) 'Politics and planning in London', in Simmie J. (ed.) *Planning for London*, London: UCL Press.

Haar, C. M. and Kayden, J. S. (eds.) *Zoning and the American Dream: Promises Still to Keep*, Chicago: Planners Press.

Hagman, D. G. and Misczynski, D. J. (1978) *Windfalls for Wipeouts: Land Value Capture and Compensation*, Washington, DC: American Society of Planning Officials.

Hall, A. (1976) 'Management in the urban fringe', *Countryside Recreation Review* 1, London: CC.

Hall, P. (ed) (1965) *Land Values*, London: Sweet & Maxwell.

Hall, P. (1974) *Urban and Regional Planning*, Harmondsworth: Penguin.

Hall, P. (1980) *Great Planning Disasters*, London: Weidenfeld & Nicolson.

Hall, P. (1988) *Cities of Tomorrow*, Oxford: Blackwell.

Hall, P. (1989) *London 2001*, London: Unwin Hyman.

Hall, P. (1997) 'The view from the London centre: twenty-five years of planning at the DoE' in Blowers, A. and Evans, B. (eds) *Town Planning into the 21st Century*, London: Routledge.

Hall, P., Gracey, H., Drewett, R., and Thomas, R. (1973) *The Containment of Urban England*, London: Allen & Unwin .

Hallett, G., Randall, P. and West, E. G. (1973) *Regional Policy for Ever? Essays on the History, Theory and Political Economy of Forty Years of Regionalism*, London: Institute of Economic Affairs.

Hardin, G. (1968) 'The tragedy of the commons', *Science* 162: 1243–48.

Harding, A. (1990) 'Public–private partnerships in urban regeneration', in Campbell, M. (ed) *Local Economic Policy*, London: Cassell.

Hardy, D. (1991) *From Garden Cities to New Towns*, London: Spon.

Hardy, D. and Ward, C. (1984) *Arcadia For All: The Legacy of a Makeshift Landscape*, London: Mansell.

Harloe, M. (1985) *Private Rented Housing in the United States and Europe*, London: Croom Helm.

Harlow, C. and Rawlings, R. (1997) *Law and Administration*, (2nd edn), London: Butterworth.

Harrison, M. L. and Mordey, R. (eds) (1982) *Planning Control: Philosophies, Prospects and Practice*, London: Croom Helm.

Harvey, J. H. (1954) Paper presented to the Ancient Monuments Society; restated in Harvey, J. H. (1972) *Conservation of Buildings*, London: Baker.

Harvey, J. H. (1993) 'The origin of listed buildings', *Transactions of the Ancient Monuments Society* 37: 1–20.

Hasegawa, J. (1992) *Replanning the Blitzed City Centre*, Buckingham: Open University Press.

Hass-Klau, C. (1990) *The Pedestrian and City Traffic*, London: Belhaven.

Hass-Klau, C., Nold, I., Bocker, G. and Crampton, G. (1992) *Civilised Streets: A Guide to Traffic Calming*, Brighton: Environmental and Transport Planning.

Haughton, G. and Hunter, C. (1994) *Sustainable Cities*, London: Jessica Kingsley.

Healey, P. (1997) *Collaborative Planning: Shaping Places in Fragmented Societies*, London: UCL Press.

Healey, P. and Williams, R.H. (1993) 'European urban planning diversity and convergence', *Urban Studies* 30: 699–718.

Healey, P., Davis, J., Wood, M., and Elson, M. (1982) *The Implementation of Development Plans: Report for the Department of the Environment*, Oxford Polytechnic School of Town Planning (unpublished manuscript).

Healey, P., McNamara, P., Elson, M. and Doak, A. (1988) *Land Use Planning and the Mediation of Urban Change: The British Planning System in Practice*, Cambridge: Cambridge University Press.

Healey, P., Khakee, A., Motte, A., and Needham, B. (eds) (1997) *Making Strategic Spatial Plans: Innovation in Europe*, London: UCL Press.

Healey, R. G. (1976) *Land Use and the States*, Baltimore: Johns Hopkins University Press.

Healy, A. (1998) 'Agenda 2000 and structure fund reform', *Town and Country Planning* 67: 68–70.

Hebbert, M. (1992) 'The British garden city: metamorphosis', in Ward, S. V. (ed.) *The Garden City: Past, Present, Future*, London: Spon.

Heighway, C. M. (ed) (1972) *The Erosion of History: Archaeology and Planning in Towns*, London: Council for British Archaeology.

Henderson, R. (1984) 'The employment performance of established manufacturing industry in Scottish new towns', *Urban Studies* 21: 295–315.

Hendry, J. (1993) 'Conservation areas in Northern Ireland: an alternative approach', *Town Planning Review* 64: 415–34.

Hennessy, P. (1992) *Never Again: Britain 1945–1951*, London: Jonathan Cape (Vintage paperback edition 1993).

Heraud, B. J. (1966) 'The new towns and London's housing problem', *Urban Studies* 3: 8–21.

Heraud, B. J. (1968) 'Social class and the new towns' *Urban Studies* 5: 35–58.

Herbert-Young, N. (ed) (1999) *Law, Policy and Development in the Rural Environment*, Cardiff: University of Wales Press.

Heseltine, M. (1980) 'Statement of design standards', in DoE Circular 22/80.

Heseltine, M. (1987) *Where There's a Will*, London: Hutchinson.

Hewison, R. (1987) *The Heritage Industry: Britain in a State of Decline*, London: Methuen.

Hillman, J. (1969) 'New houses for old – when?', *The Observer*, 7 February 1969.

Hillman, J. (1990) *Planning for Beauty: The Case for Design Guidelines*, Royal Fine Art Commission, London: HMSO.

Hills, J. (1991) *Unravelling Housing Finance*, Oxford: Clarendon.

Hirst, C. (1996) 'An avenging angel of the Tory right . . . ', *Planning Week* 4: 12–13.

Hodge, I. (1998) 'Property institutions and the provision of countryside goods', *ROOTS '98 Conference Proceedings*, London: RICS.

Holdgate, M. W. (1979) *A Perspective of Pollution*, Cambridge: Cambridge University Press.

Holford, W. G. (1953) 'Design in city centres': part 3 of MHLG *Design in Town and Village*, London: HMSO.

Holliday, J. (ed.) (1973) *City Centre Redevelopment: A Study of British City Centre Planning and Case Studies of Five English City Centres*, London: Charles Knight.

Holmans, A. (1987) *Housing Policy in Britain: A History*, London: Croom Helm.

Holmans, A. (1995) *Housing Need and Demand in England 1991 to 2100*, York: Joseph Rowntree Foundation.

Hookway, R. (1967) 'The management of Britain's rural land', in *Proceedings of the Town Planning Institute Summer School, Belfast, 1967*, London: RTPI.

Horne, M. (1993) 'The listing process in Scotland and the statutory protection of vernacular building types', *Town Planning Review* 64: 375–93.

Hornsey Metropolitan Borough, (1945) *A Plan for Hornsey*, MB Hornsey.

Hough, B. (1997) 'The erosion of the concept of development: problems in establishing a material change of use', *Journal of Planning and Environment Law* 1997: 895–903.

Hough, B. (1998) 'Relevance and reasons in planning matters', *Journal of Planning and Environment Law* 1998: 625–34.

House of Commons Environment, Transport and Regional Affairs Committee (1998) *Housing* (10th Report, Session 1997–8), London: TSO.

House of Commons Expenditure Committee (1973) *Urban Transport Planning* (2nd Report, HC 57, 1972–3), London: HMSO.

House of Commons Expenditure Committee (1975) *New Towns* (13th Report, HC 616, 1974–5), London: HMSO.

House of Commons Expenditure Committee (1977) *Planning Procedures* (8th Report, HC 395, 1976–7), London: HMSO.

Howard, E. (1898) *Tomorrow: A Peaceful Path to Real Reform*, London: Swann Sonnenschein; republished 1946 and 1975 as *Garden Cities of Tomorrow*, London: Faber.

Hull, A. and Vigar, G. (1996) *Development Plans and Governance Processes: Agendas, Arenas and Alliances*, Paper to Shaping Places Conference, University of Newcastle.

Hunt Report (1969) *The Intermediate Areas* (Cmnd 3998), London: HMSO.

Hunter, M. (ed.) (1996) *Preserving the Past: The Rise of Heritage in Modern Britain*, Stroud: Sutton.

Illsley, B. and McCarthy, J. (1996) *Community Planning: A Case Study of Dundee*, Paper presented to Shaping Places Conference, University of Newcastle.

Imrie, R. and Thomas, H. (eds) (1993) *British Urban Policy and the Urban Development Corporations*, London: Paul Chapman.

Innes, J. (1996) *Consensus Building as Role-Playing and Bricolage: Toward a Theory of Collaborative Planning*, Paper to ACSP/AESOP Congress, Toronto.

Institute for European Environmental Policy (1998) *The Impact of the European Union on Town and Country Planning in the UK*, London: HMSO.

Jackson, J. N. (1963) *Surveys for Town and Country Planning*, London: Hutchinson.

Jacobs, M. (1997) 'Environmental valuation, deliberative democracy and public decision making institutions', in J. Foster (ed) *Valuing Nature?*, London: Routledge.

Jencks, C. (1990) *The Prince, The Architects and New Wave Monarchy*, London: Academy Editions.

Jones, A. (1996) 'Local planning policy – the Newbury approach' in M. Tewdwr-Jones (ed) *British Planning Policy in Transition*, London: UCL Press.

Jones, P. (1989) 'The developing programme of groundwork projects', *Journal of Environmental Management* 29: 409–14.

Joseph Rowntree Foundation (1991) *Inquiry into British Housing*, York: JRF.

Joseph Rowntree Foundation (1995) *Inquiry into Income and Wealth* (vol 1 by Barclay, P.; vol 2 by Hills, J.), York: JRF.

Jowell, J. (1973) 'The legal control of administrative discretion', *Public Law 1973:* 178–219.

Judd, D. and Parkinson, P. (eds) (1990) *Leadership and Urban Regeneration: Cities in North America and Europe*, London: Sage.

Keeble, D. E. (1980) 'Industrial decline, regional policy, and the urban–rural manufacturing shift in the United Kingdom', *Environment and Planning A* 12: 945–62

Keeble, L. (1952) *Principles and Practice of Town and Country Planning*, London: Estates Gazette (1st edn 1952; 4th edn 1969).

Keeble, L. (1961) *Town Planning at the Crossroads*, London: Estates Gazette.

Kelly, E. (1993) *Managing Community Growth*, Westport: Praeger.

Kennet, Lord W. (1972) *Preservation*, London: Temple Smith.

Kimber, R. and Richardson, J. J. (1974) *Campaigning for the Environment*, London: Routledge & Kegan Paul.

Kindred, B. (1997) 'Comment: culture, heritage and VAT – labels and priorities', *Context* 55: 3.

Kitchen, T. (1997) *People, Politics, Policies and Plans: The City Planning Process in Contemporary Britain*, London: Paul Chapman.

Knevitt, C. (1986) *Perspectives: An Anthology of 1001 Architectural Quotations*, London: Lund Humphries.

Lafferty, W. and Eckerberg, K. (1997) *From Earth Summit to Local Forum*, Oslo: Prosus.

Lagroye, J. and Wright, W. (eds). (1979) *Local Government in Britain and France: Problems and Prospects*, London: Allen & Unwin.

Laitos, J. G. (1998) *The Law of Property Rights Protection*, New York: Aspen.

Lambert, R. (1962) 'Central and local relations in mid-Victorian England: the Local Government Act Office', *Victorian Studies* VI(2): 121–51.

Land Reform Policy Group (1998) *Identifying the Problems*, Edinburgh: Scottish Office.

Larkham, P. J. (1994) 'Conservation areas and plan-led planning: how far can we go?', *Journal of Planning and Environment Law* 1994: 8–12.

Larkham, P. J. (1996a) 'Designating conservation areas: patterns in time and space', *Journal of Urban Design* 1: 315–27.

Larkham, P. J. (1996b) *Conservation and the City*, London: Routledge.

Larkham, P. J. (1997) 'Conservation areas: ideal and reality reviewed', *Transactions of the Ancient Monuments Society* 41: 23–43.

Law, C. M. (1980) *British Regional Development since World War I*, Newton Abbot: David & Charles.

Lawless, P. (1989) *Britain's Inner Cities*, London: Paul Chapman.

Leather, P. and Morrison, T. (1997) *The State of UK Housing: A Factfile on Dwelling Conditions*, Bristol: Policy Press.

Lee, N. and Wood, C. M. (1978) 'EIA – a European perspective', *Built Environment* 4: 101–10.

Leicester City Council (1975) *Planning for Leicester*, Leicester: Leicester City Council.

Leonard, P. (1982) 'Management agreements: a tool for conservation', *Journal of Agricultural Economics* 33: 351–60.

Levin, P. and Donnison, D. (1969) 'People and Planning', *Public Administration* 13: 473–9.

Lewis, N. (1992) *Inner City Regeneration: The Demise of Regional and Local Government*, Buckingham: Open University Press.

Ling, A. (1967) *Runcorn New Town*, Runcorn Development Corporation.

Lloyd, P. (1996) 'Contested governance: European exposure in the English regions', in Alden, J. and Boland, P. (eds) *Regional Development Strategies: A European Perspective*, London: Jessica Kingsley.

Local Government Management Board (1993) *Local Agenda 21: Principles and Process: A Step by Step Guide*, Luton: LGMB.

Loew, S. (1995), *Urban Conservation in France*, PhD thesis, Faculty of Urban and Regional Studies, University of Reading.

Logan, T. H. (1976) 'The Americanization of German zoning', *Journal of the American Institute of Planners* 42: 377–85.

Logie, G. (1952) *Industry in Towns*, London: Allen & Unwin.

London County Council (1951) *Development Plan: Analysis*, London: LCC.

London County Council (1962) *Development Plan: Statement*, London: LCC.

Lowenthal, D. (1985) *The Past is a Foreign Country*, Cambridge: Cambridge University Press.

Lowenthal, D. (1991) 'British national identity and the English landscape', *Rural History* 2: 205–230.

Luttrell, W. F. (1962) *The Cost of Industrial Movement*, Cambridge: Cambridge University Press.

Mabey, R. and Craig, L. (1976) 'Development plan schemes', *The Planner*, 62 (3), 70–1.

Mabileau, A., Moyser, G., Parry, G. and Quantin, P. (1989) *Local Politics and Participation in Britain and France*, Cambridge: Cambridge University Press.

McAllister, G. and McAllister, E. G. (1941) *Town and Country Planning*, London: Faber.

McAuslan, P. (1980) *The Ideologies of Planning Law*, Oxford: Pergamon.

McBride, D. (1979) 'Planning delays and development control – a proposal for reform', *Urban Law and Policy* 2: 47–64.

McCarthy, P., Prism Research and Harrison, T. (1995) *Attitudes to Town and Country Planning*, London: HMSO.

McCrone, G. (1969) *Regional Policy in Britain*, London: Allen & Unwin.

Macfarlane, R. and Mabbott, J. (1993) *City Challenge: Involving Local Communities*, London: National Council for Voluntary Organisations.

McLoughlin, J. B. (1966) 'The PAG report: background and prospect', *Journal of the Town Planning Institute*, 52 (7): 257–261.

Macnaghten, P. and Jacobs, M. (1997) 'Public identification with sustainable development', *Global Environmental Change* 71: 5–24.

Malpass, P. (ed) (1986) *The Housing Crisis*, London: Croom Helm.

Malpass, P. and Means, R. (1992) *Implementing Housing Policy*, Buckingham: Open University Press.

Malpass, P. and Murie, A. (1990) *Housing Policy and Practice* (3rd edn), London: Macmillan.

Malpass, P. and Murie, A. (1994) *Housing Policy and Practice* (4th edn), London: Macmillan.

Manchester City Council (1945) *City of Manchester Plan*, Manchester: MCC.

Mandler, P. (1996) *The Stately Homes of England: The English Country House and the National Heritage since the Eighteenth Century*, New Haven, CT: Yale University Press.

Manley, S. and Guise, R. (1998) 'Conservation in the built environment', in Greed, C. and Roberts, M. (eds) *Introducing Urban Design: Interventions and Responses*, Harlow: Longman.

Manners, G., Keeble, D., Rodgers, B. and Warren, K. (1980) *Regional Development in Britain* (2nd edn), London: Wiley.

Manser, M. (1983) 'Barriers to design', *Journal of the Royal Institute of British Architects* 86: 401–03.

Manser, M. and Adam, R. (1992) *Application of Aesthetic Control and Conservation Area Legislation in the Town and Country Planning System*, London (unpublished).

Marriott, O. (1967/1969) *The Property Boom*, London: Hamilton; 1969 reprint published by Pan.

Marsden, T. *et al.* (1993) *Constructing the Countryside: An Approach to Rural Development*, London: UCL Press.

Martin, D. (1992) 'Europe 2000: community actions and intentions in spatial planning', *The Planner* (27 November 1992) 78 (21): 18–20.

Martin, R. (1988) 'The new economics and politics of regional restructuring: the British experience', in Albrechts, L., Moulaert, F., Roberts, P., and Swyngedouw, E. (eds) *Regional Policy at the Crossroads: European Perspectives*, London: Jessica Kingsley.

Martin, R. and Townroe, P. (eds) (1992) *Regional Development in the 1990s: The British Isles in Transition*, London: Jessica Kingsley.

Meades, J. (1979) 'Aesthetic control: strangling creativity?', *Architects' Journal* 170: 1315–24.

Meadows, D. H., Meadows, D. L., Randers, J. and Behrens, W. W. (1972) *The Limits to Growth*, London: Potomac Associates.

Meadows, D. H., Meadows, D. L. and Randers, J. (1992) *Beyond the Limits: Global Collapse or Sustainable Future?*, London: Earthscan.

Meltz, R., Merriam, D. H. and Frank, R. M. (1999) *The Takings Issue*, Washington, DC: Island Press.

Merrett, S. (1979) *State Housing in Britain*, London: Routledge & Kegan Paul.

Merrett, S. and Gray, F. (1982) *Owner Occupation in Britain*, London: Routledge & Kegan Paul.

MHLG (1953) *Design in Town and Village*, London: HMSO.

MHLG (1959) *Bulletin of Selected Appeal Decisions*, London: MHLG.

MHLG (1962) *Town Centres – Approach to Renewal* (Planning Bulletin 1), London: HMSO.

MHLG (1963) *Town Centres – Cost and Control of Development* (Planning Bulletin 3), London: HMSO.

MHLG (1964), *The South East Study 1961 – 1981*, London: HMSO.

MHLG (1966), *Elevational Control* (Circular 28/66), London: HMSO.

MHLG (1968), *Town and Country Planning Act 1968 – Part V, Historic Buildings and Conservation*, (Circular 61/68) London: HMSO.

MHLG (1969) *House Condition Survey, England and Wales 1967*, London: HMSO.

MHLG (1970a) *First Report of the Preservation Policy Group* London: HMSO.

MHLG (1970b) *Development Plans: A Manual on Form and Content*, London: HMSO.

Middlesbrough County Borough (1946) *Survey and Plan*, Middlesbrough: MCB.

Middlesbrough County Borough (1952) *Middlesbrough Development Plan: Report on the Survey*, Middlesbrough: MBC.

Middlesbrough County Borough (1953) *Middlesbrough Development Plan: Written Statement*, Middlesbrough: MBC.

Miller, C. E. (1990) 'Development control as an instrument of environmental management: a review', *Town Planning Review* 61: 231–45.

Miller, C. E. and Wood, C. M. (1983) *Planning and Pollution*, Oxford: Oxford University Press.

Millichap, D. (1989a) 'Conservation areas – Steinberg and after', *Journal of Planning and Environment Law* 1989: 233–40.

Millichap, D. (1989b) 'Conservation areas and Steinberg – the Inspectorate's response', *Journal of Planning and Environment Law* 1989: 499–504.

Ministry of Health (1949) *Housing Manual*, London: HMSO.

Ministry of Housing and Local Government see MHLG.

Ministry of Local Government and Planning (MLPG) (1951) *Town and Country Planning, 1943–1951, Progress Report by the Minister of Local Government and Planning on the Work of the Ministry of Town and Country Planning* (Cmd 8204), London: HMSO.

Ministry of Town and Country Planning see MTCP.

Ministry of Transport (1967) *Better Use of Town Roads*, London: HMSO.

Moore, B., Rhodes, J., and Tyler, P. (1973) 'Evaluating the effects of British regional economic policy', *Economic Journal* 83: 87–110.

Moore, B., Rhodes, J., and Tyler, P. (1986) *The Effects of Government Regional Economic Policy*, London: HMSO.

Morgan, K. (1980) *The Reformulation of the Regional Question: Regional Policy and the British State*, Brighton: University of Sussex (Urban and Regional Studies Working Paper).

Moro, P. (1958) 'Elevational control', *Architects Journal* 127: 203.

Morphet. J. (1993) *Towards Sustainability: The EC's Fifth Action Programme on the Environment: A Guide for Local Authorities*, Luton: Local Government Management Board.

Morton, D. (1991) 'Conservation areas: has saturation point been reached?', *The Planner* 77, 17: 5–8.

Morton, D. and Ayers, J. (1993) 'Conservation areas in an era of plan led planning', *Journal of Planning and Environment Law* 1993: 211–14 (Note: author incorrectly given as Norton).

Moussis, N. (1997) *Access to the European Union: Law, Economics, Policies* (7th edn), Genval: Euroconfidentiel.

MTCP (1944) *Town and Country Planning Act 1944* (Circular No.11), London: HMSO.

MTCP (1947a) *Estate Development and Management Problems in War Damaged Areas: Report of the Central Advisory Committee on Estate Development*, London: HMSO.

MTCP (1947b) *Advisory Handbook on the Redevelopment of Central Areas*, London: HMSO.

MTCP (1948a) *Town and Country Planning Act 1947: Explanatory Memorandum, Part II – Notes on Sections*, London: HMSO.

MTCP (1948b) *The Town and Country Planning (Development Plans) Regulations 1948*, S.I. 1948, no. 1767, London: HMSO.

Murdoch J., Abram, S. and Marsden, T. (1996) *Modalities of Planning Arenas, Actors and Strategies of Persuasion in the Development Plan Review Process*, Papers in Environmental Planning Research 5, Department of City and Regional Planning, University of Wales, Cardiff.

Mynors, C. (1995) *Listed Buildings and Conservation Areas*, London: FT Law & Tax (2nd edn).

Nadin, V. and Shaw, D. (1998) 'Transnational spatial planning in Europe: the role of INTER-REG in the UK', *Regional Studies* 32: 281–99.

Nadin, V., Hawkes, P., Cooper, S., Shaw, D., and Westlake, T. (1997) *The EU Compendium of Spatial Planning Systems and Policies* (Regional Development Studies 28), Luxembourg: Office for the Official Publications of the EC.

Nairn, I. (1955) *Outrage*, London: Architectural Press.

Nairn, I. (1957) *Counter Attack against Subtopia*, London: Architectural Press.

NAO (National Audit Office) (1997a) *Wind Up of Leeds and Bristol Urban Development Corporations*, London: TSO.

NAO (1997b) *Protecting Environmentally Sensitive Areas*, London: TSO.

National Economic Development Council (1963) *Conditions Favourable for Faster Growth*, London: HMSO.

Nature Conservancy Council (1984) *Nature Conservation in Great Britain*, Shrewsbury: NCC.

Neale, C. (1984) *South Woodham Ferrers – The Essex Design Guide in Practice*, London: Royal Institution of Chartered Surveyors.

Needleman, L. (1965) *The Economics of Housing*, London: Staples.

Newby, H. (1985) *Green and Pleasant Land? Social Change in Rural England*, London: Wildwood House.

Newman, P. and Thornley, A. (1996) *Urban Planning in Europe: International Competition, National Systems, and Planning Projects*, London: Routledge.

Nicholas, J. C., Nelson, A. C. and Juergensmeyer, J. C. (1991) *A Practitioner's Guide to Development Impact Fees*, Chicago: Planners Press.

Nicholas, R. J. (1945) *City of Manchester Plan*, Manchester: Jarrold .

Nolan, Lord (1997) *Standards of Conduct in Local Government in England, Scotland and Wales* (Third Report of the Committee on Standards in Public Life, Cm 3702), London: HMSO.

Nolan, M. P. and Sedley, S. (1997) *The Making and Remaking of the British Constitution*, London: Blackstone Press.

O'Leary, J. (1997) 'Town planning and housing development', in Balchin, P. N. and Rhoden, M. *Housing: The Essential Foundations*, London: Routledge.

Osborn, F. J. and Whittick, A. (1969) *The New Towns: The Answer to Megalopolis*, London: Leonard Hill.

Owens, S. (1997) 'Giants in the path: planning, sustainability and environmental values', *Town Planning Review* 68: 293–303.

PAG (Planning Advisory Group) (1965) *The Future of Development Plans*, London HMSO.

Page, J. (1992) 'Listing of post-war buildings', *Conservation Bulletin* 16: 2–3.

Pagoda Associates (1992) *An Evaluation of the Impact of PPG 16 on Archaeology and Planning*, London: DoE.

Parfect, M. and Power, G. (1997) *Planning for Urban Quality: Urban Design in Towns and Cities*, London: Routledge.

Parker, H. R. (1965) 'The history of compensation and betterment since 1900', in Hall, P. (ed.) *Land Values*, London: Sweet & Maxwell.

Parker Morris Report (1961) *Homes for Today and Tomorrow*, London: HMSO.

Parkinson, M. (1985) *Liverpool on the Brink*, London: Hermitage.

Parkinson, M. (1992) 'City links', *Town and Country Planning* 61: 235–6.

Parr, J. (1993) 'The metropolitan area in its wider setting', in Summers, A. A., Cheshire P. C. and Lanfranco S. (eds) *Urban Change in the United States and Western Europe*, Washington DC: Urban Institute Press.

Parry, G. and Moyser, G. (1989) 'Community, locality and political action' in A. Mabileau *et al* (eds) *Local Politics and Participation in Britain and France*, Cambridge: Cambridge University Press.

Parsons, D. W. (1988) *The Political Economy of British Regional Policy*, London: Routledge.

Patten, C. (1989) 'Planning and local choice', *Municipal Journal* 13, October, 18–19.

Patten, C. (1990) Speech to the Royal Fine Art Commission, London: DoE.

Payne, B. and Brough, C. (1981) 'Dealing with hazard and risk in planning', in Griffiths, R. (ed.) *Dealing with Risk: the Planning, Management and Acceptability of Technological Risk*, Manchester: Manchester University Press.

Pepler, G. R. S. (1949) 'The 1947 Act, the first year: a symposium', *Journal of the Town Planning Institute* 35: 232–3.

Pickard, R. D. (1996) *Conservation in the Built Environment*, Harlow: Addison Wesley–Longman.

Planning Advisory Group (1965) *The Future of Development Plans*, London: HMSO.

Planning Exchange (1997) *The New Towns Record*, Glasgow: The Planning Exchange (CD-ROM).

Potter, C. (1998) 'Conserving nature: agri-environmental policy development and change', in Ibery, B. (ed.) *The Geography of Rural Change*, Harlow: Addison Wesley–Longman.

Powdrill, E. A. (1961) *Vocabulary of Land Planning*, London: Estates Gazette.

Power, M. (1997) *The Audit Society*, Oxford: Clarendon.

Priest, G. and Cobb, P. (eds) (1980) *The Fight for Bristol*, Bristol: Bristol Civic Society and the Redcliffe Press.

Prince of Wales (1988) *A Vision of Britain: A Personal View of Architecture*, London: Doubleday.

Property Advisory Group (1981) *Planning Gain*, London: HMSO.

Public Sector Management Research Unit (1988) *An Evaluation of the Urban Development Grant Programme* (DoE), London: HMSO.

Punter, J. V. (1986–7) 'A history of aesthetic control: the control of the external appearance of development in England and Wales 1909–1985', *Town Planning Review*, 57: 351–81 and 58: 29–62.

Punter, J. V. (1990a) 'The ten commandments of urban design', *The Planner*, 67 (39), 10–14..

Punter, J. V. (1990b) *Design Control in Bristol 1940–1990*, Bristol: Redcliffe Press.

Punter, J. V. (1996) *The Quality in Town and Country Initiative: A Preliminary Assessment*, Paper presented to ACSP/AESOP Conference, Toronto (mimeo).

Punter, J. V. and Bell, A. (1997) *Design Appeals in English Planning: An Introduction and Aggregate Analysis*, Cardiff, University of Cardiff, Papers in Planning Research, no. 163.

Punter, J. V. and Carmona, M. C. (1997) *The Design Dimension of Planning: Theory, Content and Best Practice for Design Policies*, London: Spon.

Purdue, M. (1982) 'Some current issues in the law on development control in England and Wales, with particular reference to the role of the courts and judicial review', in Harrison, M. L. and Mordey, R. (eds) *Planning Control: Philosophies, Prospects and Practice*, London: Croom Helm.

Purdue, M. (1989) 'Material considerations: An ever expanding concept', *Journal of Planning and Property Law*: 156–61.

Purdue, M. (1999) 'The status of the green belt', in Herbert-Young, N. *Law, Policy and Development in the Rural Environment*, Cardiff: University of Wales Press.

Radice, G. (1992) *Offshore Britain and the European Idea*, London: I. B. Tauris.

Ravenscroft, N. (1994) 'Leisure policy in the new Europe: the UK Department of National Heritage as a model of development and integration', *European Urban and Regional Studies* 1: 131–42.

Reade, E. (1991–1992) 'The little world of Upper Bangor', *Town and Country Planning* 60: 340–43; 61: 25–7 and 44–7.

Redcliffe-Maud Report (1969) *Report of the Royal Commission on Local Government in England* (Cmnd 4040), London: HMSO.

Regional Studies Association (1990) *Beyond Green Belts*, London: Jessica Kingsley.

Reith Committee (1946) *Final Report of The New Towns Committee* (Cmd 6876), London: HMSO.

Rhodes, J. and Kan, A. (1971) *Office Dispersal and Regional Policy*, London: Cambridge University Press.

Richards, J. (1994) *Façadism*, London: Routledge.

Robert, P. and Randolph, W. G. (1984) 'Beyond decentralisation: the evolution of the population distribution in England and Wales 1961–1981', *Geoforum* 14: 75–102.

Roberts, P. and Hart, T. (1994) 'Challenges and opportunities of the Europe of the regions', *Town and Country Planning* 63: 52–3.

Roberts, T. and Shearer, T. (1992) 'Land use litigation: takings and due process claims', *Urban Lawyer* 24: 833.

Robertson, M. (ed.) (1993) 'Listed buildings: the national resurvey of England', *Transactions of the Ancient Monuments Society* 37: 21–94.

Robinson, A. (1982) 'The evaluation of conservation areas', in Grant, E. and Robinson, A. *Landscape and Industry: Essays in Memory of Geoffrey Gullett*, Enfield: Middlesex Polytechnic.

Robson, B. T. (1988) *Those Inner Cities: Reconciling the Economic and Social Aims of Urban Policy*, Oxford: Clarendon Press.

Robson, B. T. (1994) 'No city, no civilisation', *Transactions of the Institute of British Geographers* (NS) 19: 131–41.

Robson, B. T. *et al.* (1994) *Assessing the Impact of Urban Policy* (DoE), London: HMSO.

Robson, B. T., Bradford, M. G. and Tye, R. (1995) *1991 Deprivation Index: A Review of Approaches and a Matrix of Results*, London: HMSO.

Robson, B. T., Bradford, M. G. and Tomlinson, R. (1998) *Updating and Revising the Index of Local Deprivation*, London: DETR.

Robson, B. T. *et al.* (1998) *The Impact of Urban Development Corporations in Leeds, Bristol and Central Manchester*, London: DETR.

Roskill Report (1971) *Report of the Commission on the Third London Airport*, London: HMSO.

Ross, M. (1996) *Planning and the Heritage* (2nd edn), London: Spon.

Rowell, C. and Robinson, J. M. (1996) *Uppark Restored*, London: National Trust.

Rowley, A. R. (1996) 'Mixed use development: ambiguous concept, simplistic analysis and wishful thinking?', *Planning Practice and Research* 11: 85–97.

Rowley, A. R. (1998) 'Private property decision makers and the quality of urban design', *Journal of Urban Design* 3: 151–74.

Royal Commission on Environmental Pollution (1976) *Air Pollution Control: An Integrated Approach* (5th Report) (Cmnd 6371), London: HMSO.

Royal Commission on Environmental Pollution (1988) *Best Practicable Environmental Option* (12th Report) (Cm 310), London: HMSO.

Royal Commission on Environmental Pollution (1994) *Transport and the Environment* (18th Report) (Cm 2674), London: HMSO.

Royal Commission on Environmental Pollution (1997) *Transport and the Environment: – Developments Since 1994* (20th Report) (Cm 3752), London: HMSO.

Royal Commission on Environmental Pollution (1998) *Setting Environmental Standards* (21st Report) (Cm 4053), London: TSO.

Royal Fine Art Commission (1985) *22nd Report 1971–1984*, London: HMSO.

Royal Institute of British Architects (1993) *Before and After Planning* (Exhibition Catalogue), London: RIBA.

Royal Institution of Chartered Surveyors (1996) *Quality in Urban Design*, London: RICS.

Royal Town Planning Institute (RTPI) (1980) 'RTPI/RIBA joint policy statement', *Planner News* 6 (April): 1.

Royal Town Planning Institute (1990) *Policy Guidance: Design and Planning Control* (mimeo), London: RTPI.

Royal Town Planning Institute (1996) *Energy Planning: A Guide for Practitioners*, London: RTPI.

Royal Town Planning Institute (1997) *Minerals, Waste Management and Environmental Protection: Education and Training Needs*, London: RTPI.

Royston, M. G. (1979) *Pollution Prevention Pays*, Oxford: Pergamon.

Russell, B. (1926) *On Education especially in early Childhood*, London: Allen & Unwin.

Russell, H., Dawson, J., Garside, P., and Parkinson, M. (1996) *City Challenge Interim National Evaluation*, London: TSO.

Rydin, Y. (1986) *Housing Land Policy*, Aldershot: Gower.

Rydin, Y. (1993) *The British Planning System: An Introduction*, London: Macmillan.

Rydin, Y. (1998) *Urban and Environmental Planning in the UK*, London: Macmillan.

SACTRA (Standing Advisory Committee on Trunk Road Assessment) *Trunk Road Proposals: A Comprehensive Framework for Appraisal* (1979); *Urban Road Appraisal* (1986); *Assessing the Environmental Impact of Road Schemes* (1992); *Trunk Roads and the Generation of Traffic* (1994), London: HMSO (see also ACTRA 1977).

Sandford Report (1974) *Report of the National Parks Policies Review Committee*, London: HMSO.

Saunders, P. (1990) *A Nation of Home Owners*, London: Unwin Hyman.

Schaffer, F. (1970) *The New Town Story*, London: Paladin.

Scheer, B. and Preiser, W. (eds) (1994) *Design Review: Challenging Urban Aesthetic Control*, New York: Chapman and Hall.

Schouten, F. F. J. (1995) 'Heritage as historical reality', in Herbert, D. T. (ed.) *Heritage, Tourism and Society*, London: Mansell.

Scott, P. (1996) *The Property Masters: A History of the British Commercial Property Sector*, London: Spon.

Scott, P., Miller, C. E. and Wood, C. M. (1998) 'Planning and pollution: an unusual perspective on central-local relations', *Environment and Planning C* 16: 529–42.

Scott Report (1942) *Report of the Committee on Land Utilisation in Rural Areas* (Cmd 6378), London: HMSO.

Scottish Office (1997) *Towards a Development Strategy for Rural Scotland*, Edinburgh: SO.

Scottish Office Environment Department (1980) *Design Guidance*, Edinburgh: SOED.

Scottish Office Environment Department (1991) *Siting and Design of New Housing in the Countryside* (Planning Advice Note 36), Edinburgh: SOED.

Scottish Office Environment Department (1994) *Fitting New Housing Development into the Landscape* (Planning Advice Note 44), Edinburgh: SOED.

Sedley, S. (1997) 'The Common Law and the constitution', in Nolan, M. P. and Sedley, S. *The Making and Remaking of the British Constitution*, London: Blackstone.

Self, P. (1957) *Cities in Flood: The Problems of Urban Growth*, London: Faber.

Self, P. (ed) (1972) *New Towns: The British Experience*, London: Charles Knight.

Selman, P. (1992) *Environmental Planning*, London: Paul Chapman.

Sharp, E. (1969) *The Ministry of Housing and Local Government*, London: Allen & Unwin.

Sharp, T. (1953) *Design in Town and Village*, London: HMSO.

Shaw, D., Nadin, V., and Westlake, T. (1996) 'Toward a supranational spatial development perspective : experience in Europe', *Journal of Planning Education and Research* 15: 135–42.

Sheail, J. (1993) 'The management of wildlife and amenity: a UK postwar perspective', *Contemporary Record* 7: 44–65.

Shoard, M. (1980) *The Theft of the Countryside*, London: Maurice Temple Smith.

Short, J., Fleming, S. and Witt, S. (1986) *Housebuilding, Planning and Community Action: The Production and Negotiation of the Built Environment*, London: Routledge & Kegan Paul.

Shutt, J. and Colwell, A. (1998) *Towards 2006: European Regional Policy and UK Local Government*, London: Local Government Information Unit.

Simpson, B. (1987) *Planning and Public Transport in Great Britain, France and West Germany*, London: Longman.

Skeffington Report (1969) *People and Planning* (Report of the Committee on Public Participation in Planning), London: HMSO.

Slater, S., Marvin, S. and Newson, M. (1994) 'Land use planning and the water sector', *Town Planning Review* 65: 375–97.

Smeed Report (1964) *Road Pricing: The Economic and Technical Possibilities*, London: HMSO.

Smith, D. L. (1974) *Amenity and Urban Planning*, London: Crosby Lockwood Staples.

Smith, L. (1981) 'A model for the development of public participation in local authority decision-making', in L. Smith and D. Jones (eds) *Deprivation, Participation and Community Action*, London: Routledge & Kegan Paul.

Smith, L. and Jones, D. (eds) (1981) *Deprivation, Participation and Community Action*, London: Routledge & Kegan Paul.

Social Exclusion Unit (SEU) (1998) *Bringing Britain Together: A National Strategy for Neighbourhood Renewal* (Cm 4045), London: TSO.

Solesbury, W. (1974) *Policy in Urban Planning*, Oxford: Pergamon.

Solesbury, W. (1976) 'The environmental agenda: an illustration of how situations may become political issues and issues may demand responses from government; or how they may not', *Public Administration* 54: 379–97

Sorensen, A. (1993) *Costing the English New Towns*, unpublished paper, London School of Economics (summarized in *Town and Country Planning*, November 1993).

South East Joint Planning Team (1971) *Strategic Plan for the South East, Studies Vol 1*, London, HMSO.

Stansfield, K. (1991) 'Imitation or imagination?', *Public Service and Local Government*, July/August: 20–1.

Starkie, D. (1982) *The Motorway Age*, Oxford: Pergamon.

Stewart, J. and Stoker, G. (1995) *Local Government in the 1990s*, London: Macmillan.

Stone, P. A. (1970) 'Housing quality: the seventies problem', *Building Societies Gazette*, June 1970.

Stone, P. A. (1973) *The Structure, Size and Costs of Urban Settlements* (National Institute of Economic and Social Research), Cambridge: Cambridge University Press.

Stuttard, R. M. (1959) *Town and Country: The Amenity Question*, Fabian Society Research Series 204, London: Fabian Society.

Suddards, R. W. and Hargreaves, J. M. (1996) *Listed Buildings* (3rd edn), London: Sweet & Maxwell.

Sutcliffe, A. R. (1981) *Towards the Planned City: Germany, Britain, the United States and France 1780–1914*, Oxford: Basil Blackwell.

Swanwick, C. (1997) 'Characterising the countryside', *Ecos* 18: 53–60.

Taylor, J. (1992) 'Regional problems and policies: an overview', in Townroe, P. and Martin, R. (eds) *Regional Development in the 1990s: The British Isles in Transition*, London: Jessica Kingsley.

Teesside County Borough (1974) *Teesside Structure Plan: Written Statement*, Middlesbrough: Teesside.

Thomas, H. (1994) 'The New Right: "race" and planning in Britain in the 1980s and 1990s', *Planning Practice and Research* 9: 353–66.

Thomas, H. (1996) 'Public participation in planning' in Tewdwr-Jones, M. (ed.) *British Planning Policy in Transition*, London: UCL Press.

Thomas, H. (1997) 'Managing the major planning projects', *Town and Country Planning* 66: 290–4.

Thomas, H. and Krishnarayan, V. (1994) 'Race, disadvantage and policy processes in British planning', *Environment and Planning A* 26: 1891–910.

Thomas, M. J. (1994) 'Values in the past: conserving heritage', in Thomas, H. (ed.) *Values and Planning* Aldershot: Avebury.

Thomas, R. (1969) *Aycliffe to Cumbernauld: A Study of Seven New Towns in their Regions*, London Political and Economic Planning, vol XXXV, Broadsheet 516.

Thomson, J. M. (1971) 'Halfway to a motorised society', *Lloyds Bank Review*, October: 16–34 [reprinted in Cullingworth, J. B. (1993) *Problems of an Urban Society, vol 3: Planning for Change*, London: Allen & Unwin].

Thornley, A. (1991) *Urban Planning under Thatcherism: The Challenge of the Market*, London: Routledge.

Thornley, A. (1993) *Urban Planning Under Thatcherism, The Challenge of the Market* (2nd edn), London: Routledge.

Tibbalds, F. (1988a) 'Mind the gap! A personal view of the value of urban design in the late twentieth century', *The Planner*, 74 (3), 11–15.

Tibbalds, F. (1988b) 'Urban design: Tibbalds offers the Prince his ten commandments', *The Planner Mid Month Supplement* 74 (12), 1.

Tillotson, J. (1996) *European Community Law, Text, Cases and Materials* (2nd edn), London: Cavendish.

Tiratsoo, N. (1990) *Reconstruction, Affluence and Labour Politics: Coventry 1945–60*, London: Routledge.

Tomlinson, P. (1986) 'Environmental assessment in the UK: implementation of the EEC directive' *Town Planning Review* 57: 458–86.

Townroe, P. and Martin, R. (eds) (1992) *Regional Development in the 1990s: The British Isles in Transition*, London: Jessica Kingsley.

Tripp, A. (1942) *Town Planning and Road Traffic*, London: Arnold.

Truelove, P. (1994) 'The illusive transport package', *Planning Week* 2 (49): 12–13.

Tugnutt, A. (1991) 'Design control or interference?' *The Planner*, 77 (38): 6–7.

Tugnutt, A. and Robertson, M. (1987) *Making Townscape: A Contextual Approach to Building in an Urban Setting*, London: Batsford.

Turok, I. (1992) 'Property-led regeneration: panacea or placebo?', *Environment and Planning A* 24: 361–80.

Tym, R. (1993) *Merry Hill Impact Study*, London: HMSO.

Tyme, J. (1978) *Motorways versus Democracy*, London: Macmillan.

UK Round Table on Sustainable Development (1996) *Energy and Planning*, UKRTSD (Ashdown House, 123 Victoria Street, London SW1E 6DE).

UK Round Table on Sustainable Development (1998) *Aspects of Sustainable Agriculture and Rural Policy*, London: UKRTSD.

Unwin, R. (1909) *Town Planning in Practice*, London: T. Fisher Unwin.

Urban Design Alliance (1997), *A Manifesto*, London: Royal Institute of British Architects.

Uthwatt Report (1942) *Expert Committee on Compensation and Betterment: Final Report* (Cmd 6386), London: HMSO.

Vogel, D. (1986) *National Styles of Regulation: Environmental Policy in Great Britain and the United States*, Ithaca, NY: Cornell University Press.

Wakeford, R. (1990) *American Development Control: Parallels and Paradoxes from an English Perspective*, London.: HMSO.

Waltham Forest London Borough (1978) *Statutory District Plan: Results of Public Consultation*, LB Waltham Forest.

Wannop, U. (1985) 'The New Towns of Strathclyde', in Butt, J. and Gordon, G. (eds) *Strathclyde: Changing Horizons*, Edinburgh: Scottish Academic Press.

Wannop, U. (1995) *The Regional Imperative: Regional Planning and Governance in Britain, Europe and the United States*, London: Jessica Kingsley.

Wannop, U. and Cherry, G. E. (1994) 'The development of regional planning in the United Kingdom', *Planning Perspectives* 9: 29–60.

Ward, I. (1996) *A Critical Introduction to European Law*, London: Butterworth.

Ward, S. V. (1994) *Planning and Urban Change*, London: Paul Chapman.

Ward, S. V. (1998) *Selling Places: The Marketing and Promotion of Towns and Cities 1850–2000*, London: Spon.

Warwickshire County Council (1971) *Coventry–Solihull–Warwickshire: A Strategy for the Sub-region*, Warwick: Warwickshire CC.

Wates, N. (1976) *The Battle for Tolmers Square*, London: Routledge & Kegan Paul.

Weekley, I. (1988) 'Rural depopulation and counterurbanization: a paradox', *Area* 20: 127–34.

Welsh Office (1996) *Planning Guidance (Wales) Technical Advice Note 12: Design (Consultation Draft)*, Cardiff: Welsh Office.

West Central Scotland Plan Team (1974) *West Central Scotland: A Programme of Action*, Glasgow: West Central Scotland Plan Steering Committee.

Whitby, M. C. (ed.) (1994) *Incentives for Countryside Management: The Case of ESAs*, Wallingford: CAB International.

Whitby, M. C. (ed.) (1996) *The European Environment and CAP Reform: Policies and Prospects for Conservation*, Wallingford: CAB International.

White Paper (1944) *The Control of Land Use* (Cmd 6537), London: HMSO.

White Paper (1963a) *Central Scotland: A Programme for Development and Growth* (Cmnd 2288), London: HMSO.

White Paper (1963b) *The North East: A Programme for Development and Growth* (Cmnd 2206), London: HMSO.

White Paper (1965) *The Land Commission* (Cmnd 2771), London: HMSO.

White Paper (1967) *Town and Country Planning* (Cmnd 3333), London: HMSO.

White Paper (1971) *Fair Deal for Housing* (Cmnd 4728), London: HMSO.

White Paper (1974) *Land* (Cmd 5730), London: HMSO.

White Paper (1975) *Food From Our own Resources* (Cmnd 6020), London: HMSO.

White Paper (1977) *Policy for the Inners Cities* (Cmd 6845), London: HMSO.

White Paper (1979) *Farming and the Nation* (Cmnd 7458), London: HMSO.

White Paper (1989a) *The Future of Development Plans* (Cm 569), London: HMSO.

White Paper (1989b) *Roads for Prosperity* (Cm 693), London: HMSO.

White Paper (1990) *This Common Inheritance, Britain's Environmental Strategy* (Cm 1200), London: HMSO.

White Paper (1994) *Sustainable Development: The UK Strategy* (Cm 2426), London: HMSO.

White Paper (1995a) *Rural England: A Nation Committed to a Living Countryside* (Cm 3016), London: HMSO.

White Paper (1995b) *Rural Scotland: People, Prosperity and Partnership* (Cm 3041), London: HMSO.

White Paper (1995c) *A Working Countryside for Wales* (Cm 3180), London: HMSO.

White Paper (1996a) *Transport: The Way Foward* (Cm 3234), London: HMSO.

White Paper (1996b) *Household Growth: Where Shall We Live?* (Cm 3471), London: HMSO.

White Paper (1998) *A New Deal for Transport: Better for Everyone* (Cm 3950), London: HMSO.

Williams, A. J. (1973) 'The role of the local planning authority in regard to waste and pollution', *Journal of Planning and Environment Law* 1973: 14–22.

Williams, R. H. (1996) *European Union Spatial Policy and Planning*, London: Paul Chapman.

Williams, R. H. and Wood, B. (1994) *Urban Land and Property Markets in the UK*, London: UCL Press.

Willmott, P. (ed) (1994) *Urban Trends 2: A Decade in Britain's Deprived Urban Areas*, London: Policy Studies Institute.

Wilson, D. (1986) *Citizen Action: Taking Action in Your Community*, London: Longman.

Winter, M. (1996) *Rural Politics: Policies for Agriculture, Forestry and the Environment*, London: Routledge.

Wood, C. M. (1976) *Town Planning and Pollution Control*, Manchester: Manchester University Press.

Wood, C. M. (1986) 'Local planning authority controls over pollution', *Policy and Politics* 14; 107–23.

Wood, C. M. (1989) *Planning Pollution Prevention*, Oxford: Butterworth Heinemann.

Wood, C. M. (1995) *Environmental Impact Assessment: a Comparative Review*, Harlow: Longman.

Wood, C. M. and Hooper, P. (1989) 'The effects of the relaxation of the planning controls in enterprise zones on industrial pollution', *Environment and Planning A* 21: 1157–67.

Woolf, H. (1992) 'Are the judiciary environmentally myopic?', *Journal of Planning and Environment Law* 1992: 1–14.

Worskett, R. (1982) 'Conservation: the missing ethic', *Monumentum* 25: 151–61.

Wright, H. M. (1948) *The Planner's Notebook*, London: Architectural Press.

Wulf-Mathies, M. (1998) Speech to the Joint European Commission and Council of Europe Seminar on European Spatial Planning, Berlin, 27 April 1998, (unpublished).

Yorkshire and Humberside Economic Planning Council (1966) *A Review of Yorkshire and Humberside* (Department of Economic Affairs), London: HMSO.

Young, S. (1996) *Promoting Participation and Community Based Partnerships in the Context of Local Agenda 21: A Report for Practitioners*, Manchester: Department of Politics, University of Manchester.

Yuill, D. *et al.* (1991) *European Regional Incentives, 1991: Directory and Review of Regional Grants and other Aid Available for Industrial and Business Expansion and Relocation in the Member States of the European Community and Sweden* (11th edn), London: Bowker-Saur.

Zigler, E. and Muenchow, S. (1992) *Head Start: The Inside Story of America's Most Successful Educational Experiment*, New York: Basic Books.

List of acronyms used in text

AJR	application for judicial review
AONB	area of outstanding natural beauty
BANANA	'build absolutely nothing anywhere near anything'
BNRR	Birmingham Northern Relief Road
CAP	Common Agricultural Policy
CDA	comprehensive development area
CEC	Commission of the European Communities
CEMAT	Conference of European Ministers of Aménagement du Territoire
CMDC	Central Manchester Development Corporation
COBA	cost benefit analysis
CoE	Council of Europe
CoR	Committee of the Regions
CSD	Committee on Spatial Development
CUPS	Centre for Urban Policy Studies
DETR	Department of the Environment, Transport and the Regions
DFEE	Department for Education and Employment
DG	Directorate General
DoE	Department of the Environment
DoT	Department of Transport
DTI	Department of Trade and Industry
EC	European Community
ECTP	European Council of Town Planners
EEC	European Economic Community
EIA	environmental impact assessment
ERDF	European Regional Development Fund
ESA	environmentally sensitive area
ESDP	European Spatial Development Perspective
EU	European Union
EZ	enterprise zone
GEAR	Glasgow Eastern Area Renewal
GIA	general improvement area

| HAA | housing action area |
| HBF | House Builders Federation |

| IDC | industrial development certificate |
| ISTEA | Intermodal Surface Transportation Efficiency Act (USA) |

LA21	Local Agenda 21
LBC	listed building consent
LDDC	London Docklands Development Corporation
LPA	local planning authority
LPH	Leeds Partnership Homes
LRT	light rapid transport

MAFF	Ministry of Agriculture, Fisheries and Food
MHLG	Ministry of Housing and Local Government
MTCP	Ministry of Town and Country Planning

NAO	National Audit Office
NEB	National Enterprise Board
NIMBY	'not in my back yard'

PAG	Planning Advisory Group
PFI	Private Finance Initiative
PPG	planning policy guidance
PTA	passenger transport authority

RCEP	Royal Commission on Environmental Pollution
REP	regional employment premium
RIBA	Royal Institute of British Architects
RICS	Royal Institution of Chartered Surveyors
RPG	regional planning guidance
RTPI	Royal Town Planning Institute

SACTRA	Standing Advisory Committee on Trunk Road Assessment
SDA	Scottish Development Agency
SERPLAN	South East Regional Planning Forum
SEU	Social Exclusion Unit
SOED	Scottish Office Environment Department
SPZ	simplified planning zone
SRB	single regeneration budget
SSSI	site of special scientific interest

TEA–21	Transportation Equity Act of the 21st Century (USA)
TEC	training and enterprise council
TPP	Transport Policy and Programmes
TSG	transport supplementary grant

UDAG	urban development action grant
UDC	urban development corporation
UDC	urban district council

| WDA | Welsh Development Agency |

Index

Page numbers in Italic indicate figures

BIRKBECK COLLEGE
Malet Street, London WC1E 7HX
020 7631 6239
If not previously recalled for another reader,
this book should be returned or renewed
before the latest date stamped below.

19.7.2000

2 1 SEP 2000

2 5 SEP 2002

1 7 APR 2003

1 6 JUN 2003